60 009246
D1438841
FROM THE LIBRARY

JOURNEY DOWN SUNSET BOULEVARD: The Films of Billy Wilder

Neil Sinyard
and
Adrian Turner

BCW PUBLISHING LIMITED / *Ryde, Isle of Wight*

First published in Great Britain, 1979 by
BCW Publishing Limited, Ryde, Isle of Wight.
Distributed by LSP Books Limited,
8 Farncombe Street, Farncombe, Godalming, Surrey

Cover design by Paul Turner, Stonecastle Graphics

ISBN 0 904159 62 0

Photoset in 11/12pt Garamond, made and printed in
Great Britain by Unwin Brothers at The Gresham Press,
Old Woking, Surrey

Contents

Acknowledgements

Many people have helped us during various stages in the writing of this book – too many to name individually. Needless to say, the faults are entirely ours. But we would particularly like to thank Jeremy Boulton, who has given so many researchers and historians invaluable assistance before his recent departure from the National Film Archive; David Meeker of the British Film Institute; Peter Kohnlechner and the staff of the Vienna Film Museum for extending warm hospitality during their 1978 Wilder retrospective; Eva Redfern who arranged screenings of *Fedora*. Students at the English Department at the West Midlands College, Walsall, have generously shared their ideas about Wilder with us and have influenced our own responses. We extend our thanks to them, and also to Bernard Burton for projecting many of the films, and Dr Don Nunes, whose critical insights and encouragement have been unfailingly helpful. David Castell and John Williams have shown faith in the project from the very beginning and have been the most patient and creative editors.

We would also like to acknowledge the following writers: Robert Mundy, Stephen Farber, Andrew Sarris, James McCourt, Raymond Durgnat, Joseph McBride and Michael Wilmington. Their contribution to the debate about Wilder has been particularly helpful to us and is discussed in our Introduction which we feel obviates the necessity for a formal bibliography.

For permission to reproduce photographs, we would like to thank the National Film Archive Stills Library, Mainline Pictures, M-G-M, Paramount, 20th Century-Fox, United Artists, Universal and Warner Brothers.

Above all, this book would not have come into being without the support of our wives, Lesley Sinyard and Andrea Turner. They have not only borne the stresses of our labours during the two years of writing the book: they have proved our sternest and most constructive critics as well as our most sympathetic and perceptive advisers. This book is dedicated to them, with much love.

Introduction

At the 1978 Cannes Film Festival, when a colleague, John Gillett, informed Billy Wilder that this book was being written, Wilder apparently commented: "Another one?"

Why another book on Wilder? Aside from our enthusiasm for the films, the immediate reason is that there have been four attempts published to date without anyone yet having succeeded in saying anything of much critical substance. Axel Madsen's 'Billy Wilder' (Secker and Warburg, London, 1968) establishes an interesting framework in the opening chapters for an argument that disappointingly fails to materialise in his rush to judgement on the films. Tom Wood's 'The Bright Side of Billy Wilder, Primarily' (Doubleday, New York, 1970) can most charitably be described as insubstantially anecdotal, gossip rather than criticism, which has the effect of trivialising its subject. Maurice Zolotow's 'Billy Wilder in Hollywood' (Putnam, New York, 1977) is a breezy travelogue across the landscape of Wilder's personality which is entertaining about the man without really offering much illumination on the films*. Steve Seidman's 'The Film Career of Billy Wilder' (G K Hall & Co, Boston, 1977) is an invaluable reference work whose format, unfortunately, gives the author insufficient room to develop in depth his weighty structural generalisations.

All of these books have had something useful to contribute about Wilder's biographical background, which does find its way interestingly and meaningfully into the heart of his films. All of them have offered the occasional interpretative insight. But none of them can really claim to initiate the extended critical investigation of Wilder's

---

*It is too elaborate to go into here, but Zolotow's biography builds quite excitingly to a spectacular sub-Freudian explanation for Wilder's filmic personality – his ostensible cynicism, and misogyny. It reads rather like a pastiche of Freud's own famous and improbably rapid diagnosis of the demons which plagued Gustav Mahler and how they affected him creatively. Considering the fun Wilder has had at the expense of psychiatrists in his films, one wonders how he must have felt on Zolotow's couch.

films which is now long overdue. We hope that his book will go some way towards filling this critical vacuum.

More encouragingly, Wilder has been the subject of some admirable magazine articles in recent years. One thinks of Stephen Farber's fine analysis in 'Film Comment' (Winter 1971); James McCourt's modest but persuasive reading of the films in the British magazine 'Framework' (Winter 1976); Joseph McBride and Michael Wilmington's 'The Private Life of Billy Wilder' in 'Film Quarterly' (Summer 1970); and Andrew Sarris's important, if incomplete, revaluation of Wilder in 'Film Comment' (July-August 1976) – certainly Sarris's original downgrading of Wilder in his polemical grouping of directors in 'The American Cinema' (Dutton, New York, 1968) was one of the most damaging as well as one of the most challenging contributions to the debate on Wilder*. Most of all, there has been Robert Mundy's pioneering article "Wilder ReAppraised" in the Cambridge graduate magazine 'Cinema' (October 1969), which attempted to re-route the critical debate on Wilder away from the barren areas of taste and towards matters of structure and theme.

Inevitably, these articles have been of limited accessibility and have therefore not had as much influence as they deserve, although the relevant ideas of all of them will be examined at appropriate stages in the book. Also, for all their virtues, these articles have been of necessity incomplete and generalised, indicating areas for more thorough investigation rather than having the space to pursue their critical intuitions to their conclusion. Indeed, it is hard to think of any Wilder film, with the possible exceptions of *Double Indemnity* and *Sunset Boulevard*, that has been subjected to the detailed scrutiny that one asks of serious film criticism nowadays; the kind of analysis which goes beyond that of competent, concise film journalism. Certain important Wilder films – like *Sabrina, Love in the Afternoon, Witness for the Prosecution*, even *The Apartment* – have attracted no critical literature of any substance whatsoever.

Robert Mundy's article postulated a different critical approach to Wilder, arriving at the meaning of his films through situation and form rather than through subjective canons of propriety and impro-

---

*Wilder was ignominously placed in Sarris's "Less Than Meets the Eye" category, alongside figures like Lewis Milestone, Fred Zinnemann and Carol Reed, as well as directors like David Lean and William Wyler, whose upgrading is also due.

priety. It is an example which now has to be renewed and extended. For one thing, Mundy's article is now ten years old, a period in which, we would argue, Wilder has made three of the greatest films of his career – *The Private Life of Sherlock Holmes, Avanti!* and *Fedora*. It is also a period in which Wilder, while refining his art to an ever richer, subtler level of expression, has increasingly lost contact with his audience. Inevitably, this has caused him considerable professional anguish. About *The Private Life of Sherlock Holmes*, Wilder has commented: "Actually, I'm saddened I made it. Why should I be glad? I surely didn't want it to flop. Any time a picture crashes, it's like someone designing a new 'plane that doesn't fly, and there are passengers on it – actors, technicians, electricians – and it eats up a great deal of time which, as life goes on, becomes more scarce." The subsequent commercial failure of *Avanti!* and the limited distribution of *Fedora* seem dispiriting evidence of a present indifference on the part of audiences and distributors to Wilder's work, even at its greatest. We feel it a matter of urgency to record and demonstrate our admiration and indeed love of these films in the hope of reclaiming them as among the decade's noblest achievements.

We also feel that these recent films throw a crucial backward light on to Wilder's previous achievements, giving a different glow to films which formerly were confined to the shadows (*Sabrina, Love in the Afternoon*) and equally consigning to the darkness more prestigious, less personal works that now appear inflated and untypical (*The Lost Weekend, The Seven Year Itch*). For example, it would be an over-simplification to say that it is only after *Avanti!* that one can fully appreciate *Sabrina*, a film which has generally been dismissed as sub-standard even by Wilder's admirers. Naturally, it has its place in the genre of Hollywood romantic comedy of the Fifties and naturally one must be fully aware of the distortions possible when, with the benefit of hindsight, one imposes a Seventies' reading on a Fifties' film. The fact that both are based on Samuel Taylor plays is also an authorial complication which must be given its due weight. Nevertheless, one can recognise now what could only have been dimly discernible then: that a film which seemed at the time a Wilder aberration looks now both characteristic and impressive and, indeed, prophetic of his later development in this crucial last decade. It assists us in reading the film's tone and ultimately, as we try to argue, arriving at the film's meaning. This would be impossible for any critic – which then meant just about *every* critic – who came to the film with various assumptions about the director's "cynicism".

'Cynical' is the adjective which has dominated critical perspectives on Wilder, the ultimate evaluation depending on whether or not the critic in question finds cynicism attractive or repellent. In interviews, Wilder himself seems in two minds whether or not to accept the description, as if the critical insistence on this image of him has persuaded him resignedly and against his better judgement to go along with it. "I have a kind of philosophy; maybe it's cynical, but I have to be true to what I feel," he told Charles Higham and Joel Greenberg in their interview with him published in 'The Celluloid Muse' (H Regnery, Chicago, 1969). But on another occasion, he has resisted the label, emphasising that honesty and realism could only be branded "cynical" by an industry which glamourises or falsifies real experience; indeed, even the truth about itself. "Sometimes I feel gay," Wilder wrote in 'Films and Filming' (February 1957). "Other times I want to make drama; or, so even my best friends tell me, I am cynical and turn out a script like *Sunset Boulevard*. Cynic maybe, but to me that film *is* Hollywood – the writer, the agent, the fading star, were all portraits from life." Certainly "cynical" is not a word that can be easily applied to "mellow masterpieces" (Andrew Sarris's phrase) like *The Private Life of Sherlock Holmes** and *Avanti!*, or to an overwhelmingly moving testament like *Fedora*. It is equally inadequate, we would argue, to apply it to a work like *Ace in the Hole*, whose Swiftian passion transcends cynicism. An artist with a so-called "brazen contempt for people" (Pauline Kael's phrase) does not get so pained nor so laceratingly angry at the sight of human fallibility.

A dictionary definition would tell us that a cynic is a man, "who shows a disposition to disbelieve in the sincerity or goodness of human motives and actions and is wont to express this by sneers and sarcasms: a sneering fault-finder." There are, to be sure, a number of

---

*Indeed, Holmes's main enemy in the film is surely Cynicism itself, the last refuge of the disillusioned romantic, and against which Holmes is struggling throughout the film. This reading is enhanced by the fact that Holmes's chief adversary is ultimately revealed as the significantly named Diogenes Club – Diogenes being the most prestigious of Cynic Philosophers in Ancient Greece. Of course, Wilder did not christen the club as such, but it was his decision to make this organisation play such a key part in the plot and thwart Holmes's romantic aspirations; and, as we try to demonstrate in our discussions of *Some Like it Hot* and *Fedora*, Wilder is never one to throw away a Classical reference.

characters in Wilder's films who are like this, but in no case is their philosophy unequivocally endorsed: to regard them as Wilder mouthpieces is crucially to misread the tone of the films. A cynic can be further characterised as a man lacking in compassion and a sense of human potential, regarding the foibles and weaknesses of man as innate and inevitable. It is striking how often the thrust of Wilder's films runs directly contrary to this. If a Wilder hero is constantly struggling between darkness and light, it is significant that his ultimate development is always, without exception, from negative to positive. A Wilder hero *never* degenerates. A cynic would admit no change in human nature for the better. A fundamental element in Wilder's structures is the possibility of redemption, a maturing of the hero towards a more humane outlook. It is a transformation which, in some cases, might come too late, but it nevertheless carries a powerful positive charge. The heroes walk out on secure material situations at the call of personal, moral principles. In every case, the hero has to choose *between* money and happiness, or peace of mind: he is always put to the acid test of sacrificing material for moral good. In every case the mark of the hero's maturity and the director's esteem (perhaps most severely tested in *The Fortune Cookie*) is towards the man who chooses the humanist rather than the materialist option. For a so-called cynic, this is an extremely strange dramatic pattern.

Still, some critics would insist that Wilder's cynicism is really revealed by his inability to dramatise these transformations convincingly. Wilder's films might end asserting certain moral values, but these endings are merely a sop to the audience – "sugar-coating the pill" is the phrase most often used – and Wilder's heart really lies elsewhere. But if these endings were insincere in that way, it seems inconceivable that Wilder should return to this structure so consistently, particularly in the cinematic climate of the last two decades, where a properly cynical conclusion would seem to be more commercially viable and acceptable than an unfashionably moral one. In an era when filmic con-men can be romanticised to the point of embarrassment in, say, *The Sting*, it seems peculiarly dogged and individual of Wilder to insist on his cheating hero's change of heart and his acknowledgement of dishonesty at the end of *The Fortune Cookie*. The one transformation which, in our view, is an undoubted failure is the 'miracle' which concludes *The Lost Weekend*, but the failure is an instructive one: it does not work precisely because it is not sufficiently rooted in the development of the hero himself but seems to be asserting that the hero will be transformed because of the arbitrary and fortuitous return of his typewriter. In all the other films of Wilder where the endings have been notoriously problematical (and we have attempted to confront these in some detail), the redemption is rooted in a change of character, not circumstance. And if the critics find these difficult to accept, in some cases they might be more profitably employed in examining their own cynicism, not Wilder's.

Inevitably, any contemporary artist like Wilder who puts feelings above finance, the individual above the group, will find his ideals tested in an increasingly acquisitive, urbanised, impersonal society. Any sensitive artist who values culture and intelligence will feel on the defensive in a system or an industry that often seems unhealthily preoccupied with the modish, the new, the commercial. James Cagney's Coca-Cola salesman in *One, Two, Three* can talk of striped toothpaste along with the Taj Mahal and the plays of Shakespeare as if they were equivalent aesthetic achievements. One cannot forget Marilyn Monroe's comment in *The Seven Year Itch* as an "actress" in toothpaste commercials: "Every time I show my teeth on television more people see me than ever saw Sarah Bernhardt. It's something to think about." It is indeed. Wilder's ambivalence can be defined as, on the one hand, a very European fascination with that sort of joyous New World vulgarity (gorgeously embodied by Monroe) and, on the other, as a sardonic disenchantment with a society that can endorse values like that with such unblinking candour. Wilder's abrasiveness becomes a species of idealism, a cry of protest against the comfortable, the safe, the complacent. It is his examination and exposure of the grotesque gracelessness of modern life that has led him into controversial areas of content and led critics into attaching a "distasteful" label to some of his films.

The discussion of Wilder's "bad taste" has been as large a critical dead-end as the discussion of his "cynicism". This is largely because accusations of bad taste – or, alternatively, the frenzied, bourgeois trendiness of "Isn't bad taste *fun*?" – ultimately reveal more of the critics' predilections than the director's. All Wilder gets out of it is the unenviable choice of being either panned or patronised. Those critics who found adultery hilarious in *Tom Jones, The Pink Panther* and *Bedtime Story* but found it offensive in Wilder's *Kiss Me, Stupid* ought to have been attacking their own contradictions rather than venting their spleen on Wilder. They might have at least looked more closely at the tone, structure, and meaning of each, on which count *Kiss Me, Stupid* could only score a resounding moral victory.

But it would always be more useful to discuss Wilder in terms of conventions rather than in terms of taste. If he has ventured into tricky areas, it has been his attempt to extend the screen's too limited range of interests and attitudes, an endeavour which makes its own implicit comment on Hollywood conservatism during all but the last decade. Several aspects of Wilder's films can be seen essentially as acts of defiance against Hollywood standardisation. His range – concentration camp comedy, *film noir*, courtroom drama, Gothic melodrama, romance, gangland farce, social problem picture, biography – evinces a refusal to submit to genre stereotyping. If Wilder makes a genre film (*Stalag 17? Some Like it Hot?*), it is likely to be so bizarre an example that it can hardly qualify as an addition to the genre in question: it looks more like a rousing critical commentary running alongside it. His use of familiar actors in unfamiliar roles (Fred MacMurray, Ray Milland, Humphrey Bogart, Gary Cooper) gives them a chance to flex hitherto untried dramatic muscles while simultaneously examining the screen image they have developed up to that point in their careers, alluding to it, commenting on it, reconstructing it. Hollywood formulae are thus – sometimes affectionately, always wittily – revised rather than reproduced, a tactic invested with authority and conviction by Wilder's clear reverence for movies. Wilder's "daring" subject-matter can be seen as an extension both of his unconventionality and his reverence. It is not "daring" for its own sake; it is only daring in a film community whose fearful notion of what a mass audience would tolerate and support compels it constantly to underestimate its public. But there is a whale of a difference between Wilder's risk-taking, which endeavours to expand an audience's perception, and the crude excesses of some modern cinema which can attempt nothing more subtle than stretching its audience's threshold of nausea. Wilder's dismissive comments on recent films like *The Exorcist* and *Shampoo* testify eloquently enough to his contempt for those who seek to shock for the sake of commercial boons. Films like these are acts of violation against the cinema and not, like Wilder's, acts towards enhancing and liberating its potential.

If the "bad-taste cynic" conception of Wilder seems limited and inadequate, then an equal fallacy which needs to be challenged is the critical endorsement of what Andrew Sarris once termed Wilder's "lack of adequate technical mastery" in his article "Notes on the Auteur Theory" ('Film Quarterly' Winter 1962-3). The fact that Wilder is unfashionable seems to have led critics into believing that he is old-fashioned. The fact that his camerawork is uninsistent has deceived critics into assuming that it is non-existent. Certainly he refuses to dazzle a spectator with superficial displays of technique – what James Agee once contemptuously described as, "wearing your art on your sleeve." Wilder has frequently expressed his dislike of camera tricks: "Why shoot a scene from a bird's eye view or a bug's? I guess they call that thing 'stylish' or 'beautifully conceived'. 'What an eye,' they say, 'shooting through parking meters!'. It's all done to astonish the bourgeois, to amaze the middle-class critic . . . " ('The Celluloid Muse'). Wilder would surely endorse Howard Hawks' definition of a good director: "Someone who doesn't annoy you."

Wilder's reticent shooting style is a mark of his artistic discretion. He believes that a close-up is all the more powerful when withheld until absolutely necessary, like a trump card in bridge. The first close-up in *Stalag 17* does not occur until midway through the film and is a wincingly well-timed shot of the hero's battered face after the savage beating he receives from his fellow prisoners – an effective shock and also arousing in us an indignation which provides an insight into and identification with the hero's pursuit of revenge which follows. The wide-ranging mood of *The Apartment* achieves maximum expression in the scene between Baxter and Miss Kubelik in his office, when he is showing her his new hat, not knowing that she has just learned of her lover's frequent infidelities. Wilder's sudden alternating close-ups of the hero's incongruous appearance and the heroine's suppressed pain bounce comedy against tragedy in a manner that is at the heart of the film's method and meaning. The impact is heightened by Wilder's technical unobtrusiveness up to that point.

Wilder's stylistic restraint reflects, most of all, a refusal to condescend to an audience. "I'll never make a badly-shot picture or a badly constructed picture or a picture where the actors behave like idiots," he once said, and this concern with intelligence determines the characteristics of his visual style. His camera, for the most part, maintains a discreet distance from the action because he likes to give his audience the chance to think about the action rather than bully them into emotional involvement. The gain in subtlety and suggestiveness easily outweighs the risk of trying the patience of the less wary or sympathetic viewer. Part of the joy of *Avanti!* is precisely this combination of ease and control, what Henry James called, "a maximum of intensity with the minimum of strain." No shot is wasted, and the rhythm and emphasis of each sequence is calculated with hairbreadth exactness. It is the kind of utter professionalism that a Hawks hero would define as, "being so good he doesn't feel he has to prove it." We would argue that, appreciated fully in their context, the film-watching scene in *Sunset Boulevard*, the Christmas party in *The Apartment*, the morgue sequence in *Avanti!*, the Oscar presentation in *Fedora* – to name but a few choice examples – are triumphs of film form by any standard and would alone establish Wilder among the most meticulous of screen stylists.

"There's more in this case than meets the eye," says Dr Watson to Holmes in *The Private Life of Sherlock Holmes*. It is an apt comment about Billy Wilder's work. Too often the critics have looked at the films without seeming properly to appreciate what they see. It serves as a fascinating parallel to the situation of 'seeing yet not seeing' which occurs so regularly in Wilder's films. We are referring not only to the use of disguise in his films or to the situations of those scheming heroes who fail to see until too late the consequences of their actions. People literally misinterpreting what they see is one of the most important recurrent motifs of *Witness for the Prosecution*, of *The Apartment*, of *The Private Life of Sherlock Holmes*. Mirror shots are also prominent in his films, enriching the density of the visual surface while commenting on the hero's confusion of his own identity, often startling him with his own self-image or indicating another side to the character that has yet to be developed. Indeed, the very act of seeing often carries great structural and thematic weight in a Wilder film (it is a characteristic often remarked on in Hitchcock, but never to our knowledge in Wilder). Norma Desmond's vision of herself as she watches her old film in *Sunset Boulevard*, the flattering image on the screen expressing her narcissism and her illusions about her age; Betty in the same film saying, "I can't look at you anymore, Joe," when her eyes are opened for the first time about the seedy situation her lover is in; Emmy putting on her glasses for the first time in *Hold Back the Dawn* to see what kind of man she has married; Orville looking bemusedly at the flickering television screen of Dino singing Orville's song at the end of *Kiss Me, Stupid* and saying, "I can't figure out any of this"; Lord X's eye-patch in *Irma la Douce*, which Irma fails to see through even when it is on the wrong eye; the newspapermen staring unseeingly through the broken window in *The Front Page* without even recognising the significance of this 'break' which has practically dumped the wanted man in their laps. And – for those with eyes to see – Pamela Piggott's sight-seeing tour in *Avanti!* is the

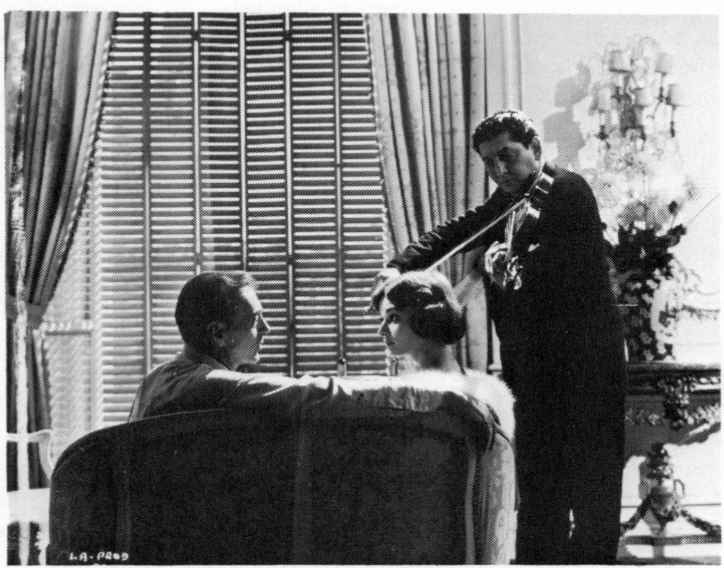

Love in the Afternoon: *Gary Cooper, Audrey Hepburn*

moment when the paradisal vision of the island is unleashed to a fresh, unjaundiced eye that can appreciate its beauty to the full. In a similar way, it is our hope that the reader's eyes will be opened to a Wilder that they do not usually see, to a world more tender, idealistic and romantic than is commonly acknowledged and with visual delights more pervasive than is usually recognised.

Something should be said about the critical assumptions underlying the book and the thematic organisation of the material. We await with interest the valuable insights on this body of work which could accrue from some of the more recent critical approaches to film, whether they come from semioticians, feminists or psycho-analysts. Nevertheless, our particular approach has been determined not only by preference but by a sense of priorities. As Andrew Sarris seems now to have recognised, the so-called 'auteur theory' could never have made complete sense while Wilder was excluded from the Pantheon. Equally important is the fact that the auteur theory cannot be laid to rest while Wilder remains unexamined in detail. Indeed, the overwhelming obviousness of Wilder's claims to be considered along these lines is the only reason we can think of to explain why it has not been properly done.

Our notion of Wilder as 'auteur' extends to an assertion of Wilder as 'artist', with all that implies about the possibility of personal expression within an industrial, commercial framework; and about the relationship of a critic to the work he is analysing and to his notions of artistry and aesthetic excellence which are obviously personal and (no doubt) culturally conditioned and class-determined. It is not the only way of approaching these films but it is, we believe, a valid one. For any further elaboration of our position, we would refer the reader to Robin Wood's chapter, "In Defense of Art", in 'Personal Views' (Gordon Fraser, London, 1976) and, in particular, his mischievously entitled section, "Schubert Replies to Colin McArthur": it would be pointless for us to reiterate something with which we so profoundly agree.

It is clear that Wilder's involvement on the production and writing of his films as well as their direction reduces one complication in the attribution of authorship to a film. Nevertheless, we have attempted to avoid some of the excesses of some auteur criticism. Because a film is recognisably the work of a particular director is not the same as saying that it is any good: we have therefore attempted to indicate relative value among the films, as well as outlining external pressures (from studios, financiers, preview audiences, even temperamental actors), certain ideological factors, and the influence on Wilder of other directors (Mitchell Leisen and Ernst Lubitsch in particular) as well as a wide variety of writers and composers. Similarly, if Wilder is the most powerful creative influence behind his films, he is not the only one. We have taken some care to acknowledge the contributions of collaborators* and also endeavoured to place the films in as wide a context as possible without losing the focus on Wilder himself. More than most, Wilder's films not only reflect but actively comment on contemporary film influences and events.

The thematic grouping of the films (rather than, say, a chronological one) seemed to us the most coherent way of discussing the work. However much they are separated in time, films like *Sunset Boulevard* and *Fedora*, for example, have so many features in common that they seem to demand a direct comparison; and this comparison surely benefits from the films having a thematic proximity in the book which enables the reader to make the necessary connections without too much searching. Of course, the categories are not intended to be rigid and exclusive. There are situations, characterisations and even inanimate objects which recur in just about every Wilder film. But one can formulate some themes which are given particular prominence and to which Wilder consistently returns, offering variations and refinements as he attempts a fresh evaluation of a favoured idea or situation.

There is the fundamental structural opposition in Wilder of Europe and America, an opposition which is felt not simply as a conflict of cultures but as a conflict of values: this tension is worked out in two contrasting ways – as deeply romantic comedies in which the Americans embrace European values, and as harsher studies of the American abroad, such as *A Foreign Affair* in which those values are resisted or debased. There are those films which focus on character reversals (in general, weak or scheming heroes who are compelled to face up to the human consequences of their scheming) and which place these reversals in the context of American society. This context is felt

---

*It is possible to talk of a Wilder team as distinctive as John Ford's or Howard Hawks' or Alfred Hitchcock's – a set of people with whom he has worked over and over again and who contribute to the identity of a Wilder film. Charles Brackett and I A L Diamond, pre-eminently, among the writers; Miklós Rózsa, André Previn, Franz Waxman and Adolph Deutsch among composers; designer Alexander Trauner; editors Doane Harrison and Daniel Mandell; cameramen like John Seitz and Joseph LaShelle; or regular Wilder actors like Cliff Osmond, Joan Shawlee or Porter Hall among the supporting players, and supreme Wilder interpreters like Jack Lemmon amd William Holden in the leads. Nearly all of his leading actors have appeared in more than one of his films: Fred MacMurray, Ray Milland, Marlene Dietrich, Audrey Hepburn, Marilyn Monroe, Shirley MacLaine, Walter Matthau. It is also a feature of his work that he has consistently coaxed fellow directors into acting – Mitchell Leisen, Erich von Stroheim, Otto Preminger – as well as obtaining glittering performances from an assortment of pets. Wilder's world is unmistakable.

physically (as in *Ace in the Hole* or *The Apartment*) and also felt ideologically (as in *Hold Back the Dawn* or *Stalag 17*). All the films in this group are essentially dramas although, as Raymond Durgnat has wisely pointed out in 'The Crazy Mirror' (Faber, London, 1969), Wilder's serious dramas have more wisecracks and witticisms than most people's comedies. Some films have plots in which the most prominent feature is disguise (*The Major and the Minor, Some Like it Hot*, for example). All the films in this category are comedies and they elaborate in a hilarious and emphatic form the motif of deception and role-playing which underlies most of Wilder's work. There are those films dominated by striking heroines whose impact on the male is traumatic (for example, *Double Indemnity* and *The Private Life of Sherlock Holmes*) and these films raise in an acute form the oft-quoted accusation against Wilder of misogyny. All the films here are dramas, though a closer definition would probably be to describe them as romantic tragedies. There are, finally, Wilder's failures and misfits. We do admit, along with Joe E Brown in *Some Like it Hot*, that, "Nobody's Perfect," though even here *The Emperor Waltz* has great thematic and some visual interest, *The Lost Weekend* has four Oscars and a lot of admirers, *The Seven Year Itch* has Marilyn Monroe, and *The Spirit of St Louis* is less of a failure than an engaging eccentricity.

Has any director of Wilder's generation maintained such a consistently high standard over so extended a period? Can any other filmmaker equal Wilder for the supply of intelligence and entertainment in equal measure? We think not. The fact that his films are so instantly enjoyable has tempted too many observers into taking them for granted, blinding them to the subtleties and riches which only close criticism could uncover. We believe the honour and admiration which his work so abundantly deserves has been too long delayed. Whatever Wilder might have said at Cannes, another book *is* necessary.

Chapter I

"ISN'T IT ROMANTIC?"

Ninotchka
Sabrina
Love in the Afternoon
Avanti!

Ninotchka (1939)

On Thursday 28 February 1933, at the age of twenty-six, Billy Wilder boarded a train from Berlin to Paris. He had with him a single suitcase and a thousand dollars hidden in the clothes he was wearing. Like Joe and Jerry in *Some Like it Hot*, who flee Chicago's mobsters in 1929, Wilder's hasty departure from Berlin was a necessary precaution to take. On the previous day unknown arsonists had set fire to the Reichstag building and within nine years most of the world was engulfed in the same inferno.

On the day of Wilder's departure the leader of the National Socialist Party told the Berlin correspondent of the London 'Daily Express': "By the decrees issued legally we have appointed tribunals which will try the enemies of the State legally, and deal with them legally in a way which will put an end to these conspiracies." It has been estimated that 10,000 people were arrested within two weeks following the publication of the decree of 28 February. It is of little consequence now who was really responsible for the Reichstag fire since Adolf Hitler, like the Emperor Nero before him, used the conflagration to gain political ground and as the basis for political and racial persecutions. Billy Wilder, like many artists and intellectuals grouped in Berlin, foresaw the coming holocaust and fled before the Nazis were fully organised.

It is highly probable that Wilder, an Austrian Jew who had moved to Berlin in 1926, would have ultimately gone to Hollywood, even without Hitler's assistance. Although he had been forging himself a successful career in the German film industry as a writer on such esteemed pictures as *Menschen am Sonntag* (1929) and *Emil und die Detektive* (1931), Hollywood had attracted many prominent European filmmakers following the First World War who had no political system to escape, only an artistic ambition to satisfy. The major

Hollywood studios were impressed by the sophistication and technical virtuosity of much European cinema and periodically sent delegations to Europe with the sole purpose of improving the American cinema by importing European talent. In Sweden, for example, Greta Garbo, Victor Sjöström and Mauritz Stiller were lured to Hollywood by Metro-Goldwyn-Mayer; from Germany, Austria and Hungary F W Murnau, Ernst Lubitsch, Fred Zinnemann and Michael Curtiz also went to Hollywood during the Twenties.

When Hitler came to power in 1933, the exodus was vastly accelerated. Robert Siodmak, Otto Preminger and Fritz Lang (who left Germany when offered the post of Head of the German film industry by Goebbels and whose banned *The Testament of Dr Mabuse*, made in 1933, had put Nazi slogans into the mouths of criminals) all eventually found their way to Hollywood and made there films of remarkable atmospheric similarity. As Colin McArthur has noted in his book 'Underworld USA' (Secker & Warburg, London, 1972), those directors whose sensibilities were, "forged in the uncertainty of Weimar Germany and decaying Austria-Hungary, were much more sour and pessimistic than the more buoyant vision of native American directors such as Ford and Capra." The refugees from Hitler's Europe had a significant influence on the American cinema, and Wilder was to make as important a contribution as any. It is, of course, open to speculation how Wilder's career might have developed had not Hitler come to power, and how the German film industry would have progressed without government interference and control. As it was, filmmaking in Germany prior to 1933 was arguably the most advanced and imaginative in the world, but the coincidental arrival of sound recording techniques would inevitably have lessened Germany's dominance, since the English-speaking market was by far the largest and Hollywood offered more facilities and opportunities than any country in Europe.

While Wilder's escape from Germany can be regarded as a tragic but shrewd piece of action, its significance on his subsequent work cannot be overestimated. His work is one of Hollywood's most thematically complex and his films struggle obsessively with the conflict between European romanticism and experience, a view inevitably tinged with melancholy, and the New World's brashness and opportunism. This is not to interpret Wilder's films in the light of his own life since, except in a general way, he has rarely used explicit biographical material as a basis for his plots (the major exception to this, perhaps, is *Hold Back the Dawn*). But the European inflection of his work is hard to escape, even for a spectator who might be unaware of his background. Numerous critics have remarked on the Expressionist *angst* to be found in Wilder's work, what Douglas McVay, in a 'Films and Filming' article (January 1960), once characterised as a, "German predilection for misery and misdeed, tinged by the 'fascination of the abomination' "; and Europe has served as an expressive backcloth for a number of Wilder's most important films. But the point of view has changed as Wilder has become assimilated into his country of adoption and deeply devoted to it. The movement from *Ninotchka* to *Avanti!* is a complicated and fascinating personal pilgrimage.

Ninotchka, Wilder's sixth Hollywood assignment as a screenwriter and his fourth in collaboration with Charles Brackett, raises specific questions of Wilder's indebtedness to Ernst Lubitsch, who directed the film. Although he worked on only two Lubitsch films (the only intermittently successful *Bluebeard's Eighth Wife* and *Ninotchka*), the *mitteleuropean* Jewish heritage of the two men is very similar and Wilder has never concealed his devotion for Lubitsch the man and the artist, particularly paying tribute to his wit and taste, his adult attitude to sexuality and yet his subtlety and discretion in portraying sexual relationships. "I always think of my style as a curious cross between Lubitsch and Stroheim", Wilder once said, implying there the tensions which animate a film of his. The polished, civilised and romantic side of his personality (the Lubitsch side) is often placed in abrupt juxtaposition with the ironic and grotesque (the Stroheim side). To appreciate the full measure and complexity of Wilder as an artist, one would need to take both into full account. Curiously, however, it is the second of these which critics have tended to stress in their approach to Wilder as so-called cynic, and the "Lubitsch side" has been regarded as either an insignificant embellishment or ignored altogether. When not ignored or undervalued, Wilder's connection with Lubitsch has been distorted. It is something of a critical commonplace to invoke Lubitsch at the expense of Wilder, to suggest that the style of 'The Master' has curdled in the hands of his grubbier-minded disciple. Thus, it is not surprising to find *Ninotchka* being used as a stick with which to beat Wilder's films, especially *One, Two, Three*. In a 'Films and Filming' article on Greta

Garbo, Richard Whitehall dismissed the trio of Russian commissars in *One, Two, Three* as "crudity itself" compared with Lubitsch's urbane treatment of Iranoff, Buljanoff and Kopalski in *Ninotchka*. "Lubitsch direction and Brackett/Wilder/Reisch screenplay add up to something much more moving and funny than Wilder direction and Wilder/Diamond screenplay," said 'Movie' at about the same time, "which again goes to show that a string of gags at machine gun rate is no substitute for concern with character.'

It should be said at once that nobody would be quicker to acknowledge the brilliance of Lubitsch than Wilder himself. "His art is lost," he said of Lubitsch in an article in 'Action' (November 1967), "That most elegant of screen magicians took his secret with him." Nevertheless, to attack Wilder for not being Lubitsch seems misguided in two essential ways. It is to underestimate the tenderness and romance in Wilder's films, which critics have wilfully persisted in misrepresenting as wholly rancid and savage. It is also to overlook the fact that times have changed and that Lubitsch himself might have experienced difficulty in remaining Lubitsch in a context of potential global annihilation – one recalls the public and critical unease and resistance when Lubitsch, however brilliantly, attempted to sustain his civilised, witty outlook against the background of Nazism in *To Be Or Not To Be* (1942). "We shall never see his like again," said Andrew Sarris in 'The American Cinema', "because the world he celebrated had died – even before he did – everywhere except in his own memory."

At the end of *Ninotchka* the hero and heroine and the three commissars (possibly modelled on the Marx Brothers) are all displaced persons, compelled to recreate in an alien land their joyous experience in Paris because what is now happening in their beloved city would make their way of life impossible. The ending makes clear the uncomfortable edge of the film's opening title, the saucy cheerfulness of which has not entirely banished a sombre, elegiac note: "This picture takes place in Paris in those wonderful days when a siren was a brunette and not an alarm . . . and if a Frenchman turned out the light it was not on account of an air-raid!". Lubitsch's world is traditionally one in which style, grace and manners are all important: a world in which pretension and pomposity and even cruelty exist in order to be satirised, but a world which nevertheless breathes an underlying idealism, Lubitsch's belief in man's innate rationalism, humour and shared standards of civilisation. Part of the poignancy of *Ninotchka* is not simply its celebration of this world, but the explicit recognition that it is on the point of collapse. Surely this is what is meant by Garbo's great speech and why we find it so moving: "The revolution is on the march . . . I know . . . wars will wash over us . . . bombs will fall . . . all civilisation will crumble . . . but not yet, please . . . wait, wait . . . what's the hurry? Let us be happy . . . give us our moment."

To put it melodramatically, Wilder is Lubitsch after the bombs have fallen. He has sustained many of Lubitsch's values, both moral and pictorial, but the world around him has grown more strident and menacing and Wilder's style could hardly avoid being correspondingly harsher, more sardonic. His world, unlike Lubitsch's, contains a powerful sense of loss (with Lubitsch, we bring the sense of loss to the films ourselves). So naturally *One, Two, Three* is more savage than *Ninotchka*, representing the ideological clash between Capitalism and Communism not in terms of romantic seduction but in terms of bullying gangsterism. *Ninotchka* is produced at a time when it is still just possible to make a joke out of a Nazi arriving at a Paris railway station. *A Foreign Affair* and *One, Two, Three* take place against a post-war Berlin background where the effects of Nazism are still evident as scars both on the landscape of the city and the psychology of the people. To expect Wilder to exhibit a Lubitsch-like sauveness and charm against that kind of devastation is to anticipate and indeed invite an insensitivity on the part of the director which Wilder, to his credit, has no intention of expressing.

Nevertheless, in arriving at the meaning of *Ninotchka* one must give careful attention to Wilder's authorial participation. Certainly the characters and situations of the film are so typical of the sort we are to see in his subsequent work that the picture is of particular interest. Admittedly, there is the problem of attributing in any precise way particular ideas and features of the film to particular people, and Wilder has gone on record as saying that the most important writer on a Lubitsch picture was Lubitsch himself, even though he never took credit for it. Is *Ninotchka* primarily a Lubitsch film, a Garbo film, an MGM film, a Brackett-Wilder film? Clearly it is all of these and the thematic focus of the film subtly shifts according to which auteur is emphasised. Naturally, this can be said of virtually every film made under studio conditions, and some might argue that all films are less the product of individuals than of ideological factors (which we shall discuss shortly), but it is important to say that *Ninotchka* has such a pronounced resemblance to Wilder's subsequent films that it seems inconceivable that his contribution to the collaborative effort was anything other than substantial.

For example, variations on the basic situation of *Ninotchka* – frosty deadpan Russian comrade (Garbo), in Paris on government business, is awakened to life and love by genial gigolo Count Leon D'Algout (Melvyn Douglas) – occur regularly in Wilder's work. Perhaps the most immediate comparison is with *Sabrina* which has a similar Cinderella theme (the transformation of the asexual heroine into a beautiful woman). In *Ninotchka* there is an equivalent to the opening Ball in *Sabrina*, the "commoner" heroine astounding the distinguished guests with her regality and ultimately even wearing a crown for the night, an idea that Wilder and Lubitsch may even have taken from Shaw's *Pygmalion* which was filmed in 1938. Paris plays a crucial part in both *Ninotchka* and *Sabrina* and the 'humanising' of a main character is a consistent Wilder concern.

In fact, one should make clear Ninotchka has as much in common with the typical Wilder hero as with his heroines. Indeed, her progress is probably closer to Humphrey Bogart's in *Sabrina* than Audrey Hepburn's in that both modify their rigid ideological positions (his Capitalist, hers Communist) when coming under the spell of romantic Paris, a city whose presence is felt symbolically more than physically. In both films, Paris is a place for those who do not quite fit in with their own society and find it difficult now to accept their national identity. "That foreign atmosphere . . . throws you out of gear," Ninotchka says to Razinin, the Commissar on the Board of Trade when she has sadly returned to Russia. Even before her Paris experience she has been wounded in love ("I kissed the Polish lancer too, before he died") and is disillusioned and wary of romantic commitment. Her submission to a rigid political system seems as much the consequence of emotional disenchantment as of ideological conviction. Her inner stability – her refusal to acknowledge feelings which burst the bonds of compartmentalisation – is maintained at a personal cost of self-denial and alienation. It is therefore a nice touch to allow the character to blossom when her stability is, in all senses, precarious: the moment when, slightly tipsy on champagne at the nightclub with Leon, she suddenly overflows with a sense of fellowship with the other people in the room. Instability is also at the root of the humour of the film's most famous scene when, "Garbo Laughs": the moment when Leon, upset at Ninotchka's refusal to laugh at his jokes, suddenly overbalances and falls off his chair and when Ninotchka's self-control is suddenly swept away by her helpless hilarity at the ridiculous spectacle of human dignity spread-eagled. It is one of the most beautiful love scenes in screen comedy and all the more effective through the film's careful build-up to this moment in terms of Ninotchka's implied receptiveness and vulnerability. The undercutting of Ninotchka's severity is even signalled at the very opening of the sequence. Her meagre order in the bistro of, "Raw beets and carrots" (this kind of restraint a clear sign in Wilder of an underdeveloped appetite for life) is contemptuously dismissed by the *patron*, "Madame", he says, affronted, "this is a restaurant, not a meadow".

Ninotchka's rejuvenation, in Garbo's glowing performance, rather undermines the parallel conversion of the hero. Consequently, despite

Ninotchka: *Greta Garbo and Melvyn Douglas at the bistro*

Melvyn Douglas's spirited playing (which itself is strikingly close to Herbert Marshall's roles in Lubitsch's *Trouble in Paradise* and *Angel*), Leon seems a somewhat slender creation compared with the later Wilder heroes whose progress is to be similar. The characterisation seems to proceed more through incidental implication than through solid development. That Leon warms to the Garbo charisma tells us little about him, since the whole film is geared to seducing its audience in a similar way. Also, the callousness of his mistress, the Grand Duchess Swana, and her treatment of Leon as a prized pet, tell us more about the weakness of the character and the wretchedness of his position than anything he is actually given to do himself. Somehow the character does not seem adequately integrated in the narrative. He remains something of an embryonic Wilder hero (and, one might uncharitably argue, a fully developed Lubitsch wastrel), a casual gigolo whose values are completely shaken up by his fascination with a remote, seemingly innocent heroine, a process which leads to his regeneration. The gigolo redeemed by love is to be more deeply developed in *Hold Back the Dawn* and *Sunset Boulevard*.

The latter film is also invoked through the Grand Duchess' devious plans to wrest her lover from the younger heroine, which anticipates the Swanson-Holden-Olson triangle of *Sunset Boulevard*. Incisively played by Ina Claire, the Grand Duchess Swana has something of Norma Desmond's narcissism: she is introduced in the film gazing at herself in the mirror and musing, "I guess one gets the face one deserves." Like Norma, she is a figure from a past era who has had her glory stolen from her and is trying to retrieve it. In fact, she is attempting to reclaim her jewels which were confiscated by the State after the Russian Revolution and which have suddenly turned up in Paris, so the Grand Duchess's rivalry with Ninotchka is not only romantically based but ideologically determined – the titled Russian refugee is unable to escape the upheavals caused by the proletariat. Inevitably, her exchanges with Ninotchka have real tension and fire and in their final scene together one is unobtrusively made aware of mirrors and clocks in the background as the Grand Duchess reveals the brutal, calculating side of her face under the veneer of 'civilisation', and Ninotchka sees her own time running out, recognising that the fulfilment of her mission means acceding to Swana's wishes and relinquishing Leon.

Because the hostility between Ninotchka and Swana is both

romantic and ideological, it would be appropriate to define the triangular structure of *Ninotchka* more closely. If Leon is torn between both women, Ninotchka is equally torn between Leon and Lenin. Interestingly, both Ninotchka and Leon have a picture of their alternative 'partner'. Leon's picture of Swana winds up in a drawer as she is displaced in his affections by Ninotchka, a gesture which even Ninotchka seems to feel as somehow furtive and callous ("Oh Leon! Don't ever ask me for a picture of myself. I couldn't bear the thought of being shut up in a drawer. I couldn't breathe. I couldn't stand it.") In contrast, Ninotchka's picture of Lenin is animated into a smile, a Lubitsch touch which, as Richard Corliss has suggested in his book 'Talking Pictures' (Overlook Press, New York, 1974), demeans the script rather than improves it. Perhaps there is an uncomfortable feeling of coyness about the moment, yet the contrasting fates of the pictures is important in what it tells us about the two characters. Leon's transformation is demonstrated by his hiding an emblem of his former life guiltily in a drawer; Ninotchka's is signalled by endowing a similar emblem of her former life with humanity. Rather than reject or hide an object which represents her ideology, she transforms it – gives it a human face.

It is a point worth bearing in mind for anyone who might regard the film's ostensible celebration of the seductiveness of capitalism as a little unsubtle. For one thing, Leon is equally seduced by Communism. Ninotchka might discover gaiety but Leon equally achieves a delicious camaraderie with the working men in the bistro, starts being nice to his servant, makes his own bed and casts off the not-so-lovable Swana, whose Imperialist insensitivity is ruthlessly exposed. One could even argue that Leon's sacrifice is the greater of the two. Even when drunk, Ninotchka does not renounce her beliefs: she starts spreading Communist doctrine to the ladies in the powder room. At the end of the film she is insistent about attempting to reconcile her awakened humanity with being, "a good Russian," whereas Leon seems stateless and somehow more isolated. All this curiously blurs the film's political focus so that, for example, Maurice Zolotow's confident description of it as "anti-Soviet" and "anti-Communist" is hard to credit against evidence from the film. (Even Ninotchka's May Day march in Moscow, seen in the context of Wilder's subsequent work, has its closest parallel in the very different ideological climate of *The Apartment*, where Bud Baxter's career march has similar implications of stifled individuality.) It remains somewhat ambiguous whether this 'blurring' arises from a deliberate narrative strategy or from an injudicious balance in the sympathies of the film, Garbo's charisma submerging not only Melvyn Douglas but also what he stands for.

However, this 'blurring' becomes somewhat clearer when one considers the film's explicit hostility towards Fascism. That the film's main enemy is not Communism or Capitalism but Fascism is demonstrated in several ways. Most explicitly, perhaps, but less powerfully, are the few direct references to the rise of Hitler: the opening caption which casts the shadow of war over Paris and the comic *Sieg Heils* at the railway station. More significant is Ninotchka's speech on the dance floor in which she appeals for universal brotherhood, wishing to unite the people of France against tyranny and dictatorship. The film is careful to mock Capitalism and Communism equally: for every joke about Stalin's Russia ("The last mass trials were a great success," says Ninotchka at the station. "There are going to be fewer but better Russians!") Leon's shallow existence is constantly under attack. As we have tried to demonstrate, the film does not condemn Communism as a political system and neither does it reproach Ninotchka for her belief in it; what the film does do is render Communism's representatives as human (from the animated picture of Lenin to the spontaneous party in Ninotchka's Moscow apartment). Nor does the film (obviously enough) condemn Capitalism but it does present some unacceptable faces of it. What does this strategy imply? *Ninotchka* was shot and released during 1939, when war in Europe was a fact and not just a genuine fear. The United States government, then three years away from direct military involvement, was nevertheless advocating support for those nations threatened by Germany, and the American film industry, largely controlled by Jewish interests and, as we have seen, containing a sizeable and significant European and Jewish creative contingent, would wish to support its government's policy in the only way open to it. *Ninotchka* therefore stands up as a clear example of discreet propaganda, advocating solidarity between America and the Soviet Union in the struggle against Hitler. If the ideology of Communism has to be softened a little and the lures of Capitalism informed with a certain sourness, the reconciliation between them is no less moving or meaningful. It is not what each of them represents that is important, but what each of them opposes.

The urgency of the film's message and the fear of its going unheeded might account for the gathering melancholia which overtakes the second half, particularly in the memorable stretch where the intoxicated, self-crowned Ninotchka, having bestowed universal love and equal royalty on her subjects, awakens to the grey reality of the morning, her diadem gone. Wilder, it might be said, has inherited not only Lubitsch's crown but Ninotchka's hangover. We will have to wait fifteen years before Lubitsch's champagne world can be evoked again, and we eavesdrop on Sabrina as she writes a letter home from her apartment in Paris.

Sabrina (1954)

"Sabrina fair
Listen where thou art sitting
Under the glassy, cool, translucent wave
In twisted braids of lilies knitting
The loose train of thy amber-dropping hair;
Listen for dear honour's sake,
Goddess of the silver lake
Listen and save"

(John Milton, *Comus*, lines 859-866)

"That name! That name!"

(Larrabee Senior, having heard his son David refer to Sabrina once too often)

* * *

In her apartment in Paris, Sabrina Fairchild (Audrey Hepburn) is writing a letter to her father (John Williams). She has been sent to Paris for two years to achieve a diploma in *haute cuisine.* More particularly, she has been sent there to recover from her unrequited love for David Larrabee (William Holden), the more wayward of the two sons of the rich Larrabee family for whom Fairchild is chauffeur. In the letter she writes of a new-found acceptance of life. "I have learned how to live . . . how to be *in* the world and *of* the world," she writes; and Wilder tracks slowly from medium-shot to close-up, stopping at the moment when Sabrina says she now feels part of life, and looks up from her writing. In that close-up, exquisitely timed in terms of gesture and camera movement, the feeling of a positive embracing of life is unforgettably crystallised.

Because it is less wilfully abrasive and assertive than its two immediate predecessors (*Ace in the Hole* and *Stalag 17*), *Sabrina* has been unfairly neglected in articles on Wilder and in interviews: even as perceptive a Wilder critic as Robert Mundy has dismissed the film as "mediocre" when what really seems to be meant is that the film appears "uncharacteristic". But looking at it now from the vantage points of *The Private Life of Sherlock Holmes* and *Avanti!*, we can see that its mellowness seems more characteristic than ever; but even then, the dreaming lightness of *Sabrina* was not unprecedented, being traceable in Wilder's work back to *Ein Blonder Traum* and *Midnight* and to the tradition of glossy Paramount comedies of the Thirties.

Joseph McBride has singled out this early letterwriting scene in *Sabrina* as one of Wilder's most successful attempts before *Avanti!* at catching the mellow, bittersweet tone of his mentor, Lubitsch. Certainly the scene is bathed throughout in an unmistakably romantic glow. At one stage Sabrina interrupts her writing to open her window more widely so that she can hear the strains of "La Vie en Rose" from a nearby accordionist. The mood is intensified by the way in which we *hear* Sabrina's voice narrating the contents of the letter over the soundtrack. This contrasts with the way in which Wilder has staged her earlier suicide note (which we *see* her laboriously writing, her grief over David's indifference appropriately internalised) but recalls the very opening of the film where her narration about the Larrabee household begins "Once upon a time . . ." and we are taken on a documentary tour, narrated by Sabrina, of the Larrabee's Long Island stronghold, noting the two tennis courts and the collection of automobiles. It is a tribute to Wilder's structural sense that these seemingly casual details, like those of the opening narration of *The Apartment*, have a later importance: but the thing we note immediately is the *tone* of the narration, which is that of a child telling a fairy-story.

Two points need to be made here. One must always be wary of taking at face value the narration in a Wilder film (a device he uses often) and not recognising that, for example, Gillis's narration in *Sunset Boulevard*, Baxter's in *The Apartment*, and Sabrina's here are intended as revelations of character and not as unadorned statements of fact. Also the casting of Audrey Hepburn is surely intended to reinforce the idea of fairy-tale, coming, as she did, fresh from her stage triumph in 'Ondine' – about the romance between a knight and a beautiful young sea nymph – and her Oscar-winning performance as the runaway Princess in William Wyler's *Roman Holiday* (1953)*. If those evocations of fairy-tale and romance are not enough, the name of the character, Sabrina Fairchild, which is constantly alluded to during the course of the film, invokes the character of Sabrina in Milton's 'Comus', who is also a water-nymph and who, like the character here, comes to the aid of two brothers.

What Wilder is doing here, then, is establishing a character with the habit of turning life into romance. This tendency can be seen both in her big gestures (the romantic excess of her suicide attempt) and in small details (at one stage, she even manages to convert "Yes, we have no bananas" into a romantic song). The opening of the film plays overtly with these fairy-tale associations – the full moon; the servant girl perched in the tree gazing longingly at the glittering array of Sachs clothing and Tiffany jewelry and, transformed by her experience in Paris, eventually going to the ball with Prince Charming – before bringing them to a climax at the dance between David and Sabrina and then fascinatingly reworking them.

If it is unexpected that Wilder should establish this romantic aura with such gravity and affection, even more surprising is the way in which it is developed. Subjected to stress and ridicule throughout the film (one recalls how Linus Larrabee, played by Humphrey Bogart, exasperatedly describes Sabrina early on as "the last of the romantics"), romanticism ultimately triumphs. The intense realisation of the letter-writing scene in Paris sets up not only the emotional tone of the film but its spiritual centre. "La Vie en Rose" (I'm looking at life through rose-coloured glasses) begins to dominate the film's beautifully arranged soundtrack. Indeed, one way of reading the film is to notice how that song begins to contend for prominence over its rival, Rodgers and Hart's "Isn't It Romantic?", the two being woven together in an ingenious orchestral arrangement at the film's high-point of tension (the night scene in Linus's office between him and Sabrina), and with the French melody finally ascendant at the film's finale. "Isn't It Romantic?" was first heard in Rouben Mamoulian's distinctly Lubitschian Paramount musical-comedy *Love Me Tonight*

*In a sense, one can see *Roman Holiday* as "the Wilder film that got away" and *Sabrina* as Wilder's oblique tribute to it. The structure of Wyler's film could have furnished a classic outline for a Wilder film – the European setting; the innocent heroine; the deceitful American journalist who cannot go through with his deception – and might well have been as significant an influence on *Sabrina* as the Samuel Taylor play on which it is based.

(1932) in which Maurice Chevalier courts Jeanette MacDonald in Paris and Wilder's use of it here is both an affectionate reference to the genre and, as in *A Foreign Affair* where the song accompanies shots of devastated Berlin, a sardonic acknowledgement that the kind of world celebrated by the song is becoming increasingly elusive and difficult. In *Sabrina*, "Isn't It Romantic?" adds a layer of irony to the romantic transactions, accompanying the moment, for example, when Linus tries to buy off Sabrina at the party and being predominantly connected with David's midnight trysts with available women in the deserted indoor tennis court. The victory of "La Vie en Rose" is therefore significant since, by extension, it represents a victory for Sabrina over David, for her romantic idealism over his pseudo-romantic slickness and calculation.

It could also represent a victory of Paris over America. Again, the casting of Audrey Hepburn, whose European origins would have been more evident to audiences at the time than now, would be significant here. Even the archetypal American business magnate, Linus Larrabee, who cannot even pose for a family photograph without a copy of the 'Wall Street Journal' protruding from his coat pocket, stumblingly begins to speak French towards the end of the film. It is a detail that has the same seeds of character development as Jack Lemmon's faltering Italian in *Avanti!*, both films based on Samuel Taylor plays and dealing in part with the regeneration of the American executive. And as in *Ninotchka*, Paris is idealised, representing romance, gaiety and freedom against work, intellect and repression. In Paris, Sabrina becomes a part of the world and not, as in America, a mere onlooker.

In both *Ninotchka* and *Sabrina*, the transformation of the heroines is marked when they throw open windows to let in the Parisian air, a moment of emotional and spiritual release. "Paris is a place for changing your outlook . . . for throwing open the windows," Sabrina tells the sceptical Linus aboard his yacht. Earlier, Linus has praised Sabrina's effect on David after her return from Paris: "It's as though a window has been blown open and a lovely fresh breeze has blown through this stuffy old house," he says. This is all the more ironic since Linus is the one who has rescued Sabrina from suffocating herself with the poisoned air of the Larrabee limousines – a suicide attempt striking not only at her own and her father's social standing but registering a sharp protest at the wealth and apparent indifference of the Larrabee family. Sabrina cannot breathe the Larrabee air but the Larrabees are intoxicated by hers. "Throwing open the windows" becomes an image of freedom and rejuvenation: each of the two sequences at the cookery school begins with shots through a circular window, anticipating the circular piece of unbreakable glass that Linus is so proud of. When Linus is deeply involved in his scheme to divert Sabrina away from David he orders Fairchild to drive with "two windows down" (David, of course, drives a convertible which Linus subsequently borrows); even during her suicide attempt in the garage, Sabrina opens a window to stop herself coughing. The insistent window imagery reminds us that *Sabrina* is a film about breaking down barriers, both social (Sabrina herself) and emotional (Linus). The image of life represented here by Sabrina contrasts significantly with that represented by her father (and also by Larrabee Senior, with his distaste for the social mobility of the twentieth century): he insists on knowing your place and not reaching for the moon. "I see life as a limousine," he tells his daughter, "with a front seat and a back seat, *and a window in between.*" Appropriately, this window is lowered when Sabrina's presence threatens the delicate social equilibrium. This attitude, encapsulating social rigidity and emotional claustrophobia, is vanquished by the last shot of the film of Linus and Sabrina together, out on the deck of an ocean liner transporting them to the city of romance.

If Sabrina's tendency is to turn life into romance, the inclination of Linus has been to convert romance into high finance. It is not accidental that Sabrina's letter-writing scene is placed directly after the scene between the Larrabee brothers when David storms into Linus' office to complain about the announcement of his engagement in the papers to Elizabeth Tyson (Martha Hyer) which Linus, unknown to him, has contrived. The juxtaposition of these two scenes emphasises the ideological poles represented by Sabrina and Linus and the distance the latter has to travel in the film in order to claim the girl at the end. He has indeed engineered a marriage between David and Elizabeth because she is the daughter of the owner of a large sugar-cane concern and Larrabee Plastics Co needs the sugar-cane for its new project of manufacturing unbreakable glass. In other words, it is not a marriage between David and Elizabeth, but a marriage between plastic and sugar-cane, arranged by the heads of the two industries – "I proposed and Mr Tyson accepted," is how Linus puts it. It is even going to be a summer wedding to cash in on the summer sugar-cane crop.

The reduction of people to useful objects is a pronounced characteristic of Wilder's representations of Capitalism. People are identified not by their names but by their business connections, a habit acquired by Sabrina's father who, at the opening ball, informs Sabrina that David is dancing with the Chase National Bank. Marriages are arranged not for love but for profit and amalgamation. One of the visual characteristics of the film, which signifies this theme, is its opening a scene with a shot of an object which identifies a main character – the poodle called David which introduces Sabrina's return from Paris; the fan, ice and champagne which announce the prostrate David after his accident with the wine glasses; the creaky record player which refers us to Linus aboard his yacht. These details establish the context very quickly but they also signify a world in which people are constantly in danger of being dehumanised, to the extent that the line between person and object becomes almost indistinguishable: "You need dusting," says Sabrina to that old record of "Yes, we have no bananas", a remark which causes Linus to flinch. "I didn't mean you, Linus," she hurriedly adds. Similarly, the Larrabees' tennis court exploits the sport's associations of "Love" and "Match" in making an expressive setting for David's romantic rendezvous, while simultaneously commenting on his emotional immaturity, his view of romance simply as a game. David sees women as sexual objects while Linus regards them as financial objects. Admiring Sabrina's physical attributes, David comments, "Look at those legs. Aren't they something?" to which Linus responds: "The last pair of legs that were something cost the family 25,000 dollars." The course of the film is to expose both attitudes as equally repulsive.

In fact, the ultimate expression of this blurring of human and object is in the presentation of the two brothers, which is essentially a contrast between the man of plastic and the man of glass. Wilder is clearly amused by their entrenched positions and it is important to recognise that he views them as equally inadequate, giving a certain piquancy to the exclamation at one stage of Larrabee Senior (Walter Hampden): "Have I spawned *two* idiot sons?". David's athletic vault over the garden wall to greet Sabrina at the ball might be one of the comic highpoints of the picture, David's extrovert frivolity taken to an extreme of absurdity; but, at the same occasion, there is a lovely cutaway to Linus and his assorted guests jumping up and down on the durable glass panel of which Linus is so inordinately proud. Linus's jump is clearly as silly as David's, and the film is eventually concerned with the way both of them find some sort of equilibrium. David might seem a romantic womaniser but he also has three embarrassing broken marriages on his (and his family's) conscience, and his obsessive and excessive libido seems symptomatic of sexual insecurity. Conversely, however Linus might disapprove of his brother's womanising, he has no scruples about exploiting it if a profitable marriage can be secured. While David is flashy, brittle and transparent, Linus is like his product: he does not burn, he does not scorch, he does not melt. (What is more, Linus has come up with a formula for sweet-tasting plastic, which implies how plastic represents for him the sweet smell of success.) The full significance of this is realised when David accidentally sits on a wine-glass which splinters painfully and which forces Linus into taking David's place as Sabrina's date. Prince Charming turns out to be made of glass and is replaced by a plastic model.

At this point of the film, Linus provides his injured brother with a plastic hammock so that he may rest his sore spot in comfort. This

Sabrina: *Humphrey Bogart, the man of plastic*

ostensibly generous gesture has an ulterior motive since he wants to keep David out of the way while he goes to work on Sabrina, whose effect on David since her return from Paris is threatening the arranged marriage with Elizabeth and sugar-cane. It is appropriate therefore that this scene contains a striking shot from behind the hammock, which shows Linus's face twisted by the plastic reflection, a visual indicator of how his own humanity is being twisted by his mercenary obsession with his product. He does, after all, believe that people are malleable. He twists David to his own designs and attempts to do the same thing with Sabrina, initially trying to buy her off and, when this fails, pursues his materialistic ends under the disguise of love.

Wilder's characters invariably go through a prolonged period of phoney affection and sexual attraction before they are able to love without inhibition. Typically, this feigned love or interest gives way to actual love, and deception gives way to confession, as when Linus tells Sabrina of the real significance of the two boat tickets to Paris, rather than the romantic significance which she has read into them. There is traditionally a point beyond which no Wilder hero can go and Linus's reformation is emphasised particularly here, since he confesses when he does not have to: the deception could have been continued. Ironically, the romantic meaning which Sabrina has mistakenly read into the tickets is actually to prove correct: Linus *is* to join her on the boat and not leave her to travel to Paris alone. This confirms the development of the film towards an ultimately romantic vision, but Linus's confession also indicates how, for Wilder, it is important for his flawed heroes to be humbled and humiliated before their reformation can begin. Wilder has detailed Linus's development with a typical mixture of admiration and disgust: admiration for the way he gradually comes to realise that there is more to life than the Stock Market; disgust at the way he has originally gone about his transformation. Sabrina can have no illusions about Linus at the end of the film, any more than Baxter can have any about Miss Kubelik at the end of *The Apartment*. Romance is tempered by knowledge, not sustained by naive ignorance.

Something should be said here about the unusual casting of Humphrey Bogart as Linus, an actor more familiar as a private eye or idealistic recluse than as a business magnate. Bogart was offered the role after Cary Grant proved unavailable, which necessitated a rapid re-write of the script in order to mould the part around Bogart, whose personality shared little with Grant's. (Howard Hawks has used both actors brilliantly, but Grant would be unthinkable in *The Big Sleep*, whatever Raymond Chandler might say, and Bogart hopelessly out of place in *Monkey Business*.) One suspects that the critics' neglect of *Sabrina* is partly to do with this idiosyncratic usage of Bogart but Wilder's subtle undermining and reconstruction of Bogart's image is one of the film's most interesting and engaging features. Wilder seizes on the opportunities offered by Bogart's deep-rooted personification of the mysterious loner, perfected perhaps in Michael Curtiz' *Casablanca* (1942), where one is never really certain what Bogart is or has been. At the same time, Wilder examines the darker areas of this isolation, particularly present in Bogart's films of the early 'Fifties such as Nicholas Ray's *In a Lonely Place* (1950), (where Bogart's Hollywood screenwriter offers intriguing comparisons with Gillis in *Sunset Boulevard*), Richard Brooks's *Deadline* (1952) and Edward Dmytryk's *The Caine Mutiny* (1954) when the isolation is beginning to have connotations of alienation, vulnerability and disintegration. At one stage Linus says: "No man walks alone from choice." The line is surely as much a calculated reference to Bogart's screen persona as to the character of Linus. But the point is that it takes on a satisfyingly ambiguous resonance precisely because of this: one is not sure whether the line is intended ironically or not. As such, it enlarges on Linus's own developing confusion, for a number of his statements take on this kind of double meaning. "What's at the end of a million?", he says at another stage, "Zero, zero, zero. A circle with a hole in it. Nothing." Is Linus playing the role of the disillusioned executive there, to catch Sabrina off guard, or has she genuinely made him aware of the hollowness of his way of life? Bogart's rumpled presence and Wilder's skilful deployment of its evocative associations give the film a tension that would have been absent had Cary Grant played the role, just as Wilder's similarly idiosyncratic use of Gary Cooper in the closely related *Love in the Afternoon* turns an unexpected change of casting into one of the film's greatest assets.

Of course (and this is precisely the point), Bogart is old enough to be Audrey Hepburn's father – thirty years older, in fact – but although *Sabrina* breaks with established patterns of Hollywood romance, the love between Linus and Sabrina develops quite naturally within the context Wilder provides. Coupled with the vulnerability and mystery of Linus's character, which would attract someone of

Sabrina's romantic disposition, we must also note her strong attraction to father-figures. This is seen not only in her close relationship with her own father (her suicide attempt using her father's objects of employment emphasises her crisis when the youthful David rejects her), but in her close friendship with the wise, kindly Baron who befriends her in her cookery class in Paris and is the man who inspires her return to life. (Intriguingly, when Sabrina writes to her father and friends about him they initially assume him to be Sabrina's beau.) A possible connection between the Baron (Marcel Dalio, famous for his role as the Marquise de la Chesnaye in Renoir's 1939 film *La Règle du Jeu* which *Sabrina* vaguely resembles in its social satire) and Linus has been subtly suggested early in the film; just as the Baron has inspired Sabrina's renewed commitment to life, Linus has saved her from asphyxiation in the garage. "What would have happened if I hadn't come along?", Linus has demanded, to which Sabrina has responded plaintively, "I'd have died" – a peculiarly pregnant remark in the light of the film's subsequent development. In retrospect, the relationship between Linus and Sabrina is not only convincing but inevitable. Having saved her from death, it is only natural that Sabrina should save him from a different kind of suffocation.

A word which is often used of Linus is "control". In the merger of the plastic and the sugar-cane, it is stressed that Linus keeps the "controls". Appropriately, then, his increasing humanity is signalled by his gradual loss of control towards the end of the film: his sudden irritation with his father's attempt to dislodge an olive from the bottom of a glass and shoving the olive between the old man's teeth; his uncontrolled punching of David during the most formalised of occasions, the board meeting; and his unsolicited confession to Sabrina. Linus's divesting himself of his usual emotional restraint is paralleled by the shedding of his business identity as expressed through his clothes, particularly his hat and umbrella (which, in one of the final scenes, David momentarily claims). Wilder's films often culminate in some kind of adjustment of clothing, which is equally an adjustment of identity: Daphne (Jack Lemmon) pulling off "her" wig to reveal the disguise to Osgood in *Some Like it Hot*; Baxter thrusting his bowler hat on the head of a bewildered cleaner as he walks out on his job in *The Apartment*. In *Sabrina*, although Linus suspects himself of falling in love with Sabrina, it is not until she's aboard the ocean liner bound for Europe that he finally realises and admits it. He is about to open a board meeting in a room overlooking New York harbour when David casually strolls in. Linus's first reaction has been to arrange it so that David could sail away with Sabrina and to hell with plastic and sugar-cane, but David in a rush of words now persuades Linus to take the pilot launch and join Sabrina on the boat. A complete reversal of the ending of *Casablanca* (the similarities are too obvious to think it was entirely unintentional), Linus throws his briefcase to David and walks out on capitalism. On the boat, Sabrina adjusts the brim of Linus's hat and he hooks his umbrella on to the belt of a passer-by. Only then can they embrace on equal terms. It is the shedding of Linus's "undertaker" image and signifies his entry into a new life, on a boat appropriately called the "Liberte".

This ending considerably undercuts Linus's vindication of capitalism earlier the film ("People who once had a dime now have a dollar and Puerto Rican kids can go around in shoes and have their teeth straightened," anticipating Wendell Armbruster's capitalistic boast in *Avanti!*) since the film's conclusion clearly reinforces Wilder's scepticism about all this. We are certainly not meant to view Linus's final decision to join Sabrina as irresponsible. If Paris is offered as the humane alternative to Communism in *Ninotchka*, it is offered equally forcefully as the humane alternative to Capitalism in *Sabrina*. The film's implicit indictment of American values takes it in the direction of *The Apartment*. Wilder's hilarious establishing shot of the Larrabee building is evidence enough of his sardonic view of American endeavour (the camera grandly revealing the plaques of ownership in a manner that seems to liken this acquisition of property and labour to the assembling of a Meccano set). Similarly ironic, then, must be the family portrait of the Larrabee dynasty at the beginning of the film. Wilder's camera has tracked silkily away from a wall painting of the family's illustrious and pioneering ancestors to take in the present generation, firmly planting them in the American mould – especially in the Eisenhower years – of progress and paternalism. It is this which Linus is to walk out on at the end, with Wilder's full approval, leaving his props behind him to clean-cut playboy David, the all-American executive of the future.

Although the merger is still going ahead at the end, the situation now is one of some confusion. Larrabee Senior attempts to take the vacant chair, but proves to be as brittle as David. And although David finally engineers his brother's departure from the boardroom, the fact

Sabrina: *The Larrabee Dynasty*

that he should end up as head of the company seems to summarise Wilder's ambivalence towards the American business ethic.

The movement of the film is unequivocally one of pulling Linus into a world of romance and emotion, a world in which he could well be a fish out of water (as Sabrina has been in the Larrabee world at the beginning). Earlier, the film has made high comedy out of Linus's attempt to revive his courting technique, digging out his old Yale sweater for the yacht-trip, grimacing at his sporty image in the mirror, and regarding "Yes, we have no bananas" as a suitable song for seduction. The shrewd camera placement for the final shot makes Linus look comically incongruous as he walks towards Sabrina, twirling his umbrella in a gesture that is little short of Chaplinesque*.

*Wilder may even have intended to give this scene its Chaplinesque inference as an oblique reminder of Chaplin's controversial departure from America in 1952, by ocean liner bound for Europe with a much younger wife.

The tone, though, is not one of ridicule: Wilder admires the commitment without underrating the difficulty. The Cinderella theme has been completely turned on its head. The film is no longer about a "displaced person", Sabrina, where she belongs socially and about the possibility of a chauffeur's daughter entering the Larrabee world. Wilder underplays the social theme (which might have interested *Wyler*) to throw emphasis on to the spiritual one. The film is about the entrance into the Sabrina world of the Larrabee Male, his renunciation of economic calculation and family reputation for the sake of emotional fulfilment.

Oddly enough, considering the ease and lightness of the playing and direction, *Sabrina* was a troubled production. None of its stars liked each other, to put it mildly, and in particular the tension between Bogart and Wilder has been extensively recounted (in all its lurid detail by Maurice Zolotow on one side, and by Bogart's biographer, Nathaniel Benchley, on the other). Nevertheless, as with the considerably more traumatic production of *Some Like it Hot*, these background tensions do not really concern us and have little effect on what we see on the screen. *Sabrina* is one of Wilder's most beguiling and personal films, structured around three of his favourite situations – the reluctant hero (Linus), forced into playing a role by material circumstances and finally accepting that role; a second hero (David) who comes to reject his life-style while gaining his self-respect; and a young innocent girl (Sabrina) who goes to Paris, returning as a mature woman and effecting the transformation of the two men. To say that *Sabrina* is a personal film, of course, is not necessarily to say that it is a good one, and *Sabrina* is in many ways a test case for authorship, an ostensibly frivolous work which becomes more substantial the more you know about the director. Our own impression is that this is a Wilder film which grows in stature every time we see it. In its stylistic restraint, its perfectly controlled tone, its structural coherence (particularly the tactic of repeating scenes with significant variations), it is one of Wilder's most subtly crafted works.

It is at least the equal of *Ninotchka* and seems more perfect in its stylistic precision (Richard Corliss, in 'Talking Pictures', has neatly summarised the stylistic traits of *Ninotchka* which do not wear too well). Moreover, for all the considerable wit, charm and ideological tension of *Ninotchka*, it is not very difficult to satirise Communism if it is represented in so stereotyped a way as Garbo's Commissar, nor too provocative to satirise Communism within a capitalistic mode of production. It is much more audacious for a Hollywood film like *Sabrina* to satirise Capitalism and to do so through a character like Linus who is presented in a much more sympathetic and thoughtful way. Of all Wilder's films up to that time, *Sabrina* is the one that looks forward to the serenity of *Avanti!*. It might lack that masterpiece's inclusiveness, its epic survey of the meaning of America and Europe for the Wilder hero, but it shares its unambiguous endorsement of a risky, courageous commitment to humanistic rather than material values. In this, *Sabrina* is one of Wilder's most vital, life-affirming films.

Love in the Afternoon (1957)

For Monsieur Claude Chevasse (Maurice Chevalier) the records of his private detective cases are a "sewer", charting in lurid detail the murky depths of human morality. But for his young and beautiful daughter Ariane (Audrey Hepburn) the files are a "library of romance", containing delirious tales of titled men and servant girls falling off the Matterhorn in suicidal embraces and of dashing matadors sweeping respectable ladies off their feet; particularly, the files detail the adventures of Frank Flannagan (Gary Cooper), an American whose international business interests have taken him through the bedrooms of Europe. For Chevasse the files, which line the walls of his study like trophies of misplaced enterprise, present an unsavoury reality from which he tries to shield his daughter. But for Ariane the files are almost fictions into which she escapes when her father is out all night on a case. When the romantic fiction becomes a reality for Ariane, she not only surrenders herself to its mythology, she also turns it upside-down.

Like Sabrina Fairchild before her, Ariane dreams of escaping her dull and sheltered existence – she calls herself, "A for Anonymous", at one point with intentional irony – but Ariane is more secure and resourceful than Sabrina was in the early stages of the film, before she left for her "therapeutic" cookery course in Paris. By already being a Parisienne, Ariane has a head start over Sabrina and her escape route begins in the French capital and ends, we are told, in New York. As in *Sabrina*, in which the heroine is left taking the unlikeliest man away with her to Paris by ocean liner, so Ariane is left with the unlikeliest man, bound first to the French Riviera by train and then by liner to America. In neither case are we shown their arrival or their future lives together, but the conclusions we draw are undeniably optimistic since the characters involved have reached a spiritual point of no return: as with Linus in *Sabrina*, we admire the commitment without underrating the difficulty.

In one sense, *Love in the Afternoon* reverses the customary Wilder principle of having an American humanised by a European influence and settling down in the Old World, but the film's gloriously uplifting, entirely logical and emotionally demanding climax finds Wilder, collaborating with I A L Diamond for the first time, in a conciliatory frame of mind. If the American in *Sabrina* is insensitive to anything but the profit motive, and the American in *Avanti!* obsessed with robot-like precision and speed, the American in *Love in the Afternoon* is already humanised and sophisticated, but to a vulgar and wholly irresponsible degree, and is finally persuaded by a worldly-wise but inexperienced European to reject his playboy life-style to settle down in New York as a happily married, ageing and responsible business executive.

Love in the Afternoon is one of Wilder's richest and most personal films*; again, like *Sabrina*, its greatness is only fully realised from the vantage points of *The Private Life of Sherlock Holmes* and *Avanti!* and it, too, has been unfairly neglected in articles on Wilder, even though he thinks highly of it: our inclusion here (and elsewhere in this book) of certain contemporary press comments and criticisms is not intended to ridicule those writing without the benefit of hindsight, but is intended to demonstrate what might be termed the prevailing norms as they existed and how many of Wilder's films deviated from what was regarded as socially acceptable in the commercial cinema. If the overall theme and conclusion of *Love in the Afternoon* was frowned upon by many critics it was perhaps because Wilder's devotion to the cinema of Ernst Lubitsch had somehow become coarsened in the hands of Hollywood's most famous "cynic". But as Richard Corliss observes in his book 'Talking Pictures', "It is certainly unfair to contrast 'Thirties' Lubitsch with 'Fifties' Wilder. And who is to say

---

**Love in the Afternoon* is also one of Wilder's rarest films: no prints are known to exist in Britain and the authors' first glimpse of the film was the brief extract shown in Nicolas Roeg's *The Man Who Fell to Earth* (1976) in which the alien David Bowie views several movies simultaneously to receive an impression of human behavioural patterns.

that, had Lubitsch lived to make films in the atomic age, one of his characters would not have been allowed to muse, "If people loved each other more, they'd shoot each other less'?". Indeed, *Love in the Afternoon* is Wilder's most emphatic tribute to Lubitsch: the theme of a rehabilitated playboy recalls Gary Cooper in *Bluebeard's Eighth Wife*, while the luxury Paris hotel setting recalls Ninotchka's transformation. One scene in particular could have been adapted from any number of situations in Lubitsch films (*Trouble in Paradise* particularly): next door to the hero's hotel suite a rich, middle-aged woman stays with her pet Chihuahua which she calls Picasso. While the woman is asleep, her dog keeps barking as mysterious figures pass through her room to gain access to the hero's suite by way of the outside balcony. The woman always wakes up when no-one's there and scolds Picasso for disturbing her sleep. When the hero becomes involved with the heroine, he forgets that his bath is running and the overflow seeps into the next door suite, causing Picasso to sound the alarm once more. At last, one feels, the rich woman and the hero will meet (they seem made for each other) but the woman instantly jumps to the wrong conclusions and scolds Picasso for making a mess of the carpet. This hilarious sequence, intercut with events next door, diverts attention away from the main thread of the action but adds a wry comment on the overall theme of the film: how wealth is not necessarily a passport to happiness but possibly a measure of loneliness and dehumanisation. Behind the brilliant comedy of the sequence lies the sadness of a wealthy woman reduced to sharing a lavish hotel suite with a dog whose simple demonstrations of loyalty she misunderstands. Next door to her is an ageing male who uses his wealth to buy company and sex. It's worth noting that in this, one of Wilder's most warmly funny and romantic films, everyone is something of a social outcast; it is one of Wilder's most moving films because isolation gives way to an acceptance of the community which surrounds them and a recognition of individual responsibility.

The sense of community which all three main characters are variously denied is presented at the beginning of the film, with one of those expertly assembled and thematically crucial montage sequences with which Wilder often begins his films. The opening is narrated by Chevasse, the quietly cynical private detective, who tells us, rather in the manner of the caption that opens *Ninotchka*, of the romantic charms of Paris. Like Baxter in *The Apartment*, Chevasse's work has reduced human behaviour to inhuman statistics and the course of the film will parallel the American's transformation with Chevasse's own. Chevasse tells us there are 7,000 hotels in Paris and some 220,000 hotel rooms and in approximately 40,000 of those rooms adulterers are hard at work. Love in various forms flourishes in every apartment, in every park, on every street corner; it flourishes between old people, young people, and between old and young people; even between dogs of every breed. At one point a motorised street cleaner moves down a cobbled street spraying a great torrent of cold water over a courting couple without disturbing their passionate embrace. The sequence ends in the Place Vendôme with a teasingly slow camera-tilt up the Colonne Vendôme – one of Wilder's most impudent phallic symbols – until we observe Chevasse perched high on the viewing platform peering through his telephoto lens into a hotel suite in which the notorious Flannagan is seducing the wife of Monsieur X, Chevasse's current client.

As with the montage sequences which open *Sabrina*, *The Apartment* and *Avanti!*, this Cook's Tour of romantic and perfidious Paris not only establishes the light-hearted, even whimsical tone of the film to follow, but also serves several important functions in the film's overall strategy. Firstly, it establishes Chevasse's cynical distaste for his profession which guarantees him a regular income and prepares for the time when his cynicism gives way to a complete acceptance of life, the moment when he realises that the innocent girl he has nurtured has brought the adulterer to heel, something he has never been able to achieve himself. And by presenting *affaires* between people of differing age groups and social classes, Wilder is at pains from the beginning to dispel any prejudices we might harbour concerning a romance between a fifty-six year-old playboy of the western world and a seventeen year-old French girl.

The casting is equally crucial, making *Love in the Afternoon* an allusive, self-conscious work which successfully integrates a tender subversion of stereotyping and a gleeful consolidation of genre expectations. As in *Sabrina*, both these elements are crucially connected with the film's break with established patterns of screen romance. By using specific performers, Wilder is able, in conjunction with the "liberating" influence of the prologue, to make us accept the film's basic premise: we identify strongly with both the characters and the actors playing them. Equally important is the film's dreamlike quality, and *Love in the Afternoon* is perhaps Wilder's most artificial movie – after the prologue there are only three major location sequences – in which Paris is as idealised as it is in *Ninotchka* and *Sabrina*. In order to heighten the film's artificiality Wilder reminds us constantly of the actors playing roles.

Maurice Chevalier had built an entire career out of singing about the sophisticated pleasures of Paris, invariably with a straw hat perched at an angle on his handsome head, and especially in Lubitsch's Paramount musicals of the 'Thirties: *The Love Parade, Paramount on Parade, One Hour With You, The Merry Widow*. In *The Love Parade* (1929) playboy Chevalier sings "Paris, Stay The Same" but, of course, it hasn't and Wilder's casting of Chevalier (bringing him back to Hollywood after twenty years) as the detective who makes a living from the lust he has advocated in countless songs seems to be an acknowledgement of the passing years.

When Ariane asks Flannagan during their first meeting why he needs background music for his seductions, he replies almost apologetically, "It's amazing what a couple of fiddles can do for you, especially if you're not much of a talker. And I'm not much of a talker". This immediately forces an association between Flannagan the character and Cooper the actor, for so long given to silent, dignified action, particularly in *High Noon* (1952) in which Dimitri Tiomkin's music actually speaks for him. Richard Corliss has suggested that, "Cooper's Flannagan is the logical middle-aged extension of the actor's preening, prating studs from *Morocco* through *Desire* and *Beau Geste* to *The Fountainhead*. Always too clumsy to be taken seriously as a sexual threat, never sufficiently self-aware to infuse his roles with the saving grace of vulnerability, Cooper possessed a lifelessness and an artlessness that made him the perfect image of a loathsome Lothario in decline".* Although the assertion that Flannagan is "loathsome" can be contested – Wilder seems to delight in his irresponsibility and vulgarity as much as in his conversion – Corliss

---

*This process can be detected in Cooper's subsequent work, Philip Dunne's *10 North Frederick*, and Anthony Mann's *Man of the West* (both 1958). In the former, as in *Love in the Afternoon*, Cooper is undermined by his love for a much younger woman. In *Man of the West*, Mann builds on the actor's *High Noon* image, sends him back into purgatory where the sins of his past life have to be expunged yet again, and then into advanced middle-age and responsibility, where Cooper is obliged to ignore the romantic attentions of the youthful Julie London in favour of home, family and community.

effectively refutes the orthodox view, summed up perhaps by Penelope Houston's observation in the 'Monthly Film Bulletin' that, "Gary Cooper's rich American seems tired and middle-aged; and without the charm that Humphrey Bogart brought to a not dissimilar part in *Sabrina* (*sic*), *Love in the Afternoon* itself looks jaded". Of course, this jaded quality in Cooper is precisely what Wilder is after, for Cooper's world-weary appearance is necessary if his redemption and his attraction to innocence is to have any meaning or dramatic validity (we might compare here the casting of Cooper in the Wilder-scripted *Ball of Fire* where his stuffy Professor is attracted to gangster's moll Barbara Stanwyck). Cary Grant, again Wilder's original choice for the role, would have had most of Cooper's age but certainly not his jaded look; Grant's playboy would have emphasised both the play and the boyish self-confidence, while Cooper's idea of play – hiring a gypsy quartet to enhance his sexual conquests – is largely one inspired by the movies (Chevalier in *The Merry Widow*, Cooper himself in Borzage and Lubitsch's *Desire*) and represents a melancholy aspect to his character. When Ariane asks him if he isn't a little too old for this sort of thing he replies: "That hurts. First you save my life and then you stab me. Is that kind?" Both Ariane and Flannagan come to realise that he's too old for the role he has chosen for himself, making his eventual redemption both inevitable and poignant.

Frank Flannagan is an executive millionaire ("Oil, construction business, turbo-jet engines, Pepsi-Cola," announces Ariane, who knows Flannagan's *curriculum vitae* from her father's bulging file on his exploits) who has become bored by his wealth and responsibilities ("When do you work?" asks Ariane; "Whenever I'm not busy") who seeks release in living up to Hollywood imagery, specifically the image of the romantic and potent male hero. Whereas most of Wilder's heroes are unable to equal this ideological ideal, Frank Flannagan is the vulgar apotheosis of it. If a connection can be drawn between Linus Larrabee in *Sabrina* and Flannagan, it is their discovery, from opposite poles, of the emptiness of materialistic impulses. If dedication to work has suppressed Linus's ability to embrace life, then a resentment of work has turned Flannagan into a love-making machine, devoid of genuine feelings. For both men the end of a million is just a series of zeroes until the presence of an innocent girl from Europe begins to humanise them.

In both cases the girl is played by Audrey Hepburn. We have

already discussed the casting of Audrey Hepburn in relation to *Sabrina*, and in *Love in the Afternoon* she expands on her role. We have noted how her stage performance as 'Ondine' and her role in William Wyler's *Roman Holiday* influenced Wilder's decision to cast her as Sabrina and the importance this has on an audience's expectations. Between her portrayals of Sabrina and Ariane, Hepburn had rejuvenated the disillusioned aristocrat Pierre in King Vidor's *War and Peace* (1956), in which she was a radiant Natasha, and swept even Fred Astaire off his feet in Stanley Donen's *Funny Face* (1957), in which the view of Paris is distinctly Wilderian. Later in her career she transforms William Holden's turgid screenplay into romance in Richard Quine's *Paris When it Sizzles* (1963), returned to Paris to beguile Cary Grant in Donen's *Charade* (1964), and confirmed the Pygmalion quality of her performances by playing Eliza to Rex Harrison's "confirmed old bachelor" in George Cukor's *My Fair Lady* (1964). Hepburn has made a definite speciality of captivating some of Hollywood's greatest senior citizens (Bogart, Fonda, Astaire, Cooper, Grant, Harrison) whose domination of her dazzling wide-eyed looks and velvet voice is equalled by her propensity for revealing their vulnerability: she is at once wife and daughter, which is precisely the kind of relationship she has with Chevasse and Flannagan. Just as William Holden and Jack Lemmon are the ideal Wilderian heroes, Audrey Hepburn is Wilder's perfect heroine, combining innocence and fragility with a sure sense of purpose and playfulness. As with Marilyn Monroe, other directors may have trapped Hepburn in her image but Wilder gives full reign to her vitality and range. In *Love in the Afternoon* she gives perhaps her most exquisitely timed and attractive performance. Wilder forces an association between Sabrina and Ariane early in both films by staging virtually identical sequences: Sabrina's gaze into the Larrabee world from her perch in a tree is continued by Ariane's perch on a hotel balcony, as she gazes into the Flannagan world of serenading strings and champagne seductions. And the process is the same: Ariane is destined to redeem the older man, being transformed herself from a wistful onlooker into an active participant. Just as Sabrina's trip to Paris enabled her to return to the Larrabee's on a roughly equal social standing, so Ariane's personality must change if she is to capture Flannagan's interest. The role she chooses is Mystery, since Flannagan's success in the field of sexual conquests has left him with no illusions whatsoever.

Ariane's entry into the Flannagan world is beautifully engineered. When Chevasse leaves his bird's-eye perch on the Colonne Vendôme, he goes home to develop his pictures. When Monsieur X (John McGiver) arrives, Ariane is ceremoniously shut in her room, though she is able to eavesdrop on the conversation through a window above her door (here Wilder first establishes her role as an onlooker). Monsieur X is shown the incriminating photographs of his wife with Flannagan and is naturally enraged, but Wilder evidently has little sympathy for him. Monsieur X is physically unattractive, overweight and choleric, and Wilder enjoys making fun of this oafish cuckold, a directorial attitude far removed from the painful depictions of adultery in *The Apartment* and *The Fortune Cookie*. In *Love in the Afternoon* Wilder invites us to have sympathy for Madame X and regard Flannagan's exploitation of sterile marriages as something of a public service – this constant liberalisation of moral attitudes in anticipation of the film's climax when moral order has been restored. Monsieur X pulls out a revolver, which he is obviously ill-equipped to handle, and leaves Chevasse determined to kill Flannagan in a *crime passionel*. Ariane, who has already been warned by her father of the dangers of adultery ("Do you know what happened to Lincoln? And right in the middle of a performance"), is distressed at the thought of her "fictional hero" being killed off and decides to intervene on his behalf. She climbs through Flannagan's hotel window, bundles Madame X out of it, puts on the perplexed lady's veil and takes her place on the couch just as Monsieur X bursts in through the door. After some hilarious confusions ("This is the Ritz Hotel, isn't it?", asks the apoplectic Monsieur X, after discovering that the woman with Flannagan isn't his wife), he makes an embarrassed exit, though returns a moment later for his gun ("I bought it in London, but maybe they'll take it back. I still have the sales-slip.") Flannagan's curiosity about this young girl who has saved his life and seemingly knows a good deal about him ("You don't look a bit like Abraham Lincoln"; "You *are* six foot three, aren't you?") is instantly aroused, while Ariane is irresistibly drawn to Flannagan, agreeing to meet him again but only in the afternoons because she "lives with another man". She also insists on preserving her anonymity.

Ariane is surrounded by age and experience. The settings are carefully chosen to reflect this. The Ritz Hotel, in which much of the action takes place, stands as a bastion of old-fashioned grace and elegance, its corridors and spacious suites, with their antique furnishings and ornate mirrors, locking the privileged guests firmly into *fin de siècle* Paris; the magnificent Opera House and the Conservatoire where Ariane is a 'cello student, are built on years of cultural tradition; Chevasse's home-cum-office, situated in a quiet corner of the city, is deliberately unostentatious – he can't bring himself to advertise his success as a divorce detective – yet the rooms reflect the qualities of the past. Chevasse's study is not unlike Sherlock Holmes's and like Holmes, Chevasse seems to eat and sleep amid his files, literally surrounded by a world he both despises and is addicted to. Ariane's room, adjoining the study, is invariably brightly-lit, where the study is dark. One might say that Chevasse represents a scientific intellect while Ariane represents romantic instinct (the central conflict within Holmes, the artistic scientist). Ariane habitually leaves her door open, allowing the strains of Haydn's 88th Symphony to echo through the Chevasse home.

Significantly, when Ariane's innocence and youth comes into direct contact with the world which surrounds her, Haydn's work, which she is studying, becomes confused with the popular waltz "Fascina-

Love in the Afternoon: *Maurice Chevalier, Audrey Hepburn*

tion" which Flannagan has his gypsy band play every night to aid his seductions*. As in *Sabrina*, with its symbolic battle for ascendancy between "La Vie en Rose" and "Isn't It Romantic?", Wilder's use of Haydn and "Fascination" is symbolic of the more general cultural clash – when Ariane tells Flannagan that she plays the 'cello he counters by saying that he once knew a girl who played the saxophone. As Ariane falls more deeply in love with Flannagan her 'cello practice starts to betray her thoughts, Haydn's Symphony merging with "Fascination" until the latter melody dominates her home to such an extent that Chevasse begins to hum the tune that is seducing his daughter. And when Flannagan goes to Chevasse's office the detective has to be told to stop humming "Fascination" as it's now getting on Flannagan's nerves, the American here failing to make a vital connection.

If the conflict between Haydn and "Fascination" symbolises the narrative tension, Ariane's 'cello case is to play an equally important role. While the 'cello practice comforts Chevasse in representing his daughter's pursuit of cultural and social respectability – the music soothing him as he pours over his files – Ariane uses her 'cello case to hide her various disguises, such as the mink coat, which she uses in her deception of Flannagan. When Flannagan leaves on one of his trips to Scandinavia, the hotel staff put the 'cello case with Flannagan's luggage, which Flannagan leaves outside his suite, an accident which anticipates the moment when Ariane has no need of the case but leaves with Flannagan herself. And at that moment, at the close of the film, Chevasse is left holding the 'cello case at the railway station. Once all three main characters come under the spell of "Fascination", Wilder marks their spiritual point of no return. The 'cello case, given at various points to Flannagan and Chevasse, is suggestive also of their transformations, an entirely characteristic use of an object by Wilder to punctuate the progress of his characters.

Of the characters with whom Ariane comes into contact, only her boyfriend Michel (Van Doude) is of her own generation and Wilder subjects him to the same kind of ridicule as Monsieur X. When

---

*On the film's American re-issue in 1961 (the year of Gary Cooper's death) *Love in the Afternoon* was re-titled *Fascination*. The story first appeared as a novel by Claude Anet and later a film made in 1931 by Paul Czinner. In France, because of copyright reasons, both Czinner's and Wilder's films (which share only a few ideas, notably the Opera House scene) are known as *Ariane*.

Ariane asks Flannagan if he isn't rather old to play the Casanova, he retaliates by asking her if she isn't rather young to be rescuing adulterers in distress. "I don't much care for young men," she says with Michel obviously in mind, "Never did. I find them conceited, and clumsy, and very unimaginative." Michel is clumsy and impulsive where Flannagan is calm and assured; compared with Flannagan's world-weariness, Michel is gauche, genuinely shocked by Ariane's mission to save Flannagan from being murdered but too guileless to do anything to change her mind – he can only ridicule the hat she wears to the Ritz. Michel is easily diverted by Ariane so she can meet Flannagan in private, as in the superb Opera House sequence – one of Wilder's greatest sequences – in which Michel, accompanying Ariane, "conducts" 'Tristan and Isolde' from his seat high in the gallery completely impervious to the strange looks he gets from those seated near him. Flannagan arrives late for the opera, of course, and Ariane spends her time ignoring Michel's foolish enthusiasm and observes Flannagan in the stalls through her opera glasses, echoing her father in an attempt to see Flannagan's face and the woman he is escorting. A year has passed since their last meeting – Flannagan has been away "on business" – and during the interval Ariane tells Flannagan that she hasn't missed him at all (naturally, he can barely remember her) but suggests they resume their afternoon meetings.

In Wilder's world, relationships are never begun without one or both partners being involved in some form of deception; even when a situation is most desperate, as in *The Apartment* for example, Baxter has to deceive Miss Kubelik and his neighbours before he feels able to reveal his true character and feelings. Consequently, Ariane finds it impossible to tell Flannagan the truth about herself – "A for Anonymous" would soon bore a modern Casanova – so she draws on her father's files to invent affairs for herself, relating them to Flannagan over his dictating machine. Flannagan, discovering her tape recording by accident, is naturally hooked and he romances her in his customary manner: a boating trip down the river, with his gypsy band cruising behind, followed by a champagne picnic on the river bank, and the established routine at the Ritz, dancing alone with Ariane until the woman has become sufficiently mellowed for the band to make a discreet exit. Both Flannagan and Ariane are irresistibly drawn to each other – as Stephen Farber has noted, "the most worldly characters hanker for the virgins. Wilder helplessly confesses that for all the weary cynics of his disillusioned world, the appeal of innocence (which may be partly an urge to corrupt that innocence) is indestructible" – but they must first pretend that their relationship is purely transitory.

For all Ariane's efforts to deceive Flannagan, he realises that she is an innocent and doubtless his attraction towards her reflects both sides of Farber's assertion. But as his relationship with Ariane develops, her earnestness to deceive him only forces him to recognise his own shortcomings. His sexual exploits in every European capital, which Ariane continually reminds him of as if she were comparing notes, ultimately force Flannagan to face up to the moral bankruptcy of his life, forcing him into the position where he needs to bring the "game" to an end and declare his love for Ariane. Like so many of Wilder's scheming duos, Flannagan and Ariane strive to become mirror images of each other until one of them is compelled to break the transparent deception to reveal, in this case, a sudden humanity and a romantic commitment. Inevitably, Wilder marks this important moment by having Ariane shed a significant piece of clothing. In order to impress Flannagan, she borrows an expensive, white mink coat which her father is keeping until its owner – one of his clients – comes back to claim it. Ariane hides the coat inside her 'cello case until she reaches the corridor outside Flannagan's suite. Neither are able to continue the charade any longer and Flannagan's tender removal of the coat – the unmasking of Ariane, revealing the ordinary clothes beneath – signifies the moment when their love for each other is out in the open.

It is at this point, after Ariane has run out of the Ritz in panic, that Flannagan decides to hire a private detective to discover Ariane's identity. Until now, one can regard Flannagan and Chevasse also as mirror images of each other, with Ariane torn between loyalty and love for her father and her love for Flannagan. In a sense, both men are played out – Flannagan knows he's rather too old and Chevasse seems increasingly disenchanted with his work, constantly giving warnings to his daughter but knowing instinctively that she will end up in the clutches of someone like Flannagan. Inevitably, Flannagan hires Chevasse to discover Ariane's identity – by a hilarious and beautifully worked-out coincidence, Flannagan goes to a Turkish bath and renews his acquaintance with Monsieur X, both men at this point sweating out their romantic troubles. Chevasse quickly solves the case and confronts Flannagan with the news that his daughter is deeply in love with him. In desperation, Chevasse offers to buy Flannagan off by giving him the files of his career, an action, one feels, that represents Chevasse's resignation of his own career (by dispensing with the most valuable files) and his desire to rid his home of Flannagan. Acting on the most noble of motives, Flannagan telephones Ariane to say he is leaving Paris immediately not to return.

The final scene resembles that of *Sabrina* and, as Richard Corliss has pointed out, also "evokes memories of the Bogart-Bergman estrangement in *Casablanca*, when Bogart leaves Paris on the 5 pm train, having read Bergman's farewell letter as the rain washes away her words." In *Love in the Afternoon* it is also raining as Flannagan and Ariane say farewell to each other. As the train begins to move down the platform Ariane runs alongside until Flannagan reaches down and lifts her into his compartment. Chevasse, his eyes filled with tears of joy and carrying his daughter's 'cello case, is left behind on the platform with the gypsy band serenading the lovers as the train pulls out of sight.

"That the father should stand on the platform smiling happily," wrote Penelope Houston, "after the train has carried off his much-loved daughter and the rich but worthless Flannagan seems, by any reasonable standards of taste, unacceptable." C A Lejeune, in 'The Observer,' was even harsher, ending her nineteen-line review with, "This is what is called a happy ending. I should call it something very different, and am sorry for the players involved in such a repulsive affair." But to judge the film's conclusion as a representation of reality is to ignore its fairy-tale construction and, perhaps, its measure of romantic allegory. The ending seems not only dramatically necessary but emotionally inevitable, for all three characters have been systematically humanised. Chevasse's attitude towards his profession, his cynicism and moral hypocrisy, has been replaced by a new-found faith in human nature, indeed, something to sing about; Flannagan's overbearing cynicism, his credo that "People should behave as if they're between 'planes," has been discredited and supplanted by an awareness of his responsibilities to both himself and the woman who loves him; Ariane's innocence, her life of enforced morality and suppressed emotion, has reached a peak of irresponsibility but found a new moral equilibrium. By the end of the film they have moved from various states of inhumanity and naivety to similar states of benevolence, maturity, even grace. Their progress represents not so much a tasteless perversion of life but an affirmation of it.

The attitudes on display in *Love in the Afternoon*, embodied in the climax and in the characterisations of Michel and Monsieur X, lead us, finally, to a consideration of Wilder's portrayals of innocence and experience and, as a consequence of this, his frequent use of sexual attraction between men and women of different generations. For Stephen Farber, "The encounter of American and European in Wilder's films is only a specific version of the more general drama that obsesses him – the confrontation of innocence and experience. The nature of innocence is one of his most persistent subjects. Wilder does not believe that innocence can survive unscathed. He does not believe that faith and trust are a reasonable basis for human relationships. His films chronicle the corruption of innocents, the fall from purity." Farber cites *Ninotchka, Hold Back the Dawn, A Foreign Affair, Love in the Afternoon, Kiss Me Stupid, The Fortune Cookie* and, "in their farcical way", *One, Two, Three* and *Irma la Douce* as stories of disillusionment and loss of innocence. Yet if we examine this list we find the confrontation of innocence and experience only palpably exists within an American-meets-European context or, as in *Ninotchka* and *Irma la Douce*, an exclusively European (Parisian) context. It is curious that Farber failed to cite *The Apartment* as a story of disillusionment and loss of innocence since this is the notable exception to the rule: Baxter's progress is certainly one of corrupted and exploited innocence. As a general rule in Wilder's films, however, America is the New World where notions of innocence and experience become redundant in the race for materialist success: the "innocents" are characterised as "dupes", as we hope to demonstrate in the following chapter, the slaves of success rather than its victims; Wilder's "dupes" are spineless creatures, almost literally so in the case of Harry Hinkle in *The Fortune Cookie*, for whom spiritual redemption means isolation from the community. The other American characters whom Farber might describe as fallen innocents – Neff in *Double Indemnity*, Gillis in *Sunset Boulevard*, Tatum in *Ace in the Hole* – are all morally flawed and psychologically unstable, resisting redemption rather than embracing it, except through the resignation of death. It is only when the American travels to Europe does Wilder allow the possibility of regeneration and only in the context of a romantic comedy such as *Love in the Afternoon*.

An important distinction must be made here between the dramas and the comedies. In the former all relationships tend to be doomed to failure or worse, but in the romantic comedies (and only one, *The Major and the Minor*, has an all-American setting) fulfilment is not only permissible but probable. While Farber asserts that Wilder "does not believe that faith and trust are a reasonable basis for human relationships," Wilder insists that they can be, given a particular set of circumstances. And these circumstances involve Europe – Eve Peabody in *Midnight*, Ninotchka, Sabrina, Flannagan and Ariane, Irma and Nestor, are all transformed and find happiness in Paris, Wendell Armbruster in Italy – and it is difficult to imagine Wilder staging these transformations in America without qualification, even though *Hold Back the Dawn* and *The Major and the Minor* come near to it. In the same way, it is impossible to imagine *Double Indemnity* or *Ace in the Hole* taking place anywhere *except* America. The crucial point to be made here is historical: America has no past and without this Wilder finds it impossible to hold his polarities in opposition to each other or to effect an amalgamation. Only in Europe, where the pace of life and the pace of the films is slower, does Wilder find the necessary historical and moral conducements and perspectives, placing Old against New, culture against commerce, feelings against frigidity, experience against innocence.

One method of crystallising this theme is to present relationships between men and women of differing age groups, a narrative device which, as Farber has noted, is one of Wilder's recurrent obsessions. Farber mentions Freud's famous paper "A Special Type of Choice of Object Made by Men" to explain Wilder's "persistent pairing of innocents and *roués* . . . as an attempt to fulfil the Oedipal fantasy, in which the innocent child wins the experienced, tainted mother from the father. And it is striking how often Wilder's films actually deal with a relationship of a young man or woman and aged lover."* The

---

*Farber speculates whether this obsession might relate to Wilder's experience in Berlin in the '20s where he "danced as a gigolo for a while in the Eden Hotel, and at the Adlon I served as a tea-time partner for lonely old ladies." Certainly this element, so pronounced in Wilder, rarely occurs in the work of other Hollywood directors. The Bogart-Bacall relationships in Howard Hawks' *To Have and Have Not* (1944) and *The Big Sleep* (1946) do not strike us as unusual since Bacall is the equal of Bogart's wise-cracking tough guy and the actors' real-life romance was public knowledge; in Hawks' *Rio Bravo* (1959) and *Hatari!* (1962) the considerable age difference between John Wayne and Angie Dickinson and Elsa Martinelli scarcely seems to occur to Hawks or his audience. The theme is entirely absent in Alfred Hitchcock, undetectable in

distinction between the dramas and the comedies must be made again (though this is not to imply a measure of serious intent on Wilder's part for the former category and a lack of conviction for the latter) for only in the European-based romantic comedies are the "unequal" relationships viewed with any optimism; an optimism, moreover, which is denied to couples of similar ages located elsewhere. When these "equal" partnerships look like succeeding, as Farber points out, Wilder qualifies the relationship by insisting that one character has a shadowy past. And very often this is involved with a relationship with an aged lover. In *Ninotchka*, Leon has been an elderly Countess's gigolo; in *Double Indemnity* and *Ace in the Hole* the heroines are trapped in lifeless marriages to older men and then kill their "equal" partners; in *Sunset Boulevard*, Joe Gillis rejects an "equal" relationship with Betty and falls victim to Norma Desmond's dementia; in *Witness for the Prosecution*, Leonard and Christine deceive each other until one of them is killed because of a parallel relationship with an older woman and another "equal" partner; in *The Apartment* the reconciliation between Baxter and Miss Kubelik has been contaminated by contact with the older Sheldrake; in *The Fortune Cookie*, the "equal" marriage of Harry and Sandy has irretrievably broken down. The failure of all these "equal" marriages and relationships can be ascribed to values – sexual and financial – that are central in American society.

It is undoubtedly significant that the five Wilder films which build explicitly towards marriage, regeneration and emotional fulfilment are orientated towards Europe, two of which feature ageing men revived by young women (*Sabrina, Love in the Afternoon*) and *Ninotchka, Irma la Douce* and *Avanti!* in which Wilder creates and endorses his perfect "equal" relationships, but only after Leon has shaken himself free from the Countess, after Nestor has disguised himself as a senile

---

Lubitsch and Ford, and only sporadic in Fritz Lang. It appears to a degree in Chaplin's work, especially *Monsieur Verdoux* (1947) and *Limelight* (1952) but even here the relationships seem more paternal than carnal and might reflect Chaplin's response to his arrest under the Man Act. If Wilder does have any companions in the field they are David Lean and, in the European cinema, Luis Buñuel. In Lean's *Brief Encounter* (1945) Celia Johnson's dreary husband *seems* far older than she is, as does Ann Todd's husband (Claude Rains) in *The Passionate Friends* (1949); in *Ryan's Daughter* (1970) the marriage between youthful Sarah Miles and middle-aged Robert Mitchum is doomed before it begins. In all three films the heroines have affairs with youthful men which eventually break up through feelings of guilt and the admonitions of a puritanical society. Buñuel has built his later career out of portraying the sexual passion of world-weary men for virgins, virgin nieces, and even novices, all of which end either in violence and disaster or as interrupted dreams.

English Lord, and after Wendell and Pamela have re-enacted the love affair of their deceased parents.

This has taken us a long way from our discussion of *Love in the Afternoon* but it explains the importance of Europe in Wilder's films. In Wilder's tortured, ambivalent world, human happiness is dependent on a liberation of ideology and the destruction of age and cultural barriers. It is also dependent on Europe, where his characters can triumph over cynicism. In *Ace in the Hole*, Wilder's most vicious critique of America (which was criticised in some circles for not being cynical enough), Tatum says to his editor that the youthful Herbie wants to be, "Going, going, going." "Going where?" is the editor's forlorn response. The answer might well be Europe. At the end of *Love in the Afternoon* all three characters have confirmed their belief that faith and trust *are* a reasonable basis for human relationships. It is to Wilder's great credit that he views their commitment with sufficient faith and trust that he can despatch Flannagan and Ariane to America. It is a measure of Wilder's disillusionment and loss of innocence that it will be another fifteen years before he finds another American, Wendell Armbruster in *Avanti!*, worthy of treatment at the spa called Europe.

Avanti! (1972)

Billy Wilder is a European at heart. Given his background, this is not unexpected, yet in no other Hollywood director whose background might be said to resemble Wilder's – one thinks of Lang, Preminger, Siodmak, Zinnemann – does Europe appear so regularly or so potently as in his work. When not adapting European source material like *Love in the Afternoon* or *One, Two, Three*, or transposing European material into an American setting, as with *Some Like it Hot* and *Kiss Me, Stupid*, Wilder often chooses to centre the action of his films in some expressive European location. Moreover, these are often settings which are specifically connected with his own background and his own circuitous route to America: Vienna (*The Emperor Waltz*), Berlin and Germany (*A Foreign Affair, Stalag 17*, part of *Witness for the Prosecution, One, Two, Three*), but especially France and Paris (*Bluebeard's Eighth Wife, Midnight, Ninotchka, Sabrina, Love in the Afternoon, Irma la Douce, Fedora*). This accounts for just under half of Wilder's total output and in using locations which have such personal associations Wilder is obviously lending authenticity to his films. But something more is clearly involved. A closer examination of the particular films would indicate that Wilder is exploring a geography that is more psychical than physical and has less to do with place than with values. The Paris of *Ninotchka, Sabrina* and *Love in the Afternoon* barely registers as a physical landscape but is felt as a *moral* one.

The confrontation between the values of America and those of Europe is arguably Wilder's most insistent preoccupation. Clearly, his fascination with innocence and experience, which we have discussed in relation to *Love in the Afternoon*, derives particularly from this cultural conflict. Clearly, too, Wilder's interest in America's international role, in films like *A Foreign Affair* and *One, Two, Three*, reflects not only his concern with coming to terms with the ideology and cultural identity of the country of his adoption; it is, implicitly, an attempt to come to terms with his own identity as a European in America. It is perhaps significant that in the last decade, Wilder's films, having become increasingly reflective, mellow and *personal*, have also become increasingly obsessed with Europe and the past.

In a sense, Wilder can be regarded as a sort of Henry James in reverse. Even allowing for the considerable difference between their respective artistic temperaments and cultural eras, both are equally fascinated with innocence and experience and, as a corollary of that, with America and Europe. James is the American who settles in Europe and whose work returns again and again to the theme of the impact of Europe on the American sensibility. Wilder often explores the same theme but from his particular vantage point as the European who has settled in America. So we have Wilder's bleak visions of America in *Double Indemnity, The Lost Weekend, Ace in the Hole, The Apartment, The Fortune Cookie* and *The Front Page*, contrasting with those exuberant hymns to the American past, *The Spirit of St Louis* and *Some Like it Hot*, while the American movie-past is celebrated in *Sunset Boulevard* and *Fedora*. We also have Wilder's observation of the American abroad who either transforms the place by exporting his own expertise and drive or is himself transformed by its differing tempo, style and morality. Whereas Henry James saw Europe as a place for the moral education or the moral corruption of the innocent New Worlders who voyaged to its cultural cornucopias (Florence, for instance, in 'Roderick Hudson'), Wilder's tendency is to see Europe and its values as preferable to an increasingly corrupt and materialistic American society. This system *never* works in reverse (the nearest Wilder comes to suggesting that it might is in *The Emperor Waltz*). Wilder's method could not accommodate a European setting out for the New World and transforming its society in the way that Linus is transformed in *Sabrina*. Wilder is interested in transformation and rejuvenation, ideals which are possible in Europe where cultural movements, language and history have prescribed character; in America, only assimilation is possible which explains Wilder's deep-rooted ambivalence. In Henry James the ideological confrontation between America and Europe is perhaps most keenly explored in 'The Ambassadors'. In Wilder, the conflicting values of America and Europe are most thoroughly examined in *Avanti!*

The film begins at New York's Kennedy Airport as Wendell Armbruster III (Jack Lemmon) arrives from Baltimore by private jet to catch the flight to Rome. It is a wet and windy day as Wendell, dressed in brightly-checkered trousers and a scarlet golf sweater and carrying an incongruous briefcase, hurries across the tarmac towards the airliner whose departure has been specially delayed for him. As the 'plane takes off, Wilder cuts to an exterior shot as the landing gear retreats into the fuselage, leaving American soil far below. During the flight, Wendell, whose rushed departure for Italy gave him no time to gather any luggage, persuades another traveller, Dr Fleischmann, to exchange clothes. This is effected in the toilet, much to the consternation of the passengers and crew, and both men emerge trying to retain an air of dignity in their ill-fitting outfits. "Please fasten your cigarettes and extinquish your seat-belts," says the Alitalia stewardess and as the plane begins its descent into Leonardo da Vinci airport Wilder again cuts to an exterior shot as the landing gear locks into position above St Peter's and the Colosseum. There is considerable confusion at the Immigration Desk since Wendell has forgotten to transfer his own passport to his borrowed set of clothes, and his finger-snapping anger and frustration only make the naturally nonchalant Italian officials even more unhurried and contemptuous. "I know you foreigners," Wendell complains, "I know how much you love to push Americans around." Wendell clearly has a tight schedule to meet and he encounters problems as soon as he arrives in Italy. He pushes his nose threateningly against the Immigration Desk window, but far from being intimidated by this display of executive power, the official's only response is to calmly wipe away the offending nose print with a cloth. Eventually, however, Wendell is able to leave the airport once Dr Fleischmann – who has had similar problems – has been located and passports exchanged. Wendell's journey continues by train to Naples, by hydrofoil to the off-shore island of Ischia, and by minibus to the Grand Hotel Excelsior.

Many of Wilder's films have memorable openings and *Avanti!* is no exception. To the casual viewer the opening sequences probably register as little more than a conventional, if delightfully comic, photographic record of Wendell's journey to Italy; a convenient way of introducing the romantic and sunny theme music and the credit titles over a skyscape. But just as the opening sequences of other Wilder films perform a crucial function, so this overture to *Avanti!*

offers, in retrospect, a rigorously constructed exposition of the film's thematic concerns.

The ritualised celebration of take-off and landing is no mere stylistic contrivance: Wilder is at pains to stress his hero's departure from America and his arrival in Europe. The landing gear being raised and lowered serve as conscious punctuation marks to separate Wendell's flight from the world of Kennedy to that of Leonardo; the effect is to emphasise the idea of journey as a *theme* of the film as well as a physical fact. The dull weather in New York seems to comment on Wendell's life-style, in direct contrast to the sunny transformation to come; and the credit titles coming up over the cloud layer anticipate the transportation of the hero into a new, freer atmosphere. The first thing we hear in the film is the announcement of the flight departure in *two* languages, which at once expresses the America-Europe polarity which the film is to explore. The arrival of Wendell at Kennedy Airport in his private jet instantly establishes his status and character – brash, important, rich – but Wilder's distanced, aloof shot of the event makes Wendell's executive jet look comically small alongside the Rome plane. An important split is thus suggested between the character's own sense of self-importance and the director's view of him as a tiny figure in a large and, to the hero, uncomprehended world. The rest of the film, paradoxically, is to cut Wendell down to size (throughout he is compelled to wear clothes too small for him) but at the same time chart a genuine spiritual growth.

On the 'plane there occurs the immediate exchange of clothing with Dr Fleischmann, anticipating Wendell's secondhand wardrobe for the entire film and which is a familiar Wilderian device for signalling an impending change in a character's personality. The joke about the stewardess's English – "Fasten your cigarettes . . ." – not only alerts us to the confusions of language to come (Wendell later scalds himself by confusing the hot and cold water taps) but prefigures the transference and reversals which are a central feature of the narrative, particularly concerning Wendell's character. The officialdom at the airport frustrates Wendell but at the same time becomes a potent mirror image of his own impersonal, business-like efficiency.

From the breathless take-off the film gradually slows down, from the furious pace of America to the leisurely life-style of the Europeans (compare Baxter's television dinner in *The Apartment* with the three-hour lunchbreaks of the Italians in *Avanti!*); from hard-boiled business acumen to soft-hearted romanticism. At 144 minutes many critics complained that the film was too long for a light comedy, but the length of the film is absolutely crucial: romantic luxuriance becomes not simply a feature of the style but a central theme. Wendell's transformation can be seen as a rising line on a graph of moral and spiritual regeneration, with each point representing an exhibit in Wilder's gallery of favourite characters and situations. *Avanti!* is a totally achieved masterpiece, for Wendell's journey is Wilder's own.

Wendell has been called away to Italy to collect his father's corpse and return it to America for an elaborate funeral: Dr Henry Kissinger will represent the Government and, as Wendell proudly boasts, "Work at every Armbruster plant in the country will come to a complete stop so that the 216,000 employees can watch the services on closed-circuit television in colour, except for Puerto Rico, who get it in black and white." Wendell's father has been killed in a car accident while on his annual vacation in Ischia. During his journey from Rome to Ischia, Wendell keeps noticing a plump English girl, Pamela Piggott (Juliet Mills), who seems to know all about Wendell's mission and tries to be friendly, telling a bored Wendell on the hydrofoil that the varieties of pasta have names like operas. Soon after arriving at the hotel, Wendell discovers that Pamela's mother died in the same accident and that Armbruster had been having an affair with Mrs Piggott at the same hotel for the last ten years. Wendell's outrage at this discovery has scarcely subsided when various other complications contrive to undermine his control and efficiency. Bureaucratic punctiliousness makes it doubtful for a while that two zinc-lined coffins can be found and appropriately certificated in time for the television spectacular planned by Wendell – "Oh, come on," he snaps to the hotel manager Carlo Carlucci (Clive Revill), "you can dig up a couple of coffins." The hero is then faced with a threat of blackmail by the hotel valet Bruno (Gianfranco Barra) who wishes to return to America and needs Wendell's help in obtaining an entry visa. Meanwhile, the corpses go missing, having been stolen by the Trotta family who are demanding compensation for their vineyard wall which was badly damaged in the accident. Insistent and unfortunately timed telephone calls from Wendell's wife add to his harrassment, as does the romantic euphoria of Pamela, who seems to be conspiring against him, particularly with insane schemes such as suggesting that their dead parents should be buried side by side in Ischia.

When Wendell first learned of his father's infidelity he has been beside himself with rage: "You mean all the time we thought he was over here getting cured he was getting laid? That grey-haired, self-righteous son-of-a-bitch!" Wendell's reaction here is worth characterising carefully. It is obviously more than emotional shock. Indeed, more shocking so far has been Wendell's personal indifference to his father's death and his more intense concern with the excellence of his own eulogy (first draft) which he will be delivering on network television and which he glibly dictates into a Dictaphone on the train as if he were quoting the latest Stock Market figures: "Wendell Armbruster Senior was an old-fashioned man," he says into the machine, "and I mean that in the noblest sense of the word. In these days of defeatism and disillusionment he was one who believed in duty to his country, devotion to his family and dedication to his work." The impression given by the speech at this stage is Wendell's satisfaction at his own eloquence rather than a sincere celebration of his father's values. The shock of his discovery, then, cannot simply be horror at his father's "hypocrisy". Indeed, at a later stage, Wendell makes it clear that he is not against infidelity in itself, only if it is sincere, committed, lasting, and with one person. "Miss Piggott, I have nothing against sex," he says, "Pre-marital, extra-marital, you name it and I'm for it. I mean, just because a man's married doesn't mean that he can't have a thing, you know, with a secretary or with an airline stewardess. Let's say you're at a convention in Hawaii – you meet some chick and, OK, you swing for a couple of nights, but then *aloha*." The only foreign word Wendell seems to know is the word for "Goodbye" ("I know all the Italian I need – *Ciao*"). This blood-chilling philosophy, which reduces people to objects and relationships to sex without love, commitment or responsibility, summarises the hero's emotional immaturity, identifying him with Frank Flannagan in *Love in the Afternoon* whose philosophy is for people to behave as if they were permanently between 'planes.

Wendell's values, then, are certainly no finer than his father's. His reaction is not disillusionment but a sort of covert envy. In this are the first glimmerings of a dissatisfaction with an existence which he has not only previously taken for granted but has seemed to him the epitome of wordly success: wealth, power, prestige, the statutory family, contact and influence with celebrities like Henry Kissinger and Billy Graham, an unthinking acceptance of being head of a huge plastics industry: what else does life hold? One can hardly avoid thinking of Linus Larrabee in *Sabrina*, also head of a plastics firm, who is also pointedly asked "What's it all for?", and who, like Wendell's father, is melted by European romanticism in a relationship with a woman whose working-class background gives their union strong social as well as spiritual overtones. Armbruster's relationship with Mrs Piggott might seem hypocritical considering the ostensible values he upheld and represented, but this is more justifiable than actually remaining consistent to a totally moribund existence, an image of the middle-class family man whose upstanding conservative life seems completely sterile. Wendell has swallowed all this unthinkingly, a high-powered American executive "cocooned in right-wing prejudice", as Tony Rayns put it ('Sight and Sound', Summer 1973), and is subjected to some of Wilder's most bristling satire to expose the hollowness of his ideals. At the beginning of the film he is rude, bigoted, xenophobic, wholly materialistic and with an emotional life that seems atrophied – "Kiss-kiss", he signs off at the end of telephone conversations with his wife in a voice of habitual tonelessness. Wendell's slow revaluation of his father is inevitably to become a process by which he revalues himself.

In his eulogy (second draft) Wendell, re-examining the situation, takes to paraphrasing 'Julius Caesar': "We come to bury Wendell Armbruster Senior, not to praise him." An initially surprising reference is, typically, to become apposite, since the "spirit" of Armbruster, like Caesar's, is to haunt the characters and become even more powerful after his death than when he was alive. Slowly, the relationship which Wendell so furiously condemned is to be re-enacted in his growing love for Pamela, which is inseparable from his growing infatuation with Europe itself. This is first of all signalled by the couple being compelled to wear their parents' clothes.

We have already noted the exchange of clothes between Wendell and Dr Fleischmann. It is the moment when Wendell exchanges his leisure self (the golfer) for his business self. The dark suit is not really a signifier for Wendell's grief over his father's death; it signals more his conception of propriety and decorum (one could say that, far from reflecting his feelings, it disguises his *absence* of feeling). In a brief conversation with Pamela outside the morgue, before they identify the corpses, Wendell seems most concerned with the effects the death will have on the Stock Market – Armbruster Industries are down fourteen points – and with buying Pamela off in case she should think of exploiting Wendell with her knowledge of the affair. "Moneywise, how are you fixed?", he enquires solicitously, echoing C C Baxter. He observes the flowers she is carrying. "In Italian they're called *trombochine*," she says. "What are they called in English?", he asks. "Daffodils," she replies with some astonishment. No further comment is needed on the mechanisation of Wendell's responses to nature and to human nature.

The sequence at the morgue is beautifully plotted, one of the finest in all of Wilder's work. Every shot is precisely judged for its maximum potential of comedy and warmth; indeed, in keeping the camera at a discreet distance from the action, Wilder shows respect for the moment and achieves a complex range of effects and emotions within the same shot. It is, first of all, a scene full of humour, largely through the extraordinary characterisation of the coroner who arrives – rather late – on a moped and quickly proceeds to dispatch the business in hand with robot-like precision, every item relevant to the formalities contained on his person in such a way that even a pen seems an extension of his fingers. Only at the end, when he is walking away, does the machine momentarily falter: his moistening sponge is leaking in his trousers pocket and the coroner's discomfort, his rueful wringing out of the wet sponge, is the moment when he is obliged to reveal a human response. Part of the beauty of this characterisation and performance is the witty way in which it becomes a delicate stylisation of the hero himself. The coroner is Wendell taken to a point of near absurdity and thus containing a disguised comment on the implications of the hero's attitudes. Like Wendell, the coroner knows only one word of a foreign language – "OK". Like Wendell, he wishes to dispose of his business with a mechanical, piston-like efficiency and with a flourish he rubber-stamps the bewildering mass of documents as if playing a cadenza for the xylophone. Like Wendell finally, though, the mechanism breaks down and a touch of humanity leaks through.

The morgue scene is also extremely moving. Pamela's daffodils become a dazzling spot of yellow in a predominantly grey scene, adding warmth to the cold room. She moves into close-up when she steps forward to identify her mother, though the potential sentimentality of that moment is beautifully held in check by the presence of the black-clad Wendell who noses his way into the corner of the frame to catch an inquisitive glimpse of his father's mistress. It is during this scene that Pamela suggests that the dead couple be buried on the island, a suggestion that Wendell angrily dismisses as it would disrupt his television spectacular. As Wendell prepares to leave he whispers to Carlucci, "Ask fat-ass if she wants a ride." After the stillness and beauty of what has gone before, the comment is heard by us in all its startling repulsiveness – and heard also by Pamela. "No, thank you", she says, with quiet dignity. She moves back to the coffins, with Wilder's camera again maintaining a discreet distance from the action. With the romantic theme music heard softly on the soundtrack and with a gesture which surely recalls Sabrina's when hearing "La Vie en Rose" outside her Paris apartment, Pamela moves to the window and opens it. And for the first time in the scene the screen suddenly becomes suffused with sunlight. It is a magical, cathartic moment – an infusion of light and life into a scene of darkness and death and a strangely beautiful pointer to the way the example of the dead lovers is to irradiate the lives of their descendants. It is a gesture Pamela is to repeat in the love scene between her and Wendell when they begin to re-enact their parents' love affair – opening a window to let in light and music.

When Wendell first learns that the coffins have gone missing he immediately assumes that Pamela is involved in their disappearance. A way to lower her guard and surreptitiously discover what she has done with them is to suggest they have dinner together as a kind of tribute to their late parents. Thus we have a typical Wilder situation (Linus dating Sabrina to divert her from David is another) of one person deceiving another by exploiting a romantic atmosphere. The dinner scene, on the terrace of the hotel, is infused with a sort of wordly glow: they wear the evening dress of their dead parents, sit at the same table, order (nearly) the same food (Pamela is on a diet) and are serenaded by the same music that their parents enjoyed, a romantic effusion always modified but never destroyed by our awareness of Wendell's plan and his suppressed discomfort at all this lush sentimentality. (Lemmon's underplaying here is superb.) It is at this point that the Trottas enter and Wendell is called away to negotiate with them. When he returns at dawn Pamela is dancing by herself to the music of the entranced orchestra, an oddly poignant image of romantic solitude. To round off the evening as their parents used to, Pamela suggests a swim to a rock and a sunbathe in the nude.

Wendell is horrified, even though he considers himself to be a "pretty groovy cat" who has seen 'Oh! Calcutta' twice *and Carnal Knowledge*. Eventually Pamela's determination causes him to relent, if only for her protection. Here again, though, we are not allowed to bask in the romantic aura uncritically. For one thing, Wendell and Pamela are being photographed by Bruno with his Polaroid, another blackmailing device to tempt Wendell into securing him a visa. Also, Wendell cannot find it in himself to shed his black socks (even Carlucci, when he recovers the photographs, is puzzled by this detail: "Is it because you are in mourning?")

The scene on the rock is a crucial one in their relationship. The camera is close to the characters' faces, imparting an intimacy to the scene while also suppressing an eroticism that would be inappropriate: Pamela's naked breasts signifying emotional release rather than sexuality. They discuss their lives with a new openness, Wendell telling of the emptiness of his marriage and job, Pamela telling of her attempted suicide when she tried to eat herself to death. It is not enough that Wendell should wear his father's clothes and assume his role. He must assume his father's values if he is to become human. Previously, Wendell's clothes have signalled a role that is incompatible with his inner-self. Thus, the sunbathing in the nude is an important stage in Wendell's search for his true identity, shedding the exterior trappings connected with his life-style. The process is to be completed later when he appears naked before Pamela in the bathroom. If Wilder's characters are nearly always hiding something – literally and spiritually – it is appropriate that Wendell's moments of illumination occur when, quite literally, he has nothing to conceal.

On returning to the hotel they discover that they have the wrong keys to their rooms: Wendell has Pamela's and she has his. Wendell moves towards her and the camera follows in a movement of hesitant attraction all the more beautiful for the reticence and detachment of the camerawork elsewhere. The keys are exchanged and they part. The scene fades into a joyful and ravishing montage as the bells of the island ring out the Sunday morning – Wendell is now eating his breakfast with cotton wool in his ears. The tone of the film has been so precisely calculated that Wendell's attempt to shut out the noise is sad as well as funny; it is the equivalent of his black socks in the sunbathing scene, a refusal or an inability to surrender to the spirit of the place, a suggestion of limitations and inhibitions so engrained that they could take a lifetime to eradicate. Significantly, it is to Pamela that Wilder grants the uninhibited release towards which the film has been building: an intoxicating tour around the island. The preparation for this scene has been superb. Although glimpsed on Wendell's arrival and during the visit to the morgue, the full beauty of the island has been withheld by Wilder until two-thirds of the way through the film, partly to prepare the proper emotional climate for it to be appreciated as an unleashing of the film's generous romantic spirit, and partly to indicate Wendell's blindness to these delights, which always seem on the fringes rather than at the forefront of his consciousness. It is important that the scene is viewed through Pamela's eyes and thus can be given its full emotional due. In a sense it represents a vision which Wendell, who rarely leaves the hotel except on business, might always be denied. Alternatively, however, it could be a vision of abundance and fruitfulness – emphasised by a shot of a mother breast-feeding her child in an open-air café – which a relationship with Pamela could ultimately lead him towards. As always there is an exquisite ambivalence and poignancy in the film's sense of beauty. But while Pamela is away, darker deeds are stirring at the hotel.

Bruno's plans to return to America by blackmailing Wendell have come to the notice of the maid, a volatile figure always identified by her vigorously flourished black duster and made sinister by her bizarre black moustache, a girl who is pregnant with Bruno's child and who plans to marry him at any cost. In a fit of seething Sicilian rage, deftly accompanied on the soundtrack by appropriate variations of 'Cavalleria Rusticana', she shoots Bruno while he is cleaning Pamela's room – yet another woman in Wilder's films who kills the man she loves.

Bruno has been an interesting character in the film's overall structure, representing the flip-side of Wendell's European education and, as noted earlier, the impossibility of European values being successfully exported to America: in the past Bruno has been deported from America for alleged Mafia connections (intriguingly, his line, "I love America", is almost a direct quote from the opening line of *The Godfather*), yet he has retained the immigrant's fascination with America as the land of opportunity and liberty. In addition to this, Bruno is essential to the film's dramatic development. Although practically all the hotel staff seem to be conspiring to contrive a romantic liaison between Wendell and Pamela it is, in fact, Bruno who inadvertently plays the most significant matchmaking role. It is not only his murder in Pamela's room that requires the shifting of her luggage into Wendell's room thus bringing them physically together. It is also those illicit photographs he has taken which have the greatest impact on Wendell: determinedly cutting them up as incriminating evidence after Carlucci has discreetly handed them over, and then slowly ceasing his destruction of them when he becomes drawn to certain attractions on the pictures and starts reassembling them – a nice detail and brief glance at Wendell's dawning humanity. And like the dead lovers, Bruno has more effect dead than he had when alive, for it is his lifeless body that is sent to America, enabling Wendell to accede to Pamela's romantic request that their parents be buried in Ischia. "Poor Bruno," says Pamela. "What do you mean, poor Bruno?", asks Wendell gently, "This is what he always wanted, to go back to America." Nothing more defines the film's generous spirit – or, indeed, its critique of American values and institutions – than the fact that Bruno not only returns to America but is accorded diplomatic status, full military honours, and promised a coast-to-coast televised funeral.

When Pamela learns that her luggage has been moved to Wendell's room she immediately jumps to the wrong conclusions. The misunderstandings which ensue from her assumption that this is Wendell's forthright American way of making a romantic move are both painful and funny. Wendell, who has moved some distance from this kind of behaviour, cannot understand her accusations: Wendell in the bathtub and Pamela on the rampage adds a degree of vulnerability and embarrassment to his incomprehension. Having finally grasped the situation, he tries to explain the significance of her luggage in his room but it is not until Carlucci enters, with the news of Bruno's murder, that the light dawns. Pamela's emotional deflation is similar to Sabrina's when she learns the real reason for those boat tickets. Yet, as in *Sabrina*, romanticism is to be redeemed and justified. In his 'phone calls with his wife Wendell, to cover up Pamela's embarrassingly vocal presence in his room, has always referred to her as his "interpreter". "Of course you need an interpreter," he snaps down the 'phone; and, of course, he does: in a sense, Pamela *has* become his interpreter and, at this moment, he suddenly realises that she has interpreted his desires correctly. He asks Pamela if she will stand on the bathroom scales. "Permesso," he says. "Avanti," she replies. And they kiss tenderly. It is a moment which beautifully and effortlessly gathers together numerous thematic strands leading towards a romantic culmination and transcendence. He kisses her on the scales because they are then at the same height, representing both her rise in his estimation and his indifference to her weight which he has jibed at insultingly before; the scales also signify a balance, a harmony in their coming together (in their first meeting he has been sitting, she standing; and throughout they have had difficulty, in more than one sense, in seeing eye to eye).

It is equally right that Wendell should request the kiss in Italian. As we have seen, he has resisted speaking a foreign tongue, clinging to his American identity. Yet he has been compelled to utter Italian in the hotel in order to get any service, and the film has often been sliding into Italian at several stages to indicate Wendell's diminishing control of events, particularly during the scene with the Trottas. The moment of commitment to Pamela *has* to be expressed in Italian to confirm his assimilation into the emotional atmosphere of the film ("Italy is not a country, it's an emotion," Pamela has said) and to

Avanti!: *Juliet Mills, Jack Lemmon on the bathroom scales*

express his capitulation to Europe, his surrender to the spiritual nationality of the film that is implicit in its title.

From the kiss, Wilder cuts directly to a shot of a helicopter framed against a blue sky, circling the island. It is an interruption, a violation of the landscape, a suggestion that Wendell's idyll cannot last, and also a reminder of Wendell's opening appearance and how far he has "travelled". The helicopter is carrying J J Blodgett, an American State Department official ("CIA? Never heard of them") who, when informed of his friend's difficulties, is flying in to cut through all the red tape and transport Wendell's father back to Baltimore in time for the funeral. Both the conception of the role and Edward Andrews' ripe performance have been criticised for their stridency, as if Wilder felt that the mood had become too mellow and needed gingering up in this final part. But, in fact, the conspicuous shift of tone and tempo at this point is surely calculated and meaningful. Blodgett's colourful behaviour offers a parallel with Wendell's in the early stages of the film, demonstrating the change in Wendell since his arrival in Italy and also providing a darkly satiric reminder of the world Wendell has left behind and will return to. "Speed it up a little," Blodgett cries with increasing impatience at the three-hour lunchtimes, echoing Wendell's "What are we waiting for?" in the early stages of the film. Blodgett takes over Wendell's pacing up and down and even offers a corruption of Wendell's original xenophobia, the latter's "I know you foreigners . . ." suddenly recalled in Blodgett's "I don't object to foreigners speaking a foreign language; I just wish they'd all speak the *same* foreign language." Wendell now has to tell Blodgett to relax, in just the same way as Carlucci had to calm *him* down. Indeed, Carlucci has to play the same role towards Blodgett in the scene in the hotel room as he has done towards Wendell earlier – distracting him from the true state of affairs and hiding incriminating pieces of clothing. If Blodgett is essentially a comic figure (and Edward Andrews certainly makes him so), he also represents a stylised vision of what Wendell was and might have become without his European experience. The taxi-driver sees Blodgett as a reincarnation of Mussolini, all the more pointed a delusion since Blodgett himself seems to be playing at Richard Nixon ("Let me make one thing perfectly clear"). His blundering and its evocation of Wendell at the beginning make an almost poignant contrast to the serenity of the hero at this stage of the film, stoical and calm and so much at home in this atmosphere that even his pajamas harmonise with the decor. Wendell's pajamas, however, are neatly divided between himself and Pamela who wears the top half (recalling the main narrative device of *Bluebeard's Eighth Wife*) pretending to be the hotel manicurist and fooling Blodgett whose training, perhaps, has made him blind to the obvious and alert to the devious.

But Blodgett's appearance ensures that Wendell's romance with Pamela will not have time to solidify. The insistent pace of American life has intruded. There is time, though, for the secret intimate burial of the parents at Carlucci's family plot, with the Trotta brothers serving as bizarre but sympathetic pall-bearers; and, before Wendell is swept away by the helicopter, for hero and heroine to arrange to meet each other every summer at Ischia to continue the tradition established by their parents. There is also time for a most beautiful exchange between Wendell and Pamela after the love scene, when he gently and tentatively enquires about any gifts his father might have given her mother; whether, as Pamela pointedly puts it, she was a kept woman:

Avanti!: *Juliet Mills, Jack Lemmon, Edward Andrews*

Wendell: "Well, after all, a man likes to show his gratitude – maybe an occasional present".

Pamela: "Oh yes. Every Christmas he would send her a dozen long-stemmed roses. To the Savoy Hotel".

Wendell: "Oh, then your mother was well-to-do".

Pamela: "No! She was making fifteen pounds a week, and tips".

Wendell: "On fifteen pounds a week she was living at the Savoy?"

Pamela: "She wasn't living there. She was working there as a manicurist".

Wendell: "Did my father know that?"

Pamela: "She didn't want him to know".

Wendell: "Why not?"

Pamela: "I told you the first day. She loved him. She didn't want any tips"

For Wilder, a critical and beautiful moment: for perhaps the very first time in his work, love for its own sake, the explicit freeing of love from any mercenary ties. The circle has been completed, even down to Pamela hastily adopting her mother's profession with no trace of irony in order to protect her relationship with Wendell from Blodgett's suspicious eyes. One feels that in the romantic reconciliation and the commitment between Wendell and Pamela, Wilder has finally found himself able to reconcile his own ambivalence towards America and Europe, love and greed.

The death of the parents and the regeneration of their children reminds us that the island (implicitly, Europe itself) is a place of the past, a place for revivifying people who are already old. When Wendell has his original outburst – "You mean all the time we thought he was over here getting cured he was getting laid?" – he is actually contradicting himself: his father *was* being cured. Wendell also gets cured and laid. Wendell and Pamela, in re-enacting the past, are reviving dead people and reviving themselves. In the scene at the dinner table they notice a ninety-year-old gentleman in a wheelchair who is able to rise and dance with his two beautiful young nurses. We are told that the old man has been coming to the hotel "since before World War One"; in other words, since before Europe was to tear itself apart. "This place must take years off your life," Wendell says of the hotel, referring not to encroaching death but to rejuvenation.

Perhaps this is the principal factor which distinguishes Wilder's evocation of Europe here. It not only represents certain values – humanity, romance, emotion – it also represents an age of wisdom and culture that has just gone. Indeed, the narrative structure of the film, where so many key events are either unseen or take place just out of frame (the accident; the murder of Bruno; the funeral arrangements), parallels the idea of a world just out of sight, a world that has just passed. The European "sage" figures who constantly appear in Wilder's films are always old, not only to represent wisdom and experience, but also to represent something that is decaying, disappearing (this gives a new dimension to the ending of *Sabrina*, where we can see now why it *has* to be the older man who joins the heroine in Paris and not his younger brother). One might say that Wilder himself has now become this sage figure, the European educating Americans in the right values and the ways of the world.

But the emphasis on the past explains why, at the end of the film, Wendell has to return to America. Europe, after all, is no longer in the ascendant; America is, and what Europe must do is pass on her cumulative culture, values and wisdom through sensitive vessels like Wendell – and like Wilder. At the end of *Avanti!* one feels, almost for the first time in a Wilder picture, a complete identification between hero and director. What they have achieved is a spiritually enriching reconciliation between their identities as Americans and Europeans. For Wendell, as for Wilder, America is the present, his work, his home, his wife. Europe is the past, his mistress – his heart.

Chapter II

"FRATERNISATION IS LEGAL"

— American GI in
A Foreign Affair

Five Graves to Cairo
A Foreign Affair
Witness for the Prosecution
One, Two, Three

Five Graves to Cairo (1943)

If *Ninotchka, Hold Back the Dawn* and *The Major and the Minor* can be regarded as oblique appeals to Americans to join the European fight against Hitler (especially in their evocation of a Europe being torn apart, of traditions and cultural values threatened, of America as representing both a sanctuary and a potential saviour), *Five Graves to Cairo* is more explicit propaganda, though laced with Wilder's distinctive wit that is all the more surprising and refreshing from a Jewish director at this point in history. But gravity, if you'll excuse the pun, has never been Wilder's *métier* and his sprightliness carries the film over its more earnest passages with no lapse in creative energy. *Five Graves to Cairo* is not one of Wilder's best films, but neither is it the "puerile effort" described by Charles Higham and Joel Greenberg in 'Hollywood in the Forties.'

Shot during January and February 1943, a year after America had declared war on Japan and Germany, the film is primarily concerned with the suppression of personal feelings of grief and revenge for the wider commitment to one's Allies in time of need. The film's opening caption states quite emphatically the urgency of its drama: "In June 1942 things looked black indeed for the British Eighth Army. It was beaten, scattered and in flight. Tobruk had fallen. The victorious Rommel and his Afrika Corps were pounding the British back and back toward Cairo and the Suez Canal".

Near the end of the film the British hero delivers one of the finest speeches to be heard in the American wartime cinema, addressed to the French heroine, Mouche, whose only concern has been to secure the release of her brother held in a German concentration camp: "In

Tobruk I saw them in their hundreds, in Sebastopol they were ten deep, in Athens they're dying of starvation, four hundred a day. For what, Mouche? So that somebody like you can hold a tin cup to a victorious Lieutenant begging for a Pfennig's worth of pity? It's not one brother that matters, it's a million brothers. It's not just one prison gate that might sneak open for you, it's all the gates that must go".

The film's concern with group solidarity, its argument that victory can only be achieved by selfless enterprise and the dissolution of nationalism amongst the Allied countries, would seem to place *Five Graves to Cairo* outside Wilder's customary preference for individualism* since his characters are invariably working on their own, either alienated from the community or ostracised by it. However, the way that Wilder presents his characters in *Five Graves to Cairo*, especially the heroine who is transformed from a likeable but selfish individual into a dewy-eyed martyr, is entirely characteristic. The whole film is structured around cultural tensions which are largely resolved through disguises and deceptions; in particular, the hero's impersonation of a Nazi agent which ultimately liberates the heroine from family ties to global responsibilities.

Nevertheless, it is important to demonstrate how much *Five Graves to Cairo* differs from the majority of Hollywood's propagandist entertainments of the time – America's declaration of war was Hollywood's as well. One could rationalise the film's sentiments and the problem of relating them to Wilder's work by attributing them to Paramount's wish to commit itself to the fight against fascism and regard Wilder as their instrument of communication; and certainly Wilder, as much as any director in Hollywood, would wish to make a valid contribution to the war effort. But *Five Graves to Cairo* is singularly reluctant to paint its Nazis black and its Allies white; indeed, Wilder seems so interested in exploring his own ideas about national identity and role-playing that we sometimes forget there is a war on. Rather like Jean Renoir with *La Grande Illusion*, (1937) Wilder finds his characters interesting as representatives of different cultures and social classes and not *a priori* as members of opposing armies who would blow each other's brains out given the slightest opportunity. Death and murder do occur, of course, and the film

*See our comments on *Stalag 17* in relation to the function of the group in Wilder and, by way of contrast, Howard Hawks.

delivers a powerful morale-boosting climax, but one values and remembers the film for its wit, its attention to detail and for the delicate interplay of its characters. There is none of the political compromise that afflicts a lavishly mounted drama like Michael Curtiz' *Mission to Moscow* (1943) which manages to condone the Stalinist purges in its support of the American and Soviet alliance. And though Wilder's film resembles a single-set play, lustrously photographed like Sternberg exotica, it has none of the allegorical significance which cripples Alfred Hitchcock's *Lifeboat* (1943). Also striking is the total lack of any American presence: a film like Zoltan Korda's *Sahara*, made the same year as Wilder's film and dealing with an identical subject, will introduce an all-American hero (Humphrey Bogart) to restore morale to the beaten British troops and, having established this ideological point, will strive to diminish Bogart's star image in the interests of national equality and group solidarity. In conspicuous contrast, the casting and the style of *Five Graves to Cairo* is deliberately low-key.

J J Bramble (Franchot Tone) is a British Army corporal who survives the defeat at Tobruk – "the blister on the devil's heel", as he later describes it. The film opens as Bramble's tank drifts aimlessly across the empty and untouched sand dunes, its accelerator jammed open by the dead driver. Bramble manages to free himself from the sweltering mobile coffin – the other crew members hanging in the dusty air like excavated mummies – and eventually crawls into the deserted village of Sidi Halfaya, on the border between Libya and Egypt. At the Empress of Britain Hotel he encounters the proprietor Farid (Akim Tamiroff) and the chambermaid Mouche (Anne Baxter). All the rest of the staff have fled east with the British troops. The Germans are expected at the hotel any moment so Bramble, in collusion with Farid and with the less than wholehearted support of Mouche, disguises himself as Davos, the hotel's club-footed waiter who was killed the previous night during a German air-raid. When the Germans arrive, led by Rommel (Erich von Stroheim) and Lieutenant Schwegler (Peter Van Eyck), Bramble finds himself accepted as their undercover agent and manages to bluff his way through their urgent enquiries about a certain Professor Cronstaetter and the Five Graves. Bramble decides to assassinate Rommel but comes into conflict with Mouche who wants the German alive to recommend the release of her brother. When some captured British officers arrive they order Bramble to discover the secret of the Five Graves. Eventually he learns they are underground supply dumps vital to Rommel's campaign and is able, on Rommel's own orders, to leave for Cairo where he informs the British. Following the successful counter-offensive at El Alamein, Bramble, promoted to Lieutenant, returns to Sidi Halfaya and learns that Mouche has been executed for "spreading military rumours" which were, in fact, designed to divert attention away from Bramble's mission and his increasingly threadbare impersonation.

This rather conventional plot* is given additional layers of irony and intrigue by the strength of the characterisations and by the expression of theme through cultural tensions. Bramble's heroism is not in question, though he is able to wriggle out of dangerous situations with almost as much ingenuity as Sergeant Sefton in *Stalag 17*. Franchot Tone's performance is competent – by no means an American star presence – and his underplaying serves to heighten Farid and Mouche's acceptance of his cause beyond their personal survival.

Farid appears to bend whichever way the wind blows – we first see him replacing the Union Jack with the Swastika and at the end he reverses the process – but he evidently favours British occupation, if only because they seem less class conscious than the Germans who debate which rooms they will have and which facilities. "You're Egyptian?", asks Schwegler of the gesticulating Farid, "Yes sir, but only because my parents were Egyptian". Farid seems less concerned with his own nationality than with the nationality of his current guests. His cook has run off with the British to Cairo and his wife has run off with a Greek to Casablanca. The very fact that Farid does not run – in either direction, but remains at his hotel, betrays an acute sense of national pride which circumstances oblige him to suppress.

The attitudes of Mouche, however, are founded less on temperament than on conviction. There is a revealing interview between Mouche and Schwegler that reverberates throughout the film:

Schwegler: "What's a French maid doing in Egypt?"

Mouche: "Housework"

---

*Curiously, Axel Madsen, Robert Mundy and Steve Seidman, in their brief and largely dismissive comments on the film, manage to get important details of the plot wrong; Madsen, for instance, identifies Mouche as "Alsatian".

Schwegler: "What's the matter with housework in Paris?"

Mouche: "In Paris there are one million French chambermaids. There's only one Mouche in Sidi Halfaya."

The thing that is immediately striking about this conversation (written in the style of one of Howard Hawks' wisecracking adventure dramas) is Mouche's apparent disregard for the German occupation of Paris; she seems less a refugee than a total independent.

At this point in the film Bramble's fate hangs in the balance. We have seen Mouche put on make-up before the Germans arrive and we fear she may betray Bramble to Schwegler. Hiding behind the reception desk in a state of near delirium, Bramble manages to escape to another room where he puts on Davos' clothes, pausing as he notices the built-up shoe which makes him limp – a curious portent of Neff's impersonation of the murdered Dietrichson in *Double Indemnity*. When Farid and Mouche discover him she expresses her contempt for the British whom she believes betrayed her country at Dunkirk, leaving one of her brothers killed and the other captured. When Bramble says he will need only impersonate Davos for a few days – until the British come back – Mouche says, "Come back? The British never come back!". It is a tragic statement and an ironic one, for Bramble does come back, but too late to save her. Nevertheless, to counter Mouche's grief for the loss of her brothers, Bramble asks her to forward his personal effects to his wife and children. For the moment, Mouche's determination to raise the alarm mellows and she allows Bramble to play the role of Davos. Farid buries Davos' body under the debris in the hotel basement.

Inevitably, Bramble and Mouche are obliged to share a room together, with the result that the room-service buzzer is almost always for Mouche, doing Bramble out of a job and metaphorically stripping him of half his disguise. Indeed, their close proximity to each other leads to a gradual shedding of their mutual antagonism, Bramble confesses that he has no family at all and later learns from Schwegler that Mouche's fraternisation with the Germans is an attempt to secure the release of her imprisoned brother. The two revelations tell us much about the characters and strike at the core of the film's meaning: the absence of family ties allows Bramble to commit himself fully to the war, even at the risk of his own death; Mouche's brother at first prevents her from embracing this wider commitment until Bramble effectively sabotages her only hope, releasing her to fight for the 'million brothers'.

After an abortive effort to get Rommel on her side, Mouche enlists Schwegler's sympathies. There is a hint early on that Mouche and Schwegler will become involved with each other when, at the end of their interview, he suddenly unties her apron (her uniform) to wipe the sweat from his face with and orders her to light his cigarette. The detail asserts his authority over her which she will endeavour to undermine. Schwegler is no stereotyped Nazi, however, and although we suspect him of taking advantage of Mouche (rather as likeable Claude Rains takes advantage of the Bulgarian refugee in *Casablanca*) there is no conclusive evidence to suggest he will not try to intervene on her brother's behalf until much later in the film. He promises to cable Berlin but persuades her to keep this knowledge from Rommel who evidently has no time for women and less time for servants. Rommel has made Schwegler his protege and, in the light of the denouement, when Rommel reveals to Mouche that the cables are forgeries, his disappointment seems almost as great as hers.

As the film develops Wilder contrives a curious triangle: Mouche between Bramble and Schwegler with the shadow of Rommel hanging over all of them. Bramble views Schwegler as both a dangerous enemy and a romantic rival, but because of his disguise he cannot openly compete with Schwegler for Mouche's affections; instead he warns her of the German facility for treachery and, forgetting her obsession with Dunkirk, reminds her of Munich, when the British were duped by Hitler. When Schwegler offers to help Mouche, she has to get Bramble out of earshot and Schwegler, in effect Bramble's superior officer, adopts a veneer of military and masculine supremacy over the crippled Bramble. The final, fatal, struggle between Bramble and Schwegler is as much over their sexual rivalry as their ideological opposition. With Schwegler out of the way, Bramble is free to conquer Mouche's romantic and ideological resistance to him.

If the alliance in the film between Britain, France and Egypt is never less than shaky, based on mutual tolerance more than on comradeship, Wilder establishes a curious and persistent echo in the presentations of Rommel and General Sebastiano (Fortunio Bonanova), an Italian who arrives with the Germans and who, despite his rank, is allocated a room without any private facilities – a constant source of bickering amongst Farid's guests. In many ways Sebastiano is the Axis equivalent of Farid: demonstrative, and only too aware of how his national characteristics are being suffocated by an alliance between ideologies. Sebastiano is the film's liveliest character and its main source of humour – more voluble than Farid and as extravagantly emotional as the Italians in *Avanti!* whom Wilder adores so much – but the interesting thing about him is his conspicuous irrelevance to the basic plot, beyond the fact that Bramble steals his pistol. The simply executed theft serves to underline the character's warm-hearted simplicity: when he discovers the loss of his gun the Germans don't suspect anything untoward; it merely confirms their ideas about Italian inefficiency. When the captured British officers arrive Bramble ties his dog-tag around the neck of a decanter to alert his comrades of his disguise. Sebastiano enters the bar and scares everyone by inspecting the decanters at close range but is easily persuaded to try a glass of 'bramble' – "If I didn't know it was bramble", he says, "I'd swear it was whisky." When Bramble goes to the Italian's room Sebastiano launches into a tirade against the Germans – "When you lie down with dogs you expect to wake up with fleas." Sebastiano is always bursting into arias from Italian opera (recalling Bonanova's role as the frustrated opera tutor in *Citizen Kane*) and is barely tolerated by the Germans – "Can a nation that belches understand a nation that sings?", he asks Bramble-Davos in dramatic despair. Bramble steals Sebastiano's gun whilst the general is complaining about the theft of his tooth brush and resolving not to sing any Wagner.

The operatic associations are continued when Mouche takes breakfast to Rommel's room. "I don't like women in the morning", he says, "Go away!". But Mouche pleads with Rommel for her brother's release, a story that Rommel seems to have heard a thousand times and finds "reminiscent of bad melodrama," comparing Mouche's emotional display to Italian operas in which the heroines are driven to suicide. It becomes evident, therefore, that the French and Italian characters are linked for their instinctive, emotional responses to dramatic situations and the British and the Germans for their colder, more scientific approach. Despite Sebastiano's claim, Rommel is extremely knowledgeable about Italian opera and has learnt its lessons; indeed, Rommel asks Bramble-Davos to arrange a performance of

'Aida' when he has taken Cairo, "but not the second act, which is too long and not too good."*

This joke of Rommel's is symptomatic of the film's ambivalent portrayals of the Germans. As we have already noted, Schwegler is by no means a conventional Nazi villain and neither is Rommel. If history has been kinder to Rommel than most of Hitler's men (perhaps because of his involvement in a plot against the Führer and his enforced suicide, historians emphasise his brilliance as a military commander and implacable adversary rather than condemn him for the ideology he represented), the Rommel in the film, contemporaneous with events, is presented by Wilder and Stroheim as a proud and boastful eccentric, full of Prussian arrogance, grandeur and sophistication. His best scene is the lavish dinner he gives for his British prisoners, during which Bramble-Davos is the rather curious waiter – literally waiting at the table for an indiscretion from the Germans to report back to the British. Rommel entertains his prisoners as if they were students at a military academy, moving salt cellars and pepperpots around the table to illustrate his strategic superiority over them. Although the scene is clearly intended to mock Rommel's self-esteem – he was defeated at El Alamein before the film went into production – one is also struck by Wilder's indulgence of the showman in Rommel (and in Stroheim), giving full rein to the character's bombast yet never turning him into a cartoon-like caricature of Nazi megalomania. Wilder cuts Rommel down to size – Stroheim is conspicuously shorter than everyone else – but he never denies him his dignity. Rommel boasts he will take Cairo within a matter of days – "I have my reservation in Shepheard's Hotel" – and will not be running the risk of over-extending his supply lines. "As my prisoners are not in the habit of escaping," he says laconically, "It is not the supplies who reach us, it is we who reach the supplies. Is that clear?".

If Wilder grants Rommel the intelligence not to reveal the location of his supply dumps ("I gave you twenty questions, gentlemen. That is twenty-one"), he is nevertheless duped by Bramble; he is fooled, indeed, by a scheme that *is* reminiscent of bad melodrama. After the

*The second act of Verdi's 'Aida' describes Egypt's victory celebrations over Ethiopia. In fact, the entire opera is a precursor of the film: its heroine torn between love and duty; the plot about secret battle plans; even the nations involved in Verdi's opera are significant: Egypt (Allies) resisting an invasion from Ethiopia (previously under Italian administration).

Five Graves to Cairo: *Franchot Tone waits at Erich von Stroheim's table*

dinner Rommel ceremoniously lays his map of Egypt before Bramble who explains his inability to fathom the vital clues the map contains because he is trying to look with an English mind. Indeed he is and Bramble's irony is lost on the Germans who are unable to detect an Englishman masquerading as one of their undercover agents. Bramble's disguise as Davos, whose nationality is ostensibly Alsatian but is confused by his ownership of Danish, Swiss and Rumanian passports, presents a further ethnographic barrier to perception.

Eventually, Bramble's English mind deciphers the secret of the five graves – posing as the archaeologist Cronstaetter, Rommel buried his ammunitions before the war, the five locations literally spelling E-G-Y-P-T on his map – and goes to Rommel's room to trace the map on a piece of mosquito netting. He is disturbed by Schwegler but is saved from having to dream up a convincing explanation by the miracle of an Allied air-raid. Both men rush for the safety of the hotel basement.

Until the air-raid, which comes towards the end of the film, Wilder has resisted staging any unnecessary action sequences; indeed, from the moment that Bramble arrives at the hotel there is not a single exterior shot. The air-raid, then, represents the sudden intrusion of wartime realities into a set of character studies and might be regarded as Wilder's one and only action scene in fifty years of filmmaking were it not so deliberately low-key, eschewing all the traditional elements of filmed battle – no exterior shots of the village being bombed, no scenes of Rommel's troops rushing for artillery, just noise and confusion in the basement, photographed in medium-shot and close-up. The air-raid is used for symbolic purposes and as a narrative device to enable Schwegler to discover the body of Davos. Again one is impressed by Wilder's restraint: there is no close-up of the decomposing body, nor a sudden outcry, just a shot of a club-foot protruding from the debris. The air-raid, then, heightens the immediate drama of the chase between Bramble and Schwegler through the blacked-out hotel. Bramble finally lures Schwegler into Rommel's room and after a prolonged struggle, during which we only see the beam of the German's torch dropped on the floor, Bramble manages to kill Schwegler and shines the torch on his lifeless face. It is a finely judged irony that an air-raid kills Davos and that another should reveal his corpse and betray his impersonator; it is like the dead coming back to haunt the living.

The air-raid also leads to the death of Mouche. When Bramble admits to Schwegler's murder her hatred of the British is revived once more; in effect, Bramble has killed her brother's chance of freedom. Bramble's impassioned speech about universal brotherhood and liberty, quoted earlier, has little effect on Mouche who once again determines to betray him. As she descends the staircase she witnesses Rommel violently ordering his men to search for Schwegler – it's the one moment in the film when Rommel seems capable of anything. He summons Mouche to him and informs her of Schwegler's forgery of the cables; and when Schwegler's body is found in Mouche's room, he senses that she has a motive for murder, hitting her in the face and despairing over his protegée's fraternising with servant girls. One cannot help linking Rommel's behaviour with the Keyes-Neff relationship in *Double Indemnity* (as with Neff and Keyes, Schwegler is constantly lighting Rommel's cigar): the older authority figure unable to control the younger womaniser. If Rommel is disillusioned by his protegée, Mouche is doubly victimised. Her betrayal by Schwegler, with a worthless piece of paper (the cables) evokes Munich just as Bramble's reluctant departure at this point, powerless to save Mouche from her fate, again recalls Dunkirk. When Mouche confesses to Schwegler's murder it is not Bramble's speech about the million brothers which one recalls but Mouche's proud remark to Schwegler that, "there's only one Mouche in Sidi Halfaya," which gives her not so much an independence but a greater responsibility. Her confession simultaneously condemns herself and her brother and allows Bramble to leave for Cairo.

The product of Bramble's heroic endeavour and Mouche's self-sacrifice is shown in a dissolve from Bramble leaving Sidi Halfaya by motor-cycle to a shot of a map of North Africa, sections of which explode. Montgomery's counter-offensive is sketched in a series of explanatory captions, animated maps and documentary footage until a final dissolve shows Bramble's unit marching into Sidi Halfaya. Farid shows Bramble Mouche's grave – just one amongst hundreds beside the hotel – and he delivers a last speech: "Don't worry Mouche, we're after them now. When you feel the earth shake it'll be our tanks and our guns and our lorries. Thousands and thousands of them. British, French and American. We're after them now, coming from all sides. We're going to blast the blazes out of them".

If Bramble's speech is undeniably stirring in a patriotic sense, embodying the national unity towards which the film has been striving and again laying great emphasis on numbers, it also strives to undercut our emotional involvement and our identification with the hero and the heroine. Yet Wilder finds it impossible to remain detached – the umbrella which Bramble has brought for Mouche as a present is the powerful human touch in a scene that summarises the film's equivocal response to the requirements of morale and melodrama. In 1959 Charles Brackett described the film as a "top-notch melodrama on which hangs a dreadful smell of propaganda." Placed beside the human elements in the story the film is reluctant propaganda and *Five Graves to Cairo* may well be the only anti-war statement to have emerged from Hollywood during those turbulent years.

A Foreign Affair (1948)

In a devastated Berlin just after the Second World War, Captain John Pringle (John Lund) of the occupying American army is driving his jeep to the house of his German mistress, Erika von Schluetow (Marlene Dietrich), who happened also to be the mistress of a prominent Nazi who has since gone underground. Pringle is carrying a gift of a mattress which he has acquired through the black market in exchange for a large chocolate cake sent to him by his sweetheart back home in Iowa. As he drives through the bombed-out streets we hear over the soundtrack the strains of "Isn't It Romantic?".

The astringent flavour of *A Foreign Affair*, surely evident from this brief description of an early sequence, is to be sustained almost constantly. Ordinarily, the use of "Isn't It Romantic?" over shots of a devastated city might seem over obviously ironic and incongruous, particularly when accompanying a hero's gift of a mattress for his mistress culled from the proceeds of a gift from his sweetheart. But irony and incongruity are not all that Wilder is after. "Isn't It Romantic?" is a song which has complicated overtones in Wilder's films, announcing, for example, Robert Benchley's pathetic attempts to seduce Ginger Rogers at the beginning of *The Major and the Minor* and having bittersweet associations for the eponymous heroine of *Sabrina*. Wilder's vision of the romanticism in the song seems at once heartfelt and quizzical, a romanticism that curdles at the point of expression. In the context of *A Foreign Affair*, the song is obviously ironic in one sense, but in another is a startling revelation of where, in this disorientating postwar situation, romance could be expected to be found. What it does not imply is any criticism of the Pringle-

Erika relationship. If Wilder does invoke a measure of criticism through his use of the song, it is surely directed at the romantic expectations of the audience. Post-war Berlin is not a place to harbour romantic illusions. "Isn't It Romantic?" is to be completely annihilated in the course of the film by Erika's three songs in the Lorelei nightclub which witheringly expose the reality of life in a war-torn, defeated city where illusions are now for sale, "slightly used", "second-hand". The whole film attempts to subvert conventional reactions to conquerors and conquered, substituting gritty realism for romantic expectation. The shock of Pringle's drive accompanied by that soundtrack is partly to lead the spectator to this important theme, to unsettle him, to compel him to respond afresh to the images. "There are the ruins of Berlin, but not one word to explain why the city had to be utterly destroyed," wrote an outraged Herbert G Luft in 1952: it is precisely to *suppress* that kind of response to the setting and to extend the moral argument beyond an easy condemnation of Nazism and an easy celebration of the Allied victory that explains Wilder's manipulation of the soundtrack.

A little later a committee from Congress, which has been sent on a five-day fact-finding mission to Berlin to enquire into the morale of the American troops, is taken on a guided tour by Colonel Plummer (Millard Mitchell). Plummer's unctuous commentary on the restraint and sympathy of the occupying forces and the way they have been taken to their hearts by the Berliners ("One guy christened his kid Di Maggio Schulz") is plainly contradicted by the evidence before the eyes of Congresswoman Phoebe Frost (Jean Arthur). The sight-seeing tour is merely an exercise in blinkering the eyes of the committee to what is really going on. The film's stylistic mix at this point of back projection and location shooting conveys precisely the sense of two separate worlds which don't quite harmonise, one being illusory and the other real, the committee being driven blandly *parallel* to the truth rather than through it. Plummer's 'documentary' narration is, in essence, a fiction.

Congresswoman Frost, however, is not deceived by this exercise in public relations. Plainly startled by the sight of a Fräulein wheeling a pram that sports two American flags as a sort of brazen advertisement of the child's parentage, she recognises more clearly than her colleagues the kind of 'fraternisation' that is really going on between the Americans and the Germans. Her disguise as a Fräulein named

Gretchen Gesundheit only confirms her worst suspicions, since she is instantly picked up by two GIs who transport her to the Lorelei club where American troops conduct their black market operations and cheerfully absorb the atmosphere of German decadence so potently projected through Erika's songs. But Frost's sense of reality, contrasting with the illusions of the other people from Washington, paradoxically only encapsulates a larger illusion. If Frost is rightly unable to reconcile what she is told with what she sees, she is also unable to reconcile what she has been led to believe should be the situation with the actual, ugly, inevitable reality of life in a beleaguered city. As Pringle tells her in one of the film's most forceful scenes, it is ludicrous to expect him to, "stand on what used to be a corner of what used to be a street with an open sample case of assorted freedoms." The narrowness of her values cannot adequately encompass the complexity of the world before her, the understandable human disorientation amidst the physical deterioration.

Hence, throughout the film, she always seems at odds with the environment, never quite at one with her context, until an extraordinary moment towards the end. Having fallen in love with her fellow Iowan, Pringle ("How is good old Iowa, Congresswoman?" – "Sixty-two percent Republican, thank you"), she now discovers his association with Erika. She walks from Erika's house, dazed by the revelation, and comes out into the street; and, because the camera is carefully placed at some distance from the action, she suddenly becomes absorbed into the setting, the ruins of her illusions finding an echo in the ruins of the city, giving an extra twist to Erika's comment to her at the moment of disillusionment – "Now you're one of us" – and giving the setting, for the first time in her experience, a *personal* significance. As she says at the end, "I came as an objective observer. Some things have happened that automatically disqualify me."

Clearly the setting is being used very differently from Wilder's European settings for the romantic comedies we discussed in the previous chapter. *A Foreign Affair* and *One, Two, Three* might also observe the American abroad, but here they are exploitative, unattractive figures whose impulses are directed not towards a process of self-regeneration but of subduing and overwhelming the Europeans with superior enterprise and guile. Europe here is seen almost as an American colony. Berlin in *A Foreign Affair* and *One, Two, Three* and the crucial Hamburg flashback in *Witness for the Prosecution* have not

A Foreign Affair: *Jean Arthur, John Lund, Marlene Dietrich*

the romantic associations of Paris but are locations from which to escape, cities whose identities, physical as well as cultural, have been debased or obliterated. The crumbling ruins of Berlin in *A Foreign Affair* eloquently express the precarious morality of those who inhabit them. Wilder is torn between seeing the necessity for escape, and yet scorning the self-righteous criticism of those outsiders who have not experienced for themselves the immense moral and material pressures endured by the people in their struggle for survival.

It is this kind of ambivalence which makes *A Foreign Affair* such an uncomfortable comedy. It might be true that part of one's discomfort is that the whole film does not quite work, which makes some of the questionable areas in it more questionable still. But it is also true that the discomfort arises from the film's uncompromising honesty about the way in which a war degrades the victors as well as the vanquished. The complexity of the film's tone must stem partly from Wilder's identity as a Jewish refugee from Berlin, now settled in Hollywood and looking back on the holocaust he missed.

When asked by 'Cinema' about *A Foreign Affair*, particularly its questioning of America's international role and its choice of the Berlin setting, Wilder answered: "Well, I know America and I know Berlin. It seemed a good idea to fuse my familiarity with both places . . . I lived in Berlin, I worked as a newspaper reporter there and I'm crazy about the place. I saw the devastation when I was in the army and *A Foreign Affair* was partly reminiscent." Wilder's first-hand knowledge is what gives the film its authority and conviction*. It gives particular force to what is arguably the film's principal theme – the unreasonable demand for a set of moral absolutes in a situation scarred by the aftermath of war. Wilder's position – his divided loyalty as American and as Berliner – gives him a unique appreciation of both sides; indeed, considering that Wilder himself lost relatives at Auschwitz, his refusal to portray the position in Berlin as liberating Yanks versus evil Krauts (the same restraint is present in *Five Graves to Cairo* and *Stalag 17*) is less an action of moral corruption and cynicism, as some critics would argue, than one of personal dignity and heroism. Without in any way condoning Fascism, he nevertheless invites us to admire the resilience of those Berliners who refused to wallow in feelings of guilt and trauma and who "kept going"†. Without in any way condoning American profiteering and exploitation, he nevertheless recognises that men who have been encouraged to fight ruthlessly for survival and victory cannot suddenly transform themselves overnight into guardian angels once peace breaks out. The film might be dealing with what Frost has termed a "moral malaria", but its exposure and understanding of this condition can only be ultimately more moral than a dishonest, sentimentalised view of Americans in Berlin. This would explain the curious moral emphasis of the film, where the satire is directed not so much against the Germans nor against the corrupted American troops, but against the people who insist on seeing the position in simple terms of vice and virtue, an attitude endorsed in a devastating moment early in the film

---

*The film is full of oblique biographical references. It is well known that, for a while, Wilder worked as a 'dancer' in the Eden Hotel in Berlin – the band which plays at the Lorelei calls itself the 'Hotel Eden Syncopaters'. For his military service, Wilder was attached to the Psychological Warfare Division for which, like Captain Pringle, he toured the ruins of Berlin and was engaged in similar "De-Nazification" duties.

†Germany's spectacular post-war recovery might well furnish some evidence of the psychological accuracy of Wilder's portrait.

when Frost tells Pringle that her hometown in Iowa boasted the lowest crime rate in the country until a young boy took a blowtorch to his entire family. So much for American virtue at home, and so much also for the solidity of Frost's values, where she can regard an event like that as a statistical rather than human tragedy and fails to see the harsh comment on small-town complacency and repression that such a tragedy implies. As is so often the case with Wilder's alleged "bad-taste" (and 'jokes' like the blowtorch episode encourage this description of his films, quoted out of context), the main target of his criticism is, implicitly, Hollywood itself. After all, it is Hollywood that most influentially perpetuated the myths and conventions of noble Americans and stage-villain Nazis, conventions which *A Foreign Affair* strives to undermine.

Although the film's challenge to standard Hollywood war romances comes mainly in its plot and characterisation, its visual style also endeavours to deglamourise the story – for instance, when Pringle and Frost become 'engaged' they set off on a drive through the country but Wilder refuses to visualise this, realising the potential damage such a sequence might do to the film's overall tone, but simply cuts to Pringle arriving at Erika's house after having dropped Frost at her hotel. The film never leaves the ruined city and in its graphic depiction one can detect the stylistic influence on the film of the neo-realism of Roberto Rossellini and Vittorio De Sica which eschewed studio gloss and took its cameras into the streets to photograph the life it found there. Apparently, one of Wilder's last acts for Lubitsch before the latter died in 1947 was to screen for him De Sica's *Shoeshine*, which had an enormous impact on both men; and Wilder to this day expresses his admiration for De Sica's later film *Bicycle Thieves*. Admittedly, Wilder's insistence on realism in the Los Angeles settings of *Double Indemnity* and the location sequences in New York for *The Lost Weekend* indicate already a preference for authenticity in his films. But the example of neo-realism must have convinced Wilder of the absolute necessity of having real footage of the ruins of Berlin. One cannot think of any other Hollywood film of this period that has quite the same neo-realist atmosphere of moral malaise, set against the physical wastes of war.

Some recent critical approaches have shown that such attempts at realism can only be regarded with some scepticism since the films display in most every other respect the conventions of narrative and characterisations common to studio dramas. But the elements of neo-realism in *A Foreign Affair* must be placed alongside its use of back projection and expressionist techniques in certain important sequences, such as those at the Lorelei. This leads us to the other major influence on the style of *A Foreign Affair*: *film noir*, its atmosphere of spiritual depression generated particularly by the work of European emigré directors in Hollywood whose darker cultural heritage and anguished personal experience gave their films a predominant mood of melancholy and fatalism. More will be said about *film noir* and Wilder when we consider *Double Indemnity* and *Sunset Boulevard*; and it might initially seem a contradiction to nominate a comedy as a *film noir*. Yet *A Foreign Affair* is a conspicuously *noir* comedy, set against a war-torn background and culminating in a killing; it also shares a narrative device common to *films noirs*, like *Double Indemnity, The Woman in the Window* and *Shadow of a Doubt*, where the guilty party has access to information regarding the investigation: Frost is determined to discover which American soldier is fraternising with Erika and Pringle volunteers to assist her. In addition to this, *A Foreign Affair* has a dramatic structure which is very similar to *Double Indemnity*; a morally flawed hero; an irrestistible *femme fatale*, with whom the hero's association could result in danger and death; and a severe moralist on the sidelines who is drawn to the man and fearful of the corruption of the other woman. Indeed, there is one scene that is almost identical to a moment in *Double Indemnity*: Pringle receiving a 'phone call from Erika when Frost is present with him in the room – like Neff being called by Phyllis with Keyes in the room – a situation which crystallises the hero's divided sympathies ("We went through basic training together," he explains to Frost when she enquires about the 'friend' on the other end of the line).

Film noir is characterised by heroes and heroines who find no way out, no escape from their dilemmas. The two key moments in the relationship between Pringle and Frost are moments when one corners the other, cutting off his or her exit. Of course, one should not depart too much from the tone of these moments: Pringle's resistance to the advancing Congresswoman at the end of the film is essentially a piece of neat comic business; and a number of Wilder's comedies have rather similar triangular structures. Nevertheless, the particular triangular struggle in *A Foreign Affair* is unquestionably closer to the dramas than the comedies, and the film's ending has nothing like the affirmation or exuberance that usually concludes a Wilder comedy. In contrast to the joyous release that concludes, say, *The Major and the Minor, Sabrina* or *Love in the Afternoon*, when hero and heroine are united, *A Foreign Affair* seems peculiarly tentative and brittle at its climax, for reasons which will become clear when we examine Pringle and Frost in more detail.

The two have been drawn together when the Congresswoman, appalled by the situation at the Lorelei, where the Americans excuse their behaviour by claiming that "Fraternisation is legal" and where Erika's seductiveness is at its most dangerous, undertakes to unmask Erika's Nazi associations and enlists the support of Pringle. Anxious to protect both Erika and himself from these investigations, he resolves to distract the Congresswoman, trapping her between some filing cabinets, which actually contain the incriminating evidence against Erika, so that he can make some romantic overtures. She succumbs, her investigative zeal and intuitions being now diverted by her emotional involvement with the unsuspected guilty party (as we shall see, this is one of Wilder's favourite character types). What follows is that Pringle begins to grow genuinely infatuated with her; and Congresswoman Frost is de-frosted by his charms.

It is a commonplace for critics of the film to find both of these stages hard to swallow. If the film does not succeed in making this relationship entirely convincing, it is important to argue the case more closely and not attack Wilder by misrepresenting his intentions. The casting of the uncharismatic John Lund as Pringle is clearly one factor which is carefully calculated. The actor's brisk unpleasantness is a refreshing reversal of type from the usual upright superhero (who would not usually be called something like 'Pringle' anyway). Lund's distinctly unsparkling presence assists the film in its atmosphere of deglamourisation; but, it must be admitted, it also lends a certain flatness to the scenes in which he participates. Pringle's attraction for Frost is not that incredible for a Wilder hero, whose tainted nature often finds itself drawn to a vision of purity, though not always for honourable motives (he may wish to destroy it). Indeed, one could say Pringle's shifting allegiances between the two women is only further evidence of his unsavoury shallowness as a man. Someone who has played so consistent a dual role through the film has probably lost sight of what his true feelings are. Wilder certainly gives little narrative weight to the hero's redemption, if it can be called that. No sooner does Pringle suspect his love for Phoebe than he is ordered to resume his former role as Erika's lover in order to smoke out her Nazi associate who is growing jealous of their relationship. Unfortunately, this latter twist is probably the film's major miscalculation, since the final setpiece – the hunting down of the Nazi, using Pringle as bait – smacks far too much of the heroics which the rest of the film has spent its time avoiding. The consequent shoot-out is quite exciting but the outcome leaves us curiously uninvolved. By this time, Pringle has been so thoroughly discredited as a hero – blackmailed by the army into resuming his role as Erika's stud and becoming passive target practice for her former lover – that it is difficult to be very excited over what Phoebe is actually winning: an audience would not have been too upset to have seen Pringle shot. Wilder's undercutting of the usual Hollywood hero is admirable in one way but arguably goes so far as to rob the film of dramatic tension.

The treatment of Phoebe Frost is more outrageous and considerably more interesting. When we are first introduced to her on the plane bringing the Congress committee to Berlin, Wilder has held for some time a shot of her as she puts away her notebook, spectacles and pen. The shot is sustained so long, in fact, that the effect becomes somewhat ambiguous: is she someone who is just very orderly, or someone who needs such excessive rituals to guard against disorder in her life? Everything about her, particularly her appearance, signals a rectitude *externally* applied rather than felt from within, an impression wittily reinforced by her use of the filing cabinets to keep Pringle at bay (an external symbol of order) until she finds herself caught in a trap of her own making. In an excellent analysis of the film, Stephen Farber has suggested that, "We haven't been convinced that anyone as puritanical as the Congresswoman could become quite so abandoned, quite so casual about a man who has been living with a former Nazi." This depends on the genuineness of the puritanism. We must remember that Phoebe has been in love before: significantly with a Southern Democrat who is her complete antithesis in outlook, her enemy. One can hardly avoid recalling Ninotchka and her Polish lancer; or avoid wondering about the sincerity and stability of a woman who has been overwhelmingly attracted to someone who is the opposite of what she stands for. It seems reasonable to infer that the pain of that unrequited relationship has resulted in a hardening of outlook, almost a caricature of self-righteousness to guard against being hurt in that way again. A number of critics have felt that, in falling in love with Pringle, Phoebe Frost is less humanised than corrupted, but Wilder would surely dispute that. Her previous moral stance was life-denying, limited and unforgiving, a mere filing-system of human standards and values which underestimated the range of human personality. Whether her relationship with Pringle will be successful or not, she is more alive at the end than at the beginning. Whether she is any more appealing is another matter.

This brings us to one of the film's most controversial areas – the performance Wilder draws from Jean Arthur. Andrew Sarris has never forgiven Wilder, apparently, for his "needless brutalisation" of Miss Arthur here. Richard Corliss has likened her coiffure in the film to medieval torture and has described her evening dress – which she buys on the black market in exchange for her typewriter – as the ugliest worn by any actress in a 'Forties movie. Much of this evaporates if you do not happen to share the predominant critical sentimentality over Miss Arthur. If, for example, you happen to think that her rather tiresome whining diminishes the grandeur of Howard Hawks's *Only Angels Have Wings* or think her gushing knowingness flaws her performances in the comedies of Frank Capra or George Stevens, then you might actually prefer her hesitancy here, her playing against type. If you have a sneaking sympathy for James Agee's attitude to her (rebuking an actress for "playing Jean Arthur – a tendency which even Miss Arthur must learn to curb"), then Wilder will be given credit as one of the few directors to have kept her under control.

To be more specific about details, her dress is awkward rather than especially ugly – even Phoebe herself describes it as "mourning for an elephant that died" and Erika is drawn to exclaim, "It's stunning . . . but haven't you got it on backwards?" – and testifies rather touchingly to the awkwardness of the character when having to select a garment which will do her justice. The contrast between her and the stunning Erika might seem overloaded, but on clear inspection is not: Phoebe's self-denial and clumsiness might be unbecoming, but so is Erika's selfishness and vanity. Both dress and hair are details of character which have been thought out and which fit. Phoebe's hairstyle is as expressive of her repression and tension as Ninotchka's flat shoes and dowdy clothes: her dress is a detail which has exactly the same feeling of romantic awkwardness and "foolishness" as Ninotchka's hat. It seems somewhat unfair, therefore, to salute

Lubitsch's charm and accuse Wilder of brutality*. Indeed, Leon's attitude to Ninotchka's hat could be regarded as patronising, in comparison with Pringle's to Phoebe's dress: he adjusts it so it looks better.

Also, Wilder does provide Miss Arthur with one of the most powerful, moving moments in the film. There has been a raid on the Lorelei Club and both Phoebe and Erika have been arrested: the latter uses her influence with a guard to have them both released and then invites Phoebe back to her home – "It's only a few ruins from here." It is then that she starts explaining her life and reveals her association with Pringle, whistling "Shine on Harvest Moon" – a favourite of Pringle's and Phoebe's – as she breaks the news. In the shadow we see a profile of Phoebe's face and a speck of silver light as a tear slips down her cheek – a beautifully restrained shot of inner disintegration. Hearing Pringle's jeep arrive and the signal of the horn, she tosses Erika's door key to him as he waits unsuspectingly below. "Four hours ago you were in a position to have him court-martialled and me sent to a labour-camp," says Erika to her, "Now you're one of us." The remark might seem a comment on Phoebe's corruption, yet we interpret her gesture with the key somewhat differently. Like Olivia De Havilland's refusal to betray her deceiving husband in *Hold Back the Dawn*, the gesture is an acknowledgement of her own complicity in the situation, a generous recognition of what her own vanity and blindness have led her into. "What a waltz we had," she says to Pringle and then descends the darkened staircase, in ironic contrast to her dreamy ascent of her own hotel staircase after a romantic night with Pringle some time before. The gravity of the moment is very sensitively handled and accusations of "brutalisation" in that context would be difficult to sustain. Wilder is closest to Phoebe Frost at her moment of disillusionment: a "brutal" director would have handled it with relish.

Nevertheless, although Wilder's handling of Phoebe and Pringle is more balanced and credible than he is often given credit for, he is not able to imbue them with as much warmth as he might have wished. He handles their humiliations seriously, not sadistically, but

---

*After all, Lubitsch is alleged to have described Greta Garbo as "Gary Cooper in drag – I mean, have you ever seen them in a film together?" but has never been subjected to the vilification for such ungallantry that Wilder has attracted for knotting Jean Arthur's hair.

is unable to imply anything very positive about them, Phoebe's transformation being uncompleted (the best is yet to come), Pringle's transformation being opportunistic and curiously hollow (at least in the beginning he stood for something – a frank pragmatism in an imperfect world – but by the end he seems passive, impotent). Part of Wilder's difficulty is in reconciling the redemptive structure with the solidly established atmosphere of disillusionment and disorientation. He could not really re-build Phoebe and Pringle without re-building Berlin. The war between romanticism and realism (implicit in the use of "Isn't It Romantic?" at the beginning) finally overwhelms Wilder himself, the realist in him not quite able to believe in the positive implications of the Pringle-Phoebe relationship, the romantic in him refusing to accept "moral malaria" as the inevitable state of affairs.

Still, this failure seems insubstantial beside the triumph of Marlene Dietrich's Erika. Jean Arthur and John Lund might have talent, but Miss Dietrich has charisma: and the allusiveness of her screen presence gives her an aura that makes the other two sides of the triangle look rather pale by comparison, thus unbalancing the film's main concern – the moral atmosphere of post-war Berlin – pushing the Pringle-Phoebe romance to a subordinate place in the narrative and making the film's emphasis on it seem over-extended. It is the night-club scenes of *A Foreign Affair* which are the most remarkable. Spotlit, with the composer himself at the piano, Erika performs the Friedrich Hollander songs in a smoke-filled atmosphere reeking of the decadent attraction of *The Blue Angel*: the raptness of the American audience eloquently conveys their seduction by the Berlin ambience. The songs – "Black Market", "Illusions" and "Amidst the Ruins of Berlin" – speak with silky precision of the world-weary disenchantment of the Berliners, yet also have a saving irony and toughness. In Dietrich's Erika is contained all the decadence of the pre-war era in Germany and all the defiance of its post-war survivors. Arrested at the end for her Nazi associations and in the process of being shipped off to a labour camp, there is a suggestion that her physical charms might overwhelm her American captors, as they have been disorientated by the corrupt attractions of Berlin through the film. Firstly, two policemen are assigned to look after her, then another two, and then another one: one of them even trips up the stairs in his eagerness to participate in Erika's detention. It is an intriguing ending, catching

A Foreign Affair: *Marlene Dietrich in the nightclub*

the film's pervasive moral dualism: a sly dig even at that stage at the ease of America's susceptibility to Europe's worldly charms; a grand ambiguous farewell to a great character, suggesting a possible freedom and escape route even while under arrest; and, as an extension of that, a refusal to come to a tidy moral resolution. That trip-up on the stairs says a lot about how decadence can catch you unawares and says a lot about the "stalemate between justice and corruption" which Raymond Durgnat has acutely characterised as an important aspect of Wilder's vision. Erika is willing to try one last throw: she is resilience personified, right or wrong. Marlene Dietrich's performance carries enormous force in the film, the quintessence of German expressionistic decadence – tempting, dangerous, unstaunched, unquenchable. In spite of himself, Wilder is drawn to it and pays tribute to its endurance. For all its flaws, it is fascinating – like the film.

Two final thoughts about Marlene Dietrich and *A Foreign Affair*. There is the moment in *Fedora* when the Countess is reading the telegrams of mourning and tribute for Fedora as she lies in state: she reels off the names but when she comes across Marlene Dietrich's tribute she pauses momentarily to add a tribute of her own: "Marlene – now there's a real fighter!", she says. The second thought is that moment in Peter Bogdanovich's book 'Picture Shows' when he recalls a conversation with Miss Dietrich. "You've worked for a lot of great directors," he begins at one stage, at which point she thoughtfully corrects him. "No . . . No, I only worked for two great directors. Von Sternberg and Billy Wilder."

Witness for the Prosecution (1957)

In common with *Five Graves to Cairo* and *The Spirit of St Louis, Witness for the Prosecution* is seldom mentioned in articles on Wilder or in interviews; and like *The Front Page*, also adapted from a well-known stage play, it seems to find more favour with Wilder's critics than with his staunchest admirers. This may be because – on the surface at least – the film is comparatively free of the director's fabled cynicism and devoid of his wholly repugnant characters: even the film's villain, played by Tyrone Power, possesses considerable charm and is indeed a sympathetic victim of circumstance until the startling revelations of the very last scene. It is perhaps significant in this context that a critic like Penelope Houston, who habitually finds Wilder's sense of humour unpalatable, should single out, in the 'Monthly Film Bulletin', the film's Hamburg flashback as an indulgence while enjoying the rest as an "old fashioned whodunit which grips adequately and has some pleasing humour in dialogue and characterisation."

Wilder's serious admirers on the other hand (excluding here Axel Madsen who raises the same objection as Miss Houston) have great difficulty in placing the film in Wilder's development, generally consigning it (if they mention it at all) to the uneven period when Wilder wandered from studio to studio before settling down in 1959 with the Mirisch Brothers. *Witness for the Prosecution* is not mentioned once in Robert Mundy's article, nor in his structural diagram, presumably because the film fails to provide a clear cut instance of role rejection. Stephen Farber likens Tyrone Power's relationship with the elderly widow Mrs French to the Joe Gillis-Norma Desmond relationship in *Sunset Boulevard* but makes no attempt to link the film to Wilder's other concerns. James McCourt mentions the film only *en passant*: the barrister's use of a filing drawer as a secret ashtray is cited as an example of Wilder's subversion of everyday objects, though as we shall see, *Witness for the Prosecution* elaborates extensively on this Wilder trait and with far more significance. Even Maurice Zolotow, who can normally be relied upon to provide some solid production insights or gossip, finds little worth reporting apart from the director's relationship with his script collaborator, Harry Kurnitz, and his high regard for Charles Laughton. Given such scanty evidence, supported by most contemporary reviews, the consensus of opinion seems to be that, hugely entertaining though it is, and with a bravura performance by Laughton, the film is marginal to Wilder's career; the director is "running for cover" (not for the first or last time) with a virtually guaranteed commercial success. This view strikes us as inadequate, and even though *Witness for the Prosecution* lacks the inner tension and passion readily discernible in more personal works like *Love in the Afternoon* and *The Private Life of Sherlock Holmes*, it nevertheless rewards close inspection. Familiarity with Wilder's other work reveals it to be a remarkably individual film, a work which perfectly embodies Wilder's avowed aim to please himself *and* the mass audience.

Although the peculiarly English milieu of Agatha Christie might at first appear to present a cultural collision in the non-Wilder sense, the thrillers of this extraordinarily prolific author celebrate the surprise ending, for which Wilder's films are often criticised, and are structured around the concept of the grand scheme in which dupes and rogues are endlessly interchangeable: we usually only discover whodunit on the last page when the villain – invariably the most obvious so least expected character – is unmasked by some form of *deus ex machina*. Disguise, too, is an essential device in Miss Christie's repertoire of dramatic effects, as it was of Sir Arthur Conan Doyle, whose Sherlock Holmes is the precursor of Miss Christie's variously eccentric sleuths. So given a degree of shared narrative resources, it is not surprising that Wilder should have a basic sympathy with Miss Christie's work and turn her long-running stage play 'Witness for the Prosecution' (first performed in London on 28 October 1953) into one of his most engaging films. Wilder makes few radical changes in the original (even the quintessentially Wilder flashback to war-time Germany was there in the original, requiring only amplification), yet his subtle changes of emphasis in the characterisation (notably the barrister and the additional character of his nurse) and his ingenious use of objects (none of which were in the original) make *Witness for the Prosecution* a dazzling inventory of Wilder's favourite themes and effects. Perhaps the film is ultimately prevented from being a masterwork like the closely related *Double Indemnity* and *The Private Life of Sherlock Holmes* because Wilder's material offers him too much to focus on.

The most immediately obvious example of Wilder's presence is in the Hamburg flashback in which Leonard Vole (Tyrone Power), who stands accused in London of murdering the wealthy widow Mrs French (Norma Varden), recalls how he met his wife Christine, played by Marlene Dietrich. Christine works in a nightclub entertaining the soldiers at the end of the war. Vole comes to her aid when a riot breaks out and they subsequently marry and move to London. The background of a war-torn Germany and the presence there of occupying forces recalls *A Foreign Affair* and anticipates a similar background for *One, Two, Three*. In every way it is a typical Wilder setting.

Yet is the scene an "unnecessary dalliance" as Axel Madsen and Penelope Houston claim? The more one considers it, the more complex and relevant it appears. The flashback is narrated by Leonard as he sits in his prison cell answering questions from his barrister and solicitor. In the light of the dénouement, in which Leonard is discredited, it is important to consider how reliable an impression this is. It could be a deceitful flashback, such as that exploited by Alfred Hitchcock in *Stage Fright* (1950) which, intriguingly, also stars Marlene Dietrich and which also has a narrator-hero who is revealed to be a murderer. Certainly the device of the deceptive flashback would not be new to the creator of *Sunset Boulevard*, and has been meticulously prepared for in an earlier flashback with Leonard and Mrs French in which Leonard's selfless charm is later revealed to be an act.

It is only when the film is seen again that we realise how cleverly Wilder is deceiving his audience and his characters. At first sight, the impression given in the flashback is one of innocence and virtue in the handsome form of Tyrone Power being seduced by European experience in the iconoclastic form of Marlene Dietrich. This is certainly the impression received by the barrister Sir Wilfrid Robarts

(Charles Laughton), his immediate circle of clerk and nurse, by the jury, and by us. Dietrich in the tatty nightclub evokes not only *A Foreign Affair* but also Josef von Sternberg's *The Blue Angel* (1930), in which she destroyed a hapless schoolteacher, and a great many American pictures in which she played a cabaret singer. Her indestructible image as a *femme fatale* is eventually overturned by Wilder, but in the Hamburg flashback it contributes to the broader deception. As in most of Wilder's films, the casting is of crucial importance.

The flashback sequence begins as Leonard enters the nightclub as Christine is singing a plaintive song called "I May Never Go Home Anymore" to the restless troops. Leonard buys a drink at the bar and the scene is directed from his point of view: a large pipe attached to the ceiling divides the bar area from the 'auditorium' at this camera-angle, giving the scene not only a theatrical flavour – almost a comment on watching Dietrich in an old movie – but reflects the first-person narrative. Leonard's appearance, with a bag slung over his shoulder, gives the impression that he has merely dropped in for a drink rather than come out to see a show. Suddenly the troops, presumably expecting a striptease and angered by Christine's obliviousness to their taunts, erupt on to the small stage and tear at Christine's trousers, revealing a spectacular leg. She is dragged to the floor as the military police arrive. Leonard, who has never left the bar area, places his drink out of danger and calmly leaves the club, unobserved through the chaos. When the police have closed the club and declared it "Off Limits" Leonard returns, retrieves his drink, and assists Christine who is gathering her possessions from the floor. She suggests they go to her place which turns out to be a derelict room behind the stage. When Leonard offers her supplies of blackmarket foodstuffs, his pleasant and helpful nature is confirmed, and when the flashback sequence ends with Christine kissing him as he lies on her bed we have no reason to doubt that Christine is using Leonard to escape her drab existence and to provide her with what have become luxuries. This impression of Christine as a predatory female is endorsed by the precise placing of the flashback, coming after her first appearance in the film at Sir Wilfrid's chambers when she creates an extremely unfavourable impression by seeming totally unconcerned by her husband's arrest for murder.

Indeed, Christine seizes the opportunity which Leonard has presented and is exploiting him, even committing bigamy in order to

Witness for the Prosecution: *Tyrone Power and Marlene Dietrich in the wrecked nightclub*

escape with him. But it is only on a second viewing that the deceptive qualities of the flashback reveal themselves. Before she meets Leonard, Christine is clearly intent on singing a quiet song to console the troops' frustration rather than accentuate it (rather like the song at the end of Stanley Kubrick's *Paths of Glory*, made the same year). Leonard's behaviour in retrospect seems coldly calculating, rather like a reworking of Sergeant Sefton in *Stalag 17* with his smooth exit from the nightclub, his careful treatment of his drink, and his supplies of instant coffee, sugar and powdered milk which he uses as a form of currency to purchase Christine's favours. Although Leonard hints, by his aloofness, that he is not a member of the group's camaraderie, he is more than equally on the make, like Charles Boyer in *Hold Back the Dawn*, Sefton and C C Baxter in *The Apartment*, determined to turn a desperate situation into his own material advantage. In view of the film's central theme of deception, the flashback sequence, far from being an indulgence on Wilder's part, is crucial to the film's structure. For it is here that Wilder induces us once and for all to accept Leonard as a victim and Christine as a predator. When Christine later appears as the chief prosecution witness, testifying against her husband as Christine Helm, the sudden revelation of a still valid, previous marriage in pre-war Germany forces us to combine this damning information with the impressionistic flashback. The element which completes the deception is the belief in Leonard's innocence by Sir Wilfrid who enjoys the reputation as the most skilful barrister at the Old Bailey. One of Wilder's most perverse images begins with a tilting camera-movement up the famous dome of the Central Criminal Court, with its Scales of Justice statue, and rests on a workman on a ladder giving the building a facelift, anticipating the cock-eyed justice which Sir Wilfrid's inspired advocacy is to bring about. British moral values and its mechanisms for justice are shown in the film to be an illusion, as deceptive as the flashback.

Leonard Vole can be seen to have a great deal in common with Wilder's American heroes. He is a drifter without friends, superficially charming but shallow and materialistic. He is a weak and opportunistic man who, through an accidental encounter, sees a way of promoting his self-interests but which could ultimately destroy him like Walter Neff in *Double Indemnity*, Joe Gillis in *Sunset Boulevard* and Chuck Tatum in *Ace in the Hole*. As with all these heroes, the scheme involves the exploitation of women and finally disintegrates because of sexual jealousies. "He has a way with women," says Christine of her husband, and Leonard uses his wife for her love and Mrs French for her money. Leonard is also an inventor, as he is in Agatha Christie's original play, but the inventor in Leonard underlines his scheming personality and his inventions, like his egg-beater which separates while it whisks, places him in the Wilder mould of American eagerness to promote its know-how to a world of happy consumers. A further link can be drawn between Leonard's relationship with Mrs French and *Sunset Boulevard*. As Stephen Farber has pointed out, Mrs French, like Norma Desmond, lives with a loyal servant (Janet McKenzie, played by Una O'Connor) in a house filled with the bric-a-brac from the past (in this case African trophies) whose life is disturbed by a young and attractive man on the make. There is no real hint in *Witness for the Prosecution* of any sexual relationship between Leonard and Mrs French, certainly not in the way suggested in *Sunset Boulevard*; rather, as Stephen Farber has described, it is a "parasitic Oedipal relationship motivated by greed and pity". It is like a doting mother being helped with her tax returns by a devoted son who murders her when he's managed to seduce her into changing her will in his favour*.

If the hero and heroine, then, seem quintessential Wilder types rather than figures remote from his world, this is equally true of the barrister Sir Wilfrid Robarts. He is the archetypal investigator-interrogator figure who comes to completely wrong conclusions from his investigations. The immediate parallel is with Wilder's vision of Sherlock Holmes: both characters are defined in identical ways, being given their particular vices and addictions – Holmes has his cocaine hidden in a box-file; Sir Wilfrid has his brandy camouflaged in a cocoa-flask and his cigars concealed in his walking cane, and both their 'guardians', Dr Watson and Nurse Plimsoll (Elsa Lanchester), are never fooled for a moment. Both men become involved in the story after returning to their offices which they inspect for signs of interference – Holmes comes back from a case in the country, Sir Wilfrid from hospital following a heart attack. Both men crave the excitement of a challenge to their powers of deduction. But another, equally striking parallel is with Keyes in *Double Indemnity*. Both Keyes and Sir Wilfrid are blinded by their own perceptions to the extent that they both clear the guilty party. Ironically, both have their own infallible systems which turn out to be wholly unreliable. With Keyes

---

*One might note here that the first meeting between Leonard and Mrs French takes place at a milliners: Leonard gestures his approval or disapproval with Mrs French's hats. This flashback, like the Hamburg episode, also has an element of voyeurism and a subtle comment on watching movies since Leonard sees Mrs French through the shop window. Significantly, their second – and entirely accidental – meeting takes place in a cinema, when Mrs French's new hat blocks Leonard's view of the screen. Wilder's obsession with hats (he is rarely photographed without one) finds its way into many of his films and assumes a curious importance – Ninotchka's hat symbolises her submission to Capitalism; Baxter's bowler in *The Apartment* is an emblem of his success; Ariane's boyfriend in *Love in the Afternoon* ridicules her "stupid hat"; Norma Desmond's hat is nearly knocked off her head by the sound boom in *Sunset Boulevard*; Hildy Johnson's incongruous straw boater symbolises his resignation in *The Front Page*, discarded when the story breaks; Sherlock Holmes resents his deerstalker image; *Fedora* even gets its name from a hat; while a myriad of hats and wigs are used as disguises in many other films.

it is his stomach ("I can feel it in my stomach, Walter"), but Sir Wilfrid's system is more complex. His method of assessing whether or not a client is telling the truth is to direct a beam of sunlight from his monocle into his client's eyes. If the client withstands the ordeal Sir Wilfrid can believe in the client's innocence because he refuses to avoid his own eyes. The irony here is twofold: Leonard passes the test admirably, while Christine walks to the window and pulls down a blind: in both cases, Sir Wilfrid succeeds in only blinding himself to the truth. All three characters – Sir Wilfrid, Sherlock Holmes, Keyes – are linked by their misogyny. Holmes and Keyes have been engaged but, for different reasons, these engagements have collapsed, leaving them with a sour, suspicious view of the opposite sex. Sir Wilfrid, like Keyes, is clearly a loner who in the film conducts a running battle with his nurse ("If you were a woman, Miss Plimsoll, I would strike you") and is consistently antagonistic towards the heroine, calling her "Frau Helm" throughout the trial, a contemptuous allusion to her nationality (Germans, after all, were not much liked following the war, even in 1953, when the play was written; and the British in particular resented their miraculous economic recovery) and to her first marriage. Christine embodies the deceitful and destructive female for Sir Wilfrid and like Holmes and Keyes he trusts men and does not trust women. Here the film does offer a clear-cut instance of role rejection which escaped Robert Mundy: Sir Wilfrid will come to reverse his convictions.

The theme of deception and role-playing is accommodated nowhere more gracefully in Wilder than in *Witness for the Prosecution*. This manifests itself initially in small details, characteristically in Wilder's use of objects. This idiosyncrasy is also shared by Alfred Hitchcock – one thinks of the glasses which distort a murder in *Strangers on a Train*; the cymbals that announce another murder in *The Man Who Knew Too Much*; the crop-dusting 'plane which becomes a potential killer in *North by Northwest*; the shower-bath in *Psycho* which becomes a death chamber; the potatoes which conceal a corpse in *Frenzy*; and of course *The Birds* – but Wilder's subversion and manipulation of familiar objects and appliances is more subtle. We have already discussed the filing drawer used by Sir Wilfrid as an ashtray, his cigars and brandy, and his monocle, all of which are used by Wilder to signify Sir Wilfrid's childish sense of cunning and to underline his inability to tumble the more sinister cunning of his clients. But perhaps the most memorable object in the film is the peculiar lift which enables Sir Wilfrid to reach his private apartment without straining his heart on the stairs. At first he views the lift with disdain, until Nurse Plimsoll demands that he make use of it, appealing to his childlike fascination with toys; and Laughton looks like an overgrown baby sitting in the contraption. He feels he is in control of the lift though, as he says, he is not yet familiar with the mechanism. But he is in fact *being* controlled, the lift being a precise visual metaphor for what happens to him in the film. He is manipulated back and forth by forces outside himself. It is surely not accidental that he is in the lift when Leonard visits him for the first time and also when Christine arrives after Leonard has been taken away by the police. The effect is of their catching him when he is vulnerable and off balance. Christine taunts him at this first meeting: as he is disappearing up the stairs in the lift, she enquires whether he is afraid of defending a "hopeless cause". This successfully draws him down again, much to Nurse Plimsoll's chagrin who probably shares the same attitude towards women as Sir Wilfrid, confirming that it is he who is being manipulated rather than doing the manipulating himself. (The deeper deception is hinted at here: during the trial, when Christine is testifying against Leonard, one wonders about this earlier scene and why she has seemed so determined to get the finest advocate on Leonard's side).

The subsequent trial and the sudden dénouement, therefore, is an entirely logical outcome of Wilder's mise-en-scène. In the first half of the film he lays down the groundwork for the second half – the elaborate use of objects and the ambiguous characters are linked together and later unravelled in court. Earlier in the film Sir Wilfrid, goaded beyond endurance by Nurse Plimsoll, playfully dons his wig (which has been ceremoniously taken out of mothballs) and conducts his own defence for the hypothetical murder of this irritating woman who has been forced on him by the hospital. Sir Wilfrid might be conscious of his own role-playing but he cannot see through it in other people. The most obvious instance of this occurs when Christine disguises herself as a prostitute and lures Sir Wilfrid to a station bar with the promise of incriminating letters about Mrs Vole. By this time the trial is going badly for Leonard and Sir Wilfrid: Christine has testified that Leonard had returned home late, giving him ample time to murder Mrs French, and had cut himself with a carving knife to

Witness for the Prosecution: *John Williams, Charles Laughton (in his stair-lift), Elsa Lanchester*

provide himself with an alibi. Sir Wilfrid has also experienced an exhausting examination of Janet McKenzie, proving to the court in the most malicious way that she is deaf and therefore incapable of hearing Leonard and Mrs French through the door, but stunned by the embarrassment of being told that the television, which Sir Wilfrid had contested was the source of the 'voices', was away being repaired. The trial looks like being lost for certain when he goes to the station bar in the hope of a miracle. The opening shot of the prostitute at the bar, with those shapely legs draped in a familiar pose, is unmistakably Christine, or Marlene Dietrich. But Sir Wilfrid, uncomfortable in the sleazy surroundings and desperate for a drink without fear of recriminations from Nurse Plimsoll, sees only what he expects to see and is completely deceived.* He is shown a hideous scar, supposedly inflicted by the prostitute's boyfriend who ran off with Christine, and barters for the letters which reveal a plot to give false testimony at the trial in order to get rid of Leonard. In this scene, as in all of *Witness for the Prosecution*, Wilder's camerawork is concise and unobtrusive, reflecting a seemingly rational and comprehensible world: there are no optical illusions or technical tricks, yet only in *The Apartment* are characters as completely deceived as here by the evidence of their own perceptions. Perhaps the most striking deception of all, though, is the way that Christine deceives Sir Wilfrid by telling the truth, the whole truth, and nothing but the truth. For Leonard has indeed murdered Mrs French for her money and has persuaded Christine to act – literally – as his accomplice in the Old Bailey. When Sir Wilfrid dramatically reveals to the jury the incriminating letters – by another childlike prank: he reads some especially revealing passages, tricks Christine into denying the accusation since the letter paper is not her own and then gleefully announces that the paper is a tailor's order for a pair of Bermuda shorts, then savagely reveals the genuine articles which prompt Christine's breakdown – he is unconsciously playing a major role in Leonard and Christine's scheme. His deep-rooted distrust of women has blinded him to the truth, ending his first examination of Christine by calling her a liar as loudly as possible. Since Christine's evidence has now been discredited, Leonard is declared not guilty. After the verdict has been given Sir Wilfrid accuses Christine of trying to cause a travesty of justice, only to discover that he is the one who has done that by proving the innocence of a guilty man. It takes some time for the terrible revelation to dawn on the old barrister who sits crestfallen in the now empty courtroom drinking the last of his brandy.

But now Wilder and Miss Dietrich produce the final surprise. Christine has entered the empty courtroom having been mauled by

---

*This scene has been criticised because Christine's disguise does not fool the audience for a moment while it fools Sir Wilfrid. This is precisely the point, of course. When Sir Wilfrid later realises the deception (Christine adopts her Cockney accent again after the verdict) we laugh, not because we have been fooled, but because Sir Wilfrid has been so easily tricked.

an angry crowd outside (this is another example of Wilder's hatred of mob mentality, evident in *Sunset Boulevard, Ace in the Hole* and, later, in *The Front Page*, and also recall Christine's earlier molestation in the Hamburg nightclub). Then Leonard is brought up from the dock. Again, Leonard resists Christine's display of emotion – "We fooled them Leonard", she cries – and merely thanks Sir Wilfrid for aiding and abetting his scheme and promising him a fat fee once Mrs French's will has been settled. The revelation of the husband's guilt and his wife's devotion, even to the extent of perjuring herself, is followed by the appearance of the "clinging brunette" who has been mentioned in the trial as being in the company of Leonard at an exclusive travel agents and being his possible mistress. She turns out to be the woman sitting next to Nurse Plimsoll throughout the trial (another case where the significance of appearances eludes us) and rushes up to embrace Leonard who responds with equal passion. Leonard is clearly going to enjoy Mrs French's money with this young girl and will desert Christine who has been duped into the elaborate scheme. "Now we're even," he tells Christine, "I saved you from Germany; you saved me from this." "You're not his wife and you're years older than he is," says the still-clinging brunette, suddenly placing Christine in the exact position of Mrs French. Christine's reaction is to even the score with an extra refinement: finding herself in a confused fit of love and rage, she avenges the widow by stabbing Leonard, using the very knife, conveniently on hand as an item of evidence, which he has previously used on himself.

The murderous heroine in *Witness for the Prosecution* forges obvious links with *Double Indemnity, Sunset Boulevard, Ace in the Hole* and, if one accepts metaphorical deaths, *The Private Life of Sherlock Holmes*: all of them kill the men they love. The confusion of anguish, love, and a sense of betrayal exhibited by Christine here is probably closest in feeling to Norma Desmond's shooting of William Holden in *Sunset Boulevard*, the woman being unable to accept a man walking out on her. There is a feeling of a deadly ritual to all these killings, deliberately accentuated in *Witness for the Prosecution* which partly betrays its theatrical origins but also reflects Sir Wilfrid's horror. He sits quietly at his bench as these characters complete the ritual. But *Witness for the Prosecution* displays a revision of Wilder's emphasis on male and female relationships which end in the death of one party. There is little tenderness in Phyllis Dietrichson in *Double Indemnity* and Lorraine

Minosa in *Ace in the Hole*, and Norma Desmond was pathologically insane to begin with. But Christine has been thoroughly duped from start to finish which, perhaps for the first time, undermines Sir Wilfrid's attitude towards women. "She's killed him!", cries Nurse Plimsoll. "No, she has executed him," responds Sir Wilfrid almost to himself, taking pleasure in the act since Leonard cannot be tried again, his mind already searching for precedents he can use in her defence. His faith restored in British justice, no matter how bizarrely it has been administered, he rises to leave to begin work on his new case. Sir Wilfrid and Christine are enjoined not by mutual attraction but by force of circumstance and misery. Wilder completes the reconciliation of the sexes by forcing Nurse Plimsoll to abandon her own matronly role. As Sir Wilfrid reaches the door of the court she picks up his cocoa-flask and cries, "Sir Wilfrid, you've forgotten your brandy!".

One, Two, Three (1961)

> "Don't ask me why, but I just got the feeling that I wanted to make a picture in Germany. I hadn't done it since 1948, when I did *A Foreign Affair*. And there's something else about it, I don't know what. Well, when you want to do something, you can always find plenty of reasons. And when I got Cagney interested, that was good enough for me. For me there's never been anybody better on the screen. Also, I happen to think Coca-Cola is funny. A lot of people didn't. Maybe that's why the picture bombed out. I still think it's funny. And when I drink it, it seems funnier."
>
> – Billy Wilder, talking to Garson Kanin in the latter's book, 'Hollywood' (Viking Press, New York, 1974)
>
> "Ich bin ein Berliner"
>
> – President John F Kennedy

Promotion seems assured for dynamic Coca-Cola sales representative in West Berlin, C R MacNamara (James Cagney), when he negotiates a sale of his product to the Russians – their attempt to concoct an equivalent, Kremlin-Cola, having been so dire that, rather than drink it, the Albanians have been using it as sheep-dip. As MacNamara says, Coca-Cola is on the verge of succeeding where Napoleon and Hitler failed: namely, in entering Moscow. But his progress is complicated when he is assigned to look after his boss's daughter, Scarlett Hazeltine (Pamela Tiffin). When she slips across the border into East Berlin and returns with a scruffy young Communist husband named Otto Ludwig Piffl (Horst Buchholz) – hence becoming Scarlett Piffl herself – MacNamara has the job of converting him into a smart Capitalist before the boss and his wife arrive. It is, in effect, an exercise in converting Otto into a model of the American way of life. Based on a Ferenc Molnar play, Wilder – like MacNamara at work on Piffl – does not simply adapt the original but utterly transforms it.

One, Two, Three is Wilder's sprightly and occasionally ironic and ambiguous tribute to three notable examples of American endeavour

– *Ninotchka*, James Cagney and Coca-Cola. The parallels with *Ninotchka* have been much discussed. There are the three Russian commissars dealing with the Capitalist entrepreneur; there is the young Communist being won over to the Capitalist system; even Scarlett's conciliating promise to her young Bolshevik husband – "I'll only wear my jewellery at home" – conjures up a quick mental image of Ninotchka, alone in her hotel room, wearing the diadem. But in the case of *One, Two, Three*, the Communist is not an amusingly deadpan Garbo waiting to be reduced to joyous, helpless laughter, but a boorish, arrogant figure who remains totally humourless and is given to exclaiming "From now on it's Piffl against everyone and everything!". The capitalist is not a witty, debonair Prince Charming but a rasping Little Caesar (when his plans are going awry, MacNamara murmurs to himself in the manner of Edward G Robinson, "Mother of Mercy, is this the end of Rico?") who is prepared to sacrifice his marriage and family on the altar of his career and Coca-Cola prosperity. In *One, Two, Three*, there is no mutual enrichment from this ideological interchange, only irreconcilable antagonism. The romantic interest in the plot is pushed to the background and it is the mechanistic machinations of MacNamara which are brought to the fore. The factors which make the atmosphere of the two films so very different can be stated very simply: time and place. We are not now in Paris, city of romance, love and changing your outlook, but in Berlin, a political battlefield, and a setting which, as in *A Foreign Affair*, evokes impermanence and disquiet. We are not in a pre-war era where the holocaust has so far been averted. We are in the harsh post-war era when Cold War politics are rife and the unimaginable can fearfully materialise at the press of a button. People are seduced and persuaded now not by love but by fear, torture, motives of self-aggrandisement or self-preservation. "Is everybody in this world corrupt?", cries out Piffl despairingly when he discovers that one of the three Russians negotiating with MacNamara has defected to the West. "I don't know everybody," returns the Russian with a shrug, unwilling to commit himself finally on the subject but certainly prepared to acknowledge the possibility.

The major role taken by MacNamara helps to focus attention on two important and interrelated themes: the Americanisation of Berlin and, more generally, the role of Americans abroad. An early montage of Communist parades in East Berlin, with balloons and placards proclaiming "Yankee Go Home" and "Was ist los in Little Rock?", is cut short by MacNamara's narration. "These demonstrations failed to provoke the West Berliners . . . they were too busy rebuilding". The camera pans pointedly across a huge Coca-Cola advertisement and the implication is clear: the rebuilding is being done with the help of American money and to the glory of American enterprise, and we are suddenly back in the "dollar diplomacy" world of *A Foreign Affair* with its attendant moral disintegration. Political events undoubtedly harmed the film's commercial career (the construction of the Berlin Wall took place during the actual shooting of *One, Two, Three* and clearly made the Cold War jokes too painful for some)*. But these events could hardly be more pertinent to the film's overriding concern – the disastrous political consequences of American Coca-Cola imperialism.

This allegory of American aggression is strengthened by the inspired casting of James Cagney as MacNamara. The film would be inconceivable without him. For one thing, Cagney brings important accretions of meaning from his other films. MacNamara has a wall-clock (handmade by dwarfs in the Black Forest) which chimes "Yankee Doodle Dandy" at significant intervals in the film, winding up the action as well as alluding to the most patriotic performance in Cagney's career (Michael Curtiz's *Yankee Doodle Dandy*, made in 1942, can probably be considered as the American cinema's equivalent to *Henry V* – Olivier's, if not Shakespeare's). In particular, one can hardly avoid comparing *One, Two, Three* with William Wellman's *The Public Enemy* (1931), the film in which Cagney first made his name. Wilder clinches the comparison by having MacNamara at one stage threaten Pifflf with a grapefruit – "Would you like a little fruit for dessert?". In the earlier film, Cagney as Tom Powers was connected with a corrupt Prohibition racket, selling illegal liquor to reluctant customers. Now he is a legal salesman of soft drinks, with a product rivalling the sales of draught beer, and is situated right at the heart of the American economy, attempting to spread Cola-Colonisation into all the world capitals (with varying success, it must be said: he has as yet

*In the 'American Film' interview, when asked to account for the film's failure, I A L Diamond commented candidly, "I think it was a flop because it was released after the Berlin Wall incident: I think people no longer considered that subject very funny. The problem we ran into was that right in the middle of shooting the picture, the border was suddenly closed."

been unable to persuade the authorities to install a Coke machine in the Reichstag). The significant thing is that the status has changed, not the method. He is still the salesman's equivalent of the Public Enemy, obtaining his ends through bullying, fraud and intimidation. "The ugly American", one of the Russian delegates calls him. Wilder's peculiar ambivalence about the crudity and yet vigour of American enterprise is splendidly contained in Cagney's fire-cracker performance. There is something fascinating about the energy and connivance even amidst doubts about the uses to which it is all being put. Wilder's ambivalence even extends to a detail such as MacNamara's elevator shoes, which, as his wife (Arlene Francis) acidly remarks, he only wears to the office when there is a secretary he is anxious to impress. On the one hand, a slight gag about Cagney's diminutive frame; on the other, a pointed and relevant reference, supported by the whole movement of the film, to Americans who are getting an inflated sense of their importance. "I'm remodelling him", explains MacNamara to his wife when she stares in disbelief at the army of manicurists and outfitters who are trooping in to transform Piffl. "Somebody should do a job on you," returns his wife. One thinks of *Avanti!* and how the American executive Armbruster tries to 'remodel' the Italians according to his own lights of efficiency and speed, only to be readjusted himself to their more civilising tempo. In *One, Two, Three*, as Piffl is converted into the prototype of the American executive, MacNamara compels his employees to accelerate to his speed, snapping his fingers and proclaiming, "Everybody work today!". It is hard to think of any other actor but Cagney who could generate quite the same freneticism and violent rhythm.

Tempo is extremely important in the film. Each nationality in the film has its own rhythm, which is often disrupted by or is the source of discord amongst the others. The Germans are mechanical and rigid, having a heel-clicking efficiency that exasperates MacNamara ("*Danke schön* already", he snaps testily to Fritz his chauffeur, as the latter opens the succession of doors for him with robot-like regularity). The Russians are predominantly turgid and ponderous. When MacNamara visits the three commissars at the Hotel Potemkin in East Berlin, he is greeted by a vocalist and orchestra performing "Yes, We Have No Bananas" as if it were a funeral dirge, a singularly cheerless assimilation of Western culture. However, when his secretary Ingeborg (Lilo Pulver) dances on the table and rouses the three men to unseemly and indecorous excitement, the rhythmic disruption is such that Russian stability and regularity momentarily relax and the picture of Khrushchev on the wall slips through its frame to reveal a baleful portrait of Stalin behind it. The Americans remain frantic and almost out of control, a tempo set by the use of Khachaturian's "Sabre Dance" at the outset of the film which bounces back to accompany the more hectic action.

There are moments when tempo and rhythm are adjusted to give us pause or to signal a slowing of MacNamara's momentum. Captured by East German guards when MacNamara has slipped some anti-Communist propaganda into his motorbike satchel, Piffl has been tortured and his spirit broken by the repeated playing of that most decadent example of Capitalist commercialism, the song "Itsy Bitsy Teeny Weeny Yellow Polka-Dot Bikini". But when the doctor reports to MacNamara that Scarlett is pregnant and the man realises he is going to have to spring Piffl from jail, MacNamara is tormented by a piece of European high culture – the doctor singing "Scarlett is pregnant" to the tune of Wagner's "The Ride of the Valkyries". Piffl, however, is freed when MacNamara arranges an exchange with the

One, Two, Three: *James Cagney at the Hotel Potemkin*

Russians of Pifﬂ for Ingeborg, though 'Ingeborg' is actually Schlemmer, MacNamara's right-hand man disguised in a polka-dot dress with "Yankee Go Home" balloons to augment his figure. Thereafter, it is a case of MacNamara winding everybody up to the tempo and rhythms of the "Sabre Dance". What is clear from this outline is that speed and frenzy are not simply part of the style of the film. They are also its subject, characterising particularly the energy of the American in exporting his values to Europe ("27 per cent of the population are now having Coke with their *knockwurst*") and, implicitly, the speed of American development from Virgin Land to Superpower and its disinclination to slow down and survey the possible chaos left in its wake.

One is reminded of Tatum's comment to his editor about the cub journalist in *Ace in the Hole*: "He wants to be going, going . . .", says Tatum, to which Boot has responded, "Going where?" In MacNamara's case, all this activity is expended in an endeavour to climb the Coca-Cola ladder, in particular through the kind of ingratiation with the boss that distinguishes C C Baxter's climb in *The Apartment*. Specifically, he believes he will be rewarded for his Eastern Europe export drive and his supervision of Scarlett with an executive position in London. He has even bought an umbrella in anticipation, a piece of tactical optimism which, rather like Bramble's purchase of a bowler hat a fortnight before war is declared in *Five Graves to Cairo*, turns out to be singularly misplaced.

In this context, then, it is significant that one of the pervasive motifs of the film is that of uncompleted, or thwarted, or chaotic and uncontrolled journeys. Despite all this mad energy, nobody ever seems to arrive at where he wants to go, or arrive at the time when he is expected, or arrive in the condition in which he set off, or actually discover what he expected to find when he got there. Pifﬂ is arrested during one of his motorbike rides; there are two frenzied car drives, one to return Pifﬂ to West Berlin, the other to transport him to the airport to greet his new in-laws; MacNamara's wife and children have been preparing to go on holiday to Venice before the arrival of Scarlett has cut short their plan (even here, MacNamara has queried how the children are going to move around in Venice: "Why do they *need* roller-skates in Venice? All the streets are under water").

Oddly enough, this throwaway remark – with its unexpected fusion of journey and submergence – might go some way towards explaining the film's slightly oppressive atmosphere. MacNamara's threshing around resembles that of a man struggling in quicksand. MacNamara's energy is symptomatic of his drive but might be equally so of his desperation, his cumulative frustration at his inability to reach his ultimate goal. In the past, even Benny Goodman has let him down. MacNamara was formerly head of the Middle East division, and when Goodman's 'plane was delayed and he was late for a concert, the rioting mob burned down the Coca-Cola building. Scarlett has been driving him mad and he particularly cannot comprehend her sense of direction – "Russia's to get out of, not to go to," he cries when she is thinking of settling in Moscow with Piffl. Now his boss is giving him trouble. Not only is Hazeltine arriving unexpectedly and at short notice in West Berlin, but the 'plane is ahead of schedule – "'Planes are supposed to be late, not early", claims MacNamara in exasperation and disbelief.

Ultimately, all of MacNamara's enterprise is to be wasted. He delivers Piffl on time but, far from being rewarded, he has done such a good job on the young man that Piffl is awarded the job that was promised to him. MacNamara is to wind up (or wind down) at the bottling plant in Atlanta, a place he has earlier described as "Siberia with mint juleps". In behaving like a gangster, he has ended up like one: failing in his final objective.

The film has been attacked for being, like MacNamara, a shade brash and unvaried. The tempo is partly Wilder's response to the predilection for deliberate pacing in the films of the early-'Sixties, and his own comment on those critics who, as he has put it, have mistaken slowness and solemnity for profundity. One aspect of this drive is the film's rather strenuous topicality. This is seen not only in its political references abroad but also at home ("Won't the schools be opening soon?", asks Ingeborg, wanting Scarlett off her hands. "In Georgia? You never know," returns MacNamara). It is also seen in its filmic references. "I'll start a workers' revolt," cries an incompletely clad Piffl, to which MacNamara responds contemptuously, "Put your pants on, Spartacus."

Given that the ferocious tempo of the film allows for few variations of light and shade, Wilder, Diamond and Cagney are to be credited for extracting as many surprises as they can from the ingenuity of MacNamara's self-centredness. "I'm not going to let that Communist kook ruin someone's life," explains the hero to his wife defending his part in the imprisonment of Piffl that has so shocked Scarlett. "But she loves him," replies Mrs MacNamara, to which her husband replies instantly, "Not her life. *Mine*." Later, having rescued Piffl, he is rather piqued by the young man's attitude. "That's gratitude . . . getting you out of jail." "You got me into jail," Piffl points out, to which MacNamara snaps back, "So we're even." Throughout the film, as this ping-pong logic suggests, all of MacNamara's actions are dominated by selfish motives and he is finally defeated not by a characteristic change of heart, but by circumstances. There are no moments of compassion in *One, Two, Three* which, for all its comic invention, deprives it of the subtle range of tone which gives so much richness to a film like *Some Like it Hot* or *The Apartment*. Of course, for those who resist the sentimental and romantic mode in Wilder, this could be a recommendation.

What seems necessary, though, is to enquire a little further into why this is so. Why is *One, Two, Three* so brutal and relentless in its humour? In McBride and Wilmington's article on Wilder, there is the suggestion that, "Wilder's profusion of gags seems to mask a desperation – a fear perhaps of telling the truth about his own emotions. If everything is foolish, then nothing is unbearable." As a generalisation, this is probably open to question, and McBride and Wilmington might wish to modify it now themselves, particularly in the light of Wilder's most recent work. But as a comment about *One, Two, Three*, it is worth investigating. It might go some way towards explaining Wilder's satire on that most unfunny subject of what individual Germans did during the war. MacNamara's assistant, Schlemmer (a delightful performance by Hans Lothar), explains that he worked in the underground railway and did not really know what was going on above. "Adolf who?", he asks innocently, responding to MacNamara's prompting, and it is only later that he inadvertently reveals that he was a member of the SS. In other hands, this might seem insensitive, but it is here that one is tempted – perhaps illegitimately – to draw on Wilder's biography. For a Jew who lost relatives at Auschwitz, he seems remarkably off-hand about German guilt, possibly because it is the only way he can cope with that knowledge. There is a sense in which one feels that this film keeps going and going because it is almost afraid to look back. Might this obsessive forward movement signify not only America's heedless progress, as we have suggested before, but the Americanisation of Wilder, the surrender of his

Berliner soul? Underneath the frenzy is an ache of sadness, seen most strongly in the endeavours of Mrs MacNamara to control the "Marco Polo" wanderings of her husband, to hold their marriage together, and to persuade him to return home to America. At the end of the film, everyone is saying goodbye to Berlin – perhaps even Wilder himself.

Like Stanley Kubrick's *Dr Strangelove* (1963), *One, Two, Three* makes its political point through comedy because the realities are too tragic to be serious about*. As in *Five Graves to Cairo*, Wilder has established a broadly conceived collection of national stereotypes but, much more than in the previous film, he has made them equally ridiculous, precisely to launch an attack on ideological rigidity. If we can recognise its foolishness, perhaps we can be brought to our senses. Like *Hold Back the Dawn* and *Sabrina*, it is another Wilder film dedicated to breaking down barriers. The fact that the Berlin Wall was constructed during the making of the film – rival ideologies so restricted that an actual wall is built between them – makes the satire all the more urgent and responsible.

---

*Indeed, in *Dr Strangelove* there is a moment which is not dissimilar to the final joke of *One, Two, Three*, when MacNamara is double-crossed by a Coca-Cola machine which delivers him a Pepsi. In Kubrick's film, a Coke machine momentarily controls the destiny of the world, and when it is peremptorily broken by a bullet from Keenan Wynn's gun, it retaliates by soaking him in Coca-Cola.

Chapter III

"IT'S ALL ON THE DINERS CLUB"

— Willie Gingrich in *The Fortune Cookie*

Hold Back the Dawn
Ace in the Hole
Stalag 17
The Apartment
The Fortune Cookie
The Front Page

Hold Back the Dawn (1941)

If *Midnight* is the perfect demonstration of Mitchell Leisen's flair for visual elegance and sophistication in the Lubitsch manner, *Hold Back the Dawn* demonstrates Leisen's difficulties in finding a suitable style for a much tougher subject: the seediness of the Hotel Esperanza, overrun with desperate immigrants, can hardly have made the decorative Leisen feel at home. Efficiently if rather anonymously directed, *Hold Back the Dawn* can most fruitfully be interpreted as a Billy Wilder film. One of his last writing assignments with Charles Brackett before launching his own career as a director, the film might serve as a blueprint for some of Wilder's subsequent preoccupations. Its two central themes are entirely characteristic: the regeneration of a corrupt hero; and the meaning of America.

Even the hero's situation has an overt biographical parallel to Wilder's own experience which gives the film an additional and unusual fascination. Georges Iscovescu (Charles Boyer) is a Rumanian expatriate who, at the start of World War Two, finds himself stranded in a run-down Mexican hotel awaiting a visa to allow him to enter the United States. In the same way Wilder himself was stranded in Mexico for a few months, waiting for a visa to take him to Hollywood. Just as Wilder had apparently danced his way round Europe in the company of rich ladies, so Iscovescu is a former gigolo who has made his living by ingratiating himself with wealthy women.

The parallel between the two men should not be pressed too far. For one thing, their motives for going to America are very different. Iscovescu is just following the money, now that the War is driving his lucrative ladies out of Europe. Wilder's reasons were a lot less dubious and cold-blooded than that: "I had my eye on Hollywood," he told Charles Higham and Joel Greenberg, "as that was the proper progression for a writer; my mother had lived in America and I had quite a few relatives there. I would have come here, Hitler or no Hitler, but I decided to come a little bit faster when he got into power!". Any connection between Wilder and Iscovescu is not meant to imply any idealisation of the hero out of close identification. On the contrary, considering what we know of Wilder's life and the invitation in the film to spot resemblances between Wilder and the hero, what is immediately intriguing is the *severity* with which Iscovescu is presented. Far from the biographical overtones adding an element of special pleading, the screenplay dwells so insistently on Iscovescu's initial unpleasantness as to seem almost an act of masochism on Wilder's part (one might add that a streak of spiritual masochism has been a consistent feature of Wilder's heroes throughout his career). Iscovescu's cruel calculation is seen in all its squalor. His former dancing partner, Anita (Paulette Goddard) talks of those "gigolo eyes of yours, cold . . . selfish . . ."; and we learn that, in his past, two women, mother and daughter, have been so pained and humiliated by their association with him that they have attempted suicide.

Nevertheless, Wilder's familiarity with the basic situation probably permits a greater depth and complexity to the characterisation than would otherwise be possible: if Wilder's hero seems far removed from his own sensitivities, the reasons for his present desperation clearly have a claim on Wilder's sympathies and the entire film seems designed to awaken Americans to the turmoil in Europe, forcing them to recognise the Europeans' view of their country as something like a promised land (at least where there isn't a Hitler), and inspiring America to keep the lights burning in Europe, as the end of Alfred Hitchcock's *Foreign Correspondent* (1940) puts it. In many ways, *Hold Back the Dawn*, in its gritty way, prefigures *Casablanca* by presenting people who will do anything to secure a transit visa. Without in any way minimising the hero's wretchedness, the film candidly exposes the misery of people in Iscovescu's situation, the insensitivity of their treatment and the exploitation of their woes. Iscovescu only manages to secure a room in the first place because someone has found the strain of waiting intolerable and hanged himself, an event whose horror is intensified by the hotel manager's callous opportunism.

Hearing of the suicide, he says quickly to Iscovescu, "I will have a room for you. Just wait."

The Hotel Esperanza*, gloomy and overcrowded, is a shock for the man who describes himself as one "used to the Ritz and the Savoy." When learning of the quota system of entry – only so many of each nationality are allowed into the States each year – and that he might have to wait eight years for a visa, the hero sees his waiting period as a prison sentence and the hotel as his cell room, an impression confirmed by the wire fence which separates the border between Mexico and the United States. The imagery of prison is extended when he meets his former dancing partner Anita who, learning of his stay at the hotel, comments: "I served time there." It is Anita who alerts him to a possible escape route. Why not abbreviate the waiting time and attain American citizenship by marrying an American woman and then divorcing her once he gets safely across the wire? Iscovescu's smoothly ingratiating talents seem singularly to equip him for such a task. Cold-bloodedly seeking a woman who answers to the description of single, unattractive, and American, he comes across the schoolteacher Emmy Brown. Cunningly immobilising her schoolbus, he now launches into his romantic routine, like so many Wilder heroes invoking a bruised past ("Margo, I have always hated her") which unleashes the heroine's emotional protectiveness and generosity. Emmy falls all too easily into his seductive trap. After an overnight romance they are married.

The character of Emmy, skilfully played by Olivia de Havilland, discloses Wilder's characteristically ambivalent attitude towards innocence. He is caught between admiring her decency and scorning her naivety. While not in any way condoning the hero's subterfuges, the film is far from uncritical of its gullible heroine. Our response is further complicated by the impact of Iscovescu on Emmy: if the deception has been despicable, the effect on the heroine has been liberating. Previously her life has been run according to rules, to schedules. Iscovescu has described himself and Emmy as two trains in the night going in opposite ways and which cannot change direction any more than "we can hold back the dawn." In fact, both of them

---

*A fine example of Wilder's attention to minutiae, Esperanza is a form of the Spanish word meaning 'Hopeful' and might even relate to the artificial language of Esperanto, signifying the various European nationalities gathered at the hotel with a common purpose.

Hold Back the Dawn: *Charles Boyer, Olivia de Havilland*

are to change direction as their relationship transforms their characters (significantly, Iscovescu's regeneration blossoms when, avoiding the immigration official Hammock, he drives Emmy *away* from the border into Mexico, which is a journey that simultaneously takes him away from the goal of his deception but compels him to confront the human element contained within it). The breakdown of the bus and the intervention of Iscovescu throws Emmy's tidy senses out of gear, releasing a slumbering romanticism. Indeed, the hero's effect on her is, both literally and metaphorically, to arouse her as if from a deep sleep, his proposal of marriage coming as she wakes up in the hotel. Her awakening to Iscovescu's 'love' has complex overtones: on the one hand, of a dream fulfilment which, in the cold light of day, ought to have made her more suspicious (the European charmer a little too much like the stereotype of romantic imagination); on the other, of the dawning of a new emotional life for her that has hitherto been suppressed. Nothing is more moving in the film than the moment when she rings up a colleague and former boyfriend at the school to inform him that the bus has only broken down and that she and the children are safe. "We're *alive*, Mr McAdams," she says: in Olivia de

Havilland's hands and in the light of what has happened to Emmy, the words vibrate.

If Emmy has been awakened into love, she has, like so many Wilder heroines (like Sabrina, Ariane, Fran Kubelik) still to be initiated into knowledge and experience. It is the time when she and Iscovescu return from their Mexican honeymoon that she is visited by Anita in her hotel room and pointedly informed of the true state of affairs. Anita and Emmy have exchanged roles: Iscovescu has married Emmy but it is Anita with whom he spends the night; Anita has contrived the scheme with Iscovescu to resume their dancing partnership in New York and leave Emmy adrift, but it is Emmy to whom Iscovescu ultimately commits himself and Anita who is left adrift. Indeed, Anita and Emmy seem almost two sides of the same coin, both dark, one sensual, the other inhibited, the one fire, the other water*. Anita even does a wicked impression of Emmy's voice at one point (Paulette Goddard relishing her de Havilland impersonation) and the two are similarly dressed in their scene together, even turning their heads at exactly the same moment like a mirror reflection when there is a knock at the door. The contrast between them signifies the warring elements within Iscovescu himself, and the object which binds all three together is the ring. Iscovescu had borrowed Anita's ring to give to Emmy as a wedding ring. It represents the circle of deception which he is spinning around the heroine, but also represents the circle which is being woven around himself, since it indicates how he is in a sense tied in ownership to both women. Ironically, it is the moment when Anita meets Emmy and demands the return of her ring – a gesture designed to reveal the deception, alienate Emmy from Iscovescu, and establish Anita's ownership of both the ring and Iscovescu – that the spell begins to weaken. Anita no longer has any hold over the hero and he is free to commit himself to Emmy whom he has grown to love.

Emmy's reaction to the news of Iscovescu's betrayal is the supreme test of her character – a small triumph of personal dignity and courage, which director, writers and actress realise with great sensitivity. She refuses to act out of spite and betray Iscovescu to the

---

*In the imagery of the film, Anita "carries a torch" for Iscovescu which, as she puts it, "burns out." Conversely, Emmy's purity 'cleanses' the hero – significantly, the moment of true love realised is when he sees her in the water and senses her freshness. He kisses her for the first time with genuine love: "It was like kissing fresh snow," he says.

authorities: "I asked *him* to marry me," she lies to Hammock in a gesture which acknowledges her own complicity in the relationship. She has been wilfully blind to the true nature of the romance and therefore is as much responsible for what has happened as he is. When returning the ring to Iscovescu ("I shouldn't have been so vain . . . I should have looked at your face more closely"), she puts on her glasses for the first time in the film to see him as he really is. The gesture with the glasses gives her a severe, unflattering appearance which seems instantly to restore her identity as the spinsterish schoolteacher of the early part of the film. But this stern facade cannot be maintained now a breach of her emotions has been made. On the drive home she cannot stop crying, a scene not dissimilar in feeling to Lana Turner's famous drive in *The Bad and the Beautiful* (1952), the tears seeming to dissolve her whole being. The rigid control of her former existence has been irretrievably lost; and in being overwhelmed by personal sorrow she also loses control of the car, spins off the road and is seriously injured.

If there is a suspicion of misogyny in the way in which Wilder's heroines are punished for the treachery and insensitivity of the heroes (one thinks also of the attempted suicides of Sabrina and Fran Kubelik), this narrative strategy serves also to intensify the hero's guilt and credibly take him to the point of reformation. Some of Wilder's more unscrupulous heroes remain untouched by the heroine's suffering: nothing could undermine Sheldrake's selfishness in *The Apartment*, for whom Fran's suicide attempt is little more than an untimely episode best forgotten. But for Iscovescu the tragedy of Emmy's accident provides a springboard for his redemption, the moment when an ambitious, ruthless man is compelled to acknowledge the human consequences of his actions. The narrative structure is always organised in such a way as constantly to keep the conman's deception before his (and our) eyes. He invariably finds it impossible to escape the bonds of his deception and has to go through the same lies over and over again: Baxter's constant explanations to Dr Dreyfuss in *The Apartment*; Harry Hinkle stuck in his wheelchair in *The Fortune Cookie*. The implications of Iscovescu's bogus marriage are constantly reiterated here, to the point where he has to put the ring on Emmy's finger three times in the course of the film (the ring which is the very symbol of his deceit). Emmy insists that they repeat the words of the marriage ceremony together when they are about to part for the first time in the hotel, and he has to reiterate "Till death us do part," at first a pointed contrast to his actual feelings about Emmy ("She'll brush off like a drop of rain," he says contemptuously to Anita), but the full significance of which only hits him when news of her accident reaches him. Details like this are constantly used in the film to involve Iscovescu in a series of rituals the full importance of which he does not comprehend until almost too late. When Emmy returns unexpectedly to the hotel she brings a wedding cake which she invites Iscovescu to cut with her, an invitation he accepts with a notable lack of enthusiasm. The cake itself becomes a symbol of their phoney marriage, since their piece is left uneaten (the marriage incomplete, false, unconsummated) and provides an important clue to Hammock that Iscovescu is trying the familiar dodge of marrying an American to inveigle his way into America. The use of objects in their relationship to carry expressive significance is given explicit expression at one stage when, during their drive further into Mexico, Emmy insists that the windshield wipers are talking to them both and whispering, "Together . . . together . . ." At the time, Iscovescu seems to ignore this as Emmy's romantic luxuriance, but later in the hospital he is to repeat "Together . . . together" in a kind of litany as he endeavours to revive her from another kind of sleep. The ritual which he has taken so lightly becomes the slender thread which he must use to rescue her from death.

The Mexican honeymoon is the period of conversion for him, a rejection of his past and his previous character. The particular moment of his regeneration is probably his refusal to consummate the marriage: "I had no right to touch her", he says. To this end he feigns an accident with the car which damages his shoulder, an incident which surely recalls the faked breakdown of the schoolbus which he has contrived and which has initiated the whole situation. This circle of deception has now entwined Iscovescu himself: like Emmy, he too is trapped. As so often in Wilder, the hero has discovered real love through at first pretending it. When he learns of Emmy's accident he risks everything by speeding through the border gate and past the guards to see her in Los Angeles. It is the moment when he jeopardises everything he has laboriously constructed, but it is also the moment when the circle of deception is at last broken. Iscovescu's crash entry into America is, at this juncture, an honourable one.

Although a central theme, America is seldom seen in the film.

Emmy talks a lot about her home town of Azusa, surely intended as an A to Z microcosm of the USA itself: growing, learning, a community of innocence and tolerance even though, we learn, there are some cynics there. Talking of the deceptions employed to dodge the immigrant quota, the investigator Hammock says he asks of all new marriages: "Is it love or is it immigration?". He fails to recognise that the two might not be contradictory. Iscovescu's growing love for Emmy becomes caught up with his growing love for America itself; indeed, one could interpret his transformation as a process whereby he becomes eligible in a human, rather than a statistical, sense to enter America (which is why Hammock can bend the rules on his behalf at the end of the film). Appropriately, therefore, the last shot of the film is not an embrace between hero and heroine but a shot of Iscovescu running towards the gate at which Emmy waits – running to both the heroine *and* America. "I'm dirt, but so is he," Anita has said of her association with Iscovescu. But Anita's nomadic, purposeless existence continues at the end, whereas Iscovescu is purified by Emmy's love and becomes part of her vision of America as a lake that is "clear and fresh" which "never gets stagnant when new streams are flowing in". In its feeling for the corrupt immigrant hero who will be washed clean by his country of adoption, *Hold Back the Dawn* is difficult to match in the American cinema until Elia Kazan's *America, America* (1963).

In the Hotel Esperanza with Iscovescu in the early part of the film is a mini-American society not yet in America, a group of almost too-good-to-be-true foreigners who are awaiting their visas and who know the American ideals better than the Americans themselves. They celebrate the Fourth of July with an exuberance and tradition taken lightly by the complacent Hammock, and it is he who has to be instructed about the poem on the base of the Statue of Liberty by the European professor. America is clearly seen as the place to live: one of the women in the group is pregnant and tricks her way over the border so that her child will be born an American citizen. It is America *as an ideal* that is particularly emphasised here. In contrast, those representatives we see of the actual America are portrayed in strikingly harsh terms: the unruly children in the 'bus; the guards at the border; the policeman at the hospital; the ruthless official Hammock whose relentless pursuit of the transgressors, regardless of the motives and heartache involved, anticipates the obsessive investigations of Purky in *The Fortune Cookie.* The idealised America of the Europeans – much the same, in fact, as the Italian immigrants in *The Godfather Part II* (1974) and all the more keenly felt perhaps in *Hold Back the Dawn* because of the biographical elements in the plot – contends with a more sceptical look at the actual American character which is to preoccupy Wilder in subsequent films.

Apparently, it was his experience with *Hold Back the Dawn* – clearly a screenplay of great personal significance – that confirmed Wilder's disillusionment with Mitchell Leisen as a director of his screenplays and his determination to become a director himself. As Wilder has said, although it is not important for a director to know how to write, it is important for a director to know how to read. Leisen's direction towards the end of the film, otherwise sure-footed if not especially imaginative, comes too close for comfort towards softening a tough-minded screenplay (a criticism, we must acknowledge, that Wilder himself was to receive in later years). One thinks especially of the dangerously sentimental close-up of Emmy's twitching fingers as Iscovescu talks her back to life, or of the cloying shot of the child who has been successfully born an American. Wilder's decision to direct was also determined by a desire to protect his own scripts, and certainly Leisen appears to underestimate or ignore the irony of the film's closing scenes, perhaps acting under instructions from Paramount who wished to see its films promoting American ideals and virtues in the face of an inevitable war. Beyond this, Charles Boyer had refused to do a scene where Iscovescu in his gloomy hotel room notices a cockroach on the wall and starts talking to it in the severe tones of the immigration official ("Where are you going? What is the purpose of your trip? Let's see your papers"). Boyer informed Wilder that people do not talk to cockroaches and that a serious actor like himself should not be seen playing such a scene, a decision which so enraged Wilder that he and Brackett, apparently, decided to rewrite the last part of the film and hand the dramatic stage over to the heroine.* As it happens, a touch of idosyncratic wit of this kind might well have done wonders in lightening the texture of

---

*Certainly seeing the film now with this knowledge gives an unexpectedly ironic humour to some of the later scenes. In the final part, Boyer is constantly being told to "Shut Up" and even Anita wonders about his sudden quietness. The irony was compounded by the fact that Olivia de Havilland blossomed so much in the last part of the film (as so many of Wilder's heroines do) that she was nominated for an Academy Award.

Leisen's somewhat laborious mise-en-scene, and endearing us a little more to the hero, our response to whom is rather hindered by Boyer's charmless performance.

We must, then, reject Higham and Greenberg's assertion about the film in 'Hollywood in the Forties' (Zwemmer, London, 1968) as a "success of direction" over a script that shows scarcely a trace of the subsequent talents of Wilder and Brackett. The themes articulated by the screenplay are entirely characteristic of Wilder and indeed the material anticipates *Ace in the Hole* in many of its details: the water and desert imagery; the hero with a confession *for sale*; certain religious overtones, felt in the film where Emmy and Iscovescu are 'blessed' in a Mexican church; a pervasive range of movie imagery, felt in the narrative framework of *Hold Back the Dawn* with the hero walking into Paramount Studios at the beginning and telling his story to a film director, played by Mitchell Leisen, in order to earn the five hundred dollars which Emmy has given him to make his start in California. If there seems here a final link between Wilder and his hero – the fact that America means Hollywood, emphasised by the border post, with "The United States" written on a board which resembles a cinema marquee – the endorsement by Paramount of Iscovescu's story who assign Leisen to film it is a fair indication that Wilder's more critical view of America was tactfully diluted. To borrow a phrase of Robert Mundy's concerning Wilder's contributior to *Ninotchka*, if the body of this film belongs to its director, then th bones are certainly Wilder's. With *Ace in the Hole*, with Wilder at th helm, the bones are to come hauntingly and disturbingly to life.

Ace in the Hole (1951)

"I've met a lot of hard-boiled eggs in my life," says Lorraine Minosa to news reporter Chuck Tatum, "but you, you're twenty minutes." Tatum, played by Kirk Douglas, shares with many of Wilder's heroes a pathological sense of being betrayed by the prevailing system, but his embittered and cynical view of human nature and his rampant opportunism are evidently engrained, a fundamental component of his psychological make-up rather than an assumed role. His last-minute conversion comes as much of a surprise to him as it does to us. He "chucks" everything away, as most of Wilder's scheming heroes do, and the entire construction of the film tumbles down, crushing not only Leo Minosa, the man trapped in a mountain cave-in, but our collective trust in the apparatus of truth as well.

Tatum's sudden awareness of his inhumanity naturally offers comparisons with Walter Neff's in *Double Indemnity*, Joe Gillis's in *Sunset Boulevard*, and the Jack Lemmon heroes of *The Apartment* and *The Fortune Cookie*, yet those seemingly abrupt conversions represent the culmination of a steadily intensifying process of disillusion and remorse, of regaining one's self respect and the shedding of an assumed role: a false, corporate identity in a business scheme. They were fighting for individual recognition and success within a monolithic system, whereas Tatum, having been fired by major city newspapers for excessive drinking and for seducing an editor's wife, is resolved to a freelance course of action. When we first meet him he is being towed in his broken-down, flashy convertible into Albuquerque, a desert town that, for Tatum at least, is either the end of the world or its beginning, a community whose sedateness Tatum is about to violate: "No chopped chicken livers, no New York Yankees, no subway smelling sweet-sour. What do you do for noise around here?", he remarks as the atmosphere stifles him, regretting even that there's "no 81st floor to jump from when you feel like it".

But Tatum does not possess the emotional range to cope with the realisation that everyone in this sleepy backwater is just as vile as he is; more tragic than Walter Neff he has no one to turn to, no dictaphone on hand – let alone a typewriter – with which to redeem himself before society. Mortally stabbed by Lorraine (and how Wilder must have relished giving one of his sourest heroines the sweetest name), he stumbles back to the peaceful offices of the 'Sun Bulletin' only to discover that the truth makes cowards of us all and we retire ungracefully to the shelter of fantasy and fabrication. "The people will think . . . What I tell them to think," is a famous dialogue exchange in Orson Welles's *Citizen Kane* (1941) which seems an appropriate method of describing the moral attitudes on display here.

Ace in the Hole is utterly uncompromising in its depiction of America as a vast hypocrisy. The people who turn out to witness the mountain rescue operation are not simply greedy for blood and disaster, but neither are their motives entirely benevolent. They are drawn to the area by the mass-media, by Tatum's dictator-like grasp of the media's potential (it is perhaps significant that Tatum wears a black shirt as he develops his scheme), and by the promise of a little "noise" in their lives. They are like Nathanael West's locusts, and a holiday carnival is quickly assembled to keep the crowd amused and the organisers in profit. *Ace in the Hole* is not only Wilder's bleakest comment on American values, but an attack on the commercial structures of Hollywood itself and the masses which feed voraciously on its merchandise. The arid, motionless desert, where most of the action takes place, is a metaphor for the American mind; the baby rattlesnake which the corrupt local police chief keeps in a cardboard box represents a growing poison of commercial exploitation and graft which leaves no one uncontaminated. Tatum does not conjure these tensions within the community out of thin air; he is like the devil coming to town who brings the latent inhumanity and evil of the citizens to the surface.

Ace in the Hole is also Wilder's most overtly symbolic film. His use of the desert and the rattlesnake are an integral part of his epic satire; the allegory on Hollywood methodology will emerge from the analysis which follows; and the continual pounding of the rescue drill is message-relaying with a vengeance. Its roots are to found in the *film noir* tradition, with all its emotional exits firmly closed. It is a quite brilliantly organised and rigorous film which Paramount, logically enough, disowned until success in Europe prompted them to re-issue it under the title *The Big Carnival*, a choice which only compounded the vehemence of Wilder's attack by publicising the very thing which Wilder despised the most. The film was a financial disaster, a destiny which is perhaps the film's aesthetic vindication, and Wilder's remaining three years at the studio were apparently rather strained. As David Thomson wrote in his book 'America in the Dark: Hollywood and the Gift of Unreality' (Morrow, New York, 1977), "it is as un-American today as it ever was to make an entertainment film so disturbing to its audience that it keeps them away."

Like *Citizen Kane*, that greatest exploration of the American success ethic, *Ace in the Hole* uses the Press to uncover intangible truths. A key scene in *Citizen Kane* has certainly influenced Tatum's philosophy:

> **Kane:** "Look Mr Carter, here is a three-column headline in the *Chronicle*. Why hasn't the *Inquirer* got a three-column headline?"
>
> **Carter:** "The news wasn't big enough".
>
> **Kane:** "Mr Carter, if the headline is big enough it makes the news big enough".

Chuck Tatum has arrived at the end of the line and desperately needs a story big enough to force the city newspapers to hire him again. With no defence against Tatum's passion and energy – "I'm a pretty good liar," he says by way of qualification, "I was worth a thousand dollars a day. You can have me for forty dollars per" – and with perhaps only a vague notion of restoring Tatum to the human race, the meek editor Mr Boot (Porter Hall) allows Tatum to join the small staff of the 'Sun Bulletin'. The name of the paper is significant: as things turn out for the entombed Leo, the paper and its reporter become his sole link with the sun. Tatum agrees to Mr Boot's demand that he abstain from drinking and, after a year's bored service (covered by Wilder in a single dissolve), Tatum is sent with a junior reporter to cover a story about a rattlesnake race – itself a potent metaphor. When they stop for gasoline on their way across the desert they learn about Leo (Richard Benedict) who has gone searching for old Indian pottery in a cave and hasn't returned. So much is true and moderately interesting for a provincial newspaper like the 'Sun Bulletin,' but Tatum proceeds to embroider the truth, echoing the neatly embroidered motto "Tell The Truth" which hangs in the newspaper offices. Leo could be rescued within a few hours if the appropriate rescue plan was adopted but Tatum sees a way of obtaining journalistic mileage if the rescue operation were prolonged. In league with the Sheriff (Ray Teal), who is up for re-election and understands the political advantage of being seen in a situation which shows his active efficiency and compassion, Tatum whips up human interest in the story whilst ensuring that the slower alternative method of rescue (drilling through the top of the mountain) takes a few days to allow the news to spread and develop. The calculation works: crowds soon pour in to view the disaster area; food and entertainment is provided and Tatum is proclaimed a hero with leading newspapers bidding for his exclusive publication rights. The Sheriff is able to turn the disaster into a vote-catching campaign: a huge election slogan is draped across the mountain. Unfortunately for Tatum, things go wrong. Leo contracts pneumonia and as the overhead drilling has made a second cave-in likely, he cannot be reached by the direct route before he dies.

Along with Willie Gingrich in *The Fortune Cookie*, Tatum is probably Wilder's most extreme portrait of avarice and ambition, but the major thrust of Wilder's scorn is directed not at him but at Leo's wife Lorraine (Jan Sterling) who views the disaster as her chance to escape her arid existence. Lorraine is a close relative of Phyllis Dietrichson in *Double Indemnity*, both blonde and icily attractive, and both married to dull, dependable men whom they want to be rid of. But whereas Phyllis seizes on Walter Neff as her passport to a wealthier and more exciting life, Lorraine has to be persuaded from running away as Tatum needs her for his own scheme for escape and success. If Lorraine remains at the accident spot, continuing to manage her husband's all-purpose trading post, Tatum can arouse human interest by presenting her as a devoted wife anxious for the safety of her beloved husband. Just as Whiplash Willie persuades Harry Hinkle's sluttish wife to feign affection so that his insurance swindle stands a better chance of succeeding, so Tatum persuades Lorraine to stay, lured by the promise of escape and wealth. "You're selling rugs to the Indians now," he tells her, "but soon you'll be selling to Mr and Mrs America." Lorraine agrees to play the role of the worried housewife (Mrs America, in fact) and since Tatum embodies the life force and sexuality which her dull existence with Leo has denied her

Ace in the Hole: *Jan Sterling selling to Mr and Mrs America*

she enters into partnership with him, neither romantic nor sexual, but based on a recognition that they need each other to get what they want. It's a business deal, straight down the line like Walter and Phyllis. Lorraine is as hard-boiled as Tatum – "Don't ask me to go to church – kneeling bags my nylons" – but after Leo dies, needlessly and pathetically, Tatum forces her to wear the birthday present Leo has bought her – a hideous fur stole – which he tightens around her neck. Physically threatened and also forced to confront their mutual involvement in Leo's death, she stabs him with a pair of scissors, disgusted by Tatum's display of remorse and angered by his failure to make their plan a success.

If the focus of Wilder's anger shifts to Lorraine – as Tatum's opportunism forces wider social perspectives – his treatment of the crowd, who swarm to the scene to turn one man's misfortune into their vicarious entertainment, is even bleaker. A personal catastrophe becomes not only news, as Tatum has calculated ("Bad news sells best," he tells the junior reporter Herbie Cook, played by Bob Arthur), it becomes another branch of showbusiness, a media event resembling a disaster-movie like *Earthquake, The Towering Inferno* or *Jaws*, in which the shark attacks become entertainment for the crowd; an entertainment complete with Ferris wheel, a folk group crooning "We're coming Leo," ice-creams, balloons, radio stations to interview the audience, and a train called the Leo Minosa Special. Wilder's loathing of mob psychology, characterised in *Sunset Boulevard* as "those heartless so-and-so's" who feed off Norma Desmond's tragedy, is at least as strong as Fritz Lang's. But whereas Lang's hatred of mobs seems specifically directed at their potential for unthinking violence and hysterical injustice, demonstrated in his first American film *Fury* (1936), Wilder despises his mobs for their blind conformity and insensitivity and their morbid fascination with suffering. The spokesmen of the crowd in *Ace in the Hole* are the grotesque Federber family – "Mr and Mrs America", as Tatum labels them – who set up camp at the foot of the mountain and are offended when others try to claim the distinction of being there first. Appropriately, Mr Federber is an insurance man (from Gallup, mentioned by Baxter in *The Apartment*), representative of those who risk and create nothing. "The Mountain of the Seven Vultures", in which Leo is trapped, becomes the mountain of the seven thousand vultures who come to gorge off both the land and Leo's misfortune. Wilder singles out the Federbers to act as the mob's spokesmen, but for the most part the mob is captured by the camera as a swirling mass that moves when told, buys when beckoned, sings when prompted, leaves when dismissed.

On the other hand Tatum, for all his unscrupulousness, is seen in more positive terms. Whilst Wilder photographs the mob *en masse*, to underline its anonymity, Tatum dominates the frame, often photographed from below against the sky, with the mountain top below his level within the frame, and with the other characters receding from him. The film's visual syntax actually resembles the outline of a mountain, marking a graph from Tatum's low, undignified arrival in Albuquerque, rising to its summit when the crowd swell and reporters are bidding for his services, and falling as the scheme disintegrates. As Tatum's plan backfires so his dominance of the frame diminishes, culminating in the final low-angle shot in which Tatum crashes to the floor. Needless to say, Tatum's enterprise is wholly selfish – Lorraine will be ditched after she has served her purpose – yet the enterprise has an audacity that arouses as much fascination as revulsion, which is one of the disturbing areas of the film.

Characteristically, Wilder provides his abrasive hero with a sympathetic companion, the cub reporter Herbie Cook, who stands as a kind of audience representative, someone to measure our responses by. He anticipates characters like Cookie in *Stalag 17* and Rudy Keppler in *The Front Page*, and has a similar relationship with the dubious main character – an adulation which is somewhat modified by the end but which still does not amount to total disillusionment and rejection. The reason why it does not is because Tatum brings excitement into people's lives. Wilder ensures, however, that we appreciate the cost of this. A pertinent shot early on in the 'Sun Bulletin' office catches Tatum with his back turned to the "Private" sign on Mr Boot's door and the embroidered "Tell The Truth" motto. Tatum is a man who habitually turns his back on the truth and has little or no respect for privacy. But he is the only person in that office who ever seems to *move*. Virtue that is as inert and complacent as Mr Boot's can scarcely be applauded, and an audience wants "the file in the loaf of bread" which Tatum is always asking for and is prepared to invent in order to stimulate our interest.

It is at the point when Tatum cannot provide the happy ending (the rescue of Leo) that he knows the story needs, that the full implications of his opportunism begin to be driven to their logical, inexorable and unbearable conclusion (appropriately in this scene, when Tatum informs the sheriff about Leo's illness, Tatum is naked to the waist, suddenly appearing vulnerable and scared). The film begins to react on *us*: we have been encouraged to identify with this force of irresponsible energy only for it to turn against us and overwhelm us. This is a familiar tactic of Wilder, as it is to a more obsessive degree in Hitchcock, which appeals to our impure emotions in order to force us to contemplate the morality of our own attitudes.

Tatum's change of heart at the end (his frenzied attempt to reach Leo, his savage remorse) has struck many critics as unconvincing. Yet it is not as compromised or as blatant as some have suggested. Leo after all is not saved, so Tatum's conversion comes too late; also, his redemption is not allowed to achieve full expression. His editor hangs up on him when he tries to confess (the "pretty good liar" has become the compulsive truth-teller, only no one wants to listen). The crowd does not turn on him so he is denied the satisfaction of the purging-by-humiliation process that overtakes a Richard Brooks hero like Lord Jim or Elmer Gantry, or destroys Nathanael West's pathetic

Homer Simpson. It is not absolutely certain that Herbie Cook will make the truth known. Tatum is back where he started ("I was worth a thousand dollars a day. You can have me for nothing") and the final shot is a virtual repetition of the one which concludes the scene when Tatum is hired. "Sell out" endings usually give more sense of release than this.

Even so, Wilder's deployment of this redemptive structure – his distinction between people who will do anything for money and those who will do *almost* anything – is so consistent as to imply a positive conviction. Wilder seems to believe in the co-existence of good and evil in human character, in conscience, and in redemption; the potential in the individual to reform his own nature. This belief is not religious in any orthodox sense, though *Ace in the Hole* has a religious emphasis that is rather unusual in Wilder's work*. Leo's parents are devout believers, his mother frequently shown (and interrupted by Tatum and Cook) in the act of prayer. Leo himself interprets the cave-in as a form of religious judgement for his desecration of the "holy mountain" of the Indians, where their dead are buried with valuable votive offerings. "They didn't want me to have it", he says. Typically, though, this religious strain is felt not so much as a positive force in its own right but as a means of highlighting, by ironic contrast, the much more pervasive atmosphere of spiritual poverty. Tatum's conversion, then, is ultimately humanist rather than religious. And if such endings seem tentative and unconvincing, this reflects not Wilder's insincerity but the precariousness of his humanism. It is an assertion of hope in basic values and dignity that seems to fly in the face of the main impulse of his films. Belief without proof, of course, is the very definition of faith. In offering a complicated optimism rather than an uncomplicated pessimism, Wilder's endings enrich and deepen his films rather than enfeeble them.

As we have already implied, the film that seems closest to *Ace in the Hole* in Wilder's work is *The Fortune Cookie*. Tatum's selfish exploits, his elaborate fakery, his verbal dexterity, seem to place him in the same family as Whiplash Willie. The lawyers who try to buy

---

*In his book 'Anatomy of Film' (St Martin's Press, New York, 1978), Bernard F Dick writes confidently of "The Genesis Myth in *Ace in the Hole*", pointing to the desert setting as a kind of Garden of Evil, the rattlesnake imagery as a kind of evil serpent, and of Lorraine eating the forbidden fruit of experience. Dick proposes Wilder's film as "an inversion of the book of Genesis, complete with a parody of the six days of creation".

off Willie are paralleled here by Tatum's dealings with the newspaper proprietors who are bidding for his services and the reporters who are begging him for a break. Yet as *Ace in the Hole* develops the more Tatum comes to resemble Harry Hinkle. The relationship which evolves between Tatum and Leo becomes strikingly similar to that between Harry and Boom-Boom Jackson. Leo, as with Boom-Boom, is being exploited by someone who becomes his best friend; indeed, the only remotely human relationship in *Ace in the Hole* is between Tatum and Leo. And like Harry Hinkle, Tatum's guilt evolves from the growing friendship and trust of the deceived man. In both cases a mercenary blonde wife stands between them, a woman who is more interested in financial gain than in her suffering husband. There are few more brutal moments in *Ace in the Hole* than Wilder's abrupt cut from the suffocating man's comment on his wife – "She's so pretty" – to Lorraine gleefully taking in more money than ever before. The effect might seem crude in other hands but it has a complex impact here, first in its blinding contrast between dark and light, and second in its perverse irony: at that precise moment Lorraine *does* look pretty – Leo's absence is doing her good.

Leo's death is, for Tatum, a personal tragedy more than a professional one. Near the end, after Tatum has been stabbed, he fetches a priest to administer the last Rites to Leo. After Leo says "Bless me father for I have sinned," Wilder cuts to Tatum as tears stream down his face, implicitly convicting him as the real sinner of the piece – the last Rites are for Tatum as well – but encompassing a far more potent and more general sense of grief and loss. This has been prepared for in the first scene between the two men which has a curious emotional emphasis. Tatum is on the trail of his scoop and when, at the end of his interview with the trapped man, he hauls out his camera to take the exclusive picture, Leo is clearly thrilled to be photographed. "My picture in the paper? No kidding!", he says, delighted by the prospect of being made famous. The overall effect of the scene, juxtaposing Tatum's inhuman opportunism and Leo's all too human response, is the reverse of cynical. Tatum brings Leo hope – and not only for immediate rescue – and throughout the film he is the only character who does.

This extends also to Tatum's relationship with the community. In a process which seems almost like irrigating the desert, he brings life to a region which has previously been dusty and arid. "A new

Ace in the Hole: *Kirk Douglas, Richard Benedict*

community is springing up," announces the radio reporter surrounded by the crowd. This revitalisation has disturbing, ambiguous implications, most notably in the "awakening" of Lorraine and the fact that the new community is essentially transient and contemptible, a swarm of locusts eagerly consuming everything in its path. Nevertheless, as with the murderer in Alfred Hitchcock's *Shadow of a Doubt* (1943), there is a perverse fascination in the way in which a character like this brings life to a community which has been stagnant and oppressive. "You might just as well be dead," someone says to the father in

Shadow of a Doubt, (1943) speaking more truthfully than he knows. Similarly, *Ace in the Hole* is about people who are being buried alive, figuratively and literally. Tatum's lust for life offers an escape (to Leo, Lorraine and Herbie Cook) from the lifeless community with its zombie-like inhabitants. When Tatum's life force is spent, the community which he has created collapses, being dismantled in an instant. In a quite stunning shot, all that is left is Leo's old father, isolated and deserted in a landscape that is empty apart from the litter. It is a shot which recalls the end of Charles Chaplin's *The Circus* (1928), in which The Tramp is left behind after the parade has gone by.

This relationship with the community would explain why Wilder's attitude to Tatum is so profoundly ambivalent. Tatum is certainly not as monstrous as Sheriff Kretzer who shows more compassion for his rattlesnake than anyone else and is exploiting Tatum's desperation. Equally, the figure of integrity represented by Mr Boot hardly offers an exciting alternative to which to aspire. Structurally similar to Keyes in *Double Indemnity*, tempting the hero back to the paths of virtue, he is much less incisive and authoritative than Keyes. He has a kind of weary wisdom more akin to resignation than values positive enough to emulate, a point made through Herbie Cook's willingness to follow Tatum's example. "He wants to be going, going," Tatum says of Herbie, to which Mr Boot responds icily, "Going where?". It is, on one level at least, a valid question: what is all this ambition and graft actually for: Success? Fame? The goals of Wilder's heroes seem not only elusive but illusions: higher and better and richer and faster for its own sake. On another level, though, Mr Boot's opposition is indicative of his conservatism, his resistance to change, his parochialism. Big city hustling is pitted against small town sterility in the same way that Europe and America are set up in opposition in other Wilder films.

What places Tatum slightly above this and relieves him from bearing the full burden of moral responsibility for Leo's death, is that he is active, alive, a creator, even an artist; an early graduate of the school which will produce Sergeant Sefton, Whiplash Willie and Walter Burns. "I don't make things happen," Tatum says defensively at one point, "All I do is write about them." Since he has contrived the entire affair, this is not strictly true, but the response to the story reflects the seamier elements in human nature outside his control. "There's that terrifying fact that people are people you know," Wilder told Charles Higham and Joel Greenberg, "People criticised me for bad taste but it really happened."* This statement of Wilder's seems very similar to Tatum's. It is in this murky area of human culpability – Tatum's entrepreneurial facility, the public's need for entertaining diversions – that *Ace in the Hole* invites comparisons with the Hollywood aesthetic and suggests a measure of identification between Wilder and the hero he has created. Wilder has not created human nature; like Tatum, he contrives a situation for that nature to manifest itself. If this director-hero identification is valid, Wilder's detailed scrutiny of Tatum and the crowd becomes an examination of his attitude to both his actual sponsors and his potential audience. *Ace in the Hole* can thus be read as a commentary on movie-going, in the same way that Alfred Hitchcock's *Rear Window* (1954) implicates its audience in the voyeurism of its director and hero.

The clearest evidence we have to suggest this is in the way that Wilder organises the crowd and its physical relationship to the spectacle. The accident spot is transformed into a kind of surrogate cinema – a drive-in to which the masses are drawn, like a Roman mob, to witness a literal life and death struggle. The cars line up in orderly rows, just as people sit in theatres, their attention focused on the mountain. The spacial relationship between the viewer and the screen is precisely echoed, and to the thousands of spectators the drama on the mountain must resemble a movie. They have to purchase a ticket (at an ever-increasing price – even Herbie Cook has to pay) to get a decent view, and Lorraine's trading post becomes the traditional popcorn kiosk, providing refreshments during the 'intervals' when nothing is happening. Wilder frequently cuts between the action and the audience gazing intently upwards, mechanically eating ice-cream and hamburgers at the same time. Audiences of *Ace in the Hole* and the film's sponsors must have been aware of this implied criticism – especially Paramount, whose famous mountain logo assumes an ironic significance in this context – and reacted accordingly.

Towards the end Tatum leaps on to one of the lifts and addresses the crowd from the mountain, rather like Moses castigating the worshippers of the Golden Calf. Tatum tells the crowd that Leo has died and that, "the circus is over." It is like an artist dismissing his

---

*Wilder is referring here to the case of Floyd Collins who died in 1925 in a cave in Kentucky in circumstances very similar to those shown in *Ace in the Hole*.

Ace in the Hole: *Kirk Douglas addresses the crowd*

own audience, having given them a truth too unpleasant to bear (even Mrs Federber bursts into tears). In a matter of minutes the place is deserted, like an empty cinema strewn with the litter of broken dreams. At the end, nobody wants to hear what Tatum has to tell them. From the heights of prosperity and success he has slumped to a total failure.

The film ends as Tatum staggers back to square one, into the 'Sun Bulletin' offices with the hope that his 'confessional' will be published; as he says, he has an even bigger story now. Wilder cuts to a studied low-angle shot as Tatum, blood seeping through his shirt (precisely echoing Walter Neff in *Double Indemnity*), crashes to the floor to die just short of the lens whilst Mr Boot and his staff stand silently above. Wilder plays his ace by dumping his hero unceremoniously into the laps of his audience. And that audience turns its back on truth and leaves the cinema once the big movie carnival has passed by.

Stalag 17 (1953)

Although *The Apartment* is perhaps Wilder's most elaborate analysis of the dehumanising effects the capitalist system can have on individuals, *Stalag 17* offers us an equally forceful expression of Wilder's attitude to the conflicting impulses in American consumerist society. Because of the restraints imposed by capitalist ideology, the characters in the films discussed in this chapter are obliged to fall back on their inventiveness and resourcefulness, often discovering their capacity for guile and the lure of corruption for the first time. In *Stalag 17*, Wilder's hero manages to conduct cut-throat capitalism in a prisoner-of-war camp. Sergeant J J Sefton (William Holden) even stages a sort of Kentucky Derby for rodents, which is one of Wilder's most impudent and literal images of the global rat-race in which all of his characters are involved. Sefton remains dehumanised to the very last, though typically he is the only dynamic character in the film.

Even at this stage in his career, spectators must have been struck by Wilder's consistently bleak choice of protagonist. He had already brought to the attention of the American movie-going public an insurance salesman who commits cold-blooded murder (Walter Neff in *Double Indemnity*), an alcoholic novelist (Don Birnam in *The Lost Weekend*), a gigolo (Joe Gillis in *Sunset Boulevard*) and a megalomaniacal journalist (Chuck Tatum in *Ace in the Hole*). The thing which distinguishes the heroes before Tatum is that they are all more victimised than villains – tragic outcasts of a social system founded on competition and ambitions realised and rewarded. Neff is trapped by his compulsion to beat the system at its own game and is fatally exploited by a deadly female. Birnam might exploit other people's kindness or steal their money, but he is essentially at the mercy of an uncontrollable passion, induced by a paranoid sense of artistic inadequacy. Gillis might believe he is exploiting a lucrative situation but

Stalag 17: *Sefton's rat-race*

he is being used by someone with identical motives – he and Norma Desmond need each other to negotiate their way back into the prevailing system. On the other hand, Tatum and Sefton are more aggressive figures, sharing with the others an enforced remoteness from society through a failure to achieve success within it, yet initiating and dominating situations for their own gain.

If in a sense all these characters are social outcasts, paradoxically they are all prisoners seeking some form of escape. In this way the prisoner-of-war camp setting of *Stalag 17* is not very different from the Hollywood of *Sunset Boulevard*: Norma Desmond's mansion is a baroque prison, complete with Germanic guard, where you get shot in the back if you try to breach its perimeter. Nor is it far removed from the Los Angeles of *Double Indemnity*, where the shadows cast by the venetian blinds in the Dietrichson home become ominous presentiments of the hero's entrapment: Neff, too, is shot attempting to escape. There is also Albuquerque and its arid environs in *Ace in the Hole* (significantly, Tatum is looking for the story with the "file in the loaf of bread") from which Tatum informs the world but from which he is never to escape alive. The principal irony of *Stalag 17* is the hero's *refusal* to escape, at least not until he has a good commercial reason for doing so and a reasonable chance of success. For if escape seems essential to a POW's conception of his identity as a soldier – the familiar movie-cliche, "It is the duty of every man to escape and hinder the enemy" – then Sefton's attitude is his conception of what it is to be an American.

Joseph McBride and Michael Wilmington have suggested that *Ace in the Hole* is more of a concentration camp film than this one; and indeed, *Stalag 17* is hardly a war film at all, being unmistakably Wilder's most successful comedy up to that date. The cleverness of *Stalag 17* lies in how Wilder is able to continue his assault on American values – the spectacular commercial failure of *Ace in the Hole* notwithstanding – in the context of a Broadway-based comedy (*Stalag 17* was a huge critical and commercial hit) without compromising his sensibility. If anything, *Stalag 17* goes further than *Ace in the Hole* since the hero's transformation is clearly a further ploy (later examples of the type are Willie Gingrich in *The Fortune Cookie* and Walter Burns in *The Front Page*, though these are darker specimens still, unpunished and unrepentant).

Dupes and rogues certainly, but Wilder has a fair measure of sympathy for them all. If they are variously wretched, weak and unscrupulous, they are also individualists seeking some form of personal enrichment and identity – in both materialist and spiritual terms – within an impersonal system which denies them this – hence Wilder's Kafkaesque vision of the insurance office in *The Apartment* and his ruthless satires on Socialist systems in *Ninotchka* and *One, Two, Three*. This is not, as Andrew Sarris suggested in his book 'The American Cinema,' "a series of tasteless gags, half anti-Left and half anti-Right, adding up to Wilder's conception of political sophistication," but a profound belief in individual liberty. In a society founded on private enterprise but which actually restricts people if they fail to achieve success, the individual has either to manipulate the system fraudulently or somehow invigorate it from within. Viewed in this light, the distance between Wilder's arch-dupe, C C Baxter, and Wilder's arch-rogue, J J Sefton, is not as great as one might expect. To be sure, Baxter is the mercilessly exploited and Sefton the merciless exploiter, yet both are striving, in their variously fallible and unethical ways, to survive. Baxter trades his apartment key for the promise of promotion, even if it means the near-suicide of the girl he loves; Sefton trades with the Nazis and swindles his comrades blind for a few home comforts, even if the Nazis are killing off some of those comrades. Wilder might not endorse his heroes' actions but he understands their motives and provides a context for them.

This struggle for survival and individuality brings to mind the comparison which is often made between Wilder's films and those of Howard Hawks. Critics have noted a similar predilection for outrageous impersonations, their witty and assertive heroines, their pungent social comedy and their lack of visual pretensions. They even have material in common (*His Girl Friday* and *The Front Page*) and Hawks has even filmed a Wilder screenplay twice (*Ball of Fire* and its disappointing remake, *A Song is Born*). However, a moment's consideration reveals that the differences between the two directors are at least as great as their points of contact (this may explain why Robin Wood, who has never written about Wilder, has the most difficulty in placing *Ball of Fire* in his Hawskian pattern). The most striking divergence is their respective attitudes to the group and to the individual. It would be extremely unwise here to oversimplify Hawks's complex notion of the group, how it is individualised and what moral values it embodies, but it seems reasonable to suggest that the groups in *Only Angels Have Wings* (1939), *Air Force* (1943), *Rio Bravo* (1959) and *Hatari!* (1962) – four of Hawks's most distinctive films, all relying on precision and discipline in action, even if only one, *Air Force*, has a conventional war setting – and the kind of empirical values they assert – of loyalty, integrity, professionalism, interdependence – can in no way be paralleled in *any* of Wilder's films, where the ethics of individualism (very often directed *against* a group rather than advocating solidarity within it) are paramount. In his book 'Personal Views', Wood argues persuasively against Peter Wollen's structuralist account of Hawks (in 'Signs and Meaning in the Cinema', Secker and

Warburg, London, 1969), particularly the latter's assertion that, "For Hawks, the highest human emotion is the camaraderie of the exclusive, self-sufficient, all-male group," by affirming that Hawks's characters express their individuality "*through* solidarity with others, perhaps, but scarcely adequately represented *by* it." If individuals in Hawks's films can only function as individuals within the context of a group (for example, Dean Martin's efforts in *Rio Bravo* to resume his place beside John Wayne by conquering his alcoholism; or John Garfield's gradual assimilation into the group in *Air Force* where, as Wood observes, "a perfect balance is achieved between individual fulfilment and the responsibility to each member of the whole"), in Wilder's universe this means the surrender of one's inner-self.

Because of this, groups in Wilder's films are rare, yet when they appear the response to them is consistent: Tatum despises the small-town reporters he works with; Lindbergh in *The Spirit of St Louis* always remains aloof from the group constructing his plane; Leonard Vole in *Witness for the Prosecution*, a close relative of Sefton, remains visibly detached from his regiment; Baxter merely uses the group of philandering executives (which itself breaks up when Sheldrake attempts to impose a hierarchy of adulterers) and never considers joining after he receives his promotion; Hildy Johnson in *The Front Page* continually disassociates himself from the pack-like reporters.

Stalag 17 presents us with Wilder's most obvious group – twenty or so men tightly packed in a prison barracks – and for the first and only time in Wilder we have a society devoid of women. Women are felt as background presences (the hilarious satire on letters from home, implying that several of the men's wives are enjoying their 'freedom'; the Russian women prisoners who aggravate the men's frustration) but their absence and lack of influence (pronounced in Wilder, either as civilising, warm-hearted influences in the comedies, or as dominant and deadly influences in the dramas) throws the men on their own resources. The split between group and individual morality becomes a major theme.

Ostensibly, the most Hawksian moment in *Stalag 17* occurs when the Nazi Commandant (Otto Preminger*) has his gleaming jack-boots

---

*The casting of Preminger as von Scherbach recalls Wilder's use of von Stroheim as Rommel in *Five Graves to Cairo* and also Stroheim's performance as the Camp Commandant in Jean Renoir's *La Grande Illusion* (1937), a work Wilder much admires and which has been compared with *Stalag 17*. Renoir's film casts Stroheim as a courtly, dignified German aristocrat recognising splashed with mud by one of the Americans standing on the parade ground. The Commandant angrily demands that the culprit stand forward and identify himself or he will punish them all. At first, one man does hesitantly step forward; then another; then all of them step forward *en masse*. It is a movement demonstrating group solidarity and responsibility. Seen in the context of the whole development of the film, however, one cannot help but see this movement as somewhat ironic: after all, *not* moving forward at this point would place one in greater danger than following the herd. Later in the film these same men are to move forward in collective, mistaken self-righteousness to beat up Sefton who is subsequently proved to be innocent ("Why not try *one at a time*", he says). Wilder's portrayal of the mob in his two previous films, *Sunset Boulevard* and *Ace in the Hole*, would not encourage an uncritical look at the way in which Wilder offers group morality in this. Indeed, Sefton receives his savage beating for a variety of reasons, not merely because he is suspected of betraying an officer to the enemy. This cautions us to consider very carefully the morality of Sefton's behaviour in the film and, more especially, the nature of his apparent conversion into a hero at the end, his seeming redemption and integration with his fellow men.

The prison camp setting is valuable for Wilder since it robs characters of choice and throws emphasis on their capacity for survival. The camp serves as a clear microcosm of the capitalist society outside. In addition to his rat-race, Sefton sets up an illicit distillery and installs a telescope so sex-starved POWs can, for a modest charge, spy on the Russian women being deloused in the showers. Sefton has no particular animosity towards anyone in the camp until Lieutenant Dunbar (Don Taylor) arrives. Dunbar immediately establishes a division between officers and enlisted men, thereby threatening Sefton's 'classless' enterprise, and we are informed early on that Dunbar

---

with regret that his way of life is over. In contrast, Wilder's Germans are ruthlessly caricatured and given no dignity whatsoever. Preminger makes cheap jokes about the author of "White Christmas" and how he stole his name from the German capital and who even puts his boots on when telephoning his superiors so that his clicking heels are heard in Berlin – obedience to a system taken to the ultimate absurdity. The cultural debasement is clinched by the characterisation of the German guard (Sig Ruman) who answers to the name of Johann Sebastian Schultz (it was Ruman who played 'Concentration Camp Erhardt' in Lubitsch's 1942 film *To Be Or Not To Be*). Schultz, in fact, is the one Nazi to show any compassion for his prisoners, but this 'weakness' is immediately exploited by the Americans. Renoir's film is a moving but slightly confected celebration of friendship and freedom; Wilder's offers camp comedy at its most coarsely astringent and inventive, condemning friendship and trust as an obstacle to freedom.

comes from a wealthy Bostonian family with all the right social connections. He has bought his position rather than earned it through ability or ingenious graft, as Sefton – the self-made man – has managed. It is the tension between Dunbar and Sefton – the polarities they represent – which propels the narrative and establishes the film's political thrust. The hero's imprisonment suddenly unleashes all the competitive urges which have lain dormant within him. The defeatism and collective weakness in the others is implied by Wilder in two ways: by showing the futility of their jointly planned escape attempts (the film opens as two men are burrowing through a tunnel, Sefton taking bets on their success, and after shots are heard, gathering up a mountain of Red Cross cigarettes which he will sell to the Germans) and in the torture scene involving Dunbar when the Nazis want his confession that he sabotaged an ammunitions train prior to his capture. Don Taylor's skilfully suave performance – the 'romantic hero' as opposed to William Holden's unshaven 'realistic' hero – suggests a hollowness when, under torture, he pleads for mercy like a child born with a silver spoon in his mouth.

Sefton is a supreme individualist – "Here you're on your own,' he comments icily to Dunbar – and in Wilder's films individualism invariably has a number of contrasting impulses held in tension. The individual hero is independent; he has no family commitments (one thinks of Neff, Gillis, Tatum, Baxter, none of whom is given any family background at all) yet at the same time he sometimes needs the company of a doting disciple (the cub reporter as Tatum's companion; Cookie as Sefton's) though rarely does Wilder provide an articulate antagonist, that role in *Ace in the Hole* being ultimately assumed by Tatum himself. And independence is not far removed from alienation: we are never quite sure whether the hero's refusal to fit in stems from a deliberate choice or a failure to do so – either way, it is a dispiriting thought. Sefton's philosophy of "dog eat dog" and "every man for himself" derives from his initial experiences as a POW when most of his possessions were stolen. Although this is Sefton's explanation and the justification for his behaviour, more than this is clearly involved.

If we are intended to regard him as alienated this is modified by his terrific energy. It is modified still further by our sense that Sefton is often the realist in a world of dreamers. When he insists on "staying put", even if it entails some bartering with the enemy to make life bearable, we feel a conflicting sense of shock and understanding. When he upbraids the Escape Committee for their schoolboy heroics, which has led to the death of the two men trying to escape, we appreciate the justice of his attack. Indeed, Wilder's opening sequence seems specifically designed to lend force to Sefton's individualism. Significantly, when he does support an escape plan it is a plan of his *own* devising, not something which has been cobbled together by the group.

This gives a certain ambiguity to Sefton's progress through the film. Like a good many Wilder heroes, he has his moment of extreme humiliation: in a typical progress he is framed, rejected and assaulted; also typically, he is ultimately redeemed through his uncovering of the real traitor in the camp. Here again, Wilder undermines the notion of group solidarity by insisting that the most trusted man of the group – Price (Peter Graves), the elected leader of the Escape Committee – should be the real traitor, acting out of a real commitment to Nazism. When Dunbar's friend tells the prisoners of Dunbar's daring exploits in order to establish his claim on their allegiance, the Nazis also hear of it. Sefton is immediately suspected as the leak – after all, he bets on the failure of escapes – and when Dunbar is removed for questioning he gets beaten up. But the group's motives are confused since it has also been revealed that Sefton has been allowed to visit the Russian prisoners whom the men have spied upon through Sefton's hastily improvised telescope. Sefton's beating, then, is as much the result of sexual jealousy and frustration, as much the result of envy at his success in beating the system, as one of patriotic outrage.

It is Sefton who unmasks Price – typically, by his awareness of objects: Price has used a chess queen as a 'letter box' and an electric light cord which he loops in various ways to alert the Nazis to an escape attempt – and is thus restored in the eyes of his camp comrades. But instead of instant assimilation into the group, Sefton remains detached and misanthropic. Now that Price has been discredited and Dunbar physically disabled, Sefton is the natural candidate for the new leader. The notion of being turned into a hero leads Sefton to devise an escape plan rather than remain in the company of men who no longer despise him. His bold plan is not only a careful calculation of the odds (he now has a useful diversion, since Price will be noisily ejected from the barracks to certain death by the machine-gunners in the look-out posts) but is also undertaken for frankly mercenary motives: Dunbar's rich family will surely pay handsomely for his rescue, and Dunbar as object rather than Dunbar as person is emphasised by the fact that he can hardly walk. The beating up of Sefton has converted him not into a patriot but into a revenge hero.

As with many of Wilder's concluding sequences, the one in *Stalag 17* has been misunderstood, arousing hostility and disbelief. Andrew Sarris, for instance, began his early assessment of Wilder in 'The American Cinema' by saying, "Billy Wilder is too cynical to believe even his own cynicism. Toward the end of *Stalag 17*, William Holden bids a properly cynical adieu to his prison-camp buddies. He ducks into the escape-tunnel for a second, then quickly pops up, out of character, with a boyish smile and a friendly wave, and then ducks down for good." But this "friendly wave", as Sarris interprets it, is surely the equivalent of 'Up Yours'. "Just let's pretend we never met before", is Sefton's parting comment to the men if they should meet after the war, a neat demolition of escape-movie clichés which insists on Sefton's denial of the group and the constraints it imposes.

The thuggish Duke (Neville Brand), whom Sefton has used throughout as a strip of sandpaper on which to ignite his matches and who does seem to ignite at the very presence of Sefton, now grins cheesily, both at the prospect of assisting in the execution of Price and in recognition of Sefton's achievement: his pathological hatred has turned into an equally exaggerated hero-worship. Cookie, who has abandoned Sefton, now smiles softly to himself and whistles "When Johnny Comes Marching Home". The last words are those of the grotesque camp clown 'Animal' (Robert Strauss) which re-assert Sefton's capitalistic impulses and leave us in no doubt as to Sefton's motives as he disappears down the tunnel with the rich Dunbar: "Maybe he just wanted to steal our wirecutters. Did you ever think of that?"

The Apartment (1960)

"On November 1st, 1959, the population of New York City was 8,042,783. If you laid all these people end to end, figuring an average height of five feet six and a half inches, they would reach from Times Square to the outskirts of Karachi, Pakistan. I know facts like these because I work for an insurance company – Consolidated Life of New York. We are one of the top five companies in the country – last year we wrote nine-point-three billion dollars worth of policies. Our home office has 31,259 employees – which is more than the entire population of Natchez, Mississippi, or Gallup, New Mexico.

"I work on the nineteenth floor, Ordinary Policy Department, Premium Accounting Division, Section W, desk number 861. My name is C C Baxter – C for Calvin, C for Clifford – however, most people call me Bud. I've been with Consolidated Life for three years and ten months. I started in the branch Office in Cincinnati, then transferred to New York. My take-home pay is $94.70 a week, and there are the usual fringe benefits.

"The hours in our department are 8.50 to 5.20 – they're staggered by floors, so that the sixteen elevators can handle the 31,259 employees without a serious traffic jam. As for myself, I very often stay on at the office and work for an extra hour or two – especially when the weather is bad. It's not that I'm overly ambitious – it's just a way of killing time, until it's all right for me to go home. You see, I have this little problem with my apartment.

"I live in the West Sixties – just half a block from Central Park. My rent is $84 a month. It used to be $80 until last July when Mrs Lieberman, the landlady, put in a second-hand air conditioning unit. It's a real nice apartment – nothing fancy but kind of cosy – just right for a bachelor. The only problem is – I can't always get in when I want to."

With this marvellous opening narration, Wilder tells us all we need to know about his hero's personality and position. Equally revealing is the imagery which accompanies Baxter's commentary. As he tells us of his world, we begin with a helicopter shot of New York, followed by a camera-tilt up the massive building in which Baxter (Jack Lemmon) and 31,258 other souls work. With a minimum of fuss, Wilder has established not only one of the basic compositional principles of the film (the conflict between the horizontal and the vertical) but also a visual analogy for one of its major themes: that of social climbing.

This theme is expounded in the contrast between the office and the elevator. The wide Panavision frame captures a vast, brightly-lit office which represents a Kafkaesque structure of uniformity and impersonality, a labyrinth of anonymous humanity which stretches to infinity. It also recalls the opening sequence of King Vidor's *The Crowd* (1928), a source acknowledged by Wilder* even though the main inspiration for *The Apartment* apparently came from David Lean's *Brief Encounter* (1945) in which the hero, played by Trevor Howard, borrows a friend's apartment so that he might have somewhere to entertain Celia Johnson.

As Baxter mechanically recites details about the 8,042,783 New Yorkers who would stretch to Karachi if laid end to end, we see the company employees who are in effect laid end to end and sandwiched together by floors. The flattened perspective gives the impression of people dehumanised and distorted by their surroundings, whilst Adolph Deutsch's wittily martial music and the clanging bell emphasise the military discipline and mechanical rhythm of the office routines. At one point, Baxter's head movements are choreographed to the electronic chatter of his calculating machine. The opening sequence continues as Baxter, long after the 5.20 stampede, arrives at his apartment to find it still engaged. It is raining and Baxter is obliged to wait by the garbage cans until Mr Kirkeby (David Lewis) has finished with Sylvia (Joan Shawlee), one of Consolidated Life's switchboard operators. Baxter loiters outside the brownstone house, his hat pulled down and the collar of his raincoat turned up, like some pathetic caricature of a *film noir* hero.

By having his group of philandering executives use Baxter's dingy apartment for their extra-marital affairs, Wilder paints a picture of inescapable mental drabness and physical stasis. The bright overhead lighting in the huge insurance office mocks the apartment reservations made surreptitiously by the executives over the internal telephone

---

*In a poll organised by the Festival Mondial du Film et des Beaux Arts de Belgique, reprinted in 'Sight and Sound' (Jul-Sep 1952), Wilder ranked *The Crowd* fifth in his Top Ten. The others, in order, were: *Battleship Potemkin* (Eisenstein, 1925), *Greed* (Von Stroheim, 1923), *Variety* (Dupont, 1925), *The Gold Rush* (Chaplin, 1924), *La Grande Illusion* (Renoir, 1937), *The Informer* (Ford, 1935), *Ninotchka* (Lubitsch, 1939), *The Best Years of Our Lives* (Wyler, 1946), *Bicycle Thieves* (De Sica, 1948).

system, while the empty bottles, the dirty glasses and the half-eaten bags of crackers which litter Baxter's dimly-lit apartment underline the essential seediness of Baxter's and his clients' situation. In a sense, Wilder is correcting an earlier mistake, for unlike Richard Sherman in *The Seven Year Itch*, the executives of *The Apartment* at least possess the nerve to consummate their menopausal fantasies. This is made explicit early on when Mr Dobisch (Ray Walston) picks up a barfly – "She looks like Marilyn Monroe!", he says excitedly to Baxter – and threatens Baxter with a poor efficiency report unless he vacates the apartment, in effect condemning Baxter to a night on a park bench in the middle of winter and a consequent heavy cold.* Even though the executives mean business, in every sense of the word, and are more 'alive' than Sherman ever could be, Wilder cannot view their clandestine activities as anything but wholly repugnant. We are a whole world and an entire culture away from the sun-drenched setting of *Avanti!*, in which Jack Lemmon's Italian affair with Juliet Mills is seen as the harassed executive's moral regeneration. *The Apartment*, with its bitter sense of comedy and low-key black and white photography, offers only moral disintegration.

The only escape from the vast general office is via the elevator which takes people down and out of the building, or alternatively – for an aspiring employee like Baxter – takes them up to the more spacious and luxurious floors with private offices, private washrooms, and names on the doors. Baxter's route out of the general office and upstairs is via his apartment key which he lends to his immediate superiors (Messrs Kirkeby, Dobisch, Vanderhof, Eichelberger) for their illicit trysts in return for a favourable word in the ear of the Director of Personnel, Mr Sheldrake (Fred MacMurray). Before long, Sheldrake is confronted with glowing reports about this 'budding' young employee – one of several connotations of Baxter's nickname. At an early stage, Mr Dobisch confuses the keys, thinking that Baxter's apartment key is actually the key to the executive washroom: Dobisch had forgotten the previous night to leave Baxter's key under the doormat, hence Baxter's freezing night in Central Park. But the

*The intrusion here of "Marilyn Monroe" into Baxter's bed-time is a comic reference to *Some Like it Hot*, in which Jack Lemmon's sleep was interrupted by the genuine article aboard the train to Florida.

confusion with the keys is significant. Baxter's own key is his passport to success: for him it *is* the key to the executive washroom. Appropriately, Baxter's self-propelled descent out into the street much later on is signalled by an inversion of this confusion: Sheldrake mistaking the key to the executive washroom, handed to him by Baxter, for the apartment key.

But the film's most inspired stroke of thematic strategy is the fact that the heroine, Miss Fran Kubelik (Shirley MacLaine), operates one of the sixteen elevators. Baxter is in love with Miss Kubelik, only gradually learning that she is Sheldrake's mistress. As the film develops, she becomes the link between Baxter and Sheldrake in more than one sense; and his acceptance of her relationship with Sheldrake is one of the factors dependent on his continuing to go up. When Baxter is summoned to Sheldrake for the first time he is told by the clerk at the next desk (Baxter's telephone is permanently engaged), "They want you upstairs." The phrase is apposite: superficially referring to possible promotion, it also carries appropriate overtones of pimping and prostitution on which Baxter's promotion is to depend. In addition to this, Miss Kubelik's comment to Baxter that "Something happens to men in elevators – must be the change of altitude" (with its unconscious reference to social climbing) is one of the understatements of the film as well as one of its main themes: What happens to a man on his way to the top, and what breed of man doesn't mind how he gets there?

If the settings of office and elevator and, as a kind of dark substructure to these, the apartment and the stairs, encapsulate one cluster of meanings in the film, Wilder is similarly adroit at using objects to carry powerful associative weight. As we have indicated, Baxter's key is not only his means of promotion but the means by which the adulterous frustrations of his superiors are unlocked. The sexual overtones of the key, beyond the obviously symbolic method of operation, are apparent in the very first scene between Baxter and Sheldrake in which the words "key" and "sexual infidelity" become practically synonymous. In a way Baxter's key becomes a symbol of his morality and pride – something to be abused or sold or bandied around the office. Being locked out of his own apartment is an expression of his denial of his own identity and self-respect. When he refuses to give his apartment key to Sheldrake at the end the symbolism is reinforced: at that stage Baxter is refusing to give *himself* to Sheldrake and is at last asserting his own integrity and humanity: "I'm all washed up around here," he says with conscious irony.

But it is Miss Kubelik's compact-case, with its fractured mirror, which starts the process by which Baxter is to be simultaneously regenerated and demoted. The compact is introduced during the scene in the Chinese restaurant where Sheldrake and Miss Kubelik are regular customers – the pianist, like Sam in *Casablanca*, has devised a signature tune for them – and we learn of their relationship's stormy history as Miss Kubelik uses the compact to tidy her make-up. It is a scene of some anguish which begins the change of the film's mood. It forces an awareness of the pain of adultery and the unpleasantness of what Baxter is implicitly condoning and exploiting. In previous scenes with Dobisch and Kirkeby, Wilder has treated infidelity with broad humour, but the sequence in the Chinese restaurant, when Sheldrake persuades Miss Kubelik to pick up the remnants of their affair, foreshadows the agony to come, establishing a darker, more complex mood which finally erupts with Miss Kubelik's suicide attempt. The encroachment of this darker mood is particularly noticeable at the end of the sequence – one of the bleakest passages in the whole of Wilder. Sheldrake has persuaded Baxter to give him the apartment key so that he has somewhere to take Miss Kubelik. Baxter has arranged to take Miss Kubelik to the theatre, using the tickets that Sheldrake no longer requires*. While Baxter is waiting outside the theatre for Miss Kubelik, staring into every taxi that pulls up, Sheldrake and Miss Kubelik are waiting outside the Chinese restaurant for a taxi to take them to his apartment – a situation Baxter has unknowingly contrived. If this were not sufficiently venomous for Wilder, the main romantic theme music is heard on the soundtrack as Sheldrake and Miss Kubelik drive off, kissing in the back of the taxi.

Subsequently, Baxter discovers the compact-case in his apartment, notices the broken mirror, and returns it to Sheldrake on the morning of his first promotion. Sheldrake enters Baxter's new office as Dobisch, Kirkeby, Vanderhof and Eichelberger are threatening Baxter with exposure since he has been "locking them out" in order to give

---

*The show concerned is 'The Music Man,' about a con-man gradually confronted by the human element involved in his deception, a parallel which demonstrates Wilder's thoroughness in developing his theme in *The Apartment*.

Sheldrake a clear calendar. When they are alone, Baxter points out to him that the mirror is broken and Sheldrake explains that his girl threw it at him. There is a shot of Sheldrake smiling at his own reflection in the cracked mirror – a man revelling in his split image, his double life. "You know how it is Baxter," he explains, "You see a girl a couple of times a week – just for laughs – and right away she thinks you're going to divorce your wife. I ask you, is that fair?". Baxter puts on an air of understanding, pretending he has experienced the same problem, but the gesture of handing over the compact at this precise juncture is emblematic of his handing Miss Kubelik over to Sheldrake as payment for his promotion. The sexual symbolism is accentuated at this point when Sheldrake asks for a duplicate key to Baxter's apartment. At this moment, Baxter is unaware of the identity of Sheldrake's mistress and, like most men in the company, is attracted to Miss Kubelik who has the reputation for being a "nice girl".

It is during the office Christmas party when Baxter discovers the identity of Sheldrake's mistress. It might be mentioned also that Wilder's grim portrayal of Christmas here elaborates one of the film's principal themes: the overwhelming of spiritual and moral values by commercial and materialist impulses. The Christmas party is a particularly harsh image of socio-sexual indulgence, an epic-scaled expansion of the sort of behaviour that Baxter's small-scale pimping encourages (indeed, even at this function, a couple are using Baxter's office for their drunken embraces and he has to throw them out). The Christmas party provides a suitably corrupt and licentious setting for the sickening impact of Baxter's discovery, a realisation which disillusions him not only about Miss Kubelik but ultimately about the implications of his own behaviour. Miss Kubelik suffers at the party as well, for here she learns from Sheldrake's secretary Miss Olsen (Edie Adams) that she is not the first to be taken to the Chinese restaurant. Miss Olsen, it transpires, was once Sheldrake's mistress who most likely became his private secretary for sexual favours given, in the same way that Miss Kubelik has been promoted from running a local elevator to one in the central lobby.

Baxter has invited Miss Kubelik to inspect his new office and his new bowler hat, not knowing of her encounter with the vindictive Miss Olsen. His office and hat (the junior executive model) are the symbols of his success and he is asking them to be admired and approved by a devastated individual who, unknown to him, is a victim of his success. Wilder cuts between the faces of the two (Baxter comically incongruous in the bowler, Miss Kubelik trying to conceal her anguish and show affection for Baxter) and, by so doing, juxtaposes the extremes of comedy and suffering through which the film moves. The visual symmetry neatly parallels the twin revelations which are to undermine them both, for Baxter's ignorance of what has shattered Miss Kubelik is to be suddenly and stunningly complemented by an unconscious revelation from Miss Kubelik which

The Apartment: *Jack Lemmon admires himself in Shirley MacLaine's compact mirror*

is to shatter Baxter. He wonders how the hat actually looks and Miss Kubelik hands him her compact-case. In a moment of great emotional power, we see Baxter's face in the cracked mirror as recognition dawns. "The mirror . . . it's broken," he says, barely controlling himself. "I know," Miss Kubelik replies, "I like it this way. It makes me look the way I feel." But the moment of recognition is appropriately presented through a reflection of Baxter's face, splintered down the middle. It is not only a precise visual image of Baxter's broken illusions; more importantly, the moment of recognition is the moment when he is forced to look at *himself*. For a while the revelation is so devastating that it seems it might even drive Baxter in the direction of his superiors, with their casual sexual encounters. Torn between ambition and self-disgust, he drifts into a noisy downtown bar and allows himself to be picked up by Margie, a lonely barfly. After the ritualised Wilder dance sequence, with its painful, deserted echoes of Norma Desmond and Joe Gillis on New Year's Eve (this is Christmas Eve), Baxter prepares to take Margie back to his apartment. While the two are listening as the juke-box in the bar plays "Oh, Come All Ye Faithful", back at the apartment Sheldrake's adulterous evening with Miss Kubelik is rising to a tragic climax. After Sheldrake has gone, Miss Kubelik takes an overdose of sleeping pills.

The small episode between Baxter and Margie serves two crucial functions. She is the first girl Baxter ever takes to his apartment, but Miss Kubelik's suicide attempt ruins his plans; secondly, the relationship between Baxter and Margie, the result of mutual loneliness rather than mutual attraction, is a premonition of the eventual reconciliation between Baxter and Miss Kubelik. As Baxter and Margie arrive at the apartment Miss Kubelik is discovered lying unconscious on Baxter's bed. Margie is unceremoniously hustled out and Dr Dreyfuss (Jack Kruschen) is hastily summoned from next door. Any doubts we might have that Baxter's disillusionment could result in an emulation of his superiors' behaviour is checked, once and for all, by Miss Kubelik's suicide attempt. It is another of the film's fine ironies that if Baxter saves her from death, it is equally true that her suicide attempt saves him.

Baxter's reaction to the tragedy is very different from Sheldrake's. When Baxter telephones his boss at his home to inform him of his mistress's suicide attempt, Sheldrade is not really concerned. He can do nothing, he says; and, after all, as his smiling countenance in the

The Apartment: *Fred MacMurray and Shirley MacLaine on Christmas Eve*

fractured mirror has indicated, his behaviour in the office building and the city has no connection with his behaviour in the tranquil and secure residential suburbs – they are two separate worlds. This has been brutally emphasised in the Christmas Eve scene between him and Miss Kubelik when they exchange presents: her personal, romantic gift of a record by the pianist in the Chinese restaurant* receives his cautious response, "We'd better keep this *here*"; while carrying an armful of presents for his family, he gives Miss Kubelik a hundred-dollar bill, wanting no trace of evidence that would tie him to this relationship in the city. Surrounded by his children on Christmas Day playing with their presents, Sheldrake tells Baxter to handle the matter himself. "As a matter of fact, I'm counting on you," he adds, with a thinly veiled threat to Baxter's career. A scandal must be avoided at all costs. At this point of crisis, both Baxter and Sheldrake are united in purpose, if not equal in responsibility. Sheldrake wants the matter hushed up for fear of losing his job and the security and

*The record is called "The Rickshaw Boy", which seems to sum up 'Buddy Boy' Baxter's role in their affair.

convenience of a home life, while Baxter must avoid an investigation which would put an end to his arrangements for furthering his career and would destroy his reputation for discretion. But from this point onwards, the morality of the two men is to diverge dramatically.

In a later 'phone conversation when Sheldrake has returned to work after the Christmas holidays, Baxter tries to persuade him to help Miss Kubelik in some way, to visit her while she is recovering in the apartment. Sheldrake dismisses this as impossible: "Put yourself in my place, Baxter," he says. In a sense, all this has happened because of Baxter's endeavours to 'put himself in Sheldrake's place' – that is, to climb the ladder to success. And at this stage, of course, this now has uncomfortable overtones: Baxter would like to put himself in Sheldrake's place in Miss Kubelik's affections. The line emphasises the occasionally eerie connection between Baxter and Sheldrake, perhaps implying that Sheldrake's route to the top was not entirely honourable. As we have seen, they both look at themselves in Miss Kubelik's mirror, with results that are meaningfully contrasted: Sheldrake grinning at his dual image; Baxter being, in more than one sense, shattered by it. Intriguingly, they both begin their first conversation with Miss Kubelik in the same way, commenting that she has had her hair cut short: Baxter likes it, though for Sheldrake it seems an act of defiance against him. Baxter echoes Sheldrake's "You see a girl a couple of times a week – just for laughs" in trying to excuse his own behaviour to Mrs Dreyfuss; and just when he is about to tell Sheldrake that he is going to take Miss Kubelik off his hands because he's fallen in love with her, Sheldrake casually tells him that he is going to marry her (unknown to Baxter, Sheldrake's wife has learned about Miss Kubelik from Miss Olsen and is suing for divorce). Baxter's relationship with Sheldrake not only provides the film with some of its sharpest dialogue exchanges, but confronts alter egos. If there are none of the sexual undercurrents of the Neff-Keyes relationship in *Double Indemnity*, it is more than just an office clerk ingratiating himself with his boss. The telephone conversations reveal Sheldrake to be the genuine brute which Baxter has tried to aspire to (Sheldrake, obliged now to live at the 'Athletic Club' after being thrown out by his wife, makes it clear to Baxter that he will 'enjoy' his temporary bachelorhood, aligning himself with Baxter) and expose the human callousness that is intimately connected with that kind of professional success. It is these telephone conversations with Sheldrake, and

Baxter's close proximity to him in the next-door office, which ultimately brings Baxter's facade crashing down, the moment when he recognises what social climbing can mean in human terms.

One of the most remarkable and satisfying aspects of *The Apartment* is Wilder's handling of the hero and the magnificent performance he elicits from Jack Lemmon. It is a performance, incidentally, that Lemmon has been giving, off and on, ever since: his roles in subsequent Wilder films, and *Days of Wine and Roses, The Odd Couple, The Prisoner of Second Avenue, The Out-of Towners* and *Save the Tiger* feed off Baxter's central tensions and owe much to the representation of contemporary America which Wilder established in *The Apartment*. To play Baxter as a cold-hearted opportunist who knows what he is doing might have alienated our sympathies; and to play him as a nice, dumb sort of guy who did not see he was being used might have stretched our credulity. Lemmon's performance takes a meticulously judged line between these two extremes. It is a portrayal that is at once comic and poignant. Wilder enhances both of these aspects by exploiting certain clown-like features of Lemmon's screen persona and Baxter's character. Baxter has feet that stick out, his clothes always seem slightly too small, and he is constantly spilling things, his inability to keep liquids in their containers anticipating his acknowledgement of a world which cannot be compartmentalised as tidily as he thought. In particular, the shaving foam on his face on Christmas Day, which Wilder leaves there for a noticeably long time, is a striking tragi-comic effect (Baxter is trying to get a shave but, as in most of his ordinary domestic routines, he is interrupted). Baxter is given here the appearance of Pagliacci, the sad clown; or even, with his 'white beard', he is Miss Kubelik's Santa Claus, contrasting sharply with the ignoble Santa Claus who has been wandering around that downtown bar on Christmas Eve and demanding to be served quickly because his sleigh is double-parked. The finest kind of collaboration between performer and director has gone into the presentation of Baxter, for Wilder and Lemmon would both recognise that the film would collapse completely if they failed to generate sympathy for and a certain measure of identification with the hero (this was to prove one of the main problems of *Kiss Me, Stupid*). Baxter's opening narration, spoken in crisp, business-like tones until the last paragraph when his voice wavers in an effort to receive our sympathy, initially encourages an identification between hero and audience which conceals a full awareness of the squalid implications of his arrangements until the situation (with the suicide attempt) blows up in his face.

"As I saw it," Lemmon has said in Don Widener's biography of the actor ('Lemmon.' MacMillan, New York, 1975), "Baxter was ambitious; a nice guy but gullible, easily intimidated and fast to excuse his behaviour. In the end he changes because he faces up to having rationalised his morals. He realises he's been had, and that's when he turns in the key." Unlike Tatum in *Ace in the Hole*, Baxter has got into the situation by accident – indeed, through his own generosity – and it has got out of control. The moral implications of his actions have scarcely occurred to him. He seems to feel he is being appropriately rewarded for doing a favour for his colleagues, a sort of unsolicited bonus for helping people out of a spot. He says as much to Sheldrake at their first meeting:

> "About six months ago I was going to night school, taking this course in Advanced Accounting . . . and one of the guys in our department was going to a banquet at the Biltmore. His wife was meeting him in town and he needed some place to change into a tuxedo. So I gave him the key, and word must have gotten around because the next thing I knew all sorts of guys were suddenly going to banquets. And when you give the key to one guy, you can't say no to another and the whole thing got out of hand."

It is clear from this that Baxter is weak rather than corrupt, though one cannot avoid appreciating the unconscious *double entendre* of Baxter's night school in Advanced Accounting – he advances without sitting for an examination. It is clear also that Baxter is a victim rather than a villain, more exploited than exploiting, a man who, in Miss Kubelik's distinction, is not so much a "taker" as one who gets "took".

Still, if Baxter is an innocent, he is also ignorant. Wilder's basic sympathy does not preclude criticism, and as well as subjecting Baxter to various indignities to cut him down to size (giving him a cold and a black eye, delivered by Miss Kubelik's brother-in-law who thinks she's living with Baxter), he also puts his hero on the receiving end of an almost incessant stream of insults: "schnook", "punk", "fink", "the nurse", "Little Lord Fauntleroy" and "Max the Knife" are a few of the more colourful. Baxter's opening narration might emphasise his naive enthusiasm, but it also establishes his obsession with statistics. And if he is not the callous lady-killer his neighbours think, he nevertheless allows them to think that way. The suicide attempt gives

Dr Dreyfuss the physical evidence of Baxter's habitual womanising and Baxter has to bluff his way through: "You know me with girls, Doc, easy come, easy go," he says at the end, almost precisely echoing Sheldrake. Dr Dreyfuss is one of Wilder's archetypal 'sage' figures who acts as a moral influence who tries to steer the wayward hero on the right path, rather like Mr Boot in *Ace in the Hole*, Keyes in *Double Indemnity*, and even Carlo Carlucci in *Avanti!* Dreyfuss as the 'European healer' might even be said to anticipate the effect of the European environment on the hero of *Avanti!*, also played by Jack Lemmon, but at the end Baxter feels unable to join the doctor's New Year's Eve party: he cannot as yet escape the trap created by his job and be integrated into this more humane community; he cannot, in Dr Dreyfuss's words, be a "mensch". Dr Dreyfuss never perceives the true situation and Baxter is unable to tell him the truth because in many ways the truth is worse than the fiction he conjures up – he is not a great lover but a pimp. Dr Dreyfuss's amazement at Baxter's apparent sexual capacities is one of the film's running jokes – the doctor even asks Baxter to donate his body for scientific research – and Dr Dreyfuss's moral homilies are directed at a screen character who is probably the most sexually abstemious since Lilian Gish but who has involuntarily unleashed all kinds of corrupt sexuality around him.

Nevertheless, there is something decidedly chilling about Baxter's tendency to view people as data. Even four executives using his apartment is not bad "percentage-wise", he says to Sheldrake proudly; the "averaging out" of people is entirely characteristic. "I know all sorts of things about you," he says to Miss Kubelik, "I know your height, your weight and your social security number," having looked up her card in the company insurance file. This is how Baxter 'knows' people and when he describes Miss Kubelik to Mr Kirkeby as "a nice, respectable girl – there are millions of them," one notices first the seeming idealism and then the glibness, that slide into a rather smug, detached generalisation. The point, of course, is that Baxter is wrong about Miss Kubelik.

The thing which reconciles us to this unattractive aspect of Baxter's nature is our awareness that this detachment is a symptom of his isolation rather than his insensitivity. The character of Bud Baxter is one of the cinema's most potent expressions of urban loneliness. "Buddy Boy", ironically, has no friends. Indeed, on two occasions he has to invent some – "Just waiting for a friend," he lies to Mrs Lieberman who finds him loitering by the garbage cans; "I have this heavy date for tonight," he brags unconvincingly to Miss Kubelik after his second promotion, when Sheldrake makes him his personal assistant once Miss Kubelik has recovered. The apartment key becomes his way of buying friendship – "Just what is it that makes you so popular?", asks Sheldrake with pointed irony, faced with those glowing reports. Probably the film's most haunting shots are of Baxter on his own: working late at the office, sleeping on a bench in Central Park, drinking alone in the crowded bar with his private circle of olive sticks. Similarly, one of the most memorable scenes in this context is the first to take place in the apartment. Baxter settles down to a frozen dinner and some televison. The programme is *Grand Hotel* (a film whose very title seems a mockery of the small apartment and its unglamorous 'guests') and the stream of advertisements which prevent the film ever getting past the opening credits is an early indication of the invasion of commercialism into people's lives at every level. But the scene is impressive not so much for its thematic relevance as for its concise and desolating evocation of urban

The Apartment: *Baxter (Jack Lemmon) watches TV*

bachelorhood. As he puts it later, Baxter is "Robinson Crusoe shipwrecked among eight million people." When he is suddenly confronted with an immovable person in his apartment he is at first confused and disconcerted; only later does he relax and act with genuine concern. These contemplative dialogue exchanges with Miss Kubelik bring a dimension of gentle poignancy to a film already rich in varieties of tone and mood. The jokes continue, of course, but they are tinged with ironic melancholy rather than sardonic astringency. The contrast between Baxter at the very beginning and at the very end is tender and touching, describing a movement from a disembodied voice intoning details about eight million New Yorkers over shots of a bleak city-scape, to a man in his bleak home with the one person in all those millions whom he really cares about. It is all the more moving because of what it has cost him.

Nothing has aroused more controversy about *The Apartment* than this ending. If Wilder had had the courage of his convictions, the film's detractors claim, Baxter would have been insensitive to Miss Kubelik's suicide attempt, would not have fallen in love with her and would have pursued his ambition with the ruthless ingenuity and self-abasement that have become necessary. Miss Kubelik would have stayed with Sheldrake and not run back to Baxter in the apartment. For some critics the climax is a classic Wilder cop-out, his deference to the box-office contriving a rosy ending and emasculating an initially candid condemnation of American opportunism. This attitude was perhaps most violently expressed by Peter John Dyer in the 'Monthly Film Bulletin' (August 1960) who thought that Wilder's "muddle-headed descent into sweetness and pathos might seem sickeningly Teutonic were it not so typical of him and so familiar; as it is, one is tempted to regard it as a characteristically cynical piece of perverse vulgarity." It is surely Dyer's review that one might regard as the 'cynical piece of perverse vulgarity'. When the sympathetic interviewers of 'Cinema' suggested to Wilder that *The Apartment* was "a little too sentimental", Wilder cut in sharply: "It was made so as not to be sentimental . . . We have a prefabricated loneliness in America – TV dinners and everything. With this loneliness goes the urge to better oneself and rise from the masses . . . I portray Americans as beasts . . . I never considered *The Apartment* to be a comedy."

Even those critics who like the ending offer only a partial defence of it. For example, Axel Madsen perpetuates some of the misunderstandings surrounding the final sequence by saying that Baxter and Miss Kubelik will be "happy, but jobless". "Jobless", yes, but "happy"? Their future together is surely very uncertain. On the most basic level, one doubts that Miss Kubelik would remain with Baxter very long because of her love for Sheldrake, a relationship that has been conducted on a much deeper, more physical level than her friendship with Baxter. Although Wilder gives us plenty of evidence to convince us of Sheldrake's insincerity, we are never in doubt about Miss Kubelik's devotion to him.

Only four sequences from the end Baxter and Miss Kubelik have a revealing dialogue which seems to draw the line between them conclusively:

Miss Kubelik: "I suppose you heard about Mr Sheldrake?"

Baxter: "You mean leaving his wife? Yeah, I'm very happy for you."

Miss Kubelik: "I never thought he'd do it."

Baxter: "I told you all along. You see, you were wrong about Mr Sheldrake."

Miss Kubelik: "I guess so."

Baxter: "For that matter, you were wrong about me, too. What you said about those who take and those who get took? Well, Mr Sheldrake wasn't using me – I was using him. See? Last month I was at desk 861 on the nineteenth floor – now I'm on the twenty-seventh floor, panelled office, three windows – so it all worked out fine. We're both getting what we want."

Miss Kubelik: "Yes. You walking to the subway?"

Baxter: "No, thank you. I have this heavy date for tonight. Aren't you meeting Mr Sheldrake?"

Miss Kubelik: "No. You know how people talk. So I decided it would be better if we didn't see each other till everything is settled, divorce-wise."

Baxter: "That's very wise."

Miss Kubelik: "Good night, Mr Baxter."

Baxter: "Good night, Miss Kubelik."

At this point Baxter is endeavouring, reasonably successfully, to convince himself that promotion is what he wants and that he allows Miss Kubelik to continue her relationship with Sheldrake without interference. But Miss Kubelik is certain of her wishes at that point. One should remember her comment to Baxter during her convalescence: "Why can't I ever fall in love with somebody nice like you?". At the end, she does not reciprocate Baxter's "Miss Kubelik, I absolutely adore you"; she simply says, "Shut up and deal." During the New Year's Eve sequence with Sheldrake in the Chinese restaurant, it seems Miss Kubelik is quite prepared to stay with Sheldrake until he tells her about Baxter's sudden resignation earlier that day: "Just walked out on me – quit – threw that big fat job right in my face. That little punk – after all I did for him. He said I couldn't bring anybody to his apartment – especially not Miss Kubelik. What's he got against you anyway?". It is this which provokes Miss Kubelik's return to Baxter, not anything that Sheldrake has done. Her rejection of Sheldrake is an impulse decision, rather like her overdose. The ecstatic travelling-shot of Miss Kubelik running back to the apartment expresses *her* sentimentailty and romanticism rather than Wilder's, the shot having the appearance of back-projection which heightens the unreality and subjectivism of the sequence. Furthermore, the surging music is not particularly reassuring considering the other contexts of romantic excess in which it has been used – Miss Kubelik's resumption of her affair with Sheldrake; her suicide attempt. In any case, the wonderful flow of the sequence, which continues as she runs across the hallway to the stairs, is abruptly halted by a loud retort which Miss Kubelik believes somewhat melodramatically is Baxter shooting himself but is actually the popping of his champagne cork. It is this aspect of Miss Kubelik's personality – her impulsiveness and emotional vulnerability – which makes her self-consciously romantic return to Baxter at once disturbing and highly characteristic, and raises doubts about the stability of their future together. She has, after all, walked out on Sheldrake before and gone back. As she has explained to Baxter, she is a "bad insurance risk" with men, having previously been infatuated with a crooked manager of a finance company and with a man who, before deserting her in favour of a drum majorette, has conducted his courtship of her in a cemetery. Every detail of Shirley MacLaine's exquisite performance testifies to a character whose emotions will always overrule her judgernent. If we can assume, then, that Baxter and Miss Kubelik are doomed to eventual separation (this assumption being based on evidence from the film, rather than idle speculation – they might become like Leo and Lorraine Minosa in

Ace in the Hole or Sandy and Harry Hinkle in *The Fortune Cookie*), all *three* of the main characters in *The Apartment* end up homeless and friendless. "Fran, where are you, Fran?" are Sheldrake's forlorn last words. "I'm on my own," says Baxter to Miss Kubelik in the final scene, to which her response isn't the natural 'No, you're not' but, "That's funny, so am I." If this is a sell-out happy ending, it is the strangest happy ending in movies.

Another critic who likes the ending but has not justified it too convincingly is Gerald Mast in his book 'The Comic Mind' (Bobbs-Merrill, New York, 1973). He interprets the last-minute reunion of Baxter and Miss Kubelik as "the conversion of a place of prostitution into a place of human love," the point when Baxter's apartment becomes "a home, not a room". This impression, though, is surely contradicted by the images. Baxter's apartment at the end looks less like a home than at any other time in the film. His possessions, apart from his tennis racquet which he has used to strain spaghetti (even now there is a strand of pasta clinging to the strings to remind him of the dinner he cooked for Miss Kubelik), are all in packing cases as the place is about to be vacated. The personal salvation of Baxter and Miss Kubelik, if one can see it as such, is considerably modified by their social precariousness. They are jobless, homeless, and with nowhere to go.

The film closes with a shot of the couple playing a hand of gin rummy amid Baxter's packing cases. There is no spontaneous embrace which one might expect. Whatever the future holds in store for them we know that their chances are slim for ever achieving success in the conventional, materialistic American manner. If it is impossible to reconcile the free enterprise ethic with basic humanity, the ending proposes that it is equally impossible to reconcile humanity with social status. Baxter and Miss Kubelik might have opted out of the rat-race and regained their self-respect in the process, but the denuded and gloomy apartment is Wilder's harsh reminder of what this rejection might involve..

In 'A History of the Cinema' (Allen Lane, London, 1976), Eric Rhode has written that *The Apartment*, "touches a depth of sadness that in all probability (Wilder) had not intended." As the foregoing analysis indicates, we would argue that this depth of sadness was very much what Wilder intended, an impression confirmed by the director's own comments on the film. Yet if *The Apartment* is a sad film, it is not a depressing one. Wilder has rarely been more sure-footed in his balancing of contrary moods, rarely more judicious in his calculation of performance. Because of the rock-solid characterisation, the meticulous narrative structure and the irrepressible leavening of spiky wit, the film can be constantly entertaining and pleasurable without the trenchancy of its criticism being in any way compromised. As director, producer and co-writer (with I A L Diamond), Wilder won three personal Academy Awards for this film. They could not have been more richly deserved.

The Fortune Cookie (1966)

Ostensibly resembling *The Apartment* in its treatment of insurance group morality, *The Fortune Cookie* does in fact mark a considerable stylistic departure for Wilder. Whereas the former film never departs from a basic realism, *The Fortune Cookie* employs various devices affecting narrative, characterisation and context which detach us from that kind of personal identification. The captions for different portions of the narrative draw attention to the film as artifice, as structure, and especially as fable. Willie Gingrich (Walter Matthau) speaks directly to the camera at one point which evokes the theatricality of a Richard III. Even the names of the characters seem deliberately unreal (Gingrich, Harry Hinkle, Boom-Boom Jackson, Chester Purkey) and would belong more appropriately to Jonsonian humours than to actual people. Indeed, the basic premise of the film is rather similar to Ben Jonson's 'Volpone,' with its exploitation of feigned infirmity for commercial ends and with Willie playing Mosca to Harry's Volpone: Willie's speech beginning, "When I wheel you into the courtroom . . .", imagining the impact the hapless Harry will have on an emotionally vulnerable jury, recalls the trial scene of the Jonson play, when the apparently helpless invalid is wheeled into court where his condition is exploited for sympathetic ends.

Thus, to criticise *The Fortune Cookie* for its stereotyped events or its two-dimensional characterisation would be rather like attacking the Seven Deadly Sins for lacking psychological depth. The film's stylistic framework is appropriate not to that of realism but to that of moral allegory. Against a background of competitive conflict and graft, Wilder presents an ideological struggle between two stylised characters, Harry Hinkle (Jack Lemmon) and Willie, one seen almost exclusively in white, the other seen almost exclusively in black: a struggle which pits weakness against strength, decency against duplicity, conscience against conmanship, love against loot, failure against success. It is essentially the archetypal Wilder dupe pitted against the archetypal rogue, placed in the foreground of the film together and given equal dramatic weight and subjected to equal critical scrutiny. In his working out of this struggle Wilder appears to be coming to terms with the tensions within his own psyche (is it a coincidence that the two films which follow *The Fortune Cookie* are the gentlest and most romantic of his career?) and tensions in his attitude towards America, a country he loves with seemingly divided feelings of affection and disappointment. The football background functions as an expressive extension to the theme of American competitiveness which occupies the heart of the film. This conscious connection between context and theme is made explicit when Harry's wife Sandy (Judi West) takes up a specific sporting reference by ace footballer Boom-Boom Jackson (Ron Rich) to extend it into the film's more general concerns: "Everybody tries for that extra five yards – and sometimes people get in our way."

At the instigation of his lawyer brother-in-law Willie, Harry has feigned the extent of his injuries sustained in a collision on the football field with Boom-Boom so that he can claim handsome damages from the insurance company and, by so doing, win back his estranged wife Sandy who has run off with a jazz musician. (Harry's occupation as a hand-held television cameraman can be regarded as a veiled metaphor for his willingness to be "directed" by Willie throughout the film until Harry himself has been filmed by Purkey, the private detective.) However, Harry's uneasy conscience has eventually surfaced, partly through recognition of his wife's grasping nature, though more especially through his sensitivity to the suffering caused to Boom-Boom who regards the accident as entirely his own fault. At the end Harry reveals the charade and Willie's corrupting influence is discarded. The final scene reunites and reconciles Harry and Boom-Boom in the virtually deserted football stadium.

This conclusion is another of those notorious "happy endings" for which Wilder is always attacked. The critical accusation is that Wilder has sugar-coated the pill. Of course, one cannot deny the spiritual uplift created by the final sequence – the two running men playing a game of football accompanied by a rousing march carries a high emotional charge. Nor would one wish to deny the film's closing affirmation of moral redemption: "No man can always be a cynic and live," said Thomas Hardy, and one of the most attractive aspects of Wilder's personality has always been his refusal to wallow in defeatism and despair. Willie's exploitation of Harry's sentimental side (the latter's need of the money to reclaim his wife) rebounds on him when it is precisely this aspect of Harry's nature (his defence of his black friend Boom-Boom) that causes the downfall of the scheme. Willie is more than adroit with the financial angle but not with the moral: he fails to allow for Harry's humanity in his devious calculations. The ending is a defiant gesture towards emotional commitment over mercenary cynicism.

At the same time, one must take note of the care and complexity with which Wilder places a moment like this, how scrupulously the optimism is qualified. If a description of the ending of *The Apartment* as "happy" seems grossly oversimplified, if not wholly inaccurate, it is equally so with *The Fortune Cookie*. At the end, Harry and Boom-Boom, like Baxter and Miss Kubelik, are unemployed with no discernible future prospects, one an exposed fraud, the other on suspension. Their game of football together at the end seems particularly precarious, a child-like gesture of innocence, jollity and defiance whose hollowness we can almost hear. Recall that at the beginning of the film Boom-Boom has been the hero of 83,000 fans and that the big moment of tribute for the 'paralysed' Harry is to be a silent prayer for his recovery with 83,000 matches flickering in the dark stadium. The actual ending is of Boom-Boom's solitary match in the dark and of a game between the two watched by three cleaners. Paradoxically, the process by which Harry eventually 'sees the light' is accompanied by images of increasing darkness. Another example of this is Harry's realisation of his wife's duplicity which, in the visual design of the film, extinguishes the "torch" that Harry has carried for her, previously so strong that, as Willie says, "it could open the next Olympic Games." Even Harry's transference of affection from Sandy to Boom-Boom conforms to the same pattern: it is a movement from blonde to black.

The closing optimism is qualified still further when one remembers what happens to the rogue. Whiplash Willie's plan to cheat the insurance company out of a million dollars has fallen through but by the end, in a devastating speech which Wilder and Diamond have rarely surpassed, the shyster lawyer succeeds in accusing all parties concerned of unethical conduct and is carving out another potentially lucrative area for himself. If the ascendancy of morality is tentative and precarious, the indestructibility of avarice is presented in solidly uncompromising terms.

By having the dupe and the rogue simultaneously present, Wilder runs the risk of dividing our attention and sympathy. This actually happens as the two characters establish themselves but paradoxically this splintering effect becomes one of the film's fascinations as well as one of its flaws. However much one admires the skill and unselfishness of Jack Lemmon's performance as Harry Hinkle, it can do little to enliven a conception of the character that seems irredeemably dull, particularly when compared with the complexity of a C C Baxter. While Harry's confinement to a private room in a hospital and, later, to a wheelchair in a gloomy apartment, is entirely consistent with the character's sense of entrapment in a scheme he never fully endorses, it does present dramatic problems which Wilder never overcomes. Unless Harry is as morbidly curious as James Stewart's incarcerated hero in Alfred Hitchcock's *Rear Window* or as raucously objectionable as the invalid of Marco Ferreri's *El Cochecito* (*The Wheelchair*), it is difficult to sustain interest in a character who is forced into such a passive role. Inevitably, Harry's feigned paralysis engages an audience's attention much less than Willie's mercurial energy. Wilder divides the screen time between the two, but the intensity of realisation is very different. Lemmon's scenes tend to sag while Matthau's crackle into life. When a scene is shared between them it's Matthau we watch and not only because he has freedom of movement: we want the scheme to succeed. Matthau's characterisation of Willie Gingrich, with all its hints of paranoia, vindictiveness and seedy charm, takes over the film, throwing off balance not only the dramatic structure but, to some extent, the moral argument as well.

A contrast between the moral atmosphere of this film and that of *The Apartment* would be revealing here. Whereas we sympathise greatly with the victim figure in *The Apartment* (Shirley MacLaine), our attitude towards Boom-Boom in *The Fortune Cookie* is more equivocal, his softness being as unattractive as Harry's. For instance, when he buys Harry his wheelchair, Wilder uses the detail of the incongruous giftwrapping to ensure that we are less moved by his sense of charity than amused and faintly embarrassed by his exaggerated sense of community spirit. If we never lose a basic identification with C C Baxter, however severely he is criticised, our impatience with Harry's passivity gives an uncomfortably potent edge to the quite blistering attacks on him by Willie, notably on his total failure to do anything for his family: "It's just that I don't want my brother-in-law to be a nobody . . . What's the matter, you afraid of a little prosperity? You're hopeless, Harry, a loser! Always have been, always will. You want to know why you lost your wife? Because you got no character – no guts. I'm surprised it didn't show up on the X-Rays." If we condemn Sheldrake's unrelieved callousness in *The Apartment*, Wilder compels us almost to indentify with Willie's in *The Fortune Cookie*.

A brief sequence from each film illustrates this last contrast very well. Near the end of *The Apartment*, Sheldrake is sitting at his desk having his shoes polished by a subservient Negro. As Baxter enters the office Sheldrake tosses the shoe-black a half-dollar with the trained indifference of a man who has got to the top by crushing all the layers in between. It is the moment just before Baxter tosses Sheldrake the key to the executive washroom and resigns his job. By juxtaposing the shoe-black sequence with Baxter's great heroic moment, Wilder emphasises Sheldrake's callousness. At the very beginning of *The Fortune Cookie*, however, Willie puts a half-dollar into a charity box in the hospital. He has second thoughts about his generosity when he needs change for the telephone and fishes the coin out when no one is looking. An act of a mean man perhaps, but Matthau's realisation of the scene endears us to the man by invoking our natural ambivalence towards charity and self-preservation. And it is perhaps significant that Wilder encourages us to address the rogue of *The Fortune Cookie* with the familiar nickname of Willie and the rogue of *The Apartment* by the much colder and remote Mr Sheldrake.

What is implied here is the existence of a radically different moral climate in the film from what is usually assumed: one that is much more troubled, unsentimental and subversive. Given a society in which everyone seems mistrustful and on the make, Wilder asks if it is really better to resign in moralistic despair or manoeuvre a situation from within to one's own advantage and purpose. Wilder's fascination with Willie is afforded a force and abrasiveness which one cannot wholly condemn. Willie might be outrageous, having no feelings for people other than contempt, but he knows how to survive and operate. Wilder's rueful admiration of this capacity seems at least equal to his appalled sense of what this implies about the corrupted values which that society rewards.

After all, the real sting in the structure of the film is not that Willie is springing a fake accident but that everyone, even down to the old Swiss surgeon Professor Winterhalter (played, naturally enough, by Sig Ruman) when the symptoms tell him otherwise, *assumes* it to be a fake. "Do you think he's telling the truth?", asks one of the insurance company detectives when Willie tells Purkey that the case has been settled; "I wouldn't put *anything* past him," comes Purkey's reply, instinctively suspicious and keeping the camera rolling. Even Keyes' cynicism about human nature in *Double Indemnity* does not extend to a ruthless examination of and spying on an apparently crippled man to test the extent of his suffering. Certainly Wilder shows no sympathy whatever for the victims of the fraud. The trio of lawyers representing the company could hardly be blander or more inhuman. Willie is incredulous that Harry could feel sorry for a fabulously rich insurance company, an incredulity Wilder clearly shares, judging from his hostile attitude to them. In his view, Willie is manipulating a suspect system to his own advantage, and in a way which he is not slow to compare with the way the economy of the country is run. Harry's injury has become the source of new prosperity for the family, his sister acquiring an expensive fur coat, his mother a holiday in Miami, his brother-in-law a new Ford Mustang which Willie intends to run in until sufficient time has elapsed for Harry to make a miraculous recovery. "Shouldn't we wait," asks Harry forlornly, "until we see the insurance money?". "Wait?" cries Willie, "Who waits nowadays? Take the Government. When they shoot a billion dollars worth of hardware into space you think they pay cash? It's all on the Diners Club!".* Willie's machinations seem the very expression of free enterprise rather than its perversion.

The values of American capitalism, then, provide the ideological frame of reference for the film. Wealth and getting ahead are the rewards of graft, greed and fraud; love is associated with weakness and is something to be exploited (even the dupe, Harry, exploits the victim, Boom-Boom); honesty is being a nobody or being thrown

---

*Dr Dreyfuss, in *The Apartment*, warns Baxter of the basic immorality of a credit card society. "Live now, pay later. Diners Club!"

into a snake-pit. Everyone is on the make in *The Fortune Cookie*, employing dirty tricks for financial gain. A client of Willie's is advised to testify that a banana skin he slipped on was ten yards further down the street, outside a particularly wealthy store; the Catholic nurses in the hospital indulge themselves in a little gambling on the football games and obtain inside information from Boom-Boom; the dressing-room attendants at the stadium amuse themselves by playing Odds and Evens on the numbers on the playing shirts and cheat by inverting No 66 for No 99; even Harry's doctor wants something for nothing or at least a means of circumventing his principles – he has quit smoking but asks Willie to "blow a little" his way. The film has an accumulation of tiny details like these which underline basic thematic questions: what kind of country is it in which success depends on the inversion of decent moral values, and where is such a country heading?* On its release in 1966, *The Fortune Cookie* seemed to be breaking no new ground but now one cannot avoid being startled by its prophetic quality and the way it has been overtaken by events. As Whiplash Willie, Walter Matthau looks at times astonishingly like Richard Nixon (to paraphrase the film, "Great lawyer, lousy President"). Indeed, the crooked lawyer's contemptuous dismissal of President Lincoln's, "You can fool some of the people all of the time, but you can't fool all of the people all of the time," which appears on television in Harry's hospital room, has unmistakeable Nixonian overtones, as has Matthau's performance in *The Front Page* which develops, of course, with the benefit of hindsight. *The Fortune Cookie* anticipates not only the paranoid atmosphere of Watergate (crystallised here in the moment when Willie stares into his cigarette case not to see his own reflection but to see what is behind him), but also its material apparatus. As Stephen Farber has remarked the most wretched character in the film is not Willie but the slimy, repulsive private investigator Purkey (Cliff Osmond), with his tapes and cameras for the purpose of gleeful voyeurism. "It is the detective," says Farber,

*These questions are made all the more poignant and urgent by the film's frequent reference to America's pioneering and cultural heritage. The references to Lincoln, Whistler, Clarence Darrow, "The Battle Hymn of the Republic" and "Wave the Flag" provide an ironic context for the squalid subversion of American ideals present in the main body of the film, as does the ending's ghostly echo of 'Huckleberry Finn,' with Harry walking out on 'civilisation' and his society's dominant ideology of self-interest and acquisitiveness in lonely support of his Negro friend.

"with his bugging devices and hidden cameras, poking genially into the most intimate activities and conversations, who represents to Wilder the most frightful possibilities of our age." One might add that Purkey's actions are only the most extreme examples of a strain running right through the film – the perversion of technology, the heartlessness of modern communications ("Let's look at that accident again on CBS's *exclusive* stop-action camera"). Even Harry's X-rays become more valuable than he is.

It is hardly surprising, therefore, that Wilder's subsequent two films should take place in Europe, leaving a Nixonian America to comment on itself (though Wilder returned to the theme, barely disguised, in *The Front Page* with its corrupt city officials). In a way he had argued himself into an impasse. Harry might have vindicated himself morally at the end of *The Fortune Cookie* but it looks disturbingly like an empty gesture, however much Wilder might like to give it more weight and authority. Willie may have been foiled, but Wilder cannot help but admire the whirlwind recuperation, the singleminded devotion of his skill and intelligence to money and success. Indeed, Willie is a character so impervious and invulnerable to insults and criticism

The Fortune Cookie: *Jack Lemmon and Walter Matthau hide from the bugging devices*

(the very opposite of Harry) that Wilder has to redirect his animus against crude materialism towards Sandi, Harry's gold-digging wife, who emerges as the most cold-blooded character in the film. Her signature tune is "You'd be so nice to come home to", a particularly barbed choice since Sandi only returns home because of the promise of wealth and is literally kicked out of her home at the end. Similarly, her telephone conversations with Harry, subtly coated by André Previn's lush music, have a romanticism constantly undercut by the presence of her lover in the shot, always with his back to us, always naked, and thus providing his own eloquent comment on Sandi's sincerity. Wilder's Panavision camera just stares impassively at these moments, refusing to cut to a close-up for dramatic effect but compelling the viewer to examine the wide-frame for its full meaning. The black-and-white photography, like that of *The Apartment*, maintains a tight stylistic rein on the comedy, and the use of Panavision, most of it in medium-shot, serves to underline the moral dichotomies Wilder is exploring. Ultimately, the camera's unflinching gaze at moral depravity is more probing than violent editing and agonised close-ups. Even so, while admiring the technical skill and artistic consistency with which this is achieved, one is a little disturbed by the utter ruthlessness of the portrait. Sandi's nature is established so quickly and reaffirmed so insistently that not only does the tension diminish but the credibility weakens as well: not even Harry would have taken that long to see through Sandi's callousness. The savagery of Wilder's exposure of Sandi is close to coldness he is purporting to condemn.

Finally, Wilder can only acknowledge the contradictions, not reconcile them. He cannot at this stage combine in a single character both the ambition needed for worldy success with the morality needed to sustain a humane outlook on life (we will need to wait for *Avanti!* and Wendell Armbruster for the ultimate embodiment of the perfect Wilder hero). Wilder's confusion accounts for the film's uneven achievement and structural awkwardness, but it is also a testament to his artistic integrity and his method of accepting the compromises in Hollywood film production that the end of *The Fortune Cookie* does not pretend to have found a solution to the issues raised. In this world, in which, to use Fran Kubelik's words, there are people who take and people who get took, there are no panaceas, only callous acceptance or idealistic resignation. Wilder would surely endorse the humanistic philosophy. But it is only a match in the dark.

The Front Page (1974)

The past and the present both play a significant role in Wilder's version of *The Front Page*. The Chicago of 1929 has been beautifully recreated by production designer Henry Bumstead, who designed *The Sting*, as a pastel-coloured lament for an age of innocence so strongly evoked in *Some Like it Hot*. The main settings, the 'Herald-Examiner' newsroom and the Criminal Court Pressroom, with their constantly jangling telephones and smoke-filled air, pay affectionate tribute to the great newspaper movies of the Thirties. Classical Hollywood narrative is also invoked in the solid structure of the Hecht and MacArthur play and Wilder's unobtrusive technical craftsmanship. However, in direct contrast to this air of nostalgia, the screenplay grimly presents a world in which innocence has been lost and in which the main political and social impulse is towards corruption and a destructive megalomania. If *The Front Page* has not been updated in terms of period or structure, it has been modernised in terms of attitude, Wilder giving it a stinging relevance to contemporary Hollywood and contemporary America. In the process, he has also offered a radical reinterpretation of the play.

The Front Page seems to have been offered to Wilder by producer Paul Monash after Joseph L Mankiewicz had turned it down. Wilder agreed to direct after Jack Lemmon and Walter Matthau were signed to play the leading roles of Hildy Johnson, the ace reporter who wants to resign his job to get married, and Walter Burns, the unscrupulous editor who will stop at nothing to prevent Hildy's departure. So after seven consecutive films for the Mirisch Corporation and United Artists (who must have been worried by Wilder's string of commercial flops), Wilder and Diamond moved to Universal Studios as a hired team who could not produce their own picture.

For Universal, a remake of *The Front Page* must have seemed an excellent prospect. They were currently enjoying a huge success with George Roy Hill's *The Sting* (1973), featuring Paul Newman and Robert Redford as a couple of con-men, and *The Front Page* probably seemed a familiar formula: not only the same period setting but also structured around a close relationship between two men. The so-called 'buddy movie,' which had emerged in the late Sixties with *Butch Cassidy and the Sundance Kid* and *Easy Rider* and developed into the Seventies with such films as *Deliverance*, *The Sting*, *The Towering Inferno*, *California Split* and *All the President's Men* offered various permutations on the notion, not necessarily homosexual, that women have no positive role and that men will find lasting spiritual relationships only with other men. In this group of films, women are either sex objects treated with contempt or too innocently attractive to offer a real alternative. These films had all been hugely successful and there was no reason to believe that *The Front Page* would not continue the trend.

Further, the assignment of Wilder as director probably seemed a shrewd commercial move. Would he not bring his own first-hand knowledge of the newspaper industry to the film? Would not his famed 'cynicism' guard against the sentimentality that had perhaps flawed the other screen adaptations of the play, Lewis Milestone's 1931 version and Howard Hawks's *His Girl Friday* (1940)? Was it not also true that many Wilder films particularly feature strong relationships between men? "It is, on the face of it, such a natural Wilder subject," wrote Clyde Jeavons in 'Sight and Sound' (Spring 1975), "that he must surely have got around to it, anyway, sooner or later."

"On the face of it," this might seem true. A moment's thought, however, would surely have raised some doubts, particularly among those expecting Wilder to provide the kind of formula reproduction of *The Front Page* that seemed required. To begin with, Wilder's own personality would surely be too distinctive and idiosyncratic to be entirely happy in faithfully adhering to an American classic. Reviewing the film in 'The New Yorker,' Pauline Kael suggested that the original play is "actor-proof and director-proof" and then criticised Wilder and Diamond for re-writing over half the original dialogue and for allowing such a raucous soundtrack: "In Wilder's *Front Page* the sound keep blasting you. The overlapping, hollering lines, which were so funny in the past because they were so precise, are bellowed chaotically now and turned into sheer noise." The deeper meaning behind Wilder's method will be considered in due course, but Kael's review does draw attention already to significant differences between what the play traditionally offers and what Wilder's film offers which, given Wilder's temperament, should not have been unexpected. Similarly, a more thorough knowledge of Wilder's work might have led a discerning observer to query those other characteristics which seemed to make him the safe, sure-fire interpreter of the *The Front Page*: namely, his 'cynicism' and his interest in male relationships. Citing *Double Indemnity*, *Ace in the Hole*, *Some Like it Hot*, *Kiss Me, Stupid*, *The Fortune Cookie* and *The Private Life of Sherlock Holmes*, Jeavons suggests that, in Wilder, "the all-male relationship has often been stronger and more interesting than the male-female." But even in the films he cites, this is far from convincing: *Double Indemnity* and *The Private Life of Sherlock Holmes* are both explorations of the *consequences* of male-female relationships, in which women are just as important as men; his assertion is certainly arguable in the case of *Some Like it Hot* and almost incomprehensible in the cases of *Ace in the Hole* and *Kiss Me, Stupid*. And what about those other Wilder films in which his suggestion is clearly repudiated – like *The Major and the Minor*, *A Foreign Affair*, *Sunset Boulevard*, *Sabrina*, *Love in the Afternoon*, *Irma la Douce* and *Avanti!* ? The more one examines the theory, the more it falls apart.

In fact, *The Front Page* is precisely a film that one could use to *question* critical notions about Wilder's cynicism and the importance of male relationships. For example, if male relationships are that crucial, why does Wilder find it necessary to expand the two female roles in *The Front Page*, even at the risk of undermining the original's intent, causing a severe structural imbalance and indeed violating the 'buddy movie' formula? Carol Burnett's unfairly criticised performance as the prostitute Molly Malloy is particularly interesting in this context because it is one area of the film in which Wilder, far from endorsing the cynicism of the original, explicitly draws back from it. Miss Burnett's playing might seem overly strident, but it does reflect Wilder's insistence on humanising the material by emphasising the role of the one person who shows genuine love and concern for the condemned anarchist Earl Williams (Austin Pendleton). This inflation of Molly's role might sour Hecht and MacArthur's flippant tone, but it is part of Wilder's refusal to view the predicament of Williams frivolously, as the original certainly encourages us to do. Molly's attempted suicide thus fits more convincingly into a Wilder framework than a Hecht-MacArthur one. In the play little more than a casual plot device, in the film she becomes another Wilder heroine (like Norma Desmond, Sabrina, Fran Kubelik, Fedora) to attempt suicide over the man she loves.

Similarly, Wilder's decision to expand the role of Peggy (Susan Sarandon), Hildy Johnson's fiancée, implies a desire to *evaluate* the relationship between Johnson and Walter Burns rather than, as in the play, simply to celebrate it, the fiancée there again being a mere plot device. Intriguingly, Howard Hawks, a director whose critical reputation rests to a large extent on his celebration of all-male group solidarity (this also being something of a generalisation), also felt uneasy about the play's presentation of the Johnson-Burns relationship and went so far as to change the sex of the hero of *The Front Page* into *His Girl Friday*. "Hell, it's better between a girl and a man than between two men," he recounted to Peter Bogdanovich. Wilder might not agree with Hawks but, like him, he finds ways to remodel the original to match his own sensibilities.

What, then, is the strategy behind Wilder's modifications and revisions of *The Front Page*? The clue is perhaps to be found in an interview he gave to Joseph McBride on the set of the film. "The time for Lubitsch is past," he said, "It's just a loss of something marvellous, the loss of a style I aspired to. The subtlest comedy you can get right now is *M*A*S*H*. Something which is warm and funny and urbane hasn't got a chance today. What good is it being a marvellous composer of polkas if nobody dances the polka anymore?" ('Sight and Sound,' Autumn 1974). The tone of this seems to reflect no desire to adapt to the modern Hollywood with his new film, more indeed to use the film to register a lament for the old values. What seems to be suggested there is a complete disillusionment with Hollywood and, by implication, its audience. *The Front Page* becomes comprehensible if we recognise it as a biting attack on the New Hollywood from a man embittered by and possibly envious of the success of films far removed from his aesthetic ideals.

This is not to deny that *The Front Page* is occasionally a very funny film. In an age of comic sloppiness on the screen (Mel Brooks, Gene Wilder), Billy Wilder shows rare skill and experience in building a cumulative comic force. The explosion of audience laughter at a small moment such as Hildy's faking of Bensinger's nose-bleed can hardly be accounted for by itself but has everything to do with context, the cunning with which this moment is placed in the action (the need for quick improvisation in a situation accelerating out of control) and with an execution crisp enough to make its dramatic point without impeding the narrative (much more concisely done here than in the play). But more pervasive than the straight humour are those moments when Wilder invites us to consider the implications of what we are finding funny. A recurrent image is a shot, from the inside, of the window of the Criminal Court's Pressroom where much of the action takes place. The reporters are gathered around the central table playing cards and drinking while they await Williams's execution. The window is closed and whenever the reporters turn to it all they see is a reflection of themselves. It is a powerful visual metaphor for the narrowness of their outlook, their obsession with the scoop, their moral blindness (indeed, this blindness is conveyed literally at some stages: when the window is spectacularly broken no-one comments on it or even seems to notice; when Williams has escaped and is hiding under the reporters' noses, no-one notices). Similarly, the 'Herald-Examiner' building offers no moral or physical perspective. Sitting in his glass-partitioned office (a familiar symbol in newspaper movies, contrasting with the private sanctums of those whom the papers seek to expose, but here used by Wilder with deliberate irony), Walter Burns sees only reflections of himself in the busy newsmen he controls or, from the reverse angle, a painted backdrop. If we take the *screen* as a window, as in the films of Hitchcock, what we see is a reflection of ourselves. This strategy, whereby the audience is implicated in the criticism along with the characters (also adopted by Wilder in *Ace in the Hole*), should make us pause. If we are laughing along with the reporters' crude jokes about Molly and her relationship with Williams, the moment when she spits at the reporters is a moment of double force: the camera placement puts us directly in the firing line. Its positioning in relation to the audience could hardly be more pointed and such tactics are clearly rather drastic if Wilder were only intent on making us laugh. Those critics, like Pauline Kael, who complain about the film's raucousness, coarseness and relentlessness – the general air of bedlam – might care to consider that the air of Bedlam is very much what Wilder is striving to create.

After all, the thin dividing line between sanity and insanity is an insistent theme. Admittedly, this element is present in the Hecht and

MacArthur original (and both the previous film versions were noted for their pace), but Wilder extends it by dramatising a scene which is only reported in the play: the interview between the psychiatrist, Dr Eggelhoffer (Martin Gabel) and Earl Williams, in which the condemned man is pronounced sane enough to hang, but where the behaviour of the psychiatrist is seen to be far more manic than that of his hapless patient – "He's crazy," is Williams's succinct comment. Further, when the Sheriff says that Williams is, "as sane as I am," the response, "Saner!" comes not from one reporter, as in the original, but from the entire group in unison, followed by smirks of self-congratulation. In the light of what develops, this has a powerful ring, for how sane is their behaviour? One minute opposing the Sheriff, next minute siding with him against Hildy to get the story; one minute toasting Hildy as he prepares to quit the newspaper "racket" to get married, the next threatening castration if he doesn't tell them where Williams is hiding; one minute using Molly as a butt for crude jokes, the next terrorising her to such a degree that she jumps out of the Pressroom window to avoid being forced to betray her lover's whereabouts. In the more savage, unstable context Wilder has provided, this moment has an inevitability lacking in the original. It seems appropriate that we have been taken not merely to the brink but over the edge. Deliberately, the soundtrack is never far away from an agonised scream, and the invented car-chase, during which Dr Eggelhoffer careers down a street on a runaway hospital stretcher yelling his intention to operate on himself (after "ordering" Williams to shoot him with the Sheriff's gun) is Keystone Cops taken to an hysterical pitch. If, as seems clear, we are meant to feel uncomfortable and on edge at these developments, then Wilder's employment of furious pacing, savage language and arch characters takes on a different meaning. He is not merely submitting to current Hollywood trends (the 'buddy movie' cycle, racy dialogue, frenzied cutting) but is actually offering a criticism of those trends as well.

No less evident is Wilder's criticism of America. Pauline Kael has suggested that the Sheriff, played by Vincent Gardenia, bears a striking resemblance to Mayor Richard Daly. And indeed the scene in which Williams seems to have escaped to the Friends of American Liberty, whose headquarters is surrounded by a noisy mob and lines of police, irresistibly recalls the Chicago Democratic Convention of 1968 when Mayor Daly called in the National Guard, with violent results, to contain the Vietnam protest movement. Richard Nixon, the Republican candidate who won the Presidential election that year, might have brought the Vietnam war to a close as far as the American military presence there was concerned, but Wilder's *The Front Page*, like several American films of the period, alludes to the Nixon legacy just as *The Fortune Cookie* seemed to anticipate it.

The shadow of Watergate lurks behind the conspiracies in *The Front Page*, both in the private sanctum of the Sheriff's office and in the 'Herald-Examiner' building. Intriguingly, the film's two scheming villains – The Mayor and Burns – both take over rooms in the Criminal Court, the former taking over the Sheriff's office, the latter installing himself in the Pressroom, locking the door and pulling down the blinds. The Sheriff is firmly under the thumb of the Mayor, played by Harold Gould with as much insidious charm as possible, and their relationship recalls that between the Sheriff and the construction engineer in *Ace in the Hole*. If the Mayor's schemes are exposed everyone in his corrupt sphere will be exposed as well. The pathetic Earl Williams, indicted for shooting a black policeman by accident and described as an anarchist, is an unwitting pawn in the unethical game of winning elections and remaining in office, a mere extension of Burns's yellow journalism whereby moral responsibility is transcended by blind ambition (to borrow the title of John Dean's autobiography) and the need to provide entertaining copy. When a temporary reprieve for Williams arrives from Washington, the Mayor sends the officious-looking Justice Department representative to an exclusive brothel so that Williams can hang on schedule to ensure the status quo is preserved and that the Mayor will be voted back into office at the forthcoming elections. The cover-up, designed by the Mayor but executed by incompetent subordinates, is discovered when the brothel is inadvertently raided by the police (recalling not only a similar event in *Irma la Douce*, but a virtual parody of the discovery of Watergate) which leads to the downfall of the Mayor and his men. But Wilder's *The Front Page* is doubly bleak since Burns, who is in jail when the plot is discovered, uses this miraculous stroke of luck to further his own unscrupulous career. The role of Johnson and Burns in uncovering this political corruption and yet their use of it to further their own interests, suggests that Wilder might be offering the two as grim parodies of the 'heroes' of Watergate, Bob Woodward and Carl Bernstein.

The film also hovers constantly on the brink of *film noir* in its intense pessimism, linking it to the revival of the form in the early Seventies and to the Wilder of *Double Indemnity, The Lost Weekend, Sunset Boulevard* and, most obviously, *Ace in the Hole.* Indeed, there is not a great deal of difference between Leo Minosa's entombment in the mountain cave in *Ace in the Hole* and Earl Williams's prolonged incarceration in a reporter's roll-top desk in the Pressroom (the fact that this desk belongs to the homosexual, Bensinger, is a further complication). Both men are there essentially because of ruthless newspapermen and their eye for the big story, and both Minosa and Williams seem to revel in the idea of becoming famous. The fact that Williams is an 'innocent' victim causes Hildy and Burns few moral qualms: their motives throughout have nothing to do with justice but everything to do with circulation figures. Both Minosa and Williams are hideously duped, though the important distinction to be made here is the moral distance America and Hollywood have travelled in just over twenty years: in *Ace in the Hole*, Tatum has to repent and die for his sins; Hildy and Burns share a brief spell in jail for unethical conduct and obstruction of justice, are instantly released when they

The Front Page: *Jack Lemmon, Walter Matthau*

tumble the Mayor's scheme, and proceed on up the ladder of success.

If Wilder cannot wholly disguise the superficial and heartless core of the original's dazzling verbal sheen, he cannot avoid but go much further than Milestone and Hawks in attempting to place the unscrupulous behaviour of Burns in a wider political context. 'Sight and Sound' chastised Wilder for diluting the wit and affection of the original but what he puts in its place is more responsible, profound and interesting – a dark, solid morality play, belonging in spirit to the 'black' films of Wilder. In *The Lost Weekend*, for example, Don Birnam's addiction to the bottle is poisoning not only his bloodstream but his whole personality and particularly his relationship with the one person he values most, his fiancée: the film is fundamentally concerned with the struggle to save him as a mature, responsible human being. Hildy's addiction to the front page story has similar implications. Far from imbuing the newspaper profession with 'wit' and 'affection,' Wilder sees it as the source of his hero's sickness, from which the man (like Birnam and his bottle) must free himself in order to survive.

The theme of Wilder's *The Front Page*, then, is not an apology for, nor a celebration of, the newspaperman's lot. It is the struggle for a man's soul*. Hildy Johnson is resigning his post to get married and settle down in Philadelphia in an advertising agency owned by his future father-in-law. The two people pulling at Hildy are his attractive fiancée Peggy and his satanic editor Walter Burns who needs Hildy to cover Williams' execution. It has been argued that the character of Peggy, although enlarged by Wilder, does not carry sufficient dramatic weight as a genuine alternative for Hildy. In one sense, this is a realistic criticism (one cannot endorse the cosy nepotism that Hildy has persuaded himself he needs), but given the life Peggy is offering to Hildy, Wilder's interest is clearly not in whether Hildy will 'divorce' Burns but how tough does Burns have to get to snap the trap shut. The sinister resonances evoked by Burns indicate clearly enough the dire consequences for Hildy if he stays. Indeed, unlike the other reporters, Hildy is not blind to the kind of hell their life represents. Great emphasis is given to his denunciation of the reporters'

---

*Maurice Zolotow has pointed out that Wilder's first produced scenario was a story about a newspaper reporter who sells his soul to the Devil, which is basically Wilder's line here.

existence, and the casting of 'heavies' such as Allen Garfield and Charles Durning among the newsmen gives the profession an appearance that is more menacing than attractive. Even the fact that Jack Lemmon looks rather overweight in the film has its point to make: Hildy, too, is on the slide, showing the incipient stages of bloated bachelorhood seen in the others. His exclamation, "Jesus Christ Almighty!", when Williams almost literally drops in his lap, is ambiguous: sympathy for the hunted creature or amazement at the greatest scoop of his career? (Considering the Faustian structure, though, Hildy's blasphemy here is disturbing.) It is around this point of crisis that the tension between the two alternatives for Hildy is crystallised. He receives phone calls almost simultaneously from Burns and Peggy and at one stage has a 'phone in each ear, trying to maintain a coherent conversation with them both. His voice keeps shifting register, which at first seems a comic *tour de force* by Lemmon, but then suddenly comes to represent the two sides of Hildy's character which these two people are drawing out – from Burns the angry, the ruthless, the bloodhunting; from Peggy the tender, the conciliating.

The crucial scene is that brief one when all three characters are present in the Pressroom for the only time in the film. Following Burns's orders and himself possessed by the scoop, Hildy is frantically tapping away at the Williams story on his typewriter while Peggy implores him to leave for the railway station (it might be said that the main tension in the second part of the film is not whether Williams can escape from the Pressroom, but whether Hildy can). It is clear that Wilder views this moment with the utmost seriousness, Burns and Peggy competing for Hildy's allegiance and exchanging hostile glances at each other.

Burns and Peggy have met before, when he visited her at the palatial picture palace where she plays the Mighty Wurlitzer between newsreels showing Commander Byrd's return from the Antarctic and Lon Chaney in *The Phantom of the Opera.* Burns's mission is to discredit Hildy in the hope that Peggy will call off the engagement and return home. In an eerie and disturbing image, he has stood at the side of the cavernous auditorium, partly in shadow, totally expressionless and detached from the audience and the show which spotlights Peggy at the organ. After Peggy has finished, he enters her dressing room and begins to spin his lies about Hildy (in perhaps the funniest of the film's dirty jokes, Burns describes Hildy as a "flasher" who molests small children, obviously getting his improvisation from the song "Button Up Your Overcoat," with which Peggy has been entertaining the audience). During the scene, Wilder has engineered a typical *film noir* image of the mirror reflection, showing us, appropriately enough, two faces of Burns at the height of his duplicity*. The fact that Burns is a figure of the shadows, like Lon Chaney, dressed in dark colours to Hildy's going-away white outfit and Peggy's shocking pink, gives their struggle an allegorical feel: Burns is Mephistopholes. His name, his preference for the electric chair over the rope, that shot of him at the cinema, his incessant profanities, all have unmistakable diabolic overtones. One can hardly fail to appreciate what is at stake for Hildy, typing out his story between these two figures.

"Cigarette me," says Hildy suddenly. Burns smiles, lights a cigarette and moves forward, the camera panning with him as if impelled to do so. He places the cigarette between Hildy's lips, leans over in a dominating position and puts his hand on Hildy's shoulder.

It is the most bloodcurdling moment in the whole film. To understand it fully, one would need to compare it with a similar moment earlier on when the homosexual Bensinger (David Wayne) has moved around to put his hand on the shoulder of the cub reporter Rudy Keppler (John Korkes) whom Burns has sent to snap an illegal picture of Williams on the gallows. Then it was an amusing moment, but when Burns does it, it is no longer funny. Also, if up to that point Wilder has invited criticism by making too easy fun of Bensinger's homosexuality (his private supply of pink toilet paper, his extrovert gayness), this moment gives a completely different dimension. Burns's hold over Hildy is far more serious. The sombre colouring clinches the mood: Burns in dark clothes hovering possessively like a vulture over the white-clad Hildy; Peggy, in pink, something tender, feminine and fragile, forcibly excluded at one side and eventually leaving the room. Burns, with one of the most violent gestures of the film, contemptuously locks the door behind her and returns to Hildy who is unaware of what has happened.

The ending follows precisely the same pattern. Hildy and Peggy

---

*On his way to Peggy's dressing room, Burns tears a star off a discarded film poster to use as an official badge. The poster advertises *All Quiet on the Western Front* (1930) – an anachronism but never mind – directed by Lewis Milestone, who made the first version of *The Front Page*.

have the chance of escape, having boarded the train to Philadelphia. But at the station in a sham gesture of regretful farewell, Burns has given his watch to Hildy as a wedding present which, typically, is a demonic object which maintains Burns's power over Hildy. "Stop the train at the next station," he says as the train pulls out of Chicago, "the son-of-a-bitch stole my watch." For Hildy there is no escape. Burns closes all exits. The end titles complete the vicious circle: we are informed that Hildy did not get married but became the editor of 'Herald-Examiner,' that Burns went on to lecture on the ethics of journalism, and that Molly and Earl survived to open a health-food store.

The conclusion must be that the subject of Wilder's film, if not that of the original play, is damnation. As we try to demonstrate in our analyses of Wilder's other films, his heroes, however wretched, are invariably redeemed by the end, even if their redemption is achievable only through death. The impossibility of redemption in *The Front Page* makes it one of Wilder's bleakest works. Wilder cannot accept Burns on the terms in which the play offers him – as a lovable rogue. His callousness and selfishness are too extreme for that. Wilder embellishes the harshness of this portrait: even his most outlandish rogues rarely strive to break up an engagement or plant a concealed camera so that a man can be "exclusively" photographed in his death agony (this latter excess recalling the technological heartlessness of Purkey in *The Fortune Cookie*, one of Wilder's most despised characters). Furthermore, the direct parallel between Burns's yellow journalism and the Mayor's political chicanery indicates Wilder's heightened disillusionment, detected in *The Fortune Cookie* and then exorcised by the sublimities of *The Private Life of Sherlock Holmes* and *Avanti!* In Wilder's work, the lure of corruption has rarely been so darkly portrayed as in *The Front Page*.

A lesser director like Lewis Milestone could blithely accept the slick irresponsibility of the Hecht and MacArthur original and make a breezy big hit out of it. But times have changed and the disquieting fascination of Wilder's version is that it is both an adaptation and a criticism. The laughter might be more muted than in orthodox interpretations, but it is also infinitely more thought-provoking.

Chapter IV

"HI! I'M DAPHNE!"

— Jack Lemmon in *Some Like It Hot*

Midnight
The Major and the Minor
Some Like It Hot
Irma la Douce
Kiss Me, Stupid

Midnight (1939)

"Don't forget – every Cinderella has a midnight"
– Eve Peabody in *Midnight*

Wilder's films are often elaborate masquerades and every masquerader has sooner or later to face the consequences of his or her masquerade. The exhilaration of the films stems from the way in which exposure is always threatened but somehow delayed until the last possible moment as the resourcefulness of the masquerader is stretched to ever more ingenious heights. The fascination of the films stems from the two-way consequences of the deception: an implicit comment on the character who adopts the disguise in the first place, the form it takes, the panache with which he projects himself into the part; and a comment on the people who respond to the disguise, those who are completely duped, those who are suspicious and try to unmask the imposter, and those who see through it but find a way of using it for their own ends. Fear of being found out is counterpointed by an apprehension of being deceived. Wilder observes with great amusement his characters' desperate attempts at self-protection, but the underlying sense of threat is what also gives the comedy its compulsion and cutting edge.

The reasons for assuming a disguise are varied. It could be escape, like Joe and Jerry from the Chicago mobsters in *Some Like it Hot*, or Susan Applegate renouncing New York in *The Major and the Minor* and dressing up as a child so that she can afford the half-fare back to Iowa. It could be assimilation, like Eve Peabody in *Midnight*, who covets a position in high society and thus passes herself off as one of its products. It could be love, like Nestor's pose as a rich client in *Irma la Douce* so that he can keep Irma to himself.

But one can also invariably characterise the main impulses behind the disguise much more bluntly: sex and/or money. One party wishes to gain either a sexual or a monetary advantage which would otherwise be unattainable if a disguise were not assumed. Thus, Joe pretends to be a millionaire to ensnare Sugar in *Some Like it Hot*, and Jerry pretends to be a woman to ensnare a millionaire in the same film. In *Midnight*, Eve, as well as being financially rewarded by Georges Flamarion for enticing playboy Jacques Picot away from his wife, is also assessing the possibility of Picot as a wealthy husband for herself. *Kiss Me, Stupid* is the most complicated of all since it is impossible to disentangle the sexual angle from the financial. Dino is the financial bait but he needs constant sexual servicing; Orville's urge to make it big as a song-writer is matched in intensity by his sexual jealousy; the whore plays the role of the wife; the wife plays the role of the whore.

Disguise or impersonation figures in just about every Wilder film in some form or other, whether it be spying in *The Private Life of Sherlock Holmes* or *Stalag 17* (or, in the latter, impersonations of screen personalities as diverse as Clark Gable and Betty Grable) or a detail in a criminal plot (Fred MacMurray's impersonation of the murdered husband in *Double Indemnity*; Marlene Dietrich's Cockney whore in *Witness for the Prosecution*) or even Norma Desmond's Charlie Chaplin routine in *Sunset Boulevard*. But one should distinguish between the effect of disguise in Wilder's comedies and his dramas. In the comedies, it tends to be initially enforced out of necessity; in the dramas, it is initially assumed out of calculated advantage (this is not a hard-and-fast rule, but a *tendency*). Also in the comedies, Wilder can permit the disguises to take physically outrageous forms so that the disguise itself becomes an integral part of the film's humour. Indeed, the very bizarreness of the disguise often illuminates the nature of those people being deceived. Irma's romantic fantasies are given an extra intensity when we see her so gullibly swallowing Nestor's extraordinary impersonation of an English Lord. Eve's bombshell impact amid the Parisian nobility testifies clearly to the sterility of life within that society when it is so startled and shaken by an intruder.

The effect on the masquerader is also pronounced. In some cases the success of the disguise is only partially fortuitous: the role is played so well because it reflects a conscious or secret desire of the character involved. Polly the Pistol's performance as Orville's respectable wife in *Kiss Me, Stupid* is convincing because it reflects a genuine yearning in her; Zelda's disguise as a whore, whatever the ostensible motives, is also a fantasy fulfilment. Susan Applegate's disguise in *The Major and the Minor* is, to some degree, a comment on her failure in New York: she needs to 'regress' in order to start again. Eve's performance as the 'Baroness Czerny' in *Midnight* expresses her genuine aspirations towards wealth and nobility.

The thematic thrust of this key motif in Wilder takes the form, first of all, of an enquiry into identity. His characters invariably assume a variety of roles, symbolised by clothes or objects, which they retain or reject as their self-knowledge develops and they become convinced of their need for personal fulfilment. It is very often only in disguise that they discover themselves and realise their full potential. Disguise often becomes a form of protection from the characters' own vulnerability or lack of confidence. A character might be a failure as 'himself' and unable to form adequate relationships (Eve in *Midnight*, Susan in *The Major and the Minor*, Jerry in *Some Like it Hot*, Polly in *Kiss Me, Stupid*). Only by pretence, through performance, can he attain some form of potency and, paradoxically, arrive at the reality of his feelings.

The disguise motif is one manifestation of Wilder's preoccupation with the deceptiveness of appearance. One of the ironies of Wilder's insistence on a lucid, uncluttered visual style is that it permits the spectator and the characters to be more comprehensively deceived by what they see: the freedom to look at something clearly seems to increase the chances of being confused. We need only think of *The Apartment*, with its absolutely transparent style and the amazing misconceptions which arise, Baxter being variously seen as innocent, ladykiller and pimp, and himself being deceived by his own observations and assumptions about the people around him. The elaboration and cunning of Wilder's visual structures should force a spectator to be more wary of easy judgments, to recognise the relativity of truth, the subjectivity of reality. The disguise motif in Wilder leads to a truth about his view of personality which might explain the fascination of his characters for us: that people are made up of what they pretend and desire to be as well as what they are; that they are also made up of what they project to other people and what other people consider them to be; and that the masquerader in a society might gain an insight into the reality of a society denied to someone comfortably, complacently ensconced inside it.

Scripted by Wilder and Brackett before *What a Life* and *Ninotchka* and stylishly directed by Mitchell Leisen, *Midnight* is a delightful early exposition of some of these themes in Wilder's work, the film essentially celebrating a glorious masquerade. Wanting to break into Parisian high society, Eve Peabody (Claudette Colbert), a chorus-girl from Indiana with a "bathtub voice," has bluffed her way into a society gathering as the "Baroness Czerny," borrowing the name from a cab driver she has met in Paris. Her disguise is seen through by one of the members of the gathering, Georges Flamarion (John Barrymore), but he also notices her effect on Jacques Picot (Francis Lederer), his wife's lover, and concocts a scheme to use Eve as a way of splitting up Jacques and Helen (Mary Astor). At a weekend party at the Flamarion country estate, Georges and Eve are congratulating themselves on how well the plan seems to be going. "Don't forget," says Eve to him – immediately before Helen is to discover the truth about Eve's identity and before the cab-driver Tibor (Don Ameche) is to enter as "Baron Czerny" – "every Cinderella has a midnight."

Abounding with felicities of wit and characterisation, the film nevertheless glows in two superbly sustained set-pieces – the society gathering into which Eve blunders, and the extraordinary weekend at Georges's country house. Both sequences combine a delightful comedy of manners with a whirlwind inventiveness as the heroine spins ever more fantastic tales to extricate herself from trouble.

The society gathering begins with a telling cameo of the rich being bored with their pleasures, attending with glum obedience a particularly dull recital; the livelier members of the audience slope off to have a more exciting game of bridge. A society which projects good form without feeling is embodied with pulverising grotesqueness by Hedda Hopper's hostess (anticipating her unsuspectingly acid self-portrait in *Sunset Boulevard*): she blunderingly introduces a performance of Chopin's 11th Prelude and has to be corrected by the exasperated painist who points out that it is 'Étude No. 12. (In a later scene at a milliner's, Hopper's extrovert gracelessness is to be crowned by a remarkable hat which splays itself across her head like a rampant tropical plant.) The impression is of a society frozen into style without meaning, decorum without dignity. In its subsequent use of a country house setting, its contrast between two societies, its exploration of masquerades and adulterous passions and its sense of the upper layer of society sustaining a facade of good form which overrides the sincere expression of feeling, *Midnight*, as John Gillett has observed, offers intriguing parallels with Jean Renoir's film of the same year, *La Règle du Jeu*, even if it does not match the Renoir film in its range of nuance and mood.

The one thing which ripples above this complacency is Helen Flamarion's affair with Jacques Picot. The society seems to know about this infidelity: indeed, it seems to countenance it as a mark of the society's charm and maturity. But there are moments when genuine feeling threatens to disrupt the sense of order. In an argument with her lover at the country house, Helen tells Jacques of her fear that she is losing him to Eve, her jealousy tremulously expressed as she pours tea. It is a precise image of decorum precariously suppressing emotion, the fragility of that society's hypocrisy and 'civilisation' when subjected to the strain of intensely felt emotions. Similarly, Georges's determination to break up his wife's affaire is played within the rules of the game: it would not do to express moral outrage and he realises he has to outmanoeuvre Jacques rather than openly challenge him. But underneath his veneer of control, his delight at manipulation, lurks again a sense of love and pain. This closed society has not entirely atrophied his feelings; indeed, Eve's eruption into it is as much an emotional as a social breaking down of barriers, anticipating Sabrina's effect on the Larrabees in *Sabrina*.

There is a beautifully observed moment when Georges is present in Eve's hotel room as an elaborate bouquet from Jacques is delivered to her. Georges looks at Jacques's florid dedication – "Hosannas to the High Gods . . ." it begins. Thoughtfully, Georges comments, "I rather resent that. To my wife he only said, 'So glad we met.' " On one level, a joke, an offhanded comment which conceals feeling behind witticism, rather like his elegant depreciation of the Picot family credentials ("a very superior income from a very inferior champagne"). But as well as a telling revelation of the superficiality of Jacques's emotions, the comment (and it is beautifully acted by Barrymore) also serves as a delicate revelation of the depth of Georges's love: he even feels stung on his wife's behalf when she is snubbed by her lover.

Eve Peabody's entry on to the scene is dramatic and significant. Alienated by Tibor's disdain of the high life and confused by his growing affection for her, she has vacated his cab and, by various stages, has found herself at the bridge game being fêted as the "Baroness Czerny." Significantly her first action at the recital has nearly disrupted the decorum entirely: she almost sits on a society dog. Her performance might express a desire to be a part of this life, but the fact that it *is* a performance suggests immediately that she does not really belong. The only time she is at ease in the film is in the scenes with Tibor, a fact which she recognises and is rather frightened by, since it seems to get in the way of her social ambitions. But her disguise does serve a useful purpose. The role has to be assumed and played out to the finish, as Eve does it, if only to find out eventually that it does not quite fit.

Unlike many Wilder masqueraders, at no time does Eve ever actually believe she *is* the part she is playing. She never loses herself in the role as Baroness Czerny and this poise between the two identities gives her an intriguing dual vision of the society. Her fascination with the glossy high-style is coupled with a total inability to take the people seriously. She has a humour that both charms and disconcerts her hosts. Her response to Helen's hat, for example, is not envy but an apprehension, she says, about the future of the ostrich plume. She cannot even take herself seriously in this society. When she is startled by her own reflection in the mirror of her suite at the Ritz Hotel, she says, with a sort of reproving mirth, "You so-and-so." It is this capacity for being in the role while simultaneously watching it from the outside that leads her to an important perception about herself and accounts for her final commitment to Tibor. She could play her part and be convincing in it to everyone except herself. She is attracted to the riches but has no respect for the people. A pursuance of the wealth could only lead to a destruction of self-respect and, with that, a destruction of identity, a point neatly revealed when some luggage from Flamarion is delivered to her at the hotel and the trunk looms larger in the frame than she does.

Ultimately, then, it is the quintessential Wilder theme of emotional instincts at war with material ones. In *Midnight*, the Paris setting has an important role to play. "So this, as they say, is Paris," says Eve on arrival, and although we see little of it, its symbolic aura of romance is clearly influential on her, as it is on several Wilder heroines. The "American gold-digger" in Eve – proclaimed by her gold lamé dress – is melted by the Parisian warmth, and the setting also takes away the bitter tinge that would have been present if this same dilemma were presented in America.

Running alongside the world of the rich is the world of the cabdrivers. There is, in fact, a nice moment when the two worlds run parallel and then collide. A cab driver, alerted by Tibor to look for Eve after she has run off, spots her in Picot's car, pulls alongside and forces it to stop. It is an indication even then of the way in which Eve's mercenary social aspirations are to be checked.

Tibor has been immediately attracted to Eve and scornful of her social ambitions, her pursuit of something for nothing. She is tired of going to dances where other people wind up with a millionaire but she winds up with a kettle drummer. But Tibor insists that he is a rich man: "I need forty francs a day. I make forty francs a day." When he takes her to the cab-driver's café, there is certainly a warm-hearted atmosphere that not only forces comparison with the café scene in *Ninotchka* (which has similar emotional overtones) but is not paralleled by any other scenes in the film. Indeed, its boisterous bustle contrasts significantly with the elegant spaciousness of the Flamarion home with its palpable impression of hollow people and spiritual emptiness. The café has an earthy vitality reminiscent of Renoir (*père et fils*) and one cannot help but relate the energetic dance in this setting to the frozen postures of the rich at that deadly recital.

Tibor's attempt to extricate Eve from the country house compares interestingly with Georges's ruse to extricate his wife from her affair. Georges can buy his support from Eve; Tibor has to use his native cunning. "I suppose love is safer in a place like this," says Tibor to Eve, and the cushioning effect of money against emotional disillusionment is suavely put by Georges: "When the love stops, the alimony begins." Georges, though, is unable to exemplify his own cynicism. His sponsorship of Eve swells from a genuine reservoir of love for his wife.

Towards the end, the film's serious undertones – its satire on class attitudes and its insights into the relationship between wealth and happiness – get somewhat submerged by the energy of its comic business. In particular, the concluding courtroom scene, where the "Baron" is being sued for divorce from a non-existent marriage and feigns insanity to keep his 'wife,' seems rather protracted (it might even have influenced Wilder in a much later decision to eliminate the courtroom scene from *Irma la Douce*). Nevertheless, there is a splendidly entertaining scene around the breakfast table, where Tibor is trying to manoeuvre Eve out of the country house. Continuing his disguise as Baron Czerny, he invents a child in Hungary who is sick;

Georges is compelled to impersonate on the 'phone the Baron's 'mother' and also their three-year old child to assure Eve that all is well and that she can stay; and Eve invents a background of mental instability in the Czerny family (the grandfather's idea of an appropriate engagement gift is a roller-skate in Thousand Island Dressing). Enraged, Tibor launches into an attack on the Flamarion society, which only confirms Eve's account of his insanity to the assembled guests, and he ends up being knocked unconscious with a saucepan, everyone being distressed by the blood streaming from his head until someone tastes it and discovers it to be gravy.

The concentration of this analysis has been on its thematic and dramatic features which relate it to Wilder's subsequent work. Nevertheless, one should pay tribute to Mitchell Leisen's accomplished direction, his response to the importance of the film's settings and to the quite expert performances he draws from the remarkable cast. Perhaps because of Leisen's fluctuating reputation, the film has had a rather curious critical history. Two of the most voluminous books on American screen comedy – Raymond Durgnat's 'The Crazy Mirror' and Gerald Mast's 'The Comic Mind' – do not even give it a mention. "The interest of the overrated *Midnight*," writes Robin Wood authoritatively in 'Personal Views,' "can safely be attributed to its Wilder/Brackett script and a very strong cast." On the other hand, John Baxter in 'Hollywood and the Thirties' (Zwemmer, London, 1968) claims that the film is "underrated . . . one of the best comedies of the Thirties . . . Leisen's masterpiece," ruining his case by both distorting the plot and the tone. His insistence on the film's "bitterness" is hard to support with evidence from the film itself. Certainly, as we have argued, it has its serious moments, but then it is the essence of fine comedy to bring serious themes and situations to harmonious conclusions, constructing an ending that is imbued with a sense of fresh beginnings. That is surely what we are given in *Midnight*. There is nothing to suggest that the audience should not endorse the film's happy ending, when Georges and his wife are re-united and Tibor and Eve run off to get married for real.

Indeed, like a number of Wilder's works, *Midnight* brings fairy-tale into reality. When Tibor, driving Eve around Paris, offers to treat her to a free meal at the café, she is suspicious and ironical. "This is a pumpkin coach. You're the fairy godmother," she says, mockingly, and it is not long before she runs off into authentic high society.

Here she discovers a more conventional 'fairy godmother' (albeit having first mistaken him for the Wolf in Red Riding Hood) in wealthy Georges, who showers her with clothes and even offers her a Prince Charming. But the 'fairy-tale' reward, in the city of romance, is not tinsel and glitter, but emotional fulfilment; not sparkling gifts, but true love. Cinderella's pumpkin coach is, truly, to be Tibor's cab.

The Major and the Minor (1942)

> "How I became a director is very interesting. When I was writing scripts with Charles Brackett, we were never allowed on the set when the film was being shot. First of all, directors didn't want writers on the set; and second, we were off writing another picture. I decided to assert myself because I wanted some control over my scripts. So I started to raise hell, and Paramount finally let me direct a picture. Actually, it was no big deal because at that time Paramount was turning out fifty pictures a year. They said, 'Let Wilder make a picture and then he'll go back to writing.' Everyone expected me to make something 'fancy-schmancy.' Yet I made something commercial. I brought back the most saleable hunk of celluloid I could – *The Major and the Minor.*"
>
> – Billy Wilder

Wilder's account of how he became a director, quoted here from Bernard F Dick's 'Anatomy of Film', might testify to his shrewd tactical sense at Paramount and his determination not to fail, but it would be wrong to infer from it that Wilder might be ashamed of his first film for being merely commercial, a crowd-pleaser, something safe to give the studio bosses the confidence to let him direct again. In terms of plot alone, *The Major and the Minor* is hardly safe material, both in moral terms and in the creative risks involved for a novice director. But the most immediately striking thing about the film is its complete assurance; it places not a foot wrong, is beautifully performed and deliciously funny, fully justifying its reputation as one of the most stylish and successful comedies of the 'Forties. Paramount must have been impressed by Wilder's work and so probably was Wilder himself.

Throughout this book we have chosen to emphasise Wilder's overall responsibility for his films; and few would dispute our claim that Wilder's personal signature is clear enough to warrant this line of approach. Nevertheless, there are sufficient reasons to consider the studio as a powerful creative influence, and in the light of Wilder's statement this needs to be examined.

Although Paramount had several stars and directors under contract to project various aspects of Americana (Bing Crosby, Bob Hope, Barbara Stanwyck, Fred MacMurray, Gary Cooper, Alan Ladd, Veronica Lake among the stars, Leo McCarey and Cecil B DeMille pre-eminently among the directors), the studio contributed rather less in this direction than did its main competitors. All the major Hollywood studios at this time had a distinctive character, deliberately cultivated and largely determined by the individual tastes of the moguls and reflected by the artists and technicians they had under contract: Metro-Goldwyn-Mayer specialised in musicals and domestic comedies; Warner Bros produced lavish biopics and tough gangster and crime thrillers; Columbia managed to maintain financial solvency and its status as a 'major' with its series of populist dramas and comedies directed by Frank Capra; Universal specialised in horror films; they all made westerns. But Paramount was rather different. As John Baxter wrote in 'Hollywood in the Thirties', "What Paramount lacked in financial stability, it made up in style. It was the direct antithesis of Metro-Goldwyn-Mayer. Metro, American-controlled and financed, expressed a typically American impulse, endorsing the virtues of money, position and honest lust. By contrast, Paramount was European in style and approach. Its key directors and technicians were European and many of its stars came, as the film-makers did, from Germany, where Paramount's sister company, UFA-EFA, provided a recruiting point and proving ground. Under the control of Hans Dreier, key Paramount art director, the studio's product achieved an opulence of surface never equalled by others, while its directors and stars brought to American film a sophistication and fantasy which it could not have achieved alone. Its cameramen were masters in the use of diffusers to spread the light, and in softening it to give the simplest film a characteristic warmth. In content as well, the films exhibited this same diffusion, subtlety and style. At Paramount the sly sexual comedy and ornate period film came into their own. Paramount's was the cinema of half-light and suggestion; witty, intelligent, faintly corrupt."

Baxter conjures up the atmosphere at Paramount and defines its essential qualities very well and Wilder, who worked first at Fox before signing with Paramount in 1937, would certainly have felt at home there: the writers' building (seen in *Sunset Boulevard*) was nicknamed 'The Tower of Babel' because of the number of different languages to be heard there. Apart from being loaned out to MGM for *Ninotchka* and to Samuel Goldwyn for *Ball of Fire*, Wilder worked exclusively for Paramount until 1954.

Paramount's leading directors were an impressive group, none more so than Josef von Sternberg, whose series of films with Marlene Dietrich had an influence on some of Wilder's films, and Ernst Lubitsch, Wilder's avowed mentor. Lubitsch, who had been brought to Hollywood in 1923, moved permanently to Paramount for his first American sound film in 1929 and was appointed the studio's head of production in 1936. Although Lubitsch announced he would not impose his 'touch' on the work of other directors he nevertheless adopted the Thalberg and Selznick procedure of close supervision and even re-shot material if he thought a sequence could be improved. Two books currently available on Lubitsch – Herman G Weinberg's 'The Lubitsch Touch' (Dover, New York, 1977) and Robert Carringer and Barry Sabath's 'Ernst Lubitsch' (G K Hall, Boston, 1978) – do not examine in any detail this crucial period at Paramount and Lubitsch's influence on the studio's output. There is clearly fertile ground for study here, and it is apparent that Paramount's glittering comedies are now remembered more than its other productions and that they were certainly, "witty, intelligent, faintly corrupt" during Lubitsch's tenure and then became somewhat tougher when directors like Wilder and Preston Sturges achieved positions of power as directors of their own scripts.

Lubitsch left Paramount in 1941 to become an independent producer-director but Wilder, whose career had flourished under the Lubitsch régime, apparently sought his advice before starting *The Major and the Minor*. Maurice Zolotow tells an amusing story of how Wilder visited Lubitsch just before shooting was due to begin: "He was running a fever, his nerves were shot, and he was suffering from diarrhoea. He said he was literally crapping in his pants. Lubitsch put an arm around him and said, 'I have directed fifty pictures and I'm still crapping in my pants on the first day.' " On Wilder's first day on the Paramount sound stage Lubitsch arranged for a European delegation to visit him – E A Dupont, Michael Curtiz, William

Dieterle and William Wyler gathered round and prevented Wilder from shooting a single foot of usable film. It's a story that testifies to the solidarity of the European colony in Hollywood and to Paramount as one of the focal points of it.

Wilder and Brackett had written a superb screenplay and they were supported by friends, some of the best technicians (Hans Dreier, responsible for most of Lubitsch's pictures, cameraman Leo Tover, who had shot *Bluebeard's Eighth Wife*, editor Doane Harrison, who would become a regular Wilder collaborator until his death after *The Fortune Cookie*) and by an efficient and sympathetic studio machine. When Wilder calls *The Major and the Minor* "a saleable hunk of celluloid" it undoubtedly was for Paramount, but this view might not have been shared by other studios. The creative atmosphere at Paramount was uniquely liberated and perhaps less ideologically motivated too (it's hard to imagine MGM or Columbia, say, sponsoring films as 'anti-American' as *A Foreign Affair* or *Ace in the Hole*) considering the strange route *The Major and the Minor* takes to endorsing traditional American values. The film's opening sequence admirably demonstrates John Baxter's definition of moral "half-light and suggestion" and, like most of Wilder's films, the opening is designed to establish not only the mood but the theme of the film that follows.

"Why don't you get out of those wet clothes and into a Dry Martini," quips Mr Osborne (Robert Benchley) to Susan Applegate (Ginger Rogers). Susan is from Stevenson, Iowa, and is trying to make a career in New York. She has a job as a hair treatment demonstrator and has come to Osborne's hotel room to massage his scalp with a special egg shampoo. As she arrives in the room we hear the strains of "Isn't It Romantic?" and we notice that Osborne has set up a dinner table for two. So confident is Osborne in his undisguised passes and innuendo, delighting in the fact that his wife is attending an air raid precaution drill, that one suspects that Susan's job might only be a facade: "Where are we going to have the treatment?" is a line that hints at something rather less decorous than a simple scalp massage. Although Wilder achieves a great deal of sly humour from the situation, gleefully contrasting Osborne's gradual realisation that Susan is on the level, with Susan's increasing anguish and clumsiness with the egg shampoo, there is an underlying sadness to the scene. We are suddenly presented with two portraits of the kind of urban loneliness and moral disintegration that will form the entire theme of *The Apartment*, Osborne describing what a lonely man he is and Susan expressing her disillusionment with New York. Only when Susan extricates herself from Osborne's room does she finally lose control: she breaks an egg over the head of the lift-boy who had earlier warned her to "mind your step" with Osborne and now says with a knowing smirk that he'll treat himself to a scalp massage at Christmas.

When Susan decides to renounce New York, as C C Baxter does, the train ride and the events which follow can be regarded as a return to primal innocence, a re-assertion of the values which have been undermined by the encounter with Osborne; it is a regression, a determination to start again. During the scene with Osborne, Susan has shown him the twenty-seven dollars and fifty cents which she keeps in an envelope in case she needs to return to Iowa. But at the station she finds that the fare has gone up. Her solution to the problem is inspired by a mother buying half-fare tickets for her children. Susan goes to the Ladies Room and shortly emerges disguised as a twelve year-old girl with pigtails and wide-eyes, stealing a girl's balloon to complete the picture of innocence she needs. As with so many of Wilder's characters, Susan's disguise arises initially from a desperate situation but becomes something far more personal, an acceptance of failure (the big city has defeated her) and an acknowledgement of loneliness and alienation: when the ticket inspectors question her she tries acting the part of a *foreign* twelve year-old, saying, "I vant to be alone" in impeccable Metro-Swedish before the balloon literally bursts. But the joke at Garbo's expense has reverberations well beyond its immediate context, alerting us, as the opening scene has done, to the fact that *The Major and the Minor* is to be a comedy not without its moments of pathos.

"You're a very peculiar child," says Major Philip Kirby (Ray Milland). "You bet I am," replies Sue-Sue. Susan has burst into Philip's compartment to escape the two conductors who have tumbled her disguise and have chased her through the train. Philip and Susan have spent the night together, he soothing her when there is a violent storm by spinning a children's story about dwarfs playing bowls and lighting pipes to explain the thunder and lightning. The scene would appear to be a rehearsal for *Some Like it Hot* – when Jack Lemmon finds himself sharing a train bunk with Marilyn Monroe but is unable to reveal his disguise as 'Daphne' – were it not for its tenderness and its wide range of emotions. On one level, Philip is simply playing the father figure ("Why, you're in absolute panic, child") whose kindness is in direct contrast to the other men in the film thus far (Osborne, the stranger on the platform who swindles Susan out of the change from her ticket, the two conductors). Whilst Philip's acceptance of Susan as Sue-Sue accounts for a great deal of humour and sexual tension, it also reflects on his character. Philip is the only person to be fooled by Susan's disguise and the amusing fact that his children's story sends *him* to sleep in Susan's arms points to an innocence that events will ultimately confirm. Like Osborne he lapses into child-talk without realising it (Osborne has gibbered about drinkey-poos, bitey-poos, rhumba-poos) and when Susan wakes up she is confronted by Philip childishly testing his bad right eye by squinting at a pencil – "I've been wondering about your eyes," she says. He explains that his bad eye is preventing him from getting him a transfer to active duty, forcing him to remain a tutor at a military institute – in other words, obliging him to stay with the boys and not working with men. Then there is the unexpected arrival of Philip's fiancée Pamela (Rita Johnson) and her father Colonel Hill (Edward Fielding). Pamela immediately jumps to the wrong conclusions, thinking she has discovered Philip

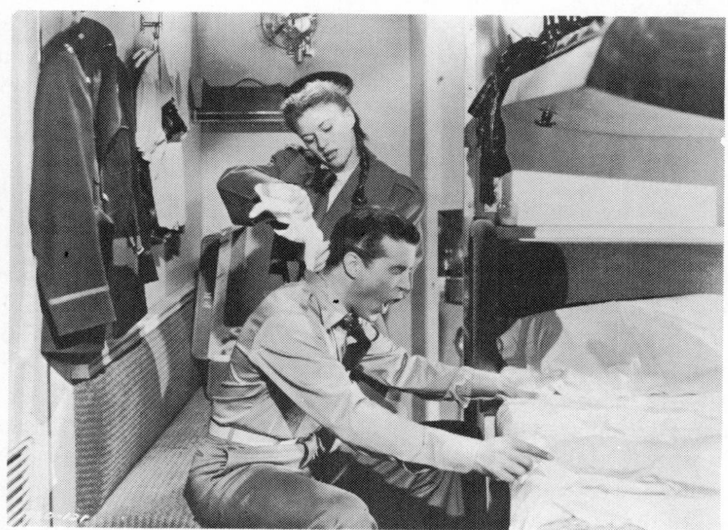

The Major and the Minor: *Ginger Rogers applies the flannel to Ray Milland*

being unfaithful to her. After an accident with a breakfast tray, which results in Philip receiving a nose-bleed and Pamela leaving the train in a jealous rage, Susan puts an iced flannel down Philip's back to stop the flow of blood. The roles have been completely reversed: the woman disguised as a child cares for a child disguised as an army Major. Philip's uncontrollable laughter caused by the icy flannel is suddenly strangled when he sees Pamela looking at him through the train window. He implores Sue-Sue to accompany him to the military institute to clear up the confusions and this "sort of grown-up foolishness."

The Hill household is presented with the same mixture of affection and ridicule as the Larrabees in *Sabrina* and the Lord household in George Cukor's *The Philadelphia Story* (1940), which *The Major and the Minor* vaguely resembles. The Hills live in some splendour: their living quarters at the Wallace Military Institute are grand and imposing, the rooms and the grounds littered with battle relics and statues of American military heroes. The institute and the house represent age, honour, tradition and fair-play (but, as Susan says, she sometimes plays half-fare). Several things are being implied here. The Hills are not only a military family in the orthodox sense; their entire way of life and thinking is conducted along military lines: when Susan is brought before a committee of senior military men as a witness in Philip's 'trial', she convinces them of Sue-Sue's authenticity without any trouble, prompting Colonel Hill to accuse the chagrined Pamela of "faulty reconnaisance work." Later on, military strategy and romantic strategy become impossible to distinguish, anticipating the indivisibility of love and finance in *Sabrina* and the all-embracing insurance jargon in *The Apartment*. Wilder implies the total spuriousness of such a mentality: that a uniform is only another kind of disguise which doesn't so much conceal a character's weaknesses as make them more conspicuous.

The similarity to *The Philadelphia Story* is evident in the presentation and function of the main characters: there is an interloper in high society (Susan); a scheduled marriage which doesn't take place but is hurriedly replaced by another; a character (Philip) trapped in a social role who is obliged to marry within his class until the interloper's presence liberates him; an insufferable bride (Pamela); and a younger sister of the bride who delights in conspiracy and whose pursuits and general disposition suggest an individualism which is forever being denied and repressed. Pamela's sister Lucy, beautifully played by Diana Lynn (who took Ray Milland's part in the sex-change remake *You're Never Too Young* in 1955), is to be Susan's staunchest ally. Susan's disguise is tumbled right away by the knowingly clever Lucy, but she doesn't tell her sister because she sees a way of exposing Pamela's meanness – "Why didn't you tell your sister?", asks Susan when she and Lucy are alone, "Because she's a stinker." It seems that Pamela has been using her influence in preventing Philip's transfer to active duty, a plot which Lucy regards as denying Philip his wishes and, perhaps, his manhood. Lucy enlists Susan's help, saying "We can work a sort of pincer movement". It's clear that Wilder views Lucy with a mixture of adoration and horror: the former for her resourcefulness and sharp wit, her irrepressible individualism, the latter for her cold-bloodedness, her scientific detachment which has given her the ambition to be "somebody like Madame Curie," surrounded by goldfish (a typical Wilder symbol for loneliness), tadpoles and test-tubes.

Lucy and Philip are comrades-in-arms because they are both dominated by Pamela and treated like children (we recall how Pamela entered Philip's compartment by bleeting "Phi, Phi, Phi, Phi, Philip"). Lucy and Susan get on (enjoying a clandestine cigarette together) because, in a sense, they are the only adults in the house. For Lucy, childhood is an unfortunate stage in the process of being accepted as an adult; for Susan it's the penalty she pays for being attracted to Philip. The consequence of this is to be continually harried by the cadets who take turns to chaperone her around the grounds and who, after the formalities of a polite salute and a doffing of caps, manoeuvre her into a quiet corner. Their methods of seduction are no different from military assault courses, provoking Susan's later description of them as "an innocent Panzer division." But if the cadets are innocent, they are also wolfish, in direct contrast to Philip who is sheepish and warm-hearted: qualities that Susan finds irresistible.

To see Philip as hen-pecked by the formidable Pamela is to appreciate his divided character – between innocent child and father figure. As he says later to Susan, "Seems I'm always off schedule twenty or thirty years." Philip might be referring at that stage to his growing attraction to Sue-Sue, but it also directly relates to his psychological state. He lacks the drive which his cadets posses to an inexhaustible degree, so his prowling the grounds to find Sue-Sue grappling with a cadet or his undisguised pleasure at dancing with her in front of the cadets can be regarded as the actions of both a worried father and a jealous lover. If Susan is protecting Philip, it is only natural that he should protect her. His fears for her virtue lead him to tell her the facts of life, clearly something he is ill-equipped to do. His adoption of the fatherly role is undermined by his evident discomfort in a tight-fitting collar. He begins by drawing an analogy between moths and light-bulbs (recalling his absurd story about dwarfs playing bowls) and tells Susan that she must put up a screen or turn out the light. "You soo, See-See?", he stutters, "You don't want to be a light-bulb, do you?" "It's never been an ambition of mine," she replies. When Philip begins his lecture he moves a photograph of Pamela to one side, subconsciously removing her while he struggles with the two sides of his character: the one side coming to terms with what he regards as a (pre-*Lolita*) paedophiliac attraction (at the dance he tells Susan how, aged twelve, he kissed his dancing teacher on the lips and then fainted) and its implied betrayal of Pamela as well as his role as father. The triangular structure, so pronounced in Wilder, emerges clearly: Philip torn between Susan and Pamela, between suppressed desire on the one hand and oppressive duty on the other. Although Philip's bad eye almost convinces him that Sue-Sue isn't quite what she appears ("At times you look almost grown-up," he says, squinting), he prefers to believe in his "good" eye, the one which shackles him to Pamela. This form of self-deception anticipates *Witness for the Prosecution*, in which Sir Wilfrid Robarts' monocle-test – his supposedly infallible way of testing his clients' honesty and character – is shown to be, literally, cockeyed. And Sir Wilfrid, like Philip, is a child disguised as an adult (again, his barrister's costume emphasises rather than conceals his naivety), dominated and deceived by women until the strength of one woman's character brings about a kind of sexual equilibrium and maturity.

It is Susan who brings about Philip's transfer and his consequent liberation and in so doing, Susan liberates herself, but not before she experiences further disillusionment and personal alienation. She and Lucy conspire to stage a temporary takeover of the institute's switchboard so that Susan can impersonate Pamela and call Washington. It's a relatively easy matter to lure the cadet away from the switchboard and what better way for Ginger Rogers to do this than by promising the excited cadet to a new dance. Earlier in the film, Philip has asked

Sue-Sue if she can dance and she replies, with a twinkle in her and her director's eye, "adequate." Susan makes the call while the cadet has gone to collect a radio, easily slipping into Pamela's shallow society talk, in which everything and everybody is "beguiling" (a fine epithet for the effect Susan has on people at the institute), and when the cadet returns the radio is playing "A Woman's a Two-Face," a wonderfully engineered comment on Susan's scheme (as Sue-Sue *and* as Pamela) and on Pamela's own selfishness.

It is at the institute dance that Susan's masquerade comes to an unfortunate end. It is an ambitious and complex sequence, when so many strands of narrative come together, and Wilder shoots the glittering scene as if it were in one of Lubitsch's mythical kingdoms, his camera craning down majestically from the high-angle establishing shot and then tracking gracefully across the dance floor. If the elegance of Lubitsch's ballroom scenes are designed to betray the sly, sexual scheming of the characters – his camera weaving around them in erotic complicity – the elegance of Wilder's sequence is undermined by the all-American dance music and the bizarre fact that it's a children's party. The adults stand by drinking, smoking and exchang-

The Major and the Minor: *Ginger Rogers is taken to the dance*

ing social gossip while the children are on the floor. Perhaps the film's funniest and sharpest visual coup is the shot of the girls who arrive from the nearby Miss Shackleford School – they are all masquerading as Veronica Lake with cowlicks over one eye. "We use them as women," says one of the cadets to Susan, sneering at the line of Veronica Lakes and preparing to dance with Sue-Sue, the only girl in the room *not* trying to look older. Inevitably, Miss Shackleford, a middle-aged spinster, is also trying to look like Veronica Lake, desperately trying to lose several years. Also inevitably, the lecherous Mr Osborne makes his anticipated reappearance – during the opening scene in his hotel room he had referred to a son training to be a soldier and Cadet Osborne proves to be as much of a lounge lizard as his father, having caused his canoe to capsize as he demonstrated the 'fall of Sedan' to Susan.

The film now displays a beautifully judged balance of contrary moods – relief and apprehension, humour and pathos. Significantly, Cadet Osborne has to *buy* a dance with Susan in the same way that his father has to purchase his pleasures. After their dance, Susan is introduced to Mr Osborne who immediately begins to question her about where they might have previously met. Susan manages to extricate herself and dances with Philip who then receives a telegram from Washington. He excitedly rushes off the dance floor to break the news to Pamela, leaving Susan to trail after him, past Mr Osborne who is desperately searching his memory. It is a sad moment when, at Philip's moment of triumph, Susan is unable to share in it, unable to admit her involvement, having to cope with Cadet Osborne's tiresome romantic overtures and his father's mental torment which might clear at any moment. Our pleasure in Pamela's barely concealed fury makes a further demand on our already divided emotions. Philip's jubilation causes a row with Pamela; he cuts in on Cadet Osborne to dance with Sue-Sue, the couple finally sharing their triumph together.

Unfortunately, Mr Osborne's furious head-scratching has finally reminded him of his scalp massage and, with the help of Pamela, the mysteries of the house guest and Philip's transfer are pieced together. Susan's decision to confront Philip with the truth after the dance is foiled by Pamela. Their final confrontation is given additional gravity by Wilder who shoots the scene like a *film noir*, casting menacing shadows across Pamela as she orders Susan from the house, refusing her permission to say goodbye to Philip. For this scene, Susan is dressed in her own clothes – until now she has been wearing Lucy's, a typical Wilder device (Jack Lemmon in *Avanti!*) for alerting us to an impending change in character – and Pamela concedes that she doesn't look bad with her finger out of her mouth. But Pamela's continued dominance over Susan is signified by her dress which has a striking moth design all over it. It is a desperate sequence, expressing the jealousy of the two women and their struggle for Philip's affections, as well as the conflicting values of military honour and duty – Pamela's exploitation of Philip's position, which would be compromised by a scandal, forces Susan to concede defeat.

Stephen Farber, in his discussion of the "mutual attraction in Wilder's films between innocence and experience," has commented that, "There are *never*, in Wilder, two completely innocent lovers." *The Major and the Minor* might well be the exception to prove the rule. The backgrounds of Susan and Philip are not sketched in any detail (Susan has left a boyfriend in Iowa, Philip is engaged), but their actions in the film are certainly those of innocents – Susan's disillusionment with New York, the ease with which she slips into childhood, her partnership with Lucy against the predatory Pamela; Philip's embarrassment over the facts of life, his alarm for his own sexuality, his feeble efforts to counter Pamela's dominance over him and her treatment of him as a child. The cadets, too, are creatures of innocence, eager for sexual experience, to be sure, but innocents nonetheless. Lucy is drawn in terms of innocence, in her dislike of the cadets (she tells Susan she won't go to the dance, "not even if they gave me an articulated skeleton") and in her defiance of her sister. Only Pamela is portrayed as corrupted, as a predator, and the film's hostility towards her might represent a conviction of Wilder's that, in this context at least, innocence must survive unscathed, for a loss of purity might deflect from the clear-cut ideological struggle ahead.

This concerns the broader context in which the action is so insistently placed: the inevitability of American involvement in the war. The Japanese bombing of Pearl Harbour occurred a month after Wilder completed shooting and three months before the film's release in September 1942. Since the war had been raging in Europe for three years (and with almost all Europe occupied by Hitler's armies), it was a major concern of both audiences and studios. In this climate it was not perhaps surprising to hear Mr Osborne refer in the opening scene to his wife's air raid drill and his own confusion at sacrificing his wife or his life – Philip, of course, *will* sacrifice his wife to the war effort. We have noted how Wilder's other films of this period – *Ninotchka, Hold Back the Dawn, Arise My Love* – implicate Americans in the struggle for Europe, but *The Major and the Minor* finally admits no European presence at all – it has become a direct concern to America's moral responsibility and its own security. The film's initially gentle references to the world outside the fabricated confines of Paramount comedy (Osborne's dialogue, Philip's uniform hanging conspicuously in his train compartment) prepare us for its most important setting – the military institute.

There is a genuinely startling – even chilling – moment early on, after Susan has been accepted as "Sue-Sue" by the top brass of the institute. She is taken out on to a balcony which overlooks the parade ground and in long-shot we see the lines of whom we imagine to be raw recruits learning their drill. When Wilder cuts to close-up we suddenly realise they are adolescents being trained for war. Clearly, Wilder's use of children is crucial to the plot, but one cannot ignore the implications of tragedy and waste as well. The choice of a military institute seems deliberate for these very reasons, since the story would have been just as effective and tightly structured if the setting were a straightforward boys' school, with Ray Milland as a teacher and his father as the headmaster.

Indeed, *The Major and the Minor* adopts such a curious attitude towards the American military establishment and its privileged children that one cannot find another Hollywood film of the time that both mocks and pities this institution with such passion. There is the very obvious correlation to be made between the harmless transparency of Susan's disguise and the possibly fatal deceptions American soldiers might encounter in the field. If the top military brass in the film are Blimp figures, easily fooled by Susan's masquerade (and we must remember that the only people who are not fooled are civilians), we are actively encouraged to fear for their reserves of perception in more dangerous circumstances – Philip's bad eye being especially worrisome here. In a way, it's the same kind of blindness and naive complacency that allowed the Japanese to catch the American Navy with its pants down at Pearl Harbour. If disguises in Wilder's films reflect various aspects or defects in the masquerader's personality, the consequences of the disguise in *The Major and the Minor* seem to warn Americans against an attitude of mock heroics and playfulness:

Susan literally makes Philip grow up and accept his responsibilities.

Perhaps one should be cautious in reading these implications into a film whose basic purpose is romantic comedy. Yet Wilder's repeated emphasis on the equation of romantic and military strategy, the very powerful impression of youth being readied for war, the play on sacrificing one's wife and/or one's life, certainly invites such an interpretation. And when one also takes into account the treatment of war in films as diverse as *Ninotchka, Hold Back the Dawn, Arise My Love, Five Graves to Cairo, A Foreign Affair, Stalag 17, Witness for the Prosecution* and *One, Two, Three*, one realises how frequently Wilder returns to the subject and how divided his emotions are. Certainly, the characters in *The Major and the Minor* are as much the target of the director's ridicule as his affection; Wilder's attitude to their innocence is a combination of deep alarm and admiration. Again, Wilder is unafraid to express his ambivalence, recognising the urgent need to fight (his condemnation of Pamela), yet lamenting the loss in human terms. Uprooted to America, whose citizens will fight to save the sinking raft of his beloved Europe, Wilder appreciates both the spirit and the sacrifice.

This goes some way to explain the tenderness of the film's closing sequences and the unique position they occupy in Wilder's work. Susan has left the institute and has returned to her small home in Stevenson, Iowa. Asked by her mother why she has taken so long to return from New York, she replies wistfully, "I went to a masquerade." Clearly, Susan has fallen deeply in love with Philip and, as she lies in a hammock on the porch of her home, she tries to balance her sense of patriotism with her romantic instincts: she stares at the light-bulb and the fluttering moths until her boyfriend, who cannot understand her mood, smashes the bulb and leaves. Although Susan can now drop her masquerade as Sue-Sue, the images of mother and daughter sitting on the porch with a full moon in the sky seems to suggest Susan's inability to escape after all; rather like Jack Lemmon at the end of *Some Like it Hot*, Susan's shedding of her disguise does not necessarily mean the full reassertion of her identity. Beside Lucy, Susan's seniority was obvious, but in the scenes with her mother Susan is reduced to being a child again. These are scenes of archetypal domesticity – the mother hulling strawberries, the daughter trying to reconcile her return to this tranquil, unchanging world with her departure from the volatile world beyond.

Susan's second escape comes unexpectedly, but not before she adopts yet another disguise. Philip telephones to say he will be at the house in a few minutes. Unwilling to confess her deception and assuming that Philip is now married to Pamela, Susan disguises herself as her mother – a double irony this, since Susan's mother is played by Ginger's *real* mother, Lela Rogers. Philip arrives and is again easily deceived, describing to 'Mrs Applegate' how her daughter made "everyone come alive, from the youngest cadet to the oldest canon." Susan asks about Pamela and Philip informs her that she married someone else, justifying this by asking what kind of life she would have had as a soldier's wife – "a wet handkerchief at the station, a letter maybe every two weeks, and then perhaps an official envelope with an identification tag." "You underestimate us women," says Susan firmly. As they sit on the porch, Philip finds himself strangely drawn to 'Mrs Applegate' – her striking resemblance to Sue-Sue, her assertion that perhaps a woman just wants to be a photograph that a soldier has above his bunk – and he even proposes marriage, claiming that Sue-Sue has accepted him as an 'Uncle' and will also accept him as a father which, in some scenes, he has been*. But 'Mrs Applegate' graciously declines, saying that she's too old – and Sue-Sue is too young – and Philip sadly takes his leave for the station, on his way to join his new regiment on the West Coast.

This wonderful scene, one of the most delicately directed of Wilder's career, is highly charged with a variety of emotions: a subdued comedy stemming from the disguise and Philip's complete acceptance of it, the bizarre touch of Lucy's gift of a frog which he has brought with him (the frog having grown up from a tadpole), and the melancholy romanticism of Philip that reflects an intense nostalgia for the events which have passed between the two characters; but perhaps most powerful of all, is the image of an American son saying farewell before marching off to war. It could be argued (as cynics might) that Wilder resists the patriotism and the grassroots philosophy implicit in such a scene by making the basis of its fraudulent (the image of American maternalism, making jam and with flour in her hair, is a phoney), but the depth of feeling is genuine enough and rare enough in Wilder's work to be taken with the utmost seriousness.

---

*The similarities to Vladimir Nabakov's *Lolita*, published in 1955, are striking here: Humbert Humbert marrying Charlotte Haze to be nearer her daughter, Lolita.

For the first and perhaps only time in his career (*The Spirit of St Louis* may be another) Wilder invites comparisons with the John Ford ethos. But there is a certain toughness and objectivity in Wilder that one misses in Ford. But by stripping down the class barriers so prevalent in the earlier part of the film (upper-crust Philip in the bosom of middle-America), Wilder identifies himself wholeheartedly with the American ideal, forging a link, too, with Frank Capra's 'democratic romances.'

The final stripping down of barriers is inevitable. Susan rushes to the railway station to confront Philip without disguise. Their circle is completed – their first meeting was aboard a train and now, as they wait for another, they meet on equal terms for the first time. The film ends as Susan accepts Philip's earlier proposal of marriage: it represents her ultimate liberation, the moment when she can assert her own identity, not as Sue-Sue or as Pamela or as her mother, but as a woman. And since she has engineered Philip's transfer to active duty, it is only natural that she should be actively supporting him in his new found responsibilities. No longer does Philip need to look at Susan with his bad eye. Their last-minute union represents not only the maturity of the couple but also the strong emotional base from which Americans went to war. It is an idealised vision of America that Wilder *would* resist in later films (in *Double Indemnity, A Foreign Affair* – in which the Iowan couple are viewed in extremely severe terms – *Ace in the Hole* and *Kiss Me, Stupid*), so that one looks for a successor to this most graceful and moving of 'Forties comedies not in Wilder's work but perhaps in William Wyler's *The Best Years of Our Lives* (1946), when the men come home to their wives, battered and bruised, and try and reconstruct the dream they left behind.

Some Like It Hot (1959)

"Very early in the structure (of *Some Like it Hot*) my friend Mr Diamond very rightly said, 'We have to find the hammerlock. We have to find the ironclad thing so that these guys trapped in women's clothes cannot just take the wigs off and say, "Look I'm a guy." It has to be a question of life and death.' And that's where the idea for the St Valentine's Day murder came. If they got out of the women's clothes, they would be killed by the Al Capone gang. That was an important invention. When we started working on the picture I had a discussion with David O Selznick, who was a very fine producer, and I very briefly told him the plot. He said, 'You mean there's going to be machine-guns and killing and blood?' I said, 'Sure.' He said, 'It's not going to be funny. No comedy can survive that kind of brutal reality.' But that's what made the picture. The two men were on the spot and we kept them there until the very end."

– Billy Wilder

The basic situation of *Some Like It Hot* – one of Wilder's most famous films and certainly one of his most widely admired – is surely familiar. Two struggling jazz musicians inadvertently witness a gangland massacre, perpetrated by Spats Columbo and his henchmen, in the Chicago of the Twenties. In order to escape the vengeful wrath of Columbo's gang they disguise themselves as members of an all-girl band, Sweet Sue's Society Syncopaters, who are on their way to Florida. Disguise is a common Wilder device and in this case is impelled by physical fear, the two men literally petrified into women, presumably in the belief that there is no fate worse than death. Complications ensue when Joe (Tony Curtis) becomes attracted to the lead singer of the band, 'Sugar' Kane (Marilyn Monroe) and has to devise a way of shedding his female disguise; when Jerry (Jack Lemmon) is relentlessly pursued by a smitten millionaire, Osgood Fielding III (Joe E Brown); and when Spats Columbo and his gang unexpectedly turn up in Florida.

Much has been written about the astonishing exuberance and

(considering the plot) surprising innocence and affection of the film which, for those commentators previously sceptical of what they characterise as Wilder's bad taste, makes *Some Like It Hot* the most endearing of his works. Some of the best writers on cinema – Stephen Farber, Richard Corliss, Gerald Mast, Molly Haskell, Robert Mundy, Joseph McBride and Michael Wilmington – have dwelled on the film at some length and supplied stimulating ideas, whose influence will no doubt be felt in this analysis. None of them, however, has really accounted for what is surely the film's most remarkable achievement: its success in sustaining and developing its central conceit of transvestism which could have gone stale and tasteless in other hands. (One awaits with dread an inevitable remake.) It accomplishes this through a cunning deployment of incident that is allowed to run wild without pulling apart either theme or structure. Indeed, for all its seeming hectic spontaneity, *Some Like It Hot* is one of the most brilliantly constructed of Wilder's films. The film is tightly organised around a consistent range of polarities – a tension between two constantly shifting worlds of male and female, gangster and musician, Chicago and Miami, romance and death, reality and unreality, dream and nightmare. It is the contrast, conflict and confrontation between these complementary worlds that provides the film with its energy, tension and coherence.

After a frantic night-time chase at the beginning of the film, in which a speeding hearse outpaces a police car, shots are exchanged between undertakers and cops, and a coffin starts leaking booze, a helpful explanatory caption appears on the screen: "Chicago, 1929." Where else? In the middle of the film, when the manager of the band, Beanstalk, is rudely awakened on his train journey by the pulling of the emergency cord, he dazedly murmurs, "Are we in Florida?". The answer is a direct cut to a shot of a coach coasting happily down the road on a sunny afternoon, with the beach in the background and with the girls' voices over the soundtrack singing, "Down among the sheltering palms." Wilder's crisp evocation of Chicago and Miami is not only a matter of indicating location: it establishes contrasting atmospheres and values just as importantly as Wendell Armbruster's journey from America to Italy in *Avanti!* Chicago is associated with night, death, violence and gangsters: it is predominantly the domain of the male. Miami, on the other hand, is immediately associated with sun, life and song: it is predominantly a female world. The millionaires lining the Miami hotel terrace are shrivelled masculine figures who snap to attention at the appearance of the women. Osgood Fielding III looks tiny beside Jerry, disguised as Daphne (or "Cinderella II" as she calls herself when Osgood is introducing himself and helping her on with 'her' shoe), and his conversation rapidly reveals a dominating mother behind the scenes who is keeping score of his disastrous marriages. In his planned seduction of Sugar, even Joe has to disguise himself as an *impotent* millionaire needing to be dominated and revived by the female. Thus, getting away from Chicago appropriately involves for Joe and Jerry not only a movement from the sound of gunfire, from a world of cacophony to a world of harmony, it involves a movement from male to female. (Appropriately, when fleeing Florida at the end becomes equally imperative for them, having witnessed *another* gangland rub-out, this involves a movement from female to male which, in the case of Jerry, is only half successful.) Thus, when Columbo's gangsters are to arrive in Miami towards the end of the film they look completely incongruous in this world of women and song. Even as the "Friends of Italian Opera" – the convention to which they have been nominally invited – both gangsters and cop seem to think that 'Rigoletto' is either the name of a nightclub or a member of the Mafia. And the gang is ultimately to be mown down to the sound of music – a lusty rendering of "For He's a Jolly Good Fellow" accompanies a hit-man who pops out of a birthday cake for Spats and starts blasting with his machine-gun.

The physical transportation from Chicago to Miami and the physical transformation from male to female is to have similarly disorientating effects on our two heroes. In Chicago Jerry has been dominated and bullied by Joe and is clearly the weaker of the two, seemingly a hypochondriac (his toothache) and with little flair with women. Joe, on the other hand, is smooth-talking, persuasive, a con-man and something of an expert with women ("Isn't he a bit of terrific?", says Jerry to the camera after Joe has made a conquest) whom he treats callously and as something to be exploited. What Wilder is to do, hilariously and sometimes movingly in the development of the film, is to explore the transformation in character which both men undergo when suffering this sexual sea-change, and to satirise the stereotyping of male and female roles, which are taken in logical stages to comically absurd conclusions. This is probably seen at its extreme in the celebrated scene on the yacht between Joe and Sugar where the erstwhile womaniser, compelled to pretend femininity to save his life and now compelled to feign impotence to further his romance, conducts a seduction scene flat on his back which can only succeed through his playing the passive feminine role himself and *being* seduced!

What has happened almost at once is that the necessitated disguise has reversed their characters. When talking man to man, their relationship stays the same: Jerry is still the dupe and Joe remains the exploiter. But in disguise they are transformed. Joe becomes quiet, sombre and inhibited, while Jerry in female garb becomes extrovert, fun-loving and generous-hearted. Even in female disguise Joe never loses sight of his own identity: he moves only from Joe to Jo-sephine. Instead of becoming Geraldine, a clear extension of his masculine self, Jerry walks into the train compartment and announces joyously to the girls, "Hi! I'm the bass fiddle, just call me Daphne!". This has been anticipated in the scene at the station where the two introduce themselves to the bandleader, Sweet Sue, and the manager, Beanstalk (whose own relationship is one of subverted roles, Sweet Sue being

Some Like it Hot: *Jack Lemmon, Tony Curtis and the girls on the train*

aggressive and demanding, Beanstalk cowardly and suppliant). "We're the new girls," says Joe, to which Jerry adds with what retrospectively seems rather like relish, "Brand new." Cautioned by Joe on the train to remember that "you're a girl" (when he is getting over-excited at the prospect of all this female company), Jerry finally loses himself in the role of Daphne to such a degree that Joe has to make him repeat, "I'm a boy." The effect on Joe of this role reversal is ultimately to make him more human and sympathetic, less callous in his attitude to women. When Jerry/Daphne is complaining about being pinched in the elevator, Joe comments seriously, "Now you know how the other half lives." Admittedly, a large element of exploitation is involved in his relationship with Sugar, but at a crucial stage, as we shall see, he finds he can no longer go through with it. Conversely, the effect on Jerry is to make him enjoy being a girl so much that he becomes engaged to Osgood, can think of no reason why the wedding shouldn't go ahead, and, to Joe's bemused query of "Why would a guy want to marry a guy?", can come up with the instant answer: "Security."

If the use of deception is a characteristic comic device of Wilder's, one can nevertheless appreciate from the outline offered so far some of the considerable risks he has undertaken. By all accounts, one of the first arguments with Marilyn Monroe was whether the film should be in colour or not: Wilder insisted on black and white, which is certainly to his purpose in creating the atmosphere of the classic gangster film but also, and perhaps more importantly, to override the otherwise insuperable make-up problems of his two heroes. Colour would have made the disguise not only implausible but crude and obvious. Clearly, the transvestism involves problems of taste, which Wilder solves partially through the pace and logic with which the film moves from one event to the next, allowing the spectator no time to reflect on possible dubious areas of content. The recurrent shots of the train wheels or the revolving indicator on the lift have the effect of winding the film up like a coiled spring, and might very well have been influenced by another very great black comedy which uses similar devices, also walks a tightrope of good taste and is similarly original in its confluence of romance and death – Charles Chaplin's *Monsieur Verdoux*.

Wilder's other main solution to the challenge is the construction of a very powerful motive for disguise. Financial or sexual gain is the usual motive behind a Wilder disguise, not shuddering fear (unless one counts indirect cases like the writer in *Sunset Boulevard*, whose various subterfuges are instigated to some degree by a pathological fear of failure). And, as Wilder and Diamond have said, structurally the main decision with *Some Like it Hot* was to find an event sufficiently powerful to keep the two men in their disguise: if they could validate this, then the issue of questionable taste would no longer arise. Hence, not only the presence of the St Valentine's Day Massacre, but also its brutal staging which echoes throughout the entire film. Wilder's visuals keep the threat before us even in the midst of the comic highjinks, the bullet-holes in Jerry's double-bass being probably the best example of this ("Where did those holes come from?", asks Sweet Sue at one stage, to which Jerry replies, none too convincingly, "Er . . . Mice?"). Much of the dialogue, too, keeps the threat of murder in the foreground: "We wouldn't be caught dead in Chicago"; "I'm a girl, I wish I was dead." The insistence on and strange fusion of death, being caught, being a girl and being a guy, keep the 'fantasy' of their disguise rooted in their struggle for survival. As Jerry points out in his Daphne outfit, they must not get themselves caught and killed: after all, what would the mortician think when he examined them? "I tell you Joe, I'd just *die* of shame." One has only to recall the Chicago scenes, with their prevailing funereal imagery, which blankets the film even before the massacre in the garage – the hearse, the coffin, the disguised speakeasy whose front is a funeral parlour, the password of "I've come for Grandma's funeral", the bald-headed organist with uncanny resemblance to Stroheim in *Sunset Boulevard*. The blood group of the two heroes (Type O) is constantly referred to, reminding us that it is in constant danger of being spilled. Even in his seduction scene with Sugar, Joe cannot forbear inventing a tale about his myopic fiancée who fell to her death when vainly attempting to kiss him above the Grand Canyon ("Eight hours later they brought her up by mule"). The linking of romance and death in this absurd little story takes us right back to the atmosphere of that massacre on St *Valentine's* Day. The grim context, like the prisoner-of-war camp in *Stalag 17*, gives the comic foreground not only an extra intensity but a peculiar resilience and sanity. Wilder's allegiance is always to characters who survive on their own wits, however disreputably, rather than characters who sink into masochistic despair.

Nevertheless, it would be an unusually timorous Wilder who did not delve into the character implications of the disguise, over and above the heroes' adoption of it in order to stay alive. Structurally, another problem must have been the one of occupying the heroes between the period when they first don the disguises and that when Spats Columbo and his gang re-appear. What happens is a fascinating investigation and contrast of character. Joe goes into reverse; Jerry regresses.

Joe's millionaire disguise in Florida, to lure Sugar, is assumed in order to gain a sexual advantage. Two lovers in Wilder rarely meet initially on equal terms and even Sugar pretends to be more of a society girl than she actually is – "My father was a conductor," she says. "Where did he conduct?", asks Joe. "On the Baltimore-Ohio" – but sadly doesn't carry the conviction needed for it. Joe takes care to conform exactly to the stereotype of the ideal man whom Sugar has described to him on the train, a stereotype which is exactly the opposite of the character we have originally seen Joe to be: shy, bespectacled, clever, very rich and totally inexperienced with women. It is close to Monroe's description of her ideal man in *The Seven Year*

Some Like it Hot: *Tony Curtis (playing Cary Grant) and Marilyn Monroe*

Itch and is Wilder's sly reference both to the character of Sugar (her search for a Sugar daddy) and to Monroe herself (quiet, bespectacled, intellectual: Wilder must have had in some part of his mind Monroe's husband and 'ideal man' of the time, Arthur Miller). If Wilder is merging the fantasy Monroe with the real one at this point, he is to perform the same service for Tony Curtis.

If Curtis might not have had any illusions about becoming Arthur Miller, he seems to have some about becoming the light-comic substitute for Cary Grant, and Wilder generously gives him an extended crack at the role, down to that unmistakable voice. "Nobody talks like that!" cries Jerry/Daphne in baffled disbelief at Joe's impersonation (and, of course, in 1929 they didn't). Indeed, Joe's performance as the heir to Shell Oil is a double reversal: of his own customary self-assurance with women; and of the screen persona of Cary Grant whose debonair romanticism has been haplessly transformed by Joe's (and Curtis's) performance into near-sighted impotence. In upending movie stereotypes, Wilder seizes the opportunity to undermine the image of the cinema's most dexterous lover by having him seduced by the cinema's ultimate sex-symbol.*

The seduction scene of Osgood Fielding's 'borrowed' yacht, then, has the appropriate sense of an event seen through the wrong end of a telescope. Everything is the reverse of what one would normally expect. Joe even has to drive to the yacht in the small launch in reverse gear as he is unable to master the gear-box ("It's an experimental model," he blusters to Sugar who is only too thrilled to be going in any direction with a millionaire). And this seduction scene in reverse – with the woman on top of the man, attempting to defrost his frigidity (one of the first signs of this is that his glasses begin to steam up) – is paralleled by events ashore, where there is a tango in reverse being performed by Daphne and Osgood, in which the

---

*One of the running jokes of Wilder's career has been his failure to procure the services of Cary Grant, despite the actor's willingness to work with the director – Wilder had written Leon in *Ninotchka*, Linus in *Sabrina* and Frank Flannagan in *Love in the Afternoon* specifically for Grant. Grant's brilliant transvestite performance in Howard Hawks' *I Was A Male War Bride* (1949) might well have been an influence on *Some Like It Hot*. By the 'Fifties, Wilder seems to have become fatalistic about the whole business and resorted to having actors in his films *impersonate* Grant: Dunbar's friend in *Stalag 17* and Curtis in *Some Like It Hot*. An uncanny coincidence Wilder would not have been aware of at the time emerged in Alfred Hitchcock's *North by Northwest*, made the same year as *Some Like It Hot*, in which Grant – like Tony Curtis in Wilder's film – walks down the platform at Chicago Station in disguise as a railway porter.

'woman' keeps assuming the dominant role ("Daphne, you're leading again").

All of this role-playing and role-reversal culminates in what is probably the film's most remarkable moment. Joe and Jerry have discovered that the gangsters have come to Miami and their detection is inevitable. Jerry/Daphne will have to desert Osgood ("I will never again find a man so good to me," he sighs) and Joe will have to resume his Josephine disguise to get out of the hotel. But instead of discarding the millionaire pose and disappearing he must, he believes, telephone Sugar with some sort of explanation. Nevertheless, the gangsters see through the disguise because of the bullet-holes in Jerry's double-bass and a furious chase through the hotel ensues, during which they witness the second gangland killings. While they are hiding in the hotel and in danger of being discovered at any moment, Joe/Josephine hears the voice of Sugar singing with Sweet Sue's band. As Daphne/Jerry telephones Osgood to suggest a rapid elopement, Joe is drawn towards the stage, attracted and saddened by Sugar's plaintive rendering of "I'm Through With Love," a song of heartbreak and loss. Indescribably moved, Joe/Josephine walks on to the stage, moves towards Sugar, kisses her passionately on her lips and, looking into her tear-stained eyes, says, "None of that Sugar. No guy is worth it."

Richard Corliss has commented potently on this moment: "Those who think of Wilder as a small-time cynic, peddling imitation Berliner *Weltschmerz*, will find their definitive refutation in the conviction, technique, assurance and audacity of a simple kiss between an ageing sex queen and a Bronx boy in drag." Corliss is absolutely right: as well as being one of the most moving moments in Monroe's screen career – the song a poignant testament to her personality both on and off the screen – it is one of the most audacious and yet most touching moments in American screen comedy. The audacity is plain enough: Hollywood's supreme sex-symbol is given her most passionate screen kiss by another woman. But it is also touching because of the exquisite rendering of the song which the kiss both celebrates and rewards, and because of the redemptive development of Joe's character. It is the moment when he decides to risk disclosure to the gangsters who are hovering in the background ("Wait a minute, that ain't no dame!" yells one of the hoods) – because the fear which has originally driven him from Chicago has been transcended by a commitment to the heartbroken Sugar. "None of that Sugar. No guy is worth it," is a renunciation of his callous, exploitative attitude towards women at the beginning of the film, which his subsequent progress has helped to exorcise. Chauvinism has given way to compassion.

A very different fate is in store for Jerry. The moment he declares, "Hi! I'm Daphne" he is effectively saying goodbye to his masculine world, his male self. Steve Seidman notes that, "in Greek mythology Daphne was a nymph who resisted the attentions of Apollo by transforming herself into a tree, a transformation which lasted for eternity." If it seems a little incongruous to invoke Greek mythology in connection with *Some Like It Hot* it is nevertheless intriguing to note that in the scene prior to the tango dance which seals Daphne's engagement to Osgood, great play is made of the character coiling 'herself' around a tree as she playfully converses with Osgood. And the central thrust of the analogy is correct: Jerry's adoption of Daphne is a role from which he cannot escape.

Perhaps a more appropriate comparison would be with Franz Kafka (ostensibly, this might seem as incongruous an analogy as Greek mythology, though Joseph McBride and Michael Wilmington, in a different context, have suggested that, "Wilder has more in common with that other Jewish humourist, Franz Kafka, than he would care to admit," and certainly his subsequent film, *The Apartment*, has distinct Kafkaesque overtones). As with Kafka, and particularly the Kafka of 'Metamorphosis', which also has a hero transformed overnight into a role he finds is impossible to shed, the world of *Some Like It Hot* is a shifting hallucination between dream and nightmare. Early in the film, before the massacre in the garage, Joe has launched into a ringing satire of Jerry's innate pessimism: "Suppose Mary Pickford divorces Douglas Fairbanks," he crows tauntingly, "suppose the Dodgers leave Brooklyn, suppose the Stock Market collapses." Through an enumeration of cataclysmic events of mounting improbability, Joe presents an ironical prediction of a world of chaos and nightmare – which, in fact, just beyond the immediate reality of the film, is ultimately to emerge. Even more strikingly, in the middle of the film when they are aboard the train, Jerry tells Joe of a childhood dream of "being locked in a pastry shop with goodies all around." He is referring to his present situation of being surrounded by all these beautiful girls. But this dream assumes a nightmarish dimension when he and Joe are trapped in the banquet hall of Little Bonaparte and his mobsters, and the huge birthday cake wheeled in for Spats turns out to contain something lethal. "Something in the cake didn't agree with him," says Little Bonaparte laconically. "Nobody leave the room until I get the recipe," says the cop. The 'goodies all around' (even the assassin plans to take some of the cake home to his child) are now stained with blood. The film's furious pace and its unceasing invention keep it just one step ahead of nightmare and desolation.

The other quality of the film that keeps the nightmare at arm's length is its tenderness. Jerry's childhood dream might eventually turn to nightmare, but on the train the dream is re-lived in all its intensity. Daphne's private conversation with Sugar gradually swells into a party in Daphne's berth for all the girls. The accumulation of people in this tiny space ('the goodies all around') invites comparison with the famous cabin scene in *A Night at the Opera* (1935), but Wilder seems to have a different object in mind. The cramped spaces and the bodies cramming themselves into it give the setting the appearance of a doll's house. Jerry's childhood dream has not only been realised but almost recreated in its original form. The scene becomes one of incredibly pure primal innocence, a blissful regression into pre-sexual childish glee.

Where is Jerry heading? As the film develops, Jack Lemmon begins to grow more and more like Marilyn Monroe (at one point, on the beach, Monroe even expresses her admiration for Lemmon's 'figure'). From the time that Daphne claims Sugar's gin flask as her own (to protect her from Sweet Sue's wrath), a strange transference starts to take place. Just as it is Daphne who finds the genuine sugar daddy that Sugar is searching for, so Sugar is on the receiving end of all Daphne's gifts from Osgood, quickly purloined by Joe in his millionaire guise. "Do you like it?", asks Sugar, displaying her gift from the millionaire, "I always did," Daphne says, recognising the diamond bracelet Osgood had given her. Can Jerry retrieve his male self? Even his disguise as a bell-boy during his flight from the gangsters is betrayed by his high-heeled shoes. Throughout the film Jerry is completely accepted as a woman. By systematically denying Jerry all traces of masculinity Wilder prepares us for one of the most celebrated of all screen dénouements.

Some Like It Hot concludes with two confessions aboard Osgood's launch. A confession sequence is typical in Wilder but these are unusual confessions, a remarkable set of variations on that characteristic moment when the hero has to extricate himself from a fraudulent or no longer tenable situation. Without going into the ramifications of his disguise as Josephine, Joe tears off his wig and explains to Sugar that he is a dissolute saxophone player and not a millionaire. Sugar's kiss betokens forgiveness in a way that matches his conciliation and also a submission to her perennial weakness for saxaphone players – jazz musicians being invariably synonomous with disreputable irresponsibility (compare, for example, the man who runs off with Harry Hinkle's wife in *The Fortune Cookie*). The honesty and passion of that kiss forestalls an audience's speculation on the future instability of the relationship. It is another dark area kept just out of sight, a fact emphasised by the couple's disappearance from the frame in the back of the launch.

Daphne has a more difficult problem with Osgood. At one stage it has been implied that a commercial motive is involved in Daphne's betrothal to the millionaire. However, this aspect is never stressed and is thrown overboard in the full confession when Daphne explains the real reason why they can never be married. "I smoke . . . I can never have children," Daphne begins hesitantly. Osgood is unperturbed – "Doesn't matter . . . We can adopt some," he counters cheerily. "Oh, you don't understand Osgood," says Daphne/Jerry, finally pulling off his wig, "I'm a man." Osgood is momentarily put off balance, but then smiles and continues driving. "Well, nobody's perfect."

If Osgood is one of the few Wilder dupes not to react to a rogue's confession, this has something to do with the extraordinary nature of the confession itself. When a Wilder hero at the end casts off some element of his clothing it usually signifies some adjustment in outlook, some renunciation of his past exploits. When Jerry removes his wig in the closing shot of *Some Like It Hot* it makes precious little difference, either to his situation or, indeed, to his physical appearance. Whereas Joe can sometimes find himself inadvertently wearing earrings in his millionaire disguise and can remove all traces of feminity with a swift, unobtrusive movement, Jerry, with elaborate flamboyance, tears off his wig to disclose his true gender – and nothing happens. Small wonder that Osgood is not only unperturbed but *unconvinced*. It exactly sustains the film's exquisitely calculated limbo at the end: Sugar precariously united with one of that breed of man who have caused her so much heartache in the past; the forthcoming 'marriage' between Osgood and Daphne which the latter will not be talked out of; the two men still on the run from the mob; the setting the open sea. The wheels of this remarkable film are still going round at the end, wilder than ever.

The film's sustained *joie de vivre* is all the more astonishing considering the well-documented headaches Wilder had in making it, notably with Marilyn Monroe who, according to most sources, was often late on the set, could never remember her lines resulting in an enormous number of takes, or was scathing about her co-stars. Wilder's exchange of barbed telegrams with Arthur Miller is probably the most famous outcome of this tension, but Wilder is nowadays a little more philosophical about the experience. "My God," he has said in a recent interview, "I think there have been more books on Marilyn Monroe than on World War II, and there's a great similarity. It was not easy. It was hell. But it was well worth it once you got in on the screen*."

In *Some Like It Hot*, Marilyn Monroe, with her unique combination of Earth Mother and frightened child, gives one of her most touching screen performances as well as one of her funniest. The role of Sugar Kane is aptly conveyed by the name. She is all sweetness (one of Jerry's "goodies"), an object to be used and abused. Like many Wilder heroines, she is a romantic who is consistently unlucky in love and almost absurdly vulnerable. Like Sabrina and like Fran Kubelik in *The Apartment*, she is easily taken in by the old romantic line. All of them fall for the man's "I don't want to discuss it" ploy, his fabricated fractured past which the gullible warm-hearted girl resolves to repair. All three have their own song which very often evokes as much romantic anguish as ecstatic release; and they are all sympathetic victim figures, Wilder revering their romanticism even while exposing its perilousness. It is often through these heroines that Wilder's own tenderness is released. What happens to them in both a cautionary and compassionate look at the fate of romanticism is a harsh modern

---

*The animosity between Wilder, Monroe and Miller is not mentioned in an interview with Wilder in the Summer-Autumn 1959 issue of 'Sight and Sound,' even though the rows were public knowledge. In London for the premiere of *Some Like It Hot*, Wilder said he was surprised by Monroe's acceptance of the role: "It's the weakest part, so the trick was to give it the strongest casting." Asked if he discussed scenes at length with Monroe, Wilder said (perhaps with unreported irony): "At short length – she gets the point right away. And she's very patient when she's working – would willingly play a scene forty times to get it right."

society in which everyone else is on the make. Because of their wholehearted emotional commitment, the heroines are often dangerously close to isolation and neuroticism: Sabrina and Fran attempt suicide, whilst Sugar has her flask of gin to solace her from her inevitable romantic disappointments. They are often amoral, a reflection of the risks they take for romance. But they also revitalise the man: one recalls Sabrina's effect on Linus and Sugar's on Joe.

Wilder's use of Monroe takes this a stage further, since the star persona informs the role to the point where it becomes difficult to disentangle one from the other (in this connection, *Some Like It Hot* becomes almost as allusive as *Sunset Boulevard*). Sugar, like Monroe, is the archetypal dumb blonde who is "not very bright"; the bighearted victim who "always gets caught"; the generous creature who always ends up with the "fuzzy end of the lollipop and the squeezed-out tube of toothpaste." If Wilder now dislikes the image of Monroe as Hollywood's sacrificial victim ("Monroe and Harlow were the lucky ones," says Fedora near the end of that film), it must be said that *Some Like It Hot* is one of those characterisations of hers (*The Misfits* is another) whose intensity gave this myth its powerful currency. No director has more effectively tapped Monroe's sense of fun. She has a blissful vulgarity, an innocent sexiness, a verve and abandon uniquely characteristic of the New World which clearly fascinates and delights Wilder. It is not surprising that she succeeds with Joe's impotence 'problem' where Professor Freud has failed ("I spent six months in Vienna with Professor Freud, flat on my back," he complains. "Have you tried American women?", Sugar asks innocently). At the same time Wilder reveals Monroe's fragility and poignancy. "I'm Through With Love" not only expresses Sugar's feelings of the moment; as Richard Corliss has said, in retrospect it, "encapsulates a tawdry childhood, three disappointing marriages, the adulation-mockery of curious fans, even a final, abortive 'phone-call".

Indeed, Wilder's use of movie mythology in *Some Like It Hot* is very important to the film's effect. As we have seen in the case of Monroe, it adds dimensions of poignancy and irony. Also, though, it adds enormously to the film's comedy. One example of this, as we have seen, is Tony Curtis's impersonation of Cary Grant. The other is Wilder's evocation of the gangster film which recreates the genre and affectionately mocks it at the same time. George Raft is not only Spats Columbo: he is also George Raft watching upstarts mimic the gestures he made famous – when Edward G Robinson Jnr absent-mindedly tosses a coin, Raft snatches it from him and snarls angrily, "Where did you pick up that cheap trick?" (Answer: from Raft himself, in *Scarface*). At a later stage, exasperated by one of his henchman's naive reiteration of their somewhat shaky alibi for St Valentine's Day ("We was with you at Rigoletto's"), he gestures to slap him across the face with a grapefruit, in emulation of James Cagney in *The Public Enemy.* Spats's obsession with his dress, a hallmark of the gangster figure ("Are your hands clean? OK, button up my spats"), reminds us that it is not only sexual stereotypes that Wilder is taking to their logical absurdity but movie stereotypes as well. Even the cop, who hovers on the edge of several scenes and leads the opening raid on the speakeasy, is played by Pat O'Brien who appeared as Hildy Johnson in Milestone's version of *The Front Page* and went on to star in several gangster movies where he represented social conscience against Cagney's social irresponsibility.

The film's self-awareness is another cushion against those tricky areas in it – the transvestism, the violence – impinging too insistently on our enjoyment. The period reconstruction is important here, giving us a sense of distance and perspective. It is the period between Prohibition and the Depression, a part of the American past with an audacity and style to which Wilder affectionately responds, and becoming in the film emblematic of all that is vital and exciting in American life. Wilder's potent imagery reinforces this concept: gangsters, dancing girls, flasks of gin hidden in a garter, a flower between your teeth for the tango. It is a period where the music is hot and, incidentally, a period whose costumes are sufficiently floppy and unrevealing to make transvestism possible without becoming too obvious. But the period setting is also important for revealing Wilder's affection for the cinema's past. *Some Like It Hot* invokes an earlier film style – a glorious opening chase reminiscent of the Keystone Cops and the pace, verve and monochrome grittiness of the classic gangster movie. These details are evocative of a mood as well as a period – an innocence, exuberance and optimism, a sense that everything was possible. As well as anything else, 1929 was, after all, the year of Wilder's entry into the film industry.

One should say finally that *Some Like It Hot* is significant for its teaming Wilder for the first time with the actor who has developed into arguably the most important performer in the Wilder arsenal:

Jack Lemmon. Without in any way underrating the brilliance of Tony Curtis and Marilyn Monroe, the miracle of the film's is Lemmon's Daphne, a drag performance of daring and dignity. And it took only some maracas to convince Lemmon of Wilder's genius.

It is the scene when Joe comes in to find Daphne stretched out on the bed after her tango with Osgood, and Osgood's proposal of marriage. Wilder apparently instructed Lemmon to do a little dance and shake the maracas after every line, a piece of direction Lemmon had admitted he was dubious about – until he saw the film with an audience. The maracas, as Lemmon acknowledged later, not only filled the space between the jokes, but were an additional comic device in themselves, as well as forging a link between that scene and the dance sequence. Of all directors, Wilder is perhaps the only one with an imagination bizarre enough and yet possessing a structural sense infallible enough to accommodate without strain or obvious contrivance – with complete dramatic logic and with total filmic authority – a world of massacres, maracas and Monroe. *Some Like It Hot* remains irresistible.

Irma La Douce (1963)

There is a moment in *The Emperor Waltz* when Bing Crosby suddenly bursts into song and, from nowhere, a group of patrolling policemen nonchalantly produce violins and proceed to accompany the hero's vocal efforts. Wilder's blithe disrespect for the formalities of musical comedy is taken a step further in *Irma la Douce*, where his solution to the problem of adapting a stage musical is to cut out all the numbers.

The attention is focused instead on the basic dramatic situation: the relationship between a prostitute, Irma (Shirley MacLaine) and her lover-cum-pimp, Nestor (Jack Lemmon), who becomes so jealous of her professional activities that he impersonates a rich English Lord in order to monopolise Irma's time and keep her away from her other clients. The film's bawdy comedy offended a number of critics (Jacques Brunius reproaching Wilder not for "bad taste" but for "*foul* taste"; Pauline Kael describing the film as a "monstrous mutation"), but their attitude seems little more sophisticated than Nestor's when he is a *gendarme* in the opening section of the film. His 'petit bourgeois' values are crushingly dealt with by the bartender Moustache (Lou Jacobi) who is the catalyst of much of the action. In any case, any pique the director might have felt at the critical reception (in fact, the majority of reviews were favourable, 'Sight and Sound' commending Wilder for having "softened up" the original musical play) was almost certainly assuaged by the box-office receipts. Perhaps surprisingly, *Irma la Douce* has proved to be not only Wilder's most commercially successful film but one of the highest grossing of all film comedies.

It is not difficult to see why Wilder was drawn to the settings and situations, if not the songs. His favoured Paris setting, to begin with, provides an expressive backcloth for the events of the film, magnif-

Irma la Douce: *Jack Lemmon, Shirley MacLaine*

icently created in a Hollywood studio by Wilder's regular designer Alexander Trauner. The emphasis on food and abundance at the beginning establishes the basic, energetic earthiness of the film's concerns – the "stomach of Paris," in which the action takes place, is a location to test the hero's appetite for life, recalling Ninotchka's conversion to capitalism over a lavish meal and Sabrina's spiritual transformation following a course in *haute cuisine*. It is a world of moral fluidity, of 'live and let live,' where the 'mecs' can peacefully co-exist with the police, and where Nestor has to be given a sharp moral lecture on the hypocrisy of a 'normalised' society that makes love illegal. It is a world of romance where a prostitute can play Scheherezade; where even the dogs drink champagne; where, given the will, you can bend iron bars; where the innocent weakling can fight the bully and win, with the aid of a billiard ball and a revolving chandelier; a world in which a green stocking might get you into prison and probably out again. In short, it is a world which, as the narrator says, might be "smelly" but is also "alive." Exuberance is the keynote, if not in the pace of the film, then certainly in its violent splashes of colour (Wilder's first work in colour since *The Spirit of St Louis*) and in its intensity of performance.

In a Wilder film people may not break into song in the ritualised way common to the musical, but they often burst into song *spontaneously* (Jack Lemmon's aria over the simmering spaghetti in *The Apartment*; Walter Matthau in *The Fortune Cookie* singing "I'm a genius" to the tune of a Rossini overture as he rushes up the stairs with the cheque from the insurance company). They also often burst into a spontaneous dance. Irma's fandango on the billiard table is a joyous expansion of an overflow of happiness which cannot be contained within a conventional or formalised emotional display. We recall the way the film has opened: "This is a story of passion, bloodshed, desire and death," intones the narrator before adding, laconically, "everything, in fact, that makes life worth living." One of Moustache's more fulsome philosophies is one that the whole tone and movement of the film supports: "Life is total war. Nobody has the right to be a conscientous objector." In the way that Bud Baxter's inability to keep liquids in their containers in *The Apartment* seems to anticipate his recognition of a world which cannot be compartmentalised as tidily as he thought, so too does Nestor's previously rigid existence spill messily over in the face of passion, desire and death. But, like Baxter, he is refreshed at the end, alive in a way previously foreign to him.

Nestor's first entrance as the righteous *gendarme* is wittily timed and utterly incongruous. His immaculate appearance and his military posture emblazon a moral rectitude and inflexibility wholly at odds with his surroundings. He is like a child in an alien land – to all intents and purposes an American (Lemmon makes no attempt to simulate a French accent) who has to learn how to become Parisian.* Even his munching of an apple (which he dutifully pays for, much to the astonishment of the stall-keeper who is used to a less scrupulous species of policeman) seems as much a sign of arrested adolescence as a premonition of his devouring the forbidden fruit of experience. His ineffectuality is taken to its extreme when, after organising a raid on the Hotel Casanova, he is first attacked by the girls in the police van who deprive him of his gun, the phallic overtones of which need no elaboration; and then deprived of his uniform and position by the apoplectic Police Commissioner who was enjoying himself in the hotel. Thereafter the relationship which develops between Nestor and Irma is effectively a process of making him more masculine, not simply in the sense of sexual experience but in the increasingly protective attitude he takes towards her and his insistence on supporting her rather than allowing her to support him.

The relationship between golden-hearted whore and puritanical pimp constitutes another variation on Wilder's fascination with Innocence and Experience. Irma's seduction of the hero into the ways of the world while she is simultaneously transformed by his love can be paralleled with a number of Wilder partnerships, notably Melvyn Douglas and Greta Garbo in *Ninotchka* and (by reversing roles, Gary Cooper and Audrey Hepburn in *Love in the Afternoon*). Nestor's sexual initiation by Irma is typical Wilder in that, at moments like these, the woman is often the predator and the man on the defensive, the former seeming much more sexually liberated than the stuffy, emasculated hero. This is largely because the heroine often has a moral and emotional transparency which contrasts with the murky motives of the male – a contrast explicitly realised in the seduction scene in *Some Like it Hot*, where the virile Tony Curtis feigns impotence in order to encourage Marilyn Monroe.

If the sexual tension implicit in such relationships has tragic consequences in, for example, *Double Indemnity* and *Sunset Boulevard*, the situation is to be treated as a source of gentle wit in *Avanti!* and in *Irma la Douce* provides the basis for the film's most charming and

*Needless to say, Wilder contrives some appropriate digs at the more traditional American tourists who fail to assimilate and behave as if they were exporting American standards to the Europeans – James Caan is more interested in American football on his transistor radio than in his Parisian companion; James Brown offers travellers' cheques as payment for the oldest profession in the world.

beautiful scene. Nestor's habit of fiddling around with his clothes and his draping newspapers on the window are at once a symptom of his shyness and apprehension and his attempt to transform Irma's room into a place of romance and love. Thus, newspapers become curtains so that no one can spy on them and the place becomes their own; his shirt becomes an impromptu lampshade for more subdued lighting; Irma's poodle is gently put out of the room in the manner of 'not in front of the children' (one is reminded of Nestor's previous police-work in a childrens' playground and his admonition of Irma as being an "unfit mother" for her pet).

Given Nestor's reserve, one might find his subsequent histrionic display as the English Lord a little hard to credit, though clearly accuracy is not something Wilder is after here, certainly no more than his caricatures of Russian trade delegates in *One, Two, Three*. As one would expect of a Wilder character, he takes his model of an Englishman predominantly from a crash course in British cinema. Wilder has always loved outrageous deceptions and Nestor's creation of Lord 'X', who lost an eye at Navarone ("I don't want to talk about it") and was rendered impotent when the bridge on the River Kwai fell on top of him, is certainly that. It is also highly characteristic that Nestor should lose himself in the role to such an extent as to start assuming the man actually exists and thus becoming jealous of *himself* (an immediate comparison is Lemmon's disguise as Daphne in *Some Like it Hot* which takes him over completely). The alter ego is so powerful indeed that Nestor's attempt to drown himself in the River Seine fails and his ghost is still stalking around at the end of the film, a supernatural dénouement which extends the film's comic logic and stylistic unity to its very limits. Can Wilder successfully accommodate the outlandishness of this disguise within the confines of character and comic realism he has established earlier? Does Lord 'X' belong in the same film as Nestor and Irma, let alone in the same world?

In the case of Nestor, the disguise is prepared for in the fact that the character has already moved from idealistic policeman to conscience-stricken pimp thus far in the film. The surreal exaggeration of the disguise (at times he seems confused about whether he is playing Professor Higgins or the husband of Lady Chatterley) dramatises the extent of a love that has taken him so far out of character. The *genuinely* noble corollary of this occurs when his assumption of this role to keep Irma to himself necessitates his sneaking out to earn money at the meat and fish markets (notice how petit bourgeois notions of monogamy and male responsibility still govern Nestor's actions, no matter how 'liberated' his life-style has become). These are achingly funny scenes, taking the consequences of Nestor's disguise to an extreme of absurdity (this is what the scheme has led to) but also to an extreme of devotion (this is the extent of his commitment to Irma). It also indicates his further assimilation into the Parisian atmosphere by his wholehearted endeavour as a worker in the "stomach of Paris." And if Nestor's sexual prowess is inevitably diminished in the process, making him too tired for love-making, his alter ego compensates by impregnating Irma after a therapy scene somewhat reminiscent of *Some Like it Hot* – Irma's tales of Baghdad being accompanied by soundtrack evocations of Rimsky-Korsakov as she plays the role of Scheherezade entertaining her 'lord'. The 'noble' birth, and the consequent reformation of Irma, are appropriate rewards for Nestor's innate nobility in endeavouring and sacrificing so much for the woman he loves. A Wilder hero traditionally has to endure extreme indignities to arrive at what he wants: the ennoblement of man through suffering is a characteristic theme.

In the same way that Nestor's outlandish disguise betokens the intensity of his love and the lengths he is prepared to go to sustain it, Irma's gullibility in being taken in by so gross a caricature demonstrates the intensity of her romantic illusions. She is deceived not because of the expertise of the impersonation but because of the extent to which she wants to believe it (a preoccupation which 'fools' Sir Wilfrid Robarts in *Witness for the Prosecution* and which blinds Sherlock Holmes to the truth). Again, Wilder has prepared for this by establishing that there has been a similarly philanthropic figure in Irma's past: she is waiting for a replica to show up. As with most other Wilder heroines, she is a romantic, a dreamer. The visions of Arabian Nights she conjures up for Lord 'X' tell us as much about her character and aspirations as they do about his. One of the central comic ironies is the contrast between the ostensibly sordid, materialistic nature of her profession and the intensely romantic vision of life she nevertheless holds. Clearly, Wilder does not invite us to make any moral condemnation of the character. He is obviously scornful of the 'How did a nice girl like you . . .' line, predominant in Hollywood cinema, which he dispatches before the end of the credit titles, blasting to smithereens the romantic clichés associated with this kind of screen character through Irma's increasingly improbable tales of her traumatic childhood. In fact, Irma is in the prostitution racket as a means of survival, the need for it disappearing when she can be convinced of the depth of Nestor's love and his determination to take care of her. Irma as wife and mother compared with Irma as prostitute is more of a change of circumstance than a change of character, since her work has scarcely touched her – "I never remember a face," she says – and the romantic idealism remains intact. Indeed, the Wilder heroine rarely changes very much during the course of a film. She is to a greater or lesser degree vulnerable at different stages, but she represents a fairly constant "humane norm," as Raymond Durgnat has put it, to which the hero must gravitate before the end. In the case of Irma, this is expressed particularly through her clothes which are fairly constant until the final sequence in which she wears a wedding dress, unlike Nestor, the human chameleon, who, in one delirious stretch towards the end of the film, moves from prisoner to policeman to dripping English Lord and finally to bridegroom in the space of about ten minutes.

Irma la Douce: *Lou Jacobi and Lord 'X' (Jack Lemmon) in the making*

As the film moves towards its climax it becomes increasingly eccentric. The action has spread out gradually from the claustrophobic settings of the early scenes, an expansion which corresponds to Nestor's widening moral horizons and the escalation of absurdities in the action. Thus, we have surely the most extraordinary wedding scene of any Hollywood comedy (with the possible exception of *The Philadelphia Story*), with prostitutes as bridesmaids, the bride herself suffering labour pains during the service, a bartender delivering the baby, and the inexplicable appearance of Lord 'X'.

Although *The Apartment* and the subsequent *Kiss Me, Stupid* make some play with the comedy of pimpmanship, the companion to *Irma la Douce* in Wilder's output is *Some Like it Hot*. Here, too, there are outrageous deceptions; an amoral heroine revitalising an impotent hero; a set of gangster figures in the background whose swaggering behaviour Wilder plainly relishes – the boss even tosses a billiard ball in imitation of George Raft. If the film is not as successful as *Some Like it Hot*, in the way in which the absurdities proceed logically and hectically from a desperate situation, this is partly to do with the pacing, which is a little languorous, and partly to do with the more overt moral context in which the film is placed. Certainly the character of Moustache – the philosophical bartender, ex-professor of Economics at the Sorbonne, ex-doctor, ex-lawyer whose bewildering variety of roles anticipate Nestor's – is crucial in determining the film's mood and moral co-ordinates. An appropriately pitched performance might have given Wilder the firm base he needed. Charles Laughton was Wilder's original choice for the role but he died shortly before the film went into production. Lou Jacobi is an agreeable and stylish performer – habitually leaving our curiosities about his past exploits dangling in mid-air with a nonchalant "But that's another story" – but he is no Laughton: the moral centre of the film is thus lacking an important charisma and imaginative audacity.

Even so, there are considerable compensations in the performances of Jack Lemmon and Shirley MacLaine; and neither must we forget that *Irma la Douce* marked the last time that Wilder could be true to himself with the full confidence that he would have a sizeable measure of public support. But that's another story. Wilder was no doubt delighted that to date his most successful way to an audience's heart has been through Paris's stomach.

Kiss Me, Stupid (1964)

It is difficult to evoke the tone and atmosphere of *Kiss Me, Stupid* in a phrase, but we would describe it as *Pillow Talk* ravaged by *Psycho.* It is a horror comedy, as indicated by the unprecedented outrage directed towards a film designed to make people laugh as well as think. The film was given a 'Condemned' rating by the Catholic Legion of Decency, and United Artists – obviously alarmed at what they had on their hands – turned over the release of the picture to a subsidiary company, Lopert Pictures, for limited American release. The American press variously described it as "the slimiest movie of the year," "a witless bore," "coarse and smutty" and "short on laughs and performances and long on vulgarity." Under the headline " 'Kiss me Stupid' wrong for Xmas in Milwaukee," 'Variety' magazine of 23 December 1964 reported that the cinema manager Jerry Gruenberg had cancelled the film as his Christmas attraction. He was supported in this by the Milwaukee archdiocesan director of the Legion, Father Raymond Parr, whose comment on Mr Gruenberg's action was: "I want to commend his sense of responsibility to the community. He contacted me to get my opinion on the film and I said that I considered it offensive, though I haven't seen it."

Supplementing the outrage was probably the film's truly terrible title. No doubt slyly intended by Wilder, this title could arouse in an unsuspecting audience expectations of one of those Doris Day vehicles of the late Fifties and early Sixties, whose titles also mixed coyness with sexual aggression – *Pillow Talk* (1959), *Lover Come Back* (1961), *Move Over Darling* (1963) – and whose main tension, as Clancy Sigal once observed, derived from whether Doris Day should or shouldn't "let Rock Hudson . . . see her without make-up on."

Wilder's rude riposte to this most spiritually desolate of Hollywood genres could scarcely have been more devastating. The Doris Day comedies play timorously around with sex while actually bending over backwards to be sentimental and inoffensive. The effect is prurient, hypocritical and deeply pornographic, since the heroine's honour is preserved only at the cost of her being morbidly preoccupied with its protection, and the films extol purity and virtue while cynically exploiting an audience's expectations of seduction. Wilder's film, on the contrary, not only candidly acknowledges the sexuality of its characters but allows them to indulge it, with results that are alternately hideous, anguished and romantic. Wilder's film not only honestly examines behaviour that might be viewed as depraved: it extends a measure of compassion and understanding to the people involved, recognising that the bleakness and aridity of their situation provoke a yearning for success that inevitably leads to confusion, despair and a distortion of values. Such tension and sympathy are completely absent from the Doris Day comedies, since their characters are already cocooned in comfort and luxury and the sexual element has nothing whatever to say about human relationships and aspirations but is merely a tease on which to hang a threadbare plot. The America projected in these films is welcoming and lush, and their plush colour, sumptuous decor and immaculately groomed characters exude a glamour that is suffocatingly unreal: the films seem more incisively decorated than directed. The Wilder film eschews such enervating gloss, setting its action in a gloomy house, hiding the sun behind Venetian blinds, dressing its characters in dowdy, ill-fitting clothes, filming the whole affair in probably the grimiest black and white photography ever seen in a film comedy, emphasising this with the wide Panavision frame, and thus giving a real edge of desperation to the characters' dream of escape.

Desperation and escape: this is where Alfred Hitchcock's *Psycho* (1960) comes in. A leading character diverted from his route and having to spend a traumatic night at a strange 'guest house'; significant actions around a gas station and a shower; a brassièred heroine preparing for an afternoon of love, the hot dry day outside being hidden from view by the window shades*; an extraordinary evocation in the opening scenes of a humdrum, listless, stagnant existence – this summary could apply equally to *Psycho* and *Kiss Me, Stupid*. Both

*As Orville comments, "If it weren't for Venetian blinds, it would be curtains for all of us."

films deal with obsessions about money and sex; both evoke an America of forbidding grey anonymity; both dig subversively at the roots of Hollywood ideology (in Hitchcock's case, the family; in Wilder's marriage). If the connection between the two films is probably coincidental (Wilder has never acknowledged any formal influence, though he has never concealed his admiration for Hitchcock), the effect of both is remarkably similar: their creators' most Dionysiac films, dream visions of fulfilment which turn into nightmares of the soul. Reflecting on the repulsive Dean Martin character in *Kiss Me, Stupid*, obsessively searching for sexual gratification in the period between night and dawn, one could even call Wilder's film The Hour of the Wolf.

It is appropriate to invoke Hollywood models as a means of understanding *Kiss Me, Stupid*, since one of the subjects of the film is Hollywood. Its subversion of the conventions of Hollywood romance – the initial provocation for the critical assault on the film – is all part of its conscious critique of Hollywood's false gods. Wilder is at his most mischevious here. Make the star repulsive; make the wife, not the husband, the dominant figure in the household; make a prostitute the most morally sympathetic character in the film. Make success dependent on venality, not virtue; make materialism more important than marriage. It is the most anti-Hollywood film that can be imagined in its conception and operation. But, the critical reaction notwithstanding, to evaluate the film as anti-Hollywood is not the same as saying that it is immoral. After all, is it not insufferable moral complacency to perpetuate a belief that success automatically rewards virtue, that the world is populated by beautiful people? The skill and intensity with which Hollywood peddles these illusions might celebrate an ideal but it might also make it that much more difficult for people to accept their own lives, which would explain the confusion and disorientation when Dino arrives in Climax, Nevada.

"Climax" as a name might seem an over-obvious sexual signal for the events of the film and the baseness of the actions to take place: but it also means The End. For most people, living in Climax is the end of the line, a prison, a cemetery even, where the choice is between escape or the endurance of a living death, exactly like the place in *Ace in the Hole* (this film's spiritual kin). The paralysing desolation of this desert town is aggravated by its geographical position midway between those two pillars of American glamour, Las Vegas and Los Angeles.

The action centres on the attempt of various characters to escape from "being buried alive in Climax, Nevada," towards one or other of the cities which symbolise success – a success which is also presented as thoroughly corrupt, disreputable and spiritually empty. If one were asked to name the Hollywood film which seemed closest in spirit to Nathanael West's great and terrifying Hollywood novel 'The Day of the Locust,' it would not be *Sunset Boulevard* and it would certainly not be John Schlesinger's film of West's novel. It would be *Kiss Me, Stupid.* Even though the setting is some way removed from Hollywood, the lure of Hollywood is strongly felt, and the film's sympathy, like West's novel, concentrates on the outsiders, the cheated, the desperate figures who are prepared to try anything to enter the realm of success that it always eluding them. The film is a mockery and indictment of Hollywood's influence, icons and ideology, a criticism which finds its centre in Dean Martin's quite extraordinary performance as the loathsome star singer, Dino Martini.

Towards the end of the film, there is one of the most remarkable single shots in the whole of Wilder's work. The citizens of Climax congregate outside Pringle's Hardware store to watch colour television. This, we are told, is the main diversion that the town has to offer, outside of a bowling alley and a seedy night-club called The Belly Button which, however, is on the outskirts of town and out of bounds for most right-minded citizens. On this particular evening they are watching Dino sing a song, "Sophia," written by two new songwriters from Climax, Millsap and Spooner. In the middle of the song, Dino pauses to say how he discovered it when passing through Climax, and to pay tribute to the composers, whose names he then proceeds to get wrong. Wilder sustains a shot seen through the window of the store, Dino singing "Sophia" on a dozen television sets with the smiling faces of the residents of Climax reflected on the window as they look in on their star, their hero. One might say that the whole thematic weight of the film is contained in this single moment.

Immediately, it marks a division between the star and his adoring public, the window in between separating the outsiders from the insiders. Indeed, it could be interpreted as an image about stardom itself, a clear picture of the star at the centre, infinitely reproduced, and surrounded by insubstantial reflections of his fans who are only identified through their devotion to him. On the television screens,

Dino is projecting his popular superstar image, the slightly drunken, slightly lecherous charmer. The film has examined the personal brute behind that public facade. If the fans project their fantasies and aspirations into Dino's star image, stardom for the man himself is merely a means whereby he has the power to cheat, manipulate, exploit, seduce and insult everyone in sight for personal satisfaction. It is one of Wilder's harshest portraits of the split between the public and the private personality; and the smiling faces in that store window would take on a different aspect if they knew how Dino had really acquired that song. But their delusion and infatuation with Dino is both chilling and significant: they are responding not to what he is but to what he represents. The repulsive reality of the figure is subsumed by the power of the image he projects – a seductive combination of ease, sex-appeal and wealth. What an emulation of that odious example might mean in moral as well as material terms is one of the film's main concerns.

The process by which that song has moved from Spooner's manuscript to nationwide television coverage is the springboard of the plot: an American success story achieved through adultery, exploitation and prostitution. Barney Millsap (Cliff Osmond) and Orville J Spooner (Ray Walston) have plotted to interest Dino in their songs when he has found himself stranded in Climax. To this end, they have ejected Spooner's wife Zelda (Felicia Farr) from the house and hired Polly the Pistol (Kim Novak) from The Belly Button to take her place for the night so that Dino's insatitable sexual appetite can be satisfied without reducing Spooner to apoplectic jealousy. In fact, the plot has wildly misfired, so this moment of nationwide triumph is surprising and oddly paltry and anticlimactic: Wilder's image of success at this juncture is noticeably flickering, wispy, distanced. In watching that song being performed and not knowing of Zelda's encounter with Dino, Spooner is suddenly uncomfortable and confused. Having ejected Zelda and subtituted Polly, Spooner has gradually found himself unable to go through with his scheme. "Does he think my wife can be bought for a song?", he has cried, throwing Dino out and himself spending the night with Polly, his 'substitute wife.' Why, then, is Dino now singing his song, as if in payment for services rendered? What does this success mean and what has it cost him? "I can't figure out any of this," he says, to

Kiss Me, Stupid: *Dean Martin, Ray Walston, Kim Novak*

which his wife responds, "Kiss me, stupid." It is obviously wiser not to ask too many questions, to stay in the dark.

Ostensibly, this ending might seem to be endorsing everything that the rest of the film has been satirising. While criticising the success-at-any-price mentality of the characters, Wilder has contrived an ending where each character seems to achieve what he wants: Dino his hit song, Polly her car, husband and wife a reconciliation. The fact that immorality is not overtly punished is Wilder's further subversion of the Hollywood ending, which was another source of the critics' seething hatred of the film. In fact, Wilder's assault on Hollywood ideology is taken a step further. He does not punish Spooner's indiscretion with failure: he rewards it with a success so hollow that the massiveness of Spooner's sacrifice looks all the more anguished. Spooner's success *is* his punishment: its price his peace of mind. If he could live with his own guilt about his adultery with Polly, he must now come to terms with suspicions about his wife, the possibility that his plans to protect her while furthering his own ambitions have brought about the very horror he wished to avoid. Unlike *The Apartment*, whose hero is morally vindicated while materially impoverished, *Kiss Me, Stupid* equally pointedly balances material success with moral chaos. That last line of the film is a positively bloodcurdling variation on 'kiss and make up,' in its suggestion of the hero's sexual enslavement and the wife's dominant determination to make something of him, even to the point of the ends justifying the means. To Polly's comment, "You've got a good husband there, Zelda," Zelda has replied, "He'll be an even better husband when I get through with him."

The role played by the wife in the film is one of its more remarkable aspects, aided immeasurably by Felicia Farr's performance, an incisive blend of domesticity and sensuality. The contrast between wife and whore in *Kiss Me, Stupid* might seem to share features of the conflicts over their men between Olivia de Havilland and Paulette Goddard in *Hold Back the Dawn* and Jean Arthur and Marlene Dietrich in *A Foreign Affair*. But in the earlier films the conflict was one of Innocence versus Experience, the complications arising from Wilder's ambivalence towards these qualities. In *Kiss Me, Stupid*, the contrast is more intricate. Indeed, the two roles occasionally merge. When they meet in Polly's trailer, it is the wife who has been given five hundred dollars by Dino for sexual favours; it is the whore who is wearing the wedding ring. "If I were you . . . and I *was*," says Polly, recommending a reconciliation between husband and wife. The emotional tone of the scene is curious: the softness and romance coming from the whore; the clear-headed calculation and practicality coming from the wife. But the exchange of ring and money – the symbols of their respective roles – suggests that Wilder perceives a connection between the two women. It is certainly not the crude one that Maurice Zolotow describes in the film: "that there is a slut crying to get out of every responsible woman's soul, and a respectable woman inside every whore's epidermis." It is that their attitudes are determined by their differing responses to the same situation: that of being treated as objects rather than individuals. The whore might be an object to be abused and the wife an object to be cossetted, but the underlying attitude is the same: a suppression of the woman's unique personality.

Woman as object in this society is asserted through one of the film's most startling symbols – Zelda's dressmaker's dummy. In one way, nothing could be more suggestive of innocent domesticity – Zelda sews her own clothes (though even this, of course, might have disturbing undercurrents. Zelda makes her own clothes because her husband cannot afford to buy them for her; the stereotyping of Zelda as the innocent domestic makes her night of love with Dino all the more outrageous). In another way, the image could hardly be more explicit in its summary of Dino's vision of woman as a mere prop, shape, with no personality nor distinction. Indeed, his first comment on seeing the dummy is to ask, "This your wife?". It is entirely appropriate that Orville deceives him with a 'dummy' wife. Women might just as well be dummies for him.

The confusion of people and objects becomes a key element of the film, as materialism overwhelms humanity. The dummy is a concise, disturbing image of the domesticated American female, a Stepford wife, a creature to be adored and adorned but not trusted or respected. It strikes not only at feminine servitude and passivity but at masculine sexist insecurity. That Orville also identifies the dummy with Zelda is proved by his concealment of it from the leering eyes of Dino, even putting his sweater over it for protection, a gesture of puritanism that recalls the Victorian habit of delicately draping a cloth over a suggestive piano leg. (We recall that Orville does teach the piano, and that the seduction between Dino and Polly, with Orville as chaperone, takes place on an extraordinary Victorian chair.)

The implications of a society which can jeopardise marriage for materialism comes to a head in the two scenes of adultery which climax the evening. They are scenes of total moral confusion. Having got drunk at the Belly Button and resting in Polly's trailer, Zelda is startled when Dino enters and she is confronted by her singing idol. There is a noticeable tracking shot towards her starstruck face, a romantic response all the more ironic considering what we have seen of him. She encourages him to sing "Sophia" and in the scene which ensues, it is very difficult to sort out who is seducing whom. Is Zelda's infidelity with Dino a fulfilment of romantic fantasy? – Wilder has described *Kiss Me, Stupid* as a "romantic film," although the romanticism inherent in an archetypal American housewife committing adultery with a rake is surely dubious. Is it a beautiful example of a woman's love – the wife being a whore for the night for her husband's sake? Or is it Zelda's act of individuality and self-assertion, reacting against Orville's uxoriousness? Her behaviour at this point seems precariously poised between self-indulgence and sacrifice, the typical balancing point of a Wilder deceiver between self-destruction and self-realisation.

Orville's infidelity with Polly is similarly confused. On the one hand, it could represent a redemptive element in his character. On the other, the *adulterous* nature of his sympathetic commitment to the abused Polly instantly undercuts any easy moral approval of his redemption. If he has resented Dino's attitude to the dressmaker's dummy, his attitude to Polly has not been very different. To him she is just a sexual object. At one point he starts unbuttoning the top of her dress to make her appear even more alluring to Dino in her disguise and it is Polly who has to correct him: "Your wife wouldn't do that." His hypocritical puritanism, triggered by his insane jealousy, moves with grotesque haste to a pushing of his 'dummy' wife into the lecher's path, a process so obvious that even Dino is puzzled by this display of Western hospitality ("What is this? Candid Camera?"). As the night draws on, however, he starts singing his songs for his 'wife's' benefit, not Dino's. When Dino makes a pass at Polly, Orville throws him out of the house. Nevertheless, his invitation to Polly to join him in the marital bed ("Coming, Mrs Spooner?"), natural and tender as it is, encloses a rather gross self-deception, Orville at this point unable to distinguish between fantasy and reality. André Previn's romantic music at this point is both moving (for Polly it is a moment of romance) and highly ironic (this is the moment of infidelity, intensified by the music being the love song written by Orville for his wife). The very quietness and unemphatic intimacy of the scene makes it all the more uncomfortable.

The ending leaves the characters in a threatening moral limbo. "Whatever he did, he did for you," Polly has said to Zelda about her husband. Partially true, but not wholly so: he did not take Polly to bed for Zelda's sake. Zelda has responded: "Whatever I did, I did for him." This is also ambiguous. She could mean she did it to help her husband or to teach him a lesson. The ending, then, has something of the unsettling mood of one of Shakespeare's dark comedies* and that flickering television shot of Dino a mocking reminder of what

*The business with the ring, the substitution of bed partners, the duped hero, the similar moral problems about means and ends, and the ambiguous role of the wife have strong overtones of 'All's Well that Ends Well' (which could serve as an alternative ironic title for the film).

this nightmare has all been for. This is perhaps what Wilder meant when, according to Axel Madsen, he described the theme of the film as, "human dignity and the sanctity of marriage." This is the kind of Hell that awaits when these two things are violated.

Orville J Spooner (the J stands for Jeremiah, he explains to Polly, to which she gently responds, "I'm sorry I asked") is one of Wilder's most penetrating studies of the emasculated male. Like Bud Baxter, he goes along with a corrupt scheme and finds it getting out of control. The real engineer of the scheme is Barney Millsap, juicily played by Cliff Osmond, whose bulk oozes a glutinous envy and ambition that would elide any moral restraint in the pursuit of materialist success. "Do you think Irving Berlin is frightened of losing his wife?", he says tauntingly to Orville, and it is this fear of the consequent effect on his marriage, of being a "nobody," that compels Orville's reluctant acquiescence. Wilder's evocation of Orville's dry existence is funny and sad. Glumly teaching piano with a transparency of Beethoven imprinted on his sweater, he simultaneously dreams of success through the composition of songs – lyrics by Millsap – with such forbidding titles as "Pretzels in the Moonlight" and "I'm a Poached Egg." The cultural dichotomy between the Beethoven on his sweater and the "poached eggs" on his manuscript is striking, but Wilder's criticism of the character's extremes does not preclude an awareness of the impulses behind his frustration and his desire to become a part of the American dream. As always with a Wilder hero, the problem is to reconcile this pursuit with human values. It is a measure of the perversity which materialism requires that the husband's love for his wife – and thus his desire to get her away from Dino – is expressed in the form of insults, hatred and antagonism. Greed and the desire for success distort Orville's most powerfully held emotions.

There is a particularly pointed scene when Zelda has retreated to her mother's home, only to hear her husband tonelessly taken apart by momma, with father bemusedly silent ("Did you say something?" – "Not recently") It is a desolate evocation of small-town gossip and morality. Wilder's mockery of the cheerless values of Climax can hardly have endeared him to middle-American audiences. What happens to Orville, a pillar of bourgeois propriety in being a music teacher and the organist at the local church, is even more outrageous, since, within hours of signing a church petition to close down the Belly Button, he has slept with a prostitute and his wife has committed adultery with a singing star. The outrage would be further compounded by the casting of an abrasive comic actor in the role whose style actually heightens the effrontery more than softens it.

It is well known that Peter Sellers was the original choice for the part of Orville, and that his heart attack in the sixth week of shooting necessitated Wilder's replacement of him by Ray Walston (the unpleasant Mr Dobisch in *The Apartment*). "With a more sympathetic lead, it could have worked," Wilder told the interviewers of 'Cinema,' "I got all I could from Ray Walston." In fact, though Walston's casting might have had a damaging effect on popular response to the film, it does have various compensations in preserving the film's integrity and toughness. Unlike *The Apartment*, this time no-one could accuse Wilder of a sympathetic softness at the centre. Walston is not an immediately appealing personality, however clever and electric a comedian, and one has to work towards sympathy for him. He is very far from the conventional Hollywood hero (crucial to the film's effect, of course): his fear of being cuckolded has a genuine edge. Walston is sufficiently anonymous to locate Orville appropriately in the structure of the film; sufficiently skilful a comedian to bring out all the seedy rattiness of the character's scheming.

Kim Novak as Polly turned out to be equally controversial, despite Wilder's evident satisfaction with her. One suspects what offended people was not Novak's performance (a sensitive and touching one, excelled only by her similarly controversial role in *Vertigo*) but the attitude the film takes towards Polly the Pistol as a character. It seems even today difficult for an American film to situate a whore in American society without some kind of moral condemnation. The call-girl heroine of Alan J Pakula's *Klute* (1971) is only ostensibly an exception: Christine Gledhill's analysis of the film in 'Women in *Film Noir*' (British Film Institute, London, 1978) is a devastatingly persuasive revelation of the ideological conservatism and anti-feminist thrust of the film. As late as Robert Aldrich's *Hustle* (1975), the director told 'Movie' magazine (Winter 1976–1977) about the necessity of making the call-girl mistress of the cop-hero European rather than American, otherwise an American audience could not have accepted the relationship. Wilder's 'foreign-ness' brings a different set of cultural assumptions to Hollywood stereotypes. For him, a whore is not a demonic sexual siren eating at the root of respectable society, but just another human being coping as best she can with life's adversities

(Polly is humanised still further by having a most unflattering, unalluring cold). Nevertheless, it is hardly surprising that Wilder would cause offence by presenting a local prostitute in small-town, middle-class America who, far from being condemned, is presented as morally superior to any other character in the film. She is the only one to be singularly unimpressed by Dino's stardom, seeing his loathsomeness for what it really is. Unlucky in love but getting by and unembittered by life, her disguise as Orville's wife involves only a minor deception since Dino does not really care who she is so long as he gets his "*action* action"; and the persuasiveness of her performance conveys an authentic emotional yearning rather than a nefarious materialism. The other characters are pretending one set of values to the community and acting out another in their homes. Polly alone remains true to herself, clinging to her sense of identity and dignity in a mean-spirited society. Wilder grants her a true night of romance.

With its plot of mistaken identities and shifting bed partners, *Kiss Me, Stupid* acknowledges a kinship with traditional farcical precedents, notably Italian sex comedies (the film is loosely based on a play, 'L'Ora Della Fantasia,' by Anna Bonacci). It also has the blatant boisterousness of Restoration Comedy and, like the best examples of Wycherley and Congreve, has a satirical view of society, character and manners that does not endorse the events it portrays but criticises by implication. The success of the film's comic strategy is difficult to assess, however, since the chances of seeing it with an audience are slim: it is rarely revived and, when exhibited, sparsely attended, sometimes even more so at the end than at the beginning. It is comedy of an excruciating rather than liberating kind. Even so, if the overall tone is difficult to gauge, the film has a great many comic moments. George Morris in 'Film Comment' (Winter 1978–1979) has done an elaborate commentary on the film's spectacular phallic imagery, ranging from drooping cactii to a protuberant Chianti bottle. However wittily and powerfully this imagery expresses the film's *mockery* of sexual obsessiveness, it cannot have endeared the film to the self-proclaimed moral guardians of America*.

---

*Recognition of this visual strategy can cut both ways, of course. It must take an impure mind to catch all the references and Wilder could always turn round and quote Freud's "Sometimes a cigar is only a cigar." Apparently the Catholic Legion of Decency even objected to the line, "She can show me her parsley," uttered by Dino when he is trying to shake off the husband and lure Zelda into the garden. "What do they want?", asked Wilder in mild astonishment, "Broccoli?".

There is a lot of pleasure to be had from the performances. Ray Walston's virtuoso displays of Orville's intense jealousy are superb and brilliantly scored by André Previn: the sudden reprise of Previn's 'jealousy motif' when Orville feels protective towards Polly now she is alone with Dino is beautifully timed, surprising an audience as much as the feeling surprises Orville himself. Nothing more cogently expresses the feeling of Orville's quest for success as a descent into the depths than his glum pursuit of Dino around the toilets, ostentatiously singing his song to catch the great man's attention, not only following him into the Gents but into the Ladies as well. Even Dino's hideous sexual energy, in its grotesque satire of the coming sexual obsessions of Hollywood, has its blackly comic side. "What's a joint like this doing in a pretty girl like you?", he crows about Polly's knee. Surveying the sorry waitresses at the Belly Button, he wrinkles his nose to observe: "I've seen better navels on oranges" (this is unfair, of course, for coming from Los Angeles he will have done). There is a comically precise contrast implied in the way the men pay the ladies for their respective roles: Dino's hundred dollar bills flamboyantly arranged in a glass; Orville's twenty-five dollars slipped surreptitiously to Polly in a primly sealed white envelope.

What is the function of the comedy in the film? Partly it reflects Wilder's amused detachment from the characters. Wilder starts from the supposition than human folly is funny: his dramatic strategy is then to take this to a point when it becomes *no longer* funny. Like Shaw, he is a moralist with a sense of humour (unlike Swift, who is a satirist without one) and it is inconceivable that Wilder could make a film without humour in it. The laughter sharpens our sense of the absurdity of human folly, but also dissolves our contempt, creating a bond between us and the screen and ensuring a delicate poise in the film between criticism and understanding.

Nevertheless, if one moment in the film encapsulates its overall mood, it is probably the sight of Zelda, drunk at the Belly Button in protest at her abominable treatment, propped up against the juke-box and pleading with it to play "Melancholy Baby", her pouting face reflected on the glass surface. All the film's sense of sadness, frustration and exclusion is contained there. For all its incidental farce, you cannot escape the sense of anguish at the centre of it: the ugly reality of life in desert towns for devitalised people, a breeding-ground of moral despair. Hideously but not surprisingly, the obnoxious Dino (like Tatum in *Ace in the Hole*) does become an activating force of hope, and Wilder observes simultaneously the tawdriness of what he represents and his understandable attraction for the people of Climax. After all, if you toss a drowning man a life-line he doesn't pause to consider the quality of the rope. But Wilder pauses: to reflect his disgust and moral outrage at the quality of contemporary life. It is striking that he has never yet come up with a romantic ending on American soil in his films – even in *The Major and the Minor*, Ray Milland is going straight off to war following his marriage. In *Kiss Me, Stupid* the closeup of Zelda's lips at the end is hardly inviting. The kiss of success at that juncture must taste bitter indeed on the lips of her husband.

Kiss Me, Stupid is an indictment of hypocrisy and materialism, but one which attempts to explain the conditions and circumstances which might lead to such behaviour. Wilder's refusal to indulge in easy condemnation was undoubtedly another reason why he was not forgiven for the film. But he recognises that his characters are humanly weak rather than inhumanly evil. Characteristically, he grants each of them a moment of grace. For Zelda, it is the moment when she walks out on her mother and trades Dino's five hundred dollar bills for the wedding ring. For Orville, it is the moment when he refuses to sell the love-song he wrote especially for his wife and throws Dino out of the house. Even Dino keeps his promise and begins to popularise the song "Sophia." Maybe the whole thing will be an isolated traumatic experience: certainly one is convinced that the success of the Millsap-Spooner song will be unrepeatable. Maybe Orville and Zelda, however imperfectly, can pick up the pieces of their marriage. But after the events of that night – and, in this, the morality of the film seems impeccable – it is only Polly who, at the end, is unequivocally driving out of Climax.

Chapter V

"A WOMAN'S A TWO-FACE"

Double Indemnity
Sunset Boulevard
The Private Life of Sherlock Holmes
Fedora

Double Indemnity (1944)

Double Indemnity is universally recognised as one of the best *American* films ever made. It is also widely regarded as both a foundation and a classic of the *film noir* and the film will be approached along these lines in due course. One of the reasons for the film's enduring popularity is the revival of interest in *film noir*, as demonstrated by critical journals and by several recent films: *Chinatown, The Long Goodbye, All the President's Men, Night Moves* – even a TV remake of *Double Indemnity* which made Wilder "throw up" – pay tribute to the special ambience of the *films noir* of the Forties and Fifties and place the genre's* thematic and stylistic constituents in a contemporary context. The *film noir* of the Forties, as exemplified by *Double Indemnity*, portrays a world of treachery, ambiguous appearance, destructive sexuality; a predominantly night-time world of guilt and paranoia, a mood of fatalism, of no escape. "The streets were dark with something more than night" is a line from one of Raymond Chandler's essays which expresses perfectly the atmosphere of pessimism and intrigue which *Double Indemnity* visualises so powerfully.

Double Indemnity, no less than *Ninotchka* or *Hold Back the Dawn*, is a test case for authorship. The film can be closely identified with the careers of James M Cain, who wrote the original novella published

---

*Whether or not *film noir* constitutes a genre is still the subject of critical enquiry (since the essential elements of *noir* are discernible in war films, westerns, melodramas as well as crime thrillers). For conflicting and valuable accounts of *film noir* see James Damico's "*Film Noir*: A Modest Proposal" 'Film Reader' No 3), Paul Schrader's "Notes on *Film Noir*" ('Film Comment' Spring 1972), and the special *film noir* issue of 'Film Comment' (Nov-Dec 1974). For a structuralist-feminist reading of *Double Indemnity* see Claire Johnston in 'Women in *Film Noir*' (British Film Institute, London, 1978).

in 1936, and Chandler, who wrote the screenplay in collaboration with Wilder. To be sure, Wilder's choice of co-writer, in preference to his regular collaborator Charles Brackett, would seem to infer on Chandler more than a fair measure of the film's atmosphere and power; after all, Wilder's reputation until that time rested largely on romantic comedies in the Lubitsch tradition. For Wilder, *Double Indemnity* was a stunning and a crucial departure.

It is well known that Wilder and Chandler did not get on personally, though Wilder has acknowledged that Chandler had a "wonderful flair" and Chandler conceded that he had learned from the experience "as much about screen writing as I am capable of learning, which is not much." On the evidence of Chandler's novels (the first of which, 'The Big Sleep', was published in 1939) one would expect him to have had a significant influence on the hard-boiled, imagistic dialogue and in projecting the slightly seedy Californian ambience, though Wilder has discussed the care he took with the visual quality of the film: "I wanted the look that Californian houses get, with the sun streaming through the shutters and showing the dust." It is the look that one associates with *film noir*, where the use of chiaroscuro (brilliantly employed in the film by the great cameraman John F Seitz) evokes a character's sense of entrapment and vulnerability. It is a style that has been convincingly (but not exclusively) traced back to German expressionism, which Wilder and other emigré directors would have been familiar with and can be detected in some of their earliest Hollywood films, notably Fritz Lang's *You Only Live Once* (1937). However, one can certainly appreciate *Double Indemnity* in terms of Chandler's novels which themselves were important influences on *film noir*, though the hero of Wilder's film is far removed from the crumpled idealism of Chandler's hero, Philip Marlowe.

The influence of James M Cain is equally unmistakable: his other filmed novels, *The Postman Always Rings Twice* and *Mildred Pierce* are structurally similar to *Double Indemnity* and all of *film noir*. However, Wilder and Chandler make several important changes to Cain's vastly overrated story (Cain himself called it "slapdash"), altering the names of the two main characters, transforming the heroine into a monstrous *femme fatale*, and completely reworking the ending: in the novella the hero and heroine's crime is discovered but they are allowed to escape by the insurance company who wish to avoid any embarrassing publicity. The novella ends with the couple aboard an ocean liner and suggests they are about to form a suicide pact. Wilder and Chandler's ending embodies a more pessimistic and poetic vision, bringing the film around full circle from its confessional opening. One might argue that Cain's ending, no matter how contrived and unsatisfying it is to read, might be regarded as more subversive than the film since Wilder and Chandler take care to restore a moral and symbolic order by having hero and heroine shoot each other and by suggesting that the heroine's step-daughter and her boyfriend will ultimately benefit from the tragedy and will take their place as respectable American citizens. But *Double Indemnity*, like most *films noirs*, conspires to undermine censorship codes by contradicting content with style: hero and heroine might not get away with their perfect murder, but *film noir* expresses a continuum of personal torment and temptation which society puts in people's way.

One must also relate the narrative structure and the characters in *Double Indemnity* to Wilder's subsequent work. He has often favoured voice-over narration and flashbacks in his films (from *Double Indemnity* to *Fedora*) and frequently employs a triangular pattern to represent the moral conflicts of his characters, often culminating when one of the characters attempts to desert the triangle altogether, with results that are usually tragic. If the three main characters in *Double Indemnity* – the *femme fatale*, the investigator, the weak murderer – are *film noir* archetypes, they are equally central to Wilder's work. Sexually aggressive, gold-digging heroines are present in many of his films, as are emotionally stunted investigators and morally culpable heroes who can resist everything but temptation.

Double Indemnity employs a cyclical narrative structure which describes a journey into the past, into the hero's memory and his subconscious. The mood of fatalism is immediately established in the opening sequence when Walter Neff (Fred MacMurray) arrives at his deserted insurance office just before dawn. Bleeding from a wound in his chest he reaches for his dictaphone machine and begins his first-person narration, addressing himself to the claims inspector Barton Keyes (Edward G Robinson): "Yes, I killed Dietrichson – me, Walter Neff, insurance salesman, thirty-five years old, unmarried, no visible scars – till a while ago, that is – I killed him for money and for a woman – it all began last May." As his confession expands, which Alfred Appel Jr, in 'Nabokov's Dark Cinema' (Oxford University Press, New York, 1974) has described as "the unfolding of a terrible, fated action, the fleshing in of the outlines of human pain and panic," so too does the fatal* and punishing bloodstain on his jacket. But we must beware of taking Neff's narration as representing the truth since his account of his own tragedy must inevitably be subjective whilst the camera is entirely objective in its selection of shots and angles. Neff's narration is in the form of a confession to Keyes, his closest colleague and his most dangerous enemy. Neff tells how he became enamoured of Phyllis Dietrichson (Barbara Stanwyck), the wife of one of his clients. Together they plot to murder Dietrichson and make it look like an accident so that they can claim on the double indemnity clause of his life insurance policy which Neff has skilfully duped the man into signing. It is only after the murder that their troubles begin.

Neff is the first of Wilder's morally weak heroes who, through motives which drift between greed, ambition, vanity and sexual enslavement, finds himself in a situation which he becomes powerless to control but which he has to see through to its tragic conclusion. The casting of Neff proved a major problem, few screen stars relishing the prospect of damaging their images by playing a vamped double murderer, but MacMurray, whose speciality at the time was romantic, happy-go-lucky saxophone players, is ideal in the role. His usual bluffness and easy charm are beautifully employed to suggest both romantic ease and emotional shallowness. Rather like his role as Keefer in *The Caine Mutiny* (1954), a similarly self-confident and righteous individual whose principles are founded on quicksand, MacMurray starts by being brash and voluble, only to grow ever more subdued as the dread events slowly overwhelm him and strike him numb.

The vulnerability and superficiality at the heart of Neff's slick salesman are clearly indicated in the beginning, when Neff decides on an impulse to visit the Dietrichson home to remind the man to renew his motor insurance. He is asked to wait in the "living room" – the room which will only witness death – but he catches a tantalising

---

*There is every reason to assume that Neff dies of his wound – Wilder's mise-en-scène, the actions and words of the characters, the poetic logic of his death and the ideological necessity for it – but it must be noted that Wilder cut twenty minutes from the end of *Double Indemnity* which showed Neff going to the gas chamber, his execution witnessed by Keyes. In one of those unfathomable coincidences, a similar sequence involving Edward G Robinson was also cut from Fritz Lang's *film noir, Scarlet Street*, made the following year.

glimpse of Phyllis above him on the landing, an image (repeated in *Sunset Boulevard*) which establishes the relationship that will develop between them – Phyllis above, dominant and sensuous, Neff below and compliant. When Phyllis joins him downstairs she is buttoning up her dress and when she pauses before a mirror there are suddenly two Barbara Stanwycks dominating one Fred MacMurray. He is, of course, to remain ignorant of her duplicity, her 'two faces,' until tragically late in the picture. However, Neff is pleased with his performance and returns to see her the following afternoon when the plot to kill Dietrichson is insinuatingly planted by her. Before she does so, Neff makes himself ostentatiously comfortable on the couch, happy to be served iced tea until he considers the time is right to make his sexual advance. But Neff's air of ease and control is wholly deceptive: Phyllis's pose on the couch, her penetrating, imposing looks assert a quiet authority over him which events will ultimately confirm. Neff might rise and walk out in righteous indignation over the woman's murderous scheme and her consequent assessment of his character, but the final shot of the sequence has Phyllis with her back to the camera, dominating the frame, whilst Neff retreats to the door, becoming ever smaller; it is as if Phyllis is shrinking him before our eyes. But Neff's incrimination and enslavement are inevitable; his snaky promiscuity is made the hapless servant of the heroine's sexual determination. For all his earlier superior decisiveness Neff returns to his apartment and stands passively by the window, turning the wheels of the scheme in his mind, wondering if this might be the opportunity to beat the system he had always longed for.* There is a ring: Phyllis is at the door. When they kiss Neff's fate is sealed, Wilder emphasising this in a beautifully judged cut from medium-shot to close-up which, in its timing, has exactly the feeling of a trap clicking shut.

The image that Neff and Phyllis frequently use to denote their relationship is "straight down the line." It has connotations of commitment, equality, trust and fulfilment. Yet as an image of

---

*Andrew Sarris detects a dramatic flaw in *Double Indemnity* since he has "never been able to perceive the motivational moment in which Fred MacMurray's breezy insurance investigator (*sic*) and devil-may-care womaniser is transformed into a purposeful murderer." As Neff waits by the window Sarris must surely recognise this critical moment, when Neff's material and sexual ambition gets the better of him. Shortly after this sequence Wilder cuts back to Neff at his dictaphone as he confesses to Keyes his frequent thoughts of how to plan the perfect insurance fraud. There is certainly sufficient evidence in the film to characterise Neff as morally weak and easily corruptible.

fulfilment of the sexual as well as the criminal conjunction of these two characters, "straight down the line" seems remarkably mechanical, powerfully evocative of a relationship rooted in a depersonalised, exploitative obsession; sexuality merely becomes a form of currency to purchase something else. This coldness is reflected in the scene in Neff's apartment when, after their embrace, they immediately begin to discuss ways of killing Dietrichson; it is also echoed in their sharp, brittle dialogue: "There's a speed limit in this State, Mr Neff. Forty-five miles an hour," Phyllis says of his salesman's innuendo, "How fast was I going officer?", "I'd say around ninety." And, as Keyes points out, the "line" leads straight to the cemetery. Highly appropriate, then, that a train should figure so largely in their murder plot and that Wilder should track directly behind Neff as he moves down the train in his impersonation of Dietrichson. Even here, when he is without Phyllis, her deathly presence is evoked by the window shades on the observation car which recall the horizontal shadows cast by the venetian blinds in the Dietrichson living room.*

There are three things which particularly distinguish Wilder's presentation of Phyllis and take her beyond being a mere signpost of doom. The first is that she seems *actively* dangerous: Ava Gardner is invariably supine in Robert Siodmak's *The Killers* (1946) and for all Mary Astor's persistent lying in John Huston's *The Maltese Falcon* (1941) we never feel that Humphrey Bogart is in any actual danger from her, whereas we always feel that Neff is (again, a vindication of the casting of MacMurray who seems vulnerable in a way that Bogart does not). This is largely because Wilder places his heroine in a carefully defined and claustrophobic context, as confined as the goldfish in the bowl which is so prominent a feature of the Dietrichson living room. Phyllis's restless pacing up and down the room is not only an image of her domestic entrapment, her thwarted potential, but that of an animal in a cage, coiled to strike out at anyone in a bid to escape her private hell. Secondly, Wilder intensifies the portrait of the *femme fatale* by blending an American sensibility with his own Germanic expressiveness and anguish. Molly Haskell, in 'From Reverence to Rape' (Holt, Rinehart and Winston, New York, 1974), has

*So oppressive is the train imagery in the film that even the first shot shows Neff unable to escape it: as he drives to his office he has to swerve to avoid a road works. The illuminated danger sign flashes "Los Angeles Railroad Corp."

commented that Phyllis is a corruption of the European *femme fatale*, "allied not with the dark forces of nature but with the green forces of the capitalist economy." But she also notes that Phyllis's attraction to Neff is "genuinely sexual." The character thus becomes infused with a sexual drive which both intoxicates and intimidates the man (Parker Tyler's theory of impotence is certainly relevant here). It would be hard to imagine indigenous American directors like Ford or Hawks convincingly creating such a devouring female satyr, but she could emerge from the darker cultural heritages of European emigrés like Wilder, Lang, Siodmak and Preminger – arguably the foremost exponents of *film noir*. Taking into account Wilder's predilection for movie references in his films, the name Phyllis *Dietrich*son (Nirdlinger in Cain's story) can hardly be accidental: MacMurray's spiritual collapse at the hands, or anklet, of a sexual siren surely evokes Emil Jannings's downfall at the feet of Marlene Dietrich in Josef von Sternberg's *The Blue Angel* (1930), itself an important precursor of *film noir*. And one is encouraged to regard this revealing change of name as evidence of Wilder's cine-literacy since Phyllis's step-daughter is named Lola (in Cain's story as well), after Dietrich's character in *The Blue Angel*. The final distinguishing element in the presentation of Phyllis is, inevitably, the lugubrious wit Wilder gives her. The tart dialogue, with which she is every bit the equal of Neff, has already been remarked upon. A crueller joke is played when Neff visits the Dietrichsons as part of the plan to obtain the husband's signature on the life insurance policy. For this most important occasion Phyllis is ostentatiously wearing black, in barely concealed anticipation of her husband's death.

In retrospect, as we listen to the narration, the hero does not appreciate the macabre joke; neither is he too enthusiastic about the person Phyllis chooses to witness the signatures. In one of the most uncomfortable sequences in all of Wilder's career, Lola (Jean Heather) plays a game of Chinese checkers as her father is deceived into signing his death warrant by her step-mother's lover. However, Phyllis's monstrous callousness is somewhat modified by the presentation of Lola and Dietrichson. The latter is gruff, middle-aged, unattractive and entirely selfish, apparently denying Phyllis any fun in life at all. There is additional tension in the scene because Lola is being prevented from seeing her boyfriend Nino, whom Phyllis and Dietrichson disapprove of. After Neff leaves the house Lola gets a lift in his car, expressing her hatred for her family all the way into town. Neff drops her on a corner where she meets Nino (Byron Barr), who instantly adopts a hostile attitude towards Neff, anticipating the sexual jealousies which will subsequently destroy Neff and Phyllis. Although Lola is viewed with some sympathy, both by Wilder and Neff, there is a certain promiscuousness and self-confidence about her ("You're ever so sweet," she says to Neff as she follows after her boyfriend) that modifies our attitude towards her.

The staging of the murder is the culmination of the earlier presentation of the heroine and is fascinating for its disturbing revelations of character. Dietrichson has broken a leg and must take the train. The plan is to kill him in his car on the way to the station, for Neff to impersonate him on the train and jump off at a prearranged spot where his body and crutches will be dumped on the tracks. The killing in the car is conveyed in a single close-up of Phyllis's face. Of course, it is important that we do not lose all sympathy with the hero, so Wilder refrains from showing Neff in the act of breaking Dietrichson's neck from the back seat. Above all others, this scene most demonstrates the subjectivity of the narration (silence at this point) and the objectivity of the camera: with hindsight, knowing that the plan eventually falls apart, Neff could reasonably imagine Phyllis's face when he murders her husband, but the reality of his point-of-view prevents him from doing so.* It is in both Wilder's and Neff's interests that the camera records Phyllis's response during this scene. The camera stares at her, fascinated by her calm. The impression given is that of a calculating mind racing ahead to the insurance claim and perhaps to the problem of how to dispose of Neff once the plan has been fully accomplished.

It is at this juncture that the claims inspector, Keyes, begins to play a more central part. His impact is felt with disproportionate power considering his secondary role. This is partly to do with Edward G Robinson's superb performance, and also partly to do with Wilder's genuine interest in the man. There is also the mystery planted right at the beginning of the film: why should Neff feel compelled to deliver a confession to Keyes rather than escape across the border?

---

*This disjuncture between the 'real' and the 'imagined' also applies to the scene near the end of the film in which Phyllis plants a pistol in the cushions before Neff arrives at her house: the audience must be made aware of the presence of the gun and Phyllis's apparent intention to use it, whilst Neff's feelings of remorse and hatred psychologically demand it.

A Woman's A Two-Face

The investigator figure who comes to completely the wrong conclusions anticipates Wilder's subsequent portrait of Sherlock Holmes; indeed, the background of Keyes and Holmes is rather similar. Both men have had broken engagements that have made them similarly suspicious of women as creatures "not to be relied on." Keyes's disillusionment has stemmed directly from his investigative zeal since he has been unable to forbear exploring his fiancée's background and has discovered that she was "a tramp from a long line of tramps." This discovery by Keyes seems significant in two ways: implying that nobody's past bears very much looking into, and anticipating Neff's unnerving discoveries about Phyllis's lurid former exploits; and it directly aligns Keyes's professional skill with his emotional sterility, an important reservation in our assessment of his character. Both Holmes and Keyes begin their films in aloof, rather contemptuous vein and both are characterised by a razor-sharp wit; both men revel in demonstrating their superior intellects: Holmes patronises Watson whilst Keyes cruelly humiliates an inarticulate truck driver in his first scene in the film and his later demolition of the managing director's theories about the Dietrichson case is indisputably the greatest scene of Robinson's career. By the end, however, both Holmes and Keyes have been humanised by the realisation of an emotional vulnerability that has clouded their rational judgement. Both Holmes and Keyes are 'too close,' in an emotional and a physical sense, to see who the guilty party is. In a profession which discourages trust in human nature, Keyes is deceived by the one person he does trust. This fallibility is the sympathetic chink in the character's otherwise solid armour of incorruptible meanness. The trust Keyes has in Neff, which Neff betrays, is made apparent in several ways. Most noticeably there is the cigar lighting routine: Keyes chain-smokes cigars but is always without matches, so Neff always has a match ready to strike with his thumb-nail*. Keyes also displays an uncommon interest and concern for Neff's well-being, suggesting both a paternal and a sexual attraction towards the younger and more physically appealing man, a concern to which Neff habitually responds to by saying, "I love you too."

---

*Almost identical routines can be found in Howard Hawks's *Only Angels Have Wings* (1939) and *Rio Bravo* (1959) and in Wilder's *The Front Page*, all films dealing with male relationships in which this ritual signifies moral and emotional interdependence.

Even before the murder the film has constructed a triangular conflict between the three main characters which is important to define as precisely as possible. First of all, Neff's choice is clearly not a straightforward one of Good or Evil; more a choice between irresponsible licence (sexual and financial temptations) on the one hand, and excessive reason, integrity and dedication on the other; a choice between the Dionysiac and the Apollonian sides of his character. Phyllis represents a world of amorality and promiscuity, a world of sensuality; Keyes a world of control, cold intelligence and inevitable retribution. The real conflict within the triangle then becomes that between Phyllis and Keyes, with Neff the passive vessel in between, a conflict which Irving Howe, in 'Mass Culture' (Free Press, New York, 1957), has defined as that between "lawless instinct and lawful conduct." He goes on: "Since Neff's feelings about that conflict are as ambiguous as those of the audience itself, he is, in a sense, the audience brought directly into the film, the moviegoer torn between what he takes for lawless sexual desire and intelligent lawful suppression." Stated in these terms, one can see how temptingly interpretation of these three characters can move into seeing them almost as allegorical emblems of Freud's Id, Ego and Superego, and symbolic of the classic tension Freud posed in 'Civilisation and its Discontents': whether the loss of "instinctual gratification" and "emotional freedom," as Lionel Trilling summarised it in 'Beyond Culture' (Secker and Warburg, London, 1966), is "compensated for either by the security of civilised life or by the stern pleasures of the masculine moral character."

Two scenes – one prior to the murder, one following – demonstrate superbly the dilemma which is tormenting Neff. Keyes has wandered into Neff's office, as he often does, and begins to persuade Neff to become a claims investigator like himself, away from the temptations of salesmanship (with its attendant overtones of promiscuity) and even away from the lucrative commission on sales. Neff is unimpressed, but as he is about to answer he receives a phone call from Phyllis who tells him that her husband will be taking the train that night. Keyes insists on remaining in the office, so Neff cryptically finds out which colour suit he must wear and pretends, for Keyes's benefit, that Fhyllis is an old flame. As soon as Phyllis hangs up Keyes (who answered the call) expresses his distrust of women, blaming 'Margie' on the phone for Neff's resistance to a more responsible job and

A Woman's A Two-Face

Double Indemnity: *Fred MacMurray torn between the concealed, feminine world of Barbara Stanwyck and the open, masculine world of Edward G Robinson*

saying, ruefully, "I'll bet she drinks from the bottle." The second sequence contains one of the most celebrated shots in the film. Keyes has turned up unexpectedly at Neff's apartment with the news that he firmly suspects Phyllis of killing her husband; all he has to do now is discover the identity of her accomplice. As Keyes is about to leave Phyllis arrives and, hearing the conversation, hides outside Neff's door. This shot, as in the telephone sequence, is a diagrammatic display of the conflict raging within Neff: Keyes still lecturing in the corridor and asking for his ritual light; Phyllis hiding behind the opened door, giving it the slightest pull to alert Neff of her presence. Both sequences brilliantly visualise the choice before Neff: the visible, severe, hectoring, rational, *masculine* world represented by Keyes, and the concealed, exciting, sensuous, *feminine* world represented by Phyllis.

Parker Tyler's pioneering analysis, published in 'Magic and Myth of the Movies' (Holt, New York, 1947), talks penetratingly of the sexual undertones of the Neff-Keyes relationship, its complex pull between dependence and love. One could add that the characters seem to represent two sides of the same mechanism: one sells insurance, the other investigates phoney claims; one takes out a cigar, the other lights it; one warns of the dangers of women, the other ignores it. When visiting the Dietrichson home for the first time Neff actually says, "I always carry my own *keys*" (when the maid comments tartly that Dietrichson keeps the drinks locked up – Phyllis probably does drink from the bottle). The pun seems too striking to be merely fortuitous and, coupled with where he says it, is an ominous portent of Neff's schizophrenia. He is trying to enter Phyllis's intoxicating arena whilst endeavouring to retain Keyes's sober calculation. Even when deeply involved in the plot and moving away from Keyes's world, Neff comments into the dictaphone, "I was trying to think with your brains, Keyes." One stunning detail clinches this irreconcilable tension raging within Neff: on the observation car in his disguise as the disabled Dietrichson he manages to get rid of a talkative and inquisitive passenger by sending him out for some *cigars*. In the strict confines of the plot – Neff's concern to cover the smallest detail which Keyes's brain would soon discover* – we notice that

*Neff overlooks the fact, which arouses Keyes's suspicions, that Dietrichson doesn't put in a claim for his broken leg.

Dietrichson smokes cigars and that Neff smokes cigarettes: Neff's request for cigars indicates the thoroughness of his plotting. However, the emphasis on Keyes's cigar smoking brings the spectre of the investigator into the observation car just as surely as the slatted shadows evoke the presence of Phyllis. One can appreciate just how impossible and how oppressive Neff's choice is.

Neff's increasingly tenuous hold on his identity is foregrounded when he has to impersonate Dietrichson. This leads us to a consideration of the secondary triangle operating within the film's elaborate framework. As we have already noted, Keyes's regard for Neff is partly paternal and partly sexual. As the film develops we can see this relationship being echoed between Neff and Lola. Following the death of her father, Lola goes to Neff's office to betray Phyllis and, like Keyes, seeks the salesman's advice and sympathy. Lola is convinced that her mother was killed by Phyllis who, when working as a nurse, deliberately opened a window to hasten the woman's death from pneumonia (ironically, Neff is shot in the act of closing a window). Throughout the film Phyllis's cold-bloodedness and determination has unnerved Neff and Lola's accusation is just one more piece of damning evidence against Phyllis that he has to consider. In order to divert Lola's attention he takes her out a few times and when they sit above the Hollywood Bowl together, and when Lola reveals that Phyllis has been seeing Nino, he decides to kill her stepmother as well. But Lola, impatient and jealous of Nino, is irresistibly drawn towards Neff, bestowing upon him the combination of paternal trust and love that he receives from Keyes.

One can see here how the film constructs complex oedipal trajectories for its characters in the notable absence of traditional family bonds: Neff killing Lola's father and then becoming her surrogate father and potential lover – again torn, this time between Phyllis and Lola; Keyes's suppressed paternal instincts directed at a surrogate son and potential lover and against the maternal-sexual drives of the women. The vicious circle is completed when Phyllis, having killed her husband, initiates an affair with her step-daughter's boyfriend with a view to having him kill Neff – a liaison which brings Nino under Keyes's suspicions until Neff's confession automatically clears him. In a film so saturated with doubles, it is inevitable that Neff *becomes* Dietrichson, cuckolded, he believes, by Nino, adopted by the dead man's daughter and shot by his wife. Indeed, as Neff limps towards the elevator at the end of the film, the image irresistibly recalls the credit title image of a man on crutches slowly advancing towards the camera: it could be Neff or Dietrichson; and when Neff goes to a drug store after the murder he compares himself to a dead man since he cannot hear his own footsteps on the empty street.

The Los Angeles in *Double Indemnity* is pitiless, an urban hell of dark streets, desolate railroad tracks, gloomy apartments and office buildings. Appropriately, the insurance company offices resemble nothing so much as a Hollywood set for a prison, with its central open landing overlooking a void and with offices leading off from each side. One is hardly aware of any ordinary citizens going about their lives without being involved in attempts to beat the system. Unquestionably the most chillingly expressive use of location is Jerry's supermarket where Neff and Phyllis meet in secret to discuss their plans. Ostensibly the supermarket presents an image of normality and of order (significantly, it is one of the film's few daytime locations) but this only heightens the incongruity of murder being discussed over cans of baby food. A closer examination reveals the supermarket

Double Indemnity: *The Supermarket (Barbara Stanwyck, Fred MacMurray)*

to be not so much a contrast to the clandestine criminality of Neff and Phyllis but a confirmation of it. The sign on the supermarket wall – 'WE DELIVER – MORE FOR LESS' – is a concentrated statement of merchandise, money and commercialism which precisely mirrors the driving impulses of the hero and heroine. Indeed, Wilder seems to take the setting closer to metaphor than to realism, this emphasised still further by the lady customer who complains about never being able to reach the goods she wants in the presence of a couple who are also going to over-reach themselves. The image of selling (Neff's characterisation of Keyes's moralising is "the speech with the two-dollar words in it") is a fundamental one in the film's portrayal of a society in which everyone is compulsively on the make: even the witness on the train, who comes to see Keyes, tries to fiddle his expenses.

In a world governed by money and exploitation, love and tenderness have little place. Neither has art. One of the most forlorn scenes in the film is that between Neff and Lola on the hill overlooking the Hollywood Bowl. Whilst the romantic strains of Schubert's Unfinished Symphony float up to them, Neff sits with his back to the concert drawing out information about Phyllis and Nino. It is a pointed contrast between the spiritual and aesthetic aspirations and achievements of man (the reference to Schubert) and the mean-spirited, grasping individuals who turn their backs on that potential. There are few more desperate visions of a loveless, materialist America than *Double Indemnity*.

Yet to label the film as being "without a single trace of pity or love" (Higham and Greenberg), however highly you might value the film for that, is not strictly true. There are, to be precise, two such traces. There is the moment when Phyllis suddenly stops in her tracks, unable to fire the second bullet into Neff, as mystified by her indecision as we are, halted perhaps by an involuntary pang of warmth and possibly love for the man who has given her, however fleetingly and morally debased, some excitement and hope. As the strains of the popular song "Tangerine" drift through the Dietrichson living room, Neff and Phyllis have a final embrace – Phyllis claiming she has never loved him and the wounded Neff, never more certain than now, whispering "Goodbye, baby" before he fires two bullets into her. He has submitted, finally, to the world of Keyes in which trust is outlawed and retribution is inevitable. Before he starts his drive to the insurance office Neff ensures that Lola and Nino, who turns up at the Dietrichson house, will be reconciled.

And there is the wonderful final scene between Neff and Keyes, played out on the mezzanine as Neff collapses on the floor, unable to reach the elevator. Accounting for Keyes's unusual failure to fathom the case, Neff says "The guy you wanted was too close – right across the desk." "Closer than *that*, Walter," says Keyes. "I love you too," whispers Neff with a reluctant and ironic smile. He fumbles for a cigarette and Keyes, reversing the usual procedure, strikes the match with his thumb-nail. This final, small spark of human compassion is all the more moving through having to wait for it across the film's desolate stretches of human greed.

Sunset Boulevard (1950)

One evening, in the cluttered living room of a vast Hollywood mansion, two people are watching an old movie. They are Joe Gillis, a young ex-newspaperman trying to make a career as a screenwriter, and Norma Desmond, a star of the silent screen whose career, like many others, was abruptly halted by the arrival of sound. The film they are watching, inevitably one of Miss Desmond's silent triumphs, is being projected by her butler and chauffeur, an ex-film director and former husband of Norma's called Max von Mayerling. Whilst Joe's dry disregard for the performance is amply conveyed by his casual posture and lounge suit, Norma is wrapped in a romantic aura, elaborately costumed as if for a premiere at Grauman's Chinese Theatre. She can scarcely contain her excitement at her own youthful image flickering on the screen, unconsciously clutching at Joe's hand, possessed by the patterns of reflected light. "Still wonderful isn't it? And no dialogue," she comments ironically and reprovingly at the budding writer beside her, "We didn't need dialogue – we had faces."

On the most basic level this extraordinary scene, from about the middle of *Sunset Boulevard*, can be considered a witty, if rather macabre, examination of what movie people do with their spare time: they roll up the conspicuously large painting and on the concealed screen of private dreams they watch themselves with the same childlike wonder and emotional rapture as the mass public for whom the film was made. Joe's respite from his mammoth ghosting job on Norma's horrendous "Salome" screenplay, which she believes will launch her comeback, is to be allowed to watch her old movies once or twice a week. When Norma suspects Joe of getting bored with his prolonged sojourn in the mansion she entertains him with her own ghostly movies or with impressions of a Mack Sennett bathing beauty or by disguising herself as Charlie Chaplin, himself a Sennett product.

This scene also indicates how the cinema has become more than a profession to these people: the movies infiltrate their homes, their lives, their personalities. If Norma is obsessed with cinema, her obsession is matched by Joe's, though in a different way. When he slips away from the mansion for a while to work with Betty Schaefer on a screenplay, it makes him think of himself as a twelve-year-old sneaking out of his parents' house to see a gangster picture. Characters in *Sunset Boulevard* are constantly defining their actions and experience in relation to cinematic models. Joe discovers that Betty is equally ensnared by filmic imagery. She works as a reader for Paramount and in an early scene upsets Joe by criticising one of his treatments for being impersonal and lacking a political statement. They meet later at a party where she apologises for her tactlessness and praises a brief flashback sequence which Joe drew from his personal experience. Their relationship begins through their comic adoption of stereotyped roles from a melodrama – she playing Lady Agatha to his love-starved soldier. Since Betty is the daughter of studio employees, the movies are in her bloodstream, forcing her to regard life as a script. "Look at this street," she says as they stroll through the deserted backlot at night, "all cardboard, all phoney, all done with mirrors. You know I like it better than any street in the world."

The cinematic allusiveness of *Sunset Boulevard* becomes even more evocative when we consider the casting. Joe Gillis, the writer desperately in need of a break, is played by William Holden who until *Sunset Boulevard* made him famous was a Paramount contract player given small romantic roles in minor films. Norma Desmond is played by Gloria Swanson, herself a legend of the silent era, whose career had receded gracefully in the period of the Talkies and who, in *Sunset Boulevard* is making a dramatic comeback, though Norma prefers to think of it as a "Return".* The film she and Joe are watching is not simply a mock-up of a Norma Desmond picture; it is *Queen Kelly*, starring Gloria Swanson and directed in 1928 by Erich von Stroheim, the director of the 1925 classic, *Greed* (surely a palpable influence on

*For a lively account of the problems encountered by Wilder in casting the roles of Joe and Norma, see "Billy Wilder in Hollywood" by Maurice Zolotow.

Wilder's desert picture *Ace in the Hole*) whose career as a director barely survived the coming of sound. Indeed, *Queen Kelly* was partly financed by Gloria Swanson and production was terminated halfway through because, it is said, sound would have left it instantly obsolete and without an audience. Inevitably, it is Stroheim who plays the butler and ex-film director Max von Mayerling (a name that is possibly an ingenious merging of Mayer and 'underling' – M-G-M, under Louis B. Mayer and Irving Thalberg, had destroyed Stroheim's original version of *Greed*). Thus, what is being watched on that private screen, by Joe and by us, is both a Norma Desmond film and a Gloria Swanson film, both a Max von Mayerling and an Erich von Stroheim creation.

In his "Biographical Dictionary of the Cinema" (Secker and Warburg, London, 1975) David Thomson, one of Wilder's harshest critics, detects in *Sunset Boulevard* a "care for sets untypical (*sic*) of Wilder" as being due to Stroheim's influence. Thomson writes eloquently about Stroheim, "It is hard to see now even what the studios chose to make available of Stroheim's work. But once seen, *Greed, The Wedding March* and *Queen Kelly* – no matter how palely they reflect originals – are never forgotten. They contain the essential contradictions in Stroheim's work: between melodrama and naturalism, romanticism and cynicism; psychological detail and epic perspectives. Like all great silent directors he knew how necessary it was to abandon taste for obsession." Thomson probably doesn't realise it, but in this passage he also pinpoints some essential contradictions in Wilder, especially the Wilder of *Sunset Boulevard*. Wilder is supremely aware of his intentions and his three main characters are, up to a point, playing themselves with an enthusiasm which some of Hollywood's executives – notably Mayer – found hard to stomach.

Cecil B DeMille also appears as himself, working, as he really was, on *Samson and Delilah* which, in a curious way, echoes Norma's sapping of Joe's strength. It was DeMille who gave Gloria Swanson her big break in films, directing her in *Don't Change Your Husband* in 1919, and who greets Norma Desmond with the words "Hello youngfellow" just as he used to call Gloria Swanson; and when, later on, we see Hedda Hopper playing herself and gloating over Norma's tragedy, we recall DeMille's embittered remark to an assistant that "A dozen press agents working overtime can do terrible things to the human spirit." Norma's regular bridge party, unkindly referred to by

Joe as the "Waxworks," also comprises actual stars of the silent era who never made the transition to sound: H B Warner, who played Christ in DeMille's *The King of Kings* (1927), Anna Q Nilsson, who starred in Raoul Walsh's first film *Regeneration* (1916), and Buster Keaton, the latter being allowed one of his few spoken words on the screen: "Pass."

Because of the film's presentation of real-life Hollywood actors and directors alongside fictional characters obsessed with movies, the line between fact and fantasy becomes progressively blurred: we are not simply watching a film about Norma Desmond but about Gloria Swanson *playing* Norma Desmond. We watch the film, it might be said, not so much on a screen as on a distorting mirror. Indeed, when Joe and Norma watch *Queen Kelly*, the screen *is* a mirror, feeding Norma's narcissism and transmitting flattering but misleading images of herself. When she leaps to her feet crying "I'll show them! I'll be back up there, so help me!", she is caught directly in the passage of light which links the projector to the screen, framing her ominously within this single path of illusion. At this moment the face of Norma Desmond in the chiaroscuro of the living room is one of the cinema's purest expressions of dementia.

Unlike many recent films made in *hommage* to Hollywood directors, the elaborate network of movie references contained in *Sunset Boulevard* is used for expressive purposes, bringing to the basic narrative structure additional layers of authenticity, poignancy and irony. Equally it contributes to the two crucial themes of the film: claustrophobia (the sense of no escape, Hollywood as a monster which devours its own creations) and the conflict between illusion and reality, where it becomes as hard for us to distinguish between Norma Desmond and Gloria Swanson as it does for Norma herself at the end to distinguish between a movie set and her own staircase, between studio lights and newsreel cameras, between a fantasy director (von Mayerling) and a real one (Cecil B DeMille).

If the inability to define or even experience emotion outside of Hollywood models is one way in which the life of these people is seen as insular and enclosed, this claustrophobia is intensified by Wilder's adoption of a cyclical narrative structure. As in *Double Indemnity* and his subsequent film, *Ace in the Hole*, the ambitious thwarted hero is dumped at his starting point, his plotting and expertise having failed to provide any tangible sense of physical or emotional release. *Sunset Boulevard* begins with Joe Gillis's corpse being discovered face down in a swimming pool and ends with the police fishing it out. The film is in the form of a flashback, narrated by Joe whom we ultimately discover is dead.

Joe's experience in the film can be interpreted as a series of failed escape plans. His motive for going to Hollywood in the first place is to escape his dull thirty-five dollar a week desk-job in a Dayton newspaper office, probably not unlike the "Sun Bulletin" in *Ace in the Hole*. Ironically, at the end of the film he is intending to escape from Hollywood to return to his job when he is shot down by Norma. The opening of the film is preoccupied with his efforts to evade the two representatives of the finance company who have orders to reclaim his car. (Losing his car would be like losing his legs, Joe has told them, as if the car symbolised his masculinity and independence – significantly, its eventual appropriation by the company does parallel Joe's emasculation as Norma beings to direct his life.) Joe initially manages to give them the slip and rushes around Hollywood trying to secure a loan from everyone he knows. Eventually he is spotted by the finance men and during the consequent car chase one of his tyres bursts and he negotiates a halting entrance into the driveway of Norma's mansion – a stroke of luck, he thinks, for the mansion has a large garage in which he can hide his car. He notices, as he could hardly fail to, the other car in the garage, which Norma is later to characterise as "not one of those cheap new things made of chromium and spit – it's an Isotta Fraschini."

The contrast between the two vehicles in the garage is nicely used by Wilder to make several important points about the characters. The magnificent old car, synonymous with the extravagant 'Twenties but now antiquated and bizarre on its blocks, is a visual anticipation of Norma Desmond herself, just as the "cheap new thing" is analogous to Joe and the role he is about to play in Norma's life. Just as Joe's car has propelled the early part of the film, Norma's is to activate later developments. When the finance men finally discover Joe's car, Norma responds casually, "And I thought it was a matter of life and death," to which Joe replies snappily, "It is to me." It seems a rather petulant reaction, yet the way in which the new useless car is pulled out of Norma's garage and hooked up by the removal truck not only reverses Joe's earlier self-satisfaction at inveigling his way into becoming Norma's expensive ghost-writer ("I dropped the hook and she snapped at it") since it is clear now that it is Joe who is hooked, not Norma. It is also a macabre premonition of his ultimate fate – he, too, is to be hooked, lifeless, out of Norma's pool and taken away. And the requisitioning of Joe's car, over and above his personal needs, is paralleled by the attempts of a Paramount assistant director to hire Norma's car, over and above her desire to be hired by Paramount for herself. Paramount have telephoned the mansion several times about the rent of her car for a new Bing Crosby picture, but Norma refuses to speak to them ("I've waited twenty years for this call," believing it to be DeMille wanting to direct her script, "now DeMille can wait until I'm good and ready."*) It is Joe, at the end, who breaks the bitter news to Norma that Paramount wanted her car, a revelation that leads directly to his murder. The effect of this is to render the cars emblematic of Joe and Norma's total uselessness. Both are discarded people who are valued less for what they are than for what they possess, both fighting for recognition and survival in a harsh and dehumanised society.

As it turns out, Joe's refuge from his creditors is a prison from which he is never to escape alive. Ominously, he is first of all mistaken by Norma for an undertaker who is expected to perform the last rites and burial of Norma's pet chimpanzee. Joe is amused by this situation, speculating typically that the dead chimp was probably "the great grandson of King Kong" (also the victim of a movie star), but he is rapidly to be transported into the situation of the chimp by becoming Norma's "pet" and winding up dead. To underline this connection, Franz Waxman's magnificent music uses a similar squealing motif for them in key contexts, notably when Joe is being pampered by Norma to the point of suffocation and nausea in the tailor's shop and where, paradoxically, the more clothes that are piled on him, the more he is stripped spiritually naked; but also when Norma leaps to her feet when watching *Queen Kelly*, linking them all in a scream of madness and excess.

To his great credit, Joe resists Norma's attempts to persuade him to stay in the mansion. As he sits reading through Norma's massive

---

*It might be worth noting here that when Norma receives the call from Paramount she is entertaining Joe with her Chaplin routine, disguised with dignity as The Tramp. Yet as she lashes out her refusal to pick up the 'phone, the Tramp's sad face is suddenly transformed into that of *The Great Dictator*, a reference, perhaps, to Chaplin's belated response to talking pictures by giving the public a torrent of words.

screenplay, drinking the champagne served by Max, he conjures a plot himself, realising the money he can earn by cutting "Salome" down to size and making it relatively coherent. Since he owes several months in rent and is concerned that the finance men may be watching his apartment he agrees to spend the night in a room over the garage. But Joe's illusion of freedom does not last long. He wakes up to find his belongings in the room with him – a constant reminder of his shabby existence – and that Norma has settled the back rent on his apartment. Norma's trap snaps shut when the roof of Joe's room begins to leak and he moves into the "husband's" room next to Norma's.

Characteristically, Wilder also conveys Joe's entrapment by making him wear clothes bought for him by Norma which exclude him from his old friends by their extravagance. When he calls into Schwabs Drugstore to buy some cigarettes for Norma (with her money), he meets some friends who are naturally inquisitive about his changed appearance, even more so when the mysterious chauffeur, Max, has to come and call him away. His friends, of course, assume he has struck lucky and Joe, like Baxter in *The Apartment*, is too torn between shame and greed to tell them the truth. Even in his scenes with Betty Schaefer (Nancy Olson), which he contrives as a release from Norma and as an attempt to fulfil himself and live his own life, Norma is still felt as an inescapable ghostly presence. For example, encouraging Betty to spice up his scenario, he tells her that "psychopaths are like hot cakes" and the remark not only refers accurately to a movie phenomenon of the time but seems to bring the spectre of Norma's own mental condition into the room. When they are working alone together in the deserted studio, Betty finds Joe's gold cigarette case with Norma's inscription "Mad about the Boy" on the inside and Joe is immediately incriminated and linked indelibly with that shady part of his life with Norma.*

---

*One cannot but marvel at Wilder's detail. "Mad about the Boy" is a song title, a choice of inscription with a theatrical flavour absolutely in character, but it also has strong implications about their relationship which Norma, in writing it, might have felt fearfully at the fringes of consciousness – the disparity of their ages ("Mad About the *Boy*") and the eventual outcome of their relationship ("*Mad* About the Boy"). The inscription can also only torment Joe: becoming Norma's "boy" has not only restricted his physical and intellectual freedom but aggravated his guilt about a relationship with a woman old enough to be his mother, a trauma of incest alienating him still further from friends who, if they knew, might be shocked by his sexual status.

Sunset Boulevard: *The dance (Gloria Swanson, William Holden)*

This pervasive sense of entrapment is amply conveyed by the powerful juxtaposition of two New Year's Eve parties and their consequences. Norma has a big party planned, getting the tiled floor on which Valentino danced polished (Waxman's main theme for Norma is a tango, placing her eloquently in the Valentino era of the 'Twenties) and hiring a palm court orchestra. Yet it is a party just for Norma and Joe, with Max stoically pouring champagne and collecting Norma's elaborate headgear tossed away as the couple dance beneath the gaze of Wilder's camera.* It is in this scene that Norma confesses

---

*Dances regularly feature in Wilder's work and in this particular scene reminds us of Wilder's employment as a "tea-room gigolo" in Berlin when he was trying to break out of journalism into screenwriting, exactly mirroring Joe in the film. Wilder's dance sequences become psycho-sexual rituals between two people, usually without anyone else around – tragically represented in *Sunset Boulevard* and *The Apartment* (Baxter dancing with the lonely barfly on Christmas Eve), romantically in *Love in the Afternoon* and *Avanti!* and between two men in *Stalag 17* and *Some Like It Hot*, the latter using a similar set-up as *Sunset Boulevard* but for comic effect. Even the ballet sequence in *The Private Life of Sherlock Holmes* leads to a confusion of sexuality. Robert Mundy has suggested that by depriving dance of its social function Wilder highlights the roles the characters are playing. This is certainly true in *Sunset Boulevard*, where Joe and Norma's lonely dance physically unites their mutual solitude and despair, the high shot revealing a floor pattern suggestive of restriction and imprisonment and also emphasising the huge room which dwarfs the characters.

her love for Joe, the moment when Joe realises that Norma's feelings towards him have gone beyond that of an employee; indeed, his work on Norma's "Salome" script has been completed by this time, yet Joe still remains in the mansion whilst Norma lavishes gifts on him. But when Norma tells Joe that she loves him his reaction is to walk out, unable to reconcile greed with passion. He escapes to a party given by Betty's fiancé Artie Green, an escape, he believes, from age to youth, from a kind of fossilised grandeur to a joyful spontaneity. At Artie Green's he might even cast off the expensive coat which represents the height of his unscrupulous fleecing of Norma ("After all, sir," smirks the salesman, "the lady's paying"). But we recall that even in his defiant gesture of walking out on Norma his watch-chain becomes entangled in the wrought-iron gates of the mansion. And beneath the overcoat he is still wearing the tails and tuxedo that Norma has bought for him. In effect, he is still in the silken and golden web woven around him by Norma's devotion and love and by his own greed and ambition. At the party he telephones Max to have his belongings moved to Artie's apartment but is told that Norma has cut her wrists with his own razor. Horrified and suddenly stricken with guilt he pushes through the throng to return to his prison, snatching up the overcoat on his way out.

Joe's return to Norma is an act of compassion which ultimately compromises his relationship with Betty and cuts him off from normal human contact for the remainder of the film. As Norma lies in bed with her wrists heavily bandaged, giving one of the most important performances of her life, Joe tries desperately to sever the relationship for ever. But to no avail; as the orchestra below play "Auld Lang Syne," he realises he must remain and surrenders to Norma's outstretched arms. Just as Max later admits to Joe that he has remained with Norma because life would not be the same without her,* Joe's acceptance of his fate is an acknowledgement of the fact that life is not worth living outside the mink-lined mansion. The wrought-iron gates, like those of Charles Foster Kane's Xanadu, become the

*Like Joe, Max's relationship with Norma has in effect emasculated him, her rejection of him as husband and self-supporting man reducing him to a role of domestic servitude. Max's feeling of impotence and frustration is probably most mischievously signalled by Wilder when he has him play Bach on Norma's organ on the morning after Joe's arrival in the house. Max's swooning delivery on the instrument conveys a release that is almost orgasmic: but the white gloves he wears acknowledge the impossibility of direct contact and, anyway, Norma tells him to stop!

doorway to a private hell rather than the gateway of opportunity. One can perceive here elements of the Faustian structure which Wilder often alludes to in his films: Joe selling his self-respect ("Don't you sometimes hate yourself?" Betty asks him at one point; "Constantly" is Joe's reply) in return for worldly gifts and resisting the attractions of a good girl trying to reclaim his soul.

Nevertheless, the Norma-Joe-Betty triangle presented here is rather difficult to interpret in terms of strict Good and Evil. Ostensibly, the two women might seem to offer a clear contrast between Norma's self-interest and Betty's devotion; between Norma's insistence on Joe's serving her and Betty's wish to serve Joe; between Norma's desire to be in front of the camera and Betty's acceptance of a role behind it. But a closer examination reveals the contrast to be much more complex than that. Betty represents a likeable but rather dull and decent conventionality, whilst Norma embodies an art and a grandeur which are always veering crazily into excess but have at least an imaginative risk and excitement. One could say that the two women in the film represent two potentialities within Joe himself, the potential of the artist (Norma) and the danger of that potential being subsumed into a normal human being (Betty). Wilder problematises the conflict still further by qualifying Betty's normality and insisting that she echoes Joe's frustration by telling him that she had her nose remodelled when she had ambitions to be an actress. In addition to this, Betty could be seen as a pale echo of Norma, seizing on Joe's comparative talent for writing (he comes up with the ideas she does the typing) as a way of developing her own career. Besides Norma, Betty *is* suffocatingly ordinary, though she obviously considers Artie Green one-dimensional and is instinctively attracted to Joe's corrupted charm. The choice before Joe is far from clear-cut and to recognise this is to appreciate why he can choose neither and has to try and start again. Thus, two often criticised scenes, towards the end of *Sunset Boulevard* – Joe's rejection of Betty, his final attempt to leave Norma – are not contradictory but inevitable. One of Wilder's literary heroes, Karl Kraus, would have understood Joe's decision perfectly, for he once wrote: "If I have to choose between the lesser of two evils I will choose neither." Joe's decision to extricate himself from an intolerable situation leads him also to attempt to save both of the women who desire him.

The impossibility of any future between Joe and Betty is perfectly

Sunset Boulevard: *Nancy Olson and William Holden at Paramount Studios*

clear, given his own compromised past and the fact that Betty is his best friend's fiancée. Norma, playing the jilted wife, has telephoned Betty to tell her the truth about Joe, but when Betty arrives at the mansion it is Joe who reveals his true self to Betty: more honourable by far to reject her in a brutal way and destroy her romantic illusions about him. As he bids farewell to Betty at the door, we see Norma above him on the balcony, looking down on the scene with sadistic pleasure. It is an image which precisely defines the relationship of Norma to Joe at that point as she sees it – that of a puppet-master controlling her puppet. Joe now goes upstairs and attempts to cut the string, telling Norma about the telephone calls from Paramount and the hundreds of fan letters which Max writes to her every week, an attempt by Joe to bring Norma crashing back to reality and also a redemptive gesture – like Walter Neff breathing his last into the dictaphone, Tatum confessing to the reporters as he bleeds to death, Baxter tossing down the key to the executive washroom, Hinkle leaping from his wheelchair to strike the private detective. Typically for a Wilder hero he has cast off the clothing and ornaments which have tied him to Norma. But his psychological technique with Norma only pushes her further into the realms of madness; he never gets past the swimming pool which he has always coveted as the ultimate status symbol ("Poor dope," Joe says at the start of the film, "He'd always wanted a pool. Well, in the end he got himself a pool, only the price turned out to be a little high.") When Norma shoots him twice in the back and once in the chest and he crashes into the water, it represents his failure to escape from Hollywood, from Norma's mansion, and, equally pertinently, a failure to escape from his own scheme concerning Norma and from Norma's obsessive fantasy world.

If Wilder's carefully measured imagery gives the film an atmosphere of deadly ritual and inevitability (repeating the same camera angle for Joe's death as the burial of the chimpanzee), then premonitions of Joe's failure to escape are cunningly signalled in the language he uses for his narration which is compulsively tied to cinematic imagery, even Hollywood clichés: "I've got a good deal here, a long-term contract with no options." Norma is similarly enwrapped by this imagery, regarding Joe's final departure as equivalent to an audience walking out in the middle of a show, an affront to her dignity as an actress. "No one *ever* leaves a star," she whispers. 'That's what makes one a star." Even at a moment of great personal triumph, when following Joe into his room after the rejection of Betty, Norma cannot resist adjusting her hair in a mirror before sweeping in for her "big" scene. This inability to distinguish genuine emotion from histrionic display emphatically relates the Hollywood setting to the larger theme of illusion and reality.

In this context we probably think first of Norma's madness, her confusion of the newsreel cameras recording her arrest for Joe's murder for the studio cameras recording her return as Salome. But Wilder undercuts an audience's sense of the reality of the Sunset Boulevard world since the narration is given by a character whom we discover is dead.* Norma's disorientation is more extreme, but we

*When asked in the 'American Film' interview whether he was concerned about having a dead narrator, Wilder replied: "Yes, but that was the only way out. I shot a whole prologue, a whole reel – that and another reel of the ending to *Double Indemnity* have never been shown. The prologue was very well shot and quite effective. A corpse is brought into the morgue downtown – and I shot it there too – and it's the corpse of Holden. There are about six other corpses there under sheets. Through a trick we see through the sheets to the faces and they are telling each other the events leading to their deaths. Then Holden starts telling his story. We previewed the picture, with the original first reel. . . . The corpse is brought in on a slab, a name tape is put on the big toe of the corpse and once the tag went on the toe, the audience broke into the biggest laugh I ever heard in my life. I said "Oh my God" and the picture just went straight down. It was a disaster. So that whole sequence went out, but we kept the notion of a man telling of the events which led to his demise."

too are baffled by appearances, by the ostensible realism of the film which in fact crumbles beneath us. Joe Gillis is a ghost writer in a more literal sense that we imagined. The device of the dead narrator clearly has several functions in the film. For one thing, it plays on Norma's strictures about talk in movies ("You made a rope of words and strangled this business") by being over-explicit in its delivery and imagery. Further, the narration – this voice from the grave – mirrors the theme of breathing life into dead careers, into waxworks, which is at the heart of the film's meaning. The 'impossibility' of the narration also has an element of the supernatural which tips *Sunset Boulevard* in the direction of the horror film, complete with old dark house, mysterious butler, wheezing organ and a manic inhabitant with nails like claws. The shot of Norma gazing down on Joe as he shows Betty the door has all the glittering decadence and sinister overtones of a James Whale or Tod Browning or Stroheim. The kiss at midnight, marking Joe's physical and emotional commitment to Norma, is faded discreetly in a style which Richard Corliss, in 'Talking Pictures,' has

Sunset Boulevard: *"Mr DeMille, I'm ready for my close-up" (Gloria Swanson)*

compared with the blood-sucking moments of *Dracula*: a vamp with her own Jonathan Harker. The characters in the mansion, however, are so bizarre that it is hard to decide whether they are really like that, deliberately exaggerating their eccentricities, or whether Joe is seeing them in terms of movie conventions as he almost imperceptibly moulds them into characters for a film script, or that the grotesquerie reflects his own deepening psychosis.

The narration could be Joe's new screenplay, a B-picture certainly (his language is certainly not Wilder's and the tawdry talk reveals his opportunism more than his talent). But what kind of picture? Appropriately for a film about Hollywood, all kinds of genres are explored and intermingled as Joe tries to make sense and coherence out of his experience. *Sunset Boulevard* begins like a gangster picture – roaring police cars at dawn, the two menacing finance men, the car chase; even the narration, claiming to tell it "before you hear it all distorted and blown out of proportion, before those Hollywood columnists get their hands on it," evokes the Fox films of Louis de Rochemont (for a long time the guiding hand of 'The March of Time' which purported to tell the truth behind the veneer of pulp material), the urban 'documentary' of *The Naked City* (1948), or even Wilder's own *Double Indemnity*. This inevitably links *Sunset Boulevard* with the *film noir*, with an already doomed hero narrating a journey into the past dominated by a deadly female. Wilder's subsequent adoption of full-blooded Gothic horror consolidates the film's generical allusiveness, clearly illustrating the progress of German Expressionism once the European directors had moved to Hollywood.

When Joe sees Norma's mansion for the first time, he immediately compares it to The Manor House (or 'Satis') in 'Great Expectations', inhabited by Miss Havisham, "taking it out on the world," as Joe inelegantly puts it, "for giving her the go-by." Great expectations that are to be unfulfilled might well describe Joe's experience. And as with Dickens's Pip, who intriguingly likens Miss Havisham to a waxwork, the expected fortune from his benefactress takes a cruel and ironic form. "A grotesque tragi-comedy" was Dickens's description of his novel and it fits well the elusive tone of *Sunset Boulevard*. There is more than a touch of Miss Havisham in Norma Desmond. If Miss Havisham has beetles running out of her wedding cake, signifying a decaying, faded dream, the rats in Norma's pool before the appearance of Joe leads her to have it restored have similar connotations.* In Miss Havisham's house everything is petrified, dominated by the past. Similarly, Norma's mansion is a mausoleum for her past triumphs, the shelves stuffed with framed pictures of herself (Gloria Swanson, that is) in former days. The mansion could even be said to be emblematic of Norma herself – expansive, decrepit, full of bric-a-brac for which no one can find a use. (Joe describes it as "stricken with a kind of creeping paralysis, out of beat with the rest of the world" which could equally describe Norma: and his further description of it as "crumbling apart in slow motion" not only anticipates Norma's ultimate disintegration but, uncannily, predicts the film's final shot.) Miss Havisham has been jilted by her lover; Norma by her audience and by the technological advance of the cinema, summed up by her visit to DeMille's set when the sound boom brushes against her hat – just as the coming of sound has knocked her career sideways – and she has to push it defiantly away. Pip's first sight of Miss Havisham at her dressing table resembles Joe's first sight of Norma, and the effect the young boy and young man has on these women is a kind of grotesque rejuvenation – Norma, readying herself for her return as much as to make herself more attractive to Joe, undergoes an extensive beauty treatment. Since Norma's entire life is lived in the past, both in the mansion and her outings in the Isotta Fraschini, Joe's involvement could represent a dangerous infusion of reality and the present. In fact, it serves his own financial purpose to help sustain her fantasy, to the extent that he becomes part of that fantasy, an accomplice like the devoted Max in the film she will never make. Ironically, this plot of Joe's which is to make his fortune is the thing which is to destroy him – Salome finally has his head on a plate. Norma kills him because he threatens the only thing which is precious to her – illusion.

"You're Norma Desmond. You used to be in silent pictures. You used to be big," says Joe when he confronts this woman for the first time and recognises her. Norma straightens herself haughtily and delivers one of the most celebrated lines in movie history: "I am big.

*The direct transition from the love scene between Norma and Joe to a scene by the swimming pool, which has now been cleaned out and refilled for Joe's benefit, could imply an interpretation of the pool as Norma's womb. It is here that Joe is to meet his death. Having doomed him with her love, Norma returns Joe to the womb rather than allow her 'boy' to achieve manhood. Her weapon – the gun – has obvious phallic overtones and reinforces her total dominance over him. (We would like to acknowledge a West Midlands College student, Mary Madden, who first directed our attention to this aspect of the film.)

It's the pictures that got small." It is a dialogue exchange that draws attention to the grandeur of the old Hollywood as against the meanness of the new. As Joe at the beginning of the film hustles for a three-hundred dollar loan for the continued hire on his car, the world we are taken into is bleak, bitter and ungenerous: the move producer, Sheldrake, who turned down *Gone With the Wind* ("Who wants to see a Civil War picture?"), finds Joe unwilling to alter his script and refuses to provide the loan; Joe's glib agent on the golf course who invokes Dostoievsky and Mozart's privations as a way of refusing the loan; the "Yes-men at Metro" who say "No" to Gillis. No one who is anyone in this society is giving anything away, with the exception of Artie Green, the 'uncommitted' assistant director who almost inadvertently gives away his fiancée. This portrait of the new Hollywood (a Hollywood on the brink of a depression caused by televison) is implicitly contrasted with the quiet dignity of a Cecil B DeMille, an old-guard survivor of the silent era who treats Norma with civility and respect. Whilst newer studio employees don't recognise Norma – the man who won't open the gates for her without authorisation; a member of DeMille's cast who says, "Norma Desmond? I thought she was dead" – or regard her as a curiosity, DeMille and a few other old-timers display an awareness of their heritage and their own legends. Norma's visit to the studio is the most moving sequence in the film because it relates directly to Hollywood's past and present, to Norma's illusions and her fate. "Without me there wouldn't be any Paramount pictures," says Norma-Gloria at one point, words which pass easily through the ears of the money-men who have no sense of anything but cruel exploitation and profit. This over-view of Hollywood presented in *Sunset Boulevard* is summed up by Wilder in an interview with Charles Higham in 'Sight and Sound' when he was asked about the creative atmosphere at Paramount: "It was absolutely marvellous. You just walked across the lot and there they were: von Sternberg, Dietrich, Gary Cooper, Leo McCarey, Lubitsch. We made pictures then, we didn't make deals. Today we spent eighty per-cent of the time making deals and twenty per-cent making pictures." Although Wilder said this in 1967, he gives this same impression, or a canny prediction, in *Sunset Boulevard*. The sense of community so pronounced in the pioneering days until the 'Thirties, has become only a microcosm of the materialist rat-race, a fact of life which has implanted a bitterness in Joe which Norma fails fully to understand. "Why don't you sit here and watch," DeMille says to Norma, "You know, pictures have changed quite a bit." There is a wonderful warmth of feeling in this sequence, culminating in the moment when a technician on a catwalk recognises Norma and trains a spot-light on her, causing everyone to gather around the forgotten star. Nevertheless, Wilder cannot conceal a quiet irony in his attitude towards DeMille, mimicking the fulsome moralising of the man's later pictures and implying a certain hardness to DeMille which has allowed him to survive, a hardness we see when the director, possibly out of sympathy for Norma or for fear of getting behind schedule, orders the spot-light to be swung back on to his set. And when DeMille says goodbye to Norma at the studio door, he snaps to his assistant to find a car other than the one Norma is climbing into as if the intrusion of the old Hollywood in his own career would constitute some kind of threat. For all his affection towards Norma, there is no way in which he is going to be talked into allowing her to play Salome in a film of his. It is Wilder, in the astounding final scene, who grants her an opportunity to do that, revealing a compassion and sensitivity which lifts *Sunset Boulevard* way above the cruel and cynical portrayal of forgotten stars shown in Robert Aldrich's heavily derivative *Whatever Happened to Baby Jane?* (1962).

Norma Desmond and Gloria Swanson are "big" beside the more casual, muted and restrained acting of a modern performer like William Holden. By setting her extrovert performance against the inspired 'straight' acting of the hero, Wilder allows us time to adjust to the sheer scale of the display, permitting us to share Joe's initial amusement, his cold irony, his contempt ("Next time," he says to Norma at their first meeting, "I'll bring my autograph book along, or maybe a hunk of cement for your footprint"), and then gradually, with him, leading us into the tragedy and pity beneath the glittering facade. Study any of the stills from *Sunset Boulevard* and you will see that just as Holden is rarely doing anything demonstrative, Swanson is rarely still: her eyes are blazing, her arms and hands in some twisted, dramatic pose, her hair seemingly alight like a Medusa. Everything about her, from her house to her cigarette holder and car, is on a grand scale. Her acting does not need dialogue: her face and body tell everything. Wilder invariably keeps his camera at a distance so that her emotion is given ample range. The doors with no locks, which is a feature of her mansion, becomes symptomatic of a personality incapable of distinguishing between the public and private, the actress and the woman. The performance is a grand defiant gesture towards sustaining illusion, against age, compromise, ultimately life itself, since Normal loses all contact with reality, in the final scene completely incapable of matching object with context. "You see,"he says near the end, more to her own reflection in a mirror than to the police and Hollywood reporters in her room, "this is my life, it always will be, there's nothing else. Just us. The cameras and those wonderful people out there in the dark."

And yet Norma (and Wilder) finds majesty in madness. "So they were turning after all, those cameras," says the long-dead Joe, "Life, which can be strangely merciful, had taken pity on Norma Desmond. The dream she had clung to so desperately had enfolded her." In her magnificent descent down the staircase it is suddenly the police, the gossip columnists, the mob, who are frozen into waxworks. As the camera captures her seductive descent – "All right Mr DeMille, I'm ready for my close-up," she says to Max who 'directs' the newsreel cameras for 'Salome' – the image begins to disintegrate in an effect of extraordinary resonance, invoking the grotesque (the anticipation of the mad-woman writ large) and the merciful (the camera stopping before the horrific close-up is achieved). It is an effect which mirrors the breakdown of the heroine and of filmic illusion itself, reminding us of the strip of celluloid passing through the projector. It is an image at least as eloquent and powerful as the more celebrated (and less subtle) film-tearing moment in Ingmar Bergman's *Persona* (1966) and should forever silence any notion of Wilder's so-called formal conservatism. It is to Gloria Swanson's glory that the character's grandeur is fully realised as well as her limitations. It is to Wilder's glory, particularly in the light of Norma's rebuke of modern movies, that he can provide a context extravagant enough to nourish that performance.

The Private Life of Sherlock Holmes (1970)

"You see, but you do not observe.
The distinction is clear" –
Sherlock Holmes to Dr Watson, *A Scandal in Bohemia.*

Wilder has always been one of the most misunderstood of directors. He is, for example, regarded as technically unadventurous when what is really meant is that he is unfashionably discreet. More fundamentally, he has been branded as a sour-faced cynic whose 'sentimentality' is merely a ploy to make his cynicism palatable and commercially viable. But as Andrew Sarris has belatedly recognised, the truth is almost exactly the opposite. Wilder is a Romantic whose 'cynicism' is a defence mechanism to guard against emotional indulgence. It is also a life-belt of sanity in an increasingly unromantic, disenchanted world. The intensity of the cynicism paradoxically serves to highlight the idealism it is designed to protect.

An indication of Wilder's innate romanticism is contained in the music in his films. Much has been said about his voluminous knowledge of American popular songs and his employment of them in films as disparate as *Sabrina* and *Some Like it Hot* to express the smooth calculation or coarse vitality of the American character. But equally pervasive is Wilder's extensive use of the classical repertoire. We recall the strains of Schubert's Unfinished Symphony floating out of the Hollywood Bowl as Walter and Lola converse urgently in *Double Indemnity*; the drinking song in Verdi's 'La Traviata' inducing an alcoholic spasm in the hero of *The Lost Weekend*; Rachmaninov's Second Piano Concerto as part of the hero's seductive strategy in *The Seven Year Itch*; Rimsky-Korsakov's *Scheherezade* underlining Irma la

Douce's fantasy-spinning; Willie Gingrich whistling Rossini at moments of triumph in *The Fortune Cookie*. Of course, it is noticeable that in none of these examples (a far from exhaustive list) is the music offered completely straight. It is either a satirical or ironical comment on a situation which is usually the obverse of romantic. At the same time, the use of this motif could suggest a romanticism which is waiting to be expressed more fully. It could suggest (surely it does, in each of these examples) an aspiration and nobility which modern man is consistently ignoring or perverting.

One could make an instructive comparison here between Wilder and Gustav Mahler. The background of both is Viennese and both produce works permeated with satire, irony, self-mockery, intimations of chaos and a pervasive streak of overt sentiment which has puzzled and annoyed the critics. Mahler is attacked as the overblown Romantic while Wilder is dismissed as the schmaltzy cynic. But Mahler's romanticism is qualified and contained by his keen humour and self-criticism just as Wilder's corrosive criticism is moderated and indeed defined by an emotional yearning. When an artist uses a romantic theme in an unromantic context, as in the Wilder films cited and as in, for example, Mahler's flickering statements of noble themes past and to come amid the stormy "Ländler" and Scherzo movements of his Ninth Symphony, he is not necessarily using it to deflate the romanticism but to draw attention to its absence in the prevailing atmosphere. Far from being simply satirical, the romantic theme evokes a still-point of idealism and beauty in a context of bitterness and stagnation and, poignantly, also a palpable sense of loss.

This gives an added significance to the function of Miklós Rózsa's music for *The Private Life of Sherlock Holmes*, which is arguably Rózsa's most glorious film score and, indeed, one of the most beautiful of all film scores. In a way, it is a further example of Wilder's adaptation of a classical piece for his own purposes, for the score is based on Rózsa's own Violin Concerto, commissioned and first performed in 1953 by Jascha Heifetz and, significantly, Wilder knew and loved the music long before planning the film. Indeed, the structure of the film is essentially inspired by and follows the structure of the concerto, judiciously adapted and expanded by Rózsa. The main theme of the opening movement conjures up Holmes's enquiring and cocaine-addicted mind; the slow, central movement parallels the developing relationship between Holmes and Gabrielle Valladon as they investigate the disappearance of her husband, Emile; and the kinetic and percussive finale accompanies the characters' upsetting encounter with the Loch Ness monster. The principal theme of Rózsa's beautiful slow movement provides the film's love motif and is first heard during the credit title sequence when a dusty musical manuscript dedicated to "Ilse von H." is taken from a dispatch box* and is followed by a picture of the heroine hidden inside Holmes's watch. An intense emotion inwardly treasured to the point of personal suffocation could hardly find more powerful expression. During the course of the film, Rózsa's love theme is used to express Holmes's *hidden* emotion, either when brusquely avoiding Watson's enquiry about his experience of women, or when learning from his brother Mycroft that he has been duped by Gabrielle who is in reality the German spy, Ilse von Hoffmanstahl. Here the theme is imbued with a brooding romantic ache as when, in an unusual subjective shot, Holmes lowers a photograph of the real Gabrielle to see Mycroft standing before him, explaining the deception in tones that are cold, official and accusing. It is a grim visual premonition of the spiritual impoverishment that could lie ahead for Holmes himself following this shattering emotional disillusionment.

The credit title sequence gives the clue to the film's overall tone. Fifty years after the death of Dr Watson, his dispatch-box is opened to reveal a number of Holmes's effects: the deerstalker hat, pipe, magnifying glass, hypodermic syringe (pointing at the credits of that needle-sharp pair, Billy Wilder and I A L Diamond). The feeling is essentially one of affection and nostalgia, a tribute to the Holmes ethos rather than a parody of it. The display of tenderness and indeed love from this ostensibly abrasive director took some critics so completely by surprise that they distorted his intention, assuming a satirical failure when it is clear that satire was very far from Wilder's mind. Pauline Kael, for instance, in 'Deeper Into Movies' (Little, Brown, New York, 1974) found it, "rather like the *second class* (our italics) English comedies of the Fifties. The picture is meant to be a put-on of the Sherlock Holmes mythology, concentrating on a case Holmes fouled up. But for this idea to be comic and have suspense we need to see the clues and draw our own inferences, so that we can

*The manuscript we see corresponds exactly – and significantly – to the music we hear on the soundtrack. Rózsa himself appears in the film as the conductor of 'Swan Lake.'

spot where Holmes is going wrong and enjoy his booboos." Ms Kael's wrong-headed insensitivity towards the film might have been expected, but even one of Wilder's most perceptive critics, Stephen Farber, misread its intention: "The title is misleading; the film isn't really about Holmes' private life at all. Wilder is too fascinated with Holmes' famous powers of deduction to abandon the detective's *public* image." But there is no inconsistency in the film. *The Private Life of Sherlock Holmes* concentrates lucidly and movingly on the tragedy of a Suppressed Romantic. Everything in the film follows from that.

To appreciate this is to throw a fresh light on both the casting and the brilliant performance of Robert Stephens as Holmes. Apparently, Wilder selected Stephens on the basis of seeing him as the tortured art teacher in *The Prime of Miss Jean Brodie* and because, as Wilder said (and this is an important clue to his conception of Holmes), "He looked as if he could be hurt." Colin Blakely as Dr Watson was suggested by Stephens to Wilder who wanted someone whom Stephens had worked with in the past, so that the rapport between them would parallel that between the characters. Blakely's Watson is impressionable and volatile and more youthful than the usual conception. Clearly, Watson is there as always to provide a contrast to Holmes, but the contrast is a much deeper one than that of slow-witted companion to razor-sharp intellect embodied in several films by Nigel Bruce and Basil Rathbone. What is immediately apparent is that Wilder's Watson is incomparably more energetic than Holmes. Watson has a spontaneity and passion that may be undisciplined and unpenetrating but has an instinctive vitality to set against Holmes's moods of lethargy and melancholy that Holmes himself seems to find occasionally enviable.

Consider the sequence at the performance of 'Swan Lake,' just after the point when Holmes has extricated himself from a future assignation with the great ballerina Petrova by delicately implying a homosexual relationship between himself and Dr Watson ("Tchaikovsky was not an isolated case"). Having failed to persuade Dr Watson to return home ("Watson, are you coming?"), he pauses by the exit to watch his friend in an ecstatic and frenzied dance with some Russian ballerinas. It is a moment that could suggest Holmes's resignation and regret at the embarrassment which is subsequently to immerse Watson when he learns of Holmes's 'revelation' about their relationship. But, more than that, it becomes a suddenly expressive cameo of the isolation of the man of the mind as he surveys the purgative pleasures of the man of the senses.

The sequel to this scene is one of the most moving and sensitively directed in all of Wilder's films. Watson rushes home seething with rage and humiliation, a state of mind not relieved by Holmes's indifference ("So there'll be a little gossip about you in St Petersburg"). Then Holmes convinces Watson that his expedient is of little importance – "After all, you have an enviable record with the fair sex." Holmes's occasional envy of his friend's vitality might extend to an envy of his virility, and when Watson tries to assert Holmes's own claims in this area he instantly registers the detective's mental withdrawal: "Holmes. Let me ask you a question. I hope I'm not being presumptuous, but there *have* been women in your life?". Holmes's response is saved from being unbearably chilling (or inappropriately funny) by Rózsa's love motif, making the response profoundly moving: "The answer is yes. You're being presumptuous." The camera lingers as Holmes retreats into his room, leaving Watson moved, frightened and in almost tearful despair. For the first time, Watson is used to imply a failure, a limitation in Holmes's sensibility, and not the other way around. Watson's visible fright at the end of this scene also implies a measure of his own guilt at creating a 'fictional character' who bears little resemblance to the real man.

The strategy of Wilder throughout the film is to build on this split between the private life of Holmes and his public persona, the man of the tales who is not so much Holmes himself as a creation of Dr Watson. It is precisely this of which Holmes is complaining in the opening scene, Watson having created a star, a superhero, an image which Holmes (like Norma Desmond and Fedora) has to live up to. He is compelled to stroll around in the "improbable costume" that is expected of him through Watson's chronicles (significantly, he only appears in this costume during his investigations in London, changing into more conventional garb for the Scottish scenes where he loses his way intellectually and emotionally). Watson has made him out to be a violin virtuoso, Holmes having just received an invitation to play the Mendelssohn Concerto, when he could hardly hold his own in the orchestra pit of a second-rate music hall. He has been presented as a "hopeless drug addict," even though Dr Watson has been diluting his seven-per-cent solution for years. Most damagingly of all, he has been portrayed as a misogynist: "Actually, I don't dislike women," Holmes says, "I merely distrust them."

If Watson is used to imply Holmes's limitations and to conceal his humanity, the heroine is introduced after the 'Swan Lake' episode to *reveal* Holmes's suppressed emotions. Gabrielle Valladon (Genevieve Page) is clearly modelled on Irene Adler, the heroine of Conan Doyle's 'A Scandal in Bohemia,' only one of two cases that Holmes failed to solve. The opening paragraph of 'A Scandal in Bohemia' is particularly useful in coming to terms with Wilder's reading of Holmes's character:

> "To Sherlock Holmes she is always *the* woman. I have seldom heard him mention her under any other name. In his eyes she eclipses and predominates the whole of her sex. It was not that he felt any emotion akin to love for Irene Adler. All emotions, and that one particularly, were abhorrent to his cold, precise, but admirably balanced mind. He was, I take it, the most perfect, reasoning and observing machine that the world has ever seen: but as a lover, he would have placed himself in a false position."

Scholars have argued about the precise meaning of this opening paragraph, particularly Watson's emphasis in the first sentence. Does "*the* woman" refer to the woman who successfully outwitted Holmes – the object of his hatred? – or is "*the* woman" the only one who captured his interest in an emotional way? Watson's disclaimer of the latter possibility only raises these questions more urgently and seems to relate more to his idealisation of Holmes than to the truth. Wilder seizes on this ambiguity by having Gabrielle both outwit Holmes and capture his heart. Watson's 'presumption,' therefore, threatens to pierce through Holmes's defence mechanisms and at the end, as we shall see, he dare not 'presume' again after Holmes's professional integrity and his heart have both been broken. As the film develops we realise that Holmes has always been betrayed by women which has produced within him a profound distrust and fear of them; on the train to Scotland, Gabrielle's own 'presumption' leads Holmes to admit that the most affectionate woman he ever knew was a murderess, with whom he had "a passionate affair right in my laboratory, and all the time behind my back she was stealing cyanide to put in her husband's steak and kidney pie." He then lists the types of women he has been involved with: kleptomaniacs, nymphomaniacs, pyromaniacs. "Have you ever been cornered by a mad woman?", he asks Dr Watson following his nightmarish encounter with Petrova. The tragic connection between Petrova and Gabrielle is that, for different motives, they both want Holmes for his brain rather than for his heart – it is the man of the tales that captures their imagination.

The main tension in the film, then, is not on the detection of a particular case (which Holmes does not solve anyway) but on the character of Holmes. Indeed, the very incongruity of the plot details (involving midgets, Trappist monks, canaries, a mechanical Loch Ness monster, and Queen Victoria) seems designed to detach the viewer from any close involvement with the specific unravelling of the plot and throw his attention on the character doing the detection (what kind of man can solve *that?*). For all Holmes's deductive powers there seems another dark, secret side more consistent with suppressed romantic melancholia – the violin playing, the compulsive drug-taking. It is a conflict between the Romantic and the Artist in Holmes vying with the Scientist and the Logician. The psychological split, which is actually a confusion of identity heightened by his involvement with Gabrielle to whom his feelings are drawn, is to rend him from within and render as failures both his emotional and intellectual endeavours. Holmes is masquerading as the "perfect, reasoning and observing machine" but the very flamboyance of the performance takes the character into the realms of romance and theatricality.

The Private Life of Sherlock Holmes: *Robert Stephens, Genevieve Page, Colin Blakely*

Theatrical imagery is prevalent in the film, significantly so in a film which is exploring so intensely the dichotomy of Appearance and Reality (if Gabrielle is not what she seems, neither is Holmes). This range of imagery is quickly established when Holmes first enters his study and lifts the window blind and is continued in the scene at the ballet. During the train journey to Scotland, when Holmes and Gabrielle share a sleeping compartment disguised as Mr and Mrs Ashdown, there is a moving conversation where Holmes reveals that he was once engaged, in answer to Gabrielle's enquiry about his attitudes to women as described in Watson's chronicles: "She was the daughter of my violin teacher. We were engaged to be married, the invitations were out, I was being fitted for a tail-coat, and twenty-four hours before the wedding she died of influenza." "I'm sorry," says Gabrielle, feeling both moved and surprised by Holmes's candour. But then the curtain goes up over his emotions: "It just proves my contention that women *are* unreliable and *not* to be trusted"; the roles are reassumed ("Good night, Mrs Ashdown," "Good night, Mr Ashdown"); and each draws a blind across their bed as if concluding a performance. "The curtain is going up on the last act," announces Holmes when summoned to the castle for the dénouement. His gestures are also surprisingly histrionic for a man of supposed cold logic. When he returns to the hotel, after Mycroft's revelation of Gabrielle's treachery, he comes to her bed as she lies asleep. Using the parasol which has been of vital importance in her deception (as her signalling device to the enemy), he lifts the blanket over her naked back. This gesture with parasol and blanket, at first sight one of regretful gentleness, becomes on deeper consideration one of rebuke, a gesture which draws an eloquent and disapproving curtain over her seductiveness.

Holmes as the surrogate romantic and thwarted artist is wholly consistent with Stephens' performance, giving a precise definition to both his elaborate make-up and to the luxuriant tones with which he delivers the dialogue. This Holmes clearly sees himself as a Byron in disguise, an image completely lost on Watson. "Maybe Mrs Hudson is entertaining," says Watson, attempting to explain an unaccountable ring at the door. "I've never found her so," returns Holmes with commendable quickness that draws no response whatever from Watson, Holmes as *wit* not being part of the image. When Holmes draws attention to the quality of his logic and rationality it is always in a tone of *complaint* or deprecation rather than one of self-congratulation: "Oh, come now Watson, you must admit you have a tendency to over-romanticise. You've taken my simple exercises in logic and embellished them, embroidered them . . ." Later on he says, "How I envy you your mind Watson. It's placid, imperturbable, prosaic. But my mind rebels against stagnation. It is like a racing engine tearing itself to pieces. . . ." As we have seen, Holmes's envy of Watson, however ironically expressed, is an element which frequently occurs in the film. But equally striking is the way in which Holmes's superior mental processes are seen here as potentially self-destructive.

It is an impression that is elaborated in the wonderful scene in the graveyard near Loch Ness. Holmes, Watson and Gabrielle have been drawn there in their investigations and are surprised to find a funeral in progress. There are three coffins, two small ones and one adult one, the latter suspected to contain Gabrielle's missing husband, the engineer Emile Valladon. It is Holmes who connects this business with the case of the missing midgets which had been brought to his attention in the opening scene of the film – "boys with the faces of old men," is Holmes's description of their brothers who come to mourn at the graveside. Valladon's connection with the midgets is to be clarified later, but what is noticeable at this point is the strange mood which afflicts Holmes. Far from this intuition providing him with a source of delight and self-satisfaction, his mood is suddenly bitter and melancholy. "Some of us are *cursed* with memories like flypaper and stuck there is a staggering amount of miscellaneous data, mostly useless," he says dully. A sense of anguish at the fate of a man compelled to live too much in the mind seems to expand also into a twisted identification with the midgets, whose physical stuntedness echoes Holmes's emotional stuntedness. Holmes's dedication to a life of cold intellect, perpetuated by Watson's myth-making and a denial of Holmes's private-self, has made him old before his time.

The resonances of this incident extend to his meeting with Queen Victoria, who is also a midget; who, like Holmes, is playing a role which does not quite fit (imperious majesty in a ludicrously diminutive frame); who, like Holmes, is a figure of distorted myth as well as reality; and who, like Holmes, represents a Romantic personality in Victorian clothing, extolling the virtues of honour, integrity and fairness in an increasingly scientific and cynical world. She is "not amused" to learn that the Loch Ness monster is really an underwater warship, and even less so when she learns that its purpose is to destroy the enemy without being seen. The notion of a British ship firing at an enemy in such an underhand way and without first displaying its colours is abhorrent to her. Mycroft (Christopher Lee), the fanatical scientist, is momentarily thrown off balance – like Sherlock, he has been "undone by a woman." However, he soon devises an equally underhand way of complying with Victoria's orders to destroy the ship by allowing it to be captured by his present enemies, having first loosened a few bolts so that it will explode when fully submerged. In this world, Victoria's values are anachronistic.

Holmes, too, is an anachronism. Like *Ninotchka* and, in a different way, *Sunset Boulevard* and *Fedora, The Private Life of Sherlock Holmes* is an elegy for a vanished era. Holmes is out of place in a society now given over to bureaucracy, technology and frighteningly advanced weaponry. This is particularly seen in the 'Scottish safari' sequence where Holmes, Watson and Gabrielle visit numerous castles in their hunt for clues. It is a funny scene, the humour enhanced by Rózsa's music, with its romantic surges abruptly dissipated by discordant bagpipes as the search proves fruitless. But it is also a rather touching scene, Holmes's individualistic methods seeming quaint and archaic in the context of global conflict and cynicism – "Holmes, I think we're redundant here," says Watson, after they are ejected from the castle they have been looking for. Holmes is patronisingly reprimanded in precisely these terms by Mycroft when he visits him at the Diogenes Club (which itself turns out to be the Victorian equivalent of the CIA* – nothing is what it seems). "My dear Sherlock," says Mycroft, "there are certain affairs that do not come within the province of the private detective. They have to be dealt with on an altogether different level." It is another of Wilder's studies of the fate of individualism in a depersonalised society. Holmes must stay within his limits, rendered obsolete by modern government machinery. He describes his brother's mind as "Machiavellian" and, as he remarks to Watson, he and Mycroft might live in the same town but they do not live in the same world.

The limits of Holmes, though, are psychological as well as external,

---

*See the Introduction for a fuller explanation of the function and the symbolic value of the Diogenes Club in the film.

and are explored thoroughly. An early indication of Holmes's inhibitions is contained in the scene at the ballet where Rogozhin (Clive Revill) invites Holmes backstage to meet Petrova and deal with her "far from ordinary" case. "It is only the *extra*-ordinary that interests me," says Holmes complacently at the dressing-room door; but, in fact, the "extra" extraordinary nature of her particular proposal (Holmes as her stud on a Venetian gondola) is to compel him to make a summary, albeit elegant, retreat. Although Petrova needs Holmes's brain (to fertilise with her beauty) she offers him a particularly valuable violin as a fee – it is a neat encapsulation of the conflict raging within Holmes, yet his inhibitions prevent him from making a decision. There are certain *emotional* affairs which clearly do not come within his province either.

The pattern established in this scene is to inform the structure of a number of scenes in the film. Holmes will contentedly enter or often initiate a scene but is unable to push it through to its conclusion, the initiative being seized from him before the end (a structure which, as can be seen, is strongly suggestive of Holmes's impotence, both political and sexual). He breaks into the empty shop in Ashdown Street, successfully conceals himself, Watson and Gabrielle from intruders, and deduces what seems to be crucial information. "The art of concealment is being in the right place at the right time," he pronounces ringingly, only for all this to be vitiated by Gabrielle's discovery of a note from Mycroft with an instruction to meet him at the Diogenes Club – a clear suggestion that Mycroft knows Holmes's movements and, indeed, does not need to see him to know where he is. To prove this, Mycroft says, "You're looking fit, both of you," when his back is turned. At the end of this meeting with Mycroft, the latter tosses Sherlock his walking-cane with the words, "You forgot your tool-kit," another demonstration of Mycroft's ease at seeing through his brother's deceptions and a reminder of the previous scene, since this cane-cum-concealed chisel, hammer and saw is the means by which Holmes broke into Ashdown Street. Despite his disguise as Mr Ashdown, the Scottish hotel-keeper has no difficulty in recognising the great detective ("Are you sure you have the right Mr Ashdown?", "Quite sure, Mr Holmes"). Even Watson upstages him at one point by exposing a flaw in Holmes's logic when the latter is disputing whether Watson has seen the Loch Ness monster – "You're the least logical man I know! How can you say it's a figment of my imagination when for years you've been saying I have no imagination *whatsoever*?!". And in the dénouement, Holmes's confident explanation of the mystery does not penetrate to the ultimate solution and Holmes again is frustrated by Mycroft's revelation.

Even Holmes's acute perception of the similarities between this mystery and the ballet does not quite go to the heart of the matter. "We've come across this situation before. At the ballet," he says, "There's a lake and there's a castle and there's a swan that isn't really a swan. Or in this case, a monster that isn't really a monster." What Holmes fails to observe is that the swan that isn't really a swan points to the distinctly swan-like features of Gabrielle who, to compound the connection, is dressed in white during the Scottish sequences and who is not what she seems – but the German spy, Ilse von Hoffmanstahl, a monster who is not really a monster . . .

The impression, then, if of a Holmes whose deductive brilliance is flawed and sabotaged by an underdeveloped humanity. The 'mechanical monster' is, in a sense, Holmes himself. He is the half-complete man, one whose 'romantic wound' (the death of his fiancée) has built up in him a spiritual aridity. Throughout there is a highly evocative use of dust, smoke, fog, mist and veils which give the early part of the film in particular a distinct sense of claustrophobia, and which gathers wide-ranging thematic overtones. Dust is blown off Holmes's magnifying-glass during the credit title sequence; Holmes complains to his housekeeper Mrs Hudson (Irene Handl) about her sweeping the dust from his desk, informing her that it enables him to maintain an efficient filing system – "By the thickness of it I can date any document immediately" – "Well, some of the dust was *that* thick" – "That would be . . . March 1883." Holmes is almost totally consumed by clouds of smoke while researching varieties of tobacco ash and, at one point, Watson even thinks he recognises Holmes from the curling ring of smoke rising over the back of his chair. Hurrying to see Mycroft, he cannot resist pausing to catch the drooping ash from a sleeping man's cigar and analyse its contents. At first, all this serves to suggest is Holmes's own dryness; then, more seriously, implies an incipient decay. It is the entrance of the woman into Holmes's life that indicates the possibility of release from oppressive routine and bursting the dam of Holmes's emotional repression.

Wilder has been criticised for failing to convey the growing intensity of the relationship between Holmes and Gabrielle. But a close reading of the film's imagery only reveals how fully and how subtly Wilder has conveyed the developing feeling between them without having to resort to over-explicit dialogue or insistent close-ups. Given the prevailing metaphors of dust and suffocation outlined before, even a simple action like Gabrielle's instinctive tearing down of the cobwebs from the window bars of 32 Ashdown Street is charged with meaning. In the middle of the film, as her relationship with Holmes blossoms, the screen is suffused with pastoral shades, contrasting with the brooding hues earlier. It is striking how often Holmes plays the role of Gabrielle's husband and with fractionally more zeal than is absolutely necessary, sleeping in the same compartment or hotel room, though in separate beds; and, on a number of occasions, removing her wedding ring and then replacing it in a ritual strongly suggestive of marriage without consummation. The only real physical contact between them happens to be in the scene where Gabrielle seems to be still suffering from shock and comes naked into Holmes's room, pretending to mistake him for her husband. A complicated seduction scene ensues, with both playing roles: he that of the husband, she that of the wife, he deceiving her on one level (he is not the husband), she deceiving him on another (she is neither in a state of shock, nor is she Gabrielle Valladon). Paradoxically, the very artificiality of the situation seems to release in these two disenchanted lovers a genuine emotional warmth and commitment, almost a wish fulfilment. One should remember that Gabrielle/Ilsa falls in love as well as Holmes and is later to be executed under the name of Mrs Ashdown, still playing the disguised role of Holmes's wife. Holmes is the ostensibly rational man betrayed by his emotions and, as with Keyes in *Double Indemnity*, it is this fallibility which endears him to Wilder and to us and not his infallible intuitions. He is too close to the guilty party and his reasoning powers are impaired when his feelings are stirred. "I'm sorry I didn't give you a closer game," says Ilse, to which Holmes responds, "Close enough," a line which is a strong verbal echo of Keyes ("Closer than that, Walter") and similarly suggests an emotional proximity rather than an intellectual one.

When Ilse's treachery is revealed and she rides off as Mycroft's prisoner in the bright sunlight (to be exchanged for a British spy), she starts signalling "Auf Wiedersehen" to Holmes with her parasol. Watson presses Holmes for an explanation – "The public has a right to know these things. If she's a German spy, why should we concern ourselves about her feelings?". Holmes has suggested to Watson that Gabrielle would not like the story spread over the pages of 'Strand' magazine, as a way of protecting both their emotional interests. Watson's comment underestimates *Holmes's* feelings. Holmes watches her "personal message" until she and the blue sky are eventually concealed from view by the gathering dust from her coach. There is a very slow dissolve to a wintry Baker Street as Holmes and Watson slip back into their grey lives.

The final scene brings tragic news from Mycroft. In a note to Holmes, he informs him that Ilse has been arrested by Japanese intelligence for spying on naval installations and has been tried and summarily executed by firing squad. "It might interest you to know," the letter continues, "that she had been living in Japan for these past months under the name of Mrs Ashdown." Holmes rises from the breakfast table, stunned, walking to the window and staring out in an action which recalls the scene when Gabrielle, naked, had disturbed him in his room, and also the scene when he has returned to his hotel room and stared out of the window, digesting the shock of the woman's betrayal. Curious, Watson pulls the letter towards him with the sugar tongs, a detail which amusingly shows even there Watson's hesitancy in 'presuming' on Holmes's personal feelings, and a detail which also, and most beautifully, expresses the delicacy of the emotions being dealt with – emotions too precious to be contaminated by awkward human contact. As he has done at several significant points of the film, Holmes retreats into his room with the hypodermic syringe and closes the door, locked again in his private world of drugs, melancholy and self-disgust. Watson, in the meantime, starts writing up his chronicle beside the fire, perpetuating a legend whose distance from the truth is becoming increasingly tragic. One of Holmes's more pointed lines to Gabrielle suddenly takes on a poignant edge: "We all have occasional failures. Fortunately, Dr Watson doesn't write about mine." Holmes's infallibility seems, in that context, suddenly negative and sterile. It is the *private* man to whom we have responded.

"With *The Private Life of Sherlock Holmes*," Wilder has commented, somewhat bitterly, "I was prematurely reviving interest in Holmes.

Now the market is swamped with smarter brothers and seven-per-cent solutions." The film's disappointing commercial history – it was withdrawn from distribution in America after only a few weeks, though it fared better in Europe – clearly hurt him deeply, especially since United Artists forced him to cut the running time from around 200 minutes to 125 minutes*. The disappointment must have been accentuated by the fact that the film is clearly a personal one, revealing a gentler side to Wilder's personality that had rarely received such full expression before. Did *The Private Life of Sherlock Holmes* herald a new direction or a recapitulation? Perhaps both. A recapitulation in the sense that all of Wilder's Seventies' films have their heart in the past, revaluing, refining, and perfecting the territory Wilder has traversed throughout his long career. This film's failure with critics and public must have made him feel a bit like his Holmes – an individualist ill-at-ease in a modern and depersonalised system, an anachronism whose wit and intelligence are no longer enough.

What is new, though, is the tone. Previously identified with a cinema of acerbity and risk in a climate of tasteful timidity, Wilder suddenly distils a temperateness and geniality in a climate of sensationalism and shock – one need only compare Holmes's methods with those of James Bond. Only *The Front Page* has since sought to emulate the stridency of the Seventies and it is debatable whether the relentlessness of that film is an attempt to emulate contemporary fashion or offer a critical commentary on it. Of course, geniality and romance have always been important in Wilder – for every *One, Two, Three* there is a *Ninotchka*; for every *Foreign Affair* there is a *Love in the Afternoon*; for every *Ace in the Hole* there is a *Sabrina*. But the

---

*The deleted episodes would seem to strengthen our reading of the film's themes rather than weaken them. The original version begins with Watson's grandson arriving at the London bank and opening the dispatch-box. This is followed by a scene on a train in which Holmes gives a demonstration of his powers of deduction which drives a man to almost certain suicide. Then comes the opening as it now exists in the available version and the ballet episode which was to have been followed by a scene aboard a luxury ocean liner, in which Watson persuades Holmes to let him handle a murder enquiry which he bungles; a further episode involved the 'Case of the Upside-Down Room' that Watson faked to save Holmes from killing himself through boredom. Finally, at some point during the adventure with Gabrielle, there was to have been a flashback to Holmes's days as a student at Oxford, where he rowed in the University boat race and fell in love for the first time. We can only speculate on the glories of this version, yet one must emphasise the structural perfection of the present – cut – version: both episodes relate directly to each other, as we have attempted to demonstrate; and one must pay tribute to Wilder and Diamond's brilliant plotting, in which even the tiniest detail – like the case of the missing midgets which Holmes turns down in the opening scene – is followed through.

perspectives of the past, the observation of a favourite character of Wilder's, its relaxation in its handling of sexual relationships, all give *The Private Life of Sherlock Holmes* an additional reservoir of tenderness and grace. Glowingly photographed by Christopher Challis and exquisitely designed by Alexander Trauner, it is the very essence of a mature masterpiece. Breathing a serenity without sloppiness, a melancholy without rancour, a mellowness without sentimentality, its very defiance of modishness makes it one of the most beautiful of modern films.

Fedora (1978)

> "And the candle by which she had been reading the book filled with trouble and deceit, sorrow and evil, flared up with a brighter light, illuminating for her everything that before had been enshrouded in darkness, flickered, grew dim and went out forever"
>
> – Tolstoy, 'Anna Karenina.'

> "I've never tried to repeat a success of mine. But sequels are very fashionable today. The picture I'm preparing now, *Fedora*, well, I was seriously thinking to make it sound more fashionable, of calling it *Fedora II*"
>
> – Billy Wilder

It is night time at a deserted railway station. A whistle shatters the silence and a locomotive billowing a great geyser of white steam comes around a curve. The black-coated figure of a woman appears before us like an apparition, her taut, white face emerging out of that linear background giving the shot a momentary, startling reminiscence of Edvard Munch's painting "*Geschrei* – The Scream." She walks purposefully towards the advancing train and, as we hear a shout offscreen – "Fedora!" – she launches herself into its path, her figure caught for a ghostly instant in the glare of the lights before vanishing beneath the wheels. The Expressionist lighting, the enormous steam engine, and the theatrically cloaked woman, all evoke the atmosphere of the Thirties; one expects to hear the word "Cut!" and the request to do it once more please. But the event we have just witnessed is apparently real, the year is 1977, and an old movie star is involved.

"Fedora is dead," announces the brittle-blonde hostess of an American news show from a gaudy studio. "The legendary movie star was killed last night in a suburb of Paris when she either jumped or fell under a train." The programme continues with a tribute to the celebrated star, reminding viewers of her performances as Emma Bovary, Joan of Arc and Lola Montès, her retirement and her comeback in the Sixties (appropriately, in a film about resurrection entitled "The Miracle of Santa Cristi") when she amazed everyone by her youthful beauty, and concludes with coverage of Fedora's lying-in-state in her Paris mansion. Among the thousands of mourners who slowly circle the open casket is Barry Detweiler (William Holden), an independent film producer, who now takes up the story.

Perched on a balcony above the grief-stricken fans is gathered Fedora's small group of intimates: the heavily-veiled and disabled Countess Sobryanski (Hildegard Knef), the Count (Hans Jaray), the star's former dresser Miss Balfour (Frances Sternhagen) and Dr Vando (José Ferrer), a world famous cosmetic surgeon responsible for Fedora's everlasting beauty. They gaze down on the scene as if they were already dead, frozen like waxworks, waiting for Fedora to join them. And adding a faintly incongruous note to the proceedings, a palm court orchestra serenades the mourners from another balcony with specially selected mood music – Grieg's "Last Spring," Sibelius's "Valse Triste." The sense of gloom is relieved by an abundance of floral tributes. Detweiler observes all this with noticeable disdain, disparaging the reporters with their flashbulbs and their TV cameras and then begins to tell us the story of the death of the sixty-seven-year-old star, played here by Marthe Keller, who lies serenely in the coffin, wearing a pair of silken white gloves and looking not a day over forty.

This is the seductive opening of *Fedora* in which Wilder immediately establishes a connection with *Sunset Boulevard*, made almost thirty years earlier. When, at the beginning of the earlier film, Joe Gillis (William Holden) asks us if we would like to know the facts, he says we have "come to the right place." Holden is to be our guide through death once more, allowing us the privilege of being able to eavesdrop on the lives and deaths of the rich and famous before the malicious gossip columnists get their hands on the story. Once again Holden plays a man out of luck and on the make, pushing a screenplay with which he hopes to lure Fedora out of retirement a third time. The screenplay is a remake of 'Anna Karenina' but Fedora only gets to play the final scene. Like Norma Desmond, who defies reason and truth by claiming the identity of Salome, Fedora ends her life as Tolstoy's tragic heroine, playing the scene to an empty house. When Fedora throws herself under the train, Wilder chooses to freeze the frame, momentarily, as if in horror. This deliberately self-conscious effect is unusual in Wilder but a device which beautifully aligns style and theme since the whole film, like *Sunset Boulevard*, contrasts the unsuccessful endeavour of two ageing egocentrics to make time stand still with the ability of Hollywood and film (by technical means like freeze-frames, by the preservation of performance) to make time do *exactly* that.

One of the most powerful elements in *Sunset Boulevard* was its chillingly accurate prophecy of the Hollywood to come, contained in the presentation of Joe Gillis – "the cheap new thing" – and the secondary characters whose pursuit of the dollar is paramount. Thirty years later, *Fedora* is a lament for the Hollywood of today. Everyone in the film is old or, we ultimately discover, behaves much older than his or her years, and represents certain values now disdained. It is the film of an ageing Crowned Head, to borrow the title of Thomas Tryon's book which contains the original story of *Fedora*, who refuses to abdicate even if it means working in exile. It is the work of a director at the height of his powers but whose creativity is forever being frustrated by a radically altered industry and the demands of a new audience. In 1950, when he made *Sunset Boulevard*, Wilder's position was one of power and success and he could view the dilemma of the unsuccessful screenwriter with compassion but also with a certain amount of detachment. In 1978, Wilder's position is much closer to that of his hero, Detweiler, a proximity which Wilder seems to make no attempt to disguise. When Detweiler finally gets to renew his acquaintance with Fedora he tries desperately to persuade her to appear in 'Anna Karenina' since he can then finance the picture with tax-shelter money. (*Fedora*, which is officially registered as a West German – French co-production, was financed in an identical fashion since no American studio was interested in it.) Not only does "Detweiler" as a name seem an elaborate rearrangement of Wilder's own (and he does correct someone who calls him "Getwyler" – it would not do to be confused with William Wyler): William Holden even looks like Wilder at some stages and is given to wearing glasses and a very Wilderian straw hat.

The identification between Detweiler and Wilder is not complete, of course. One cannot imagine Wilder seriously proposing a remake of *Anna Karenina* under the title of "The Snows of Yesteryear," as Detweiler is doing. However sad and movingly desperate, Detweiler's complaint about the modern Hollywood – "The kids with beards have taken over. They don't need scripts, just give them a hand-held camera with a zoom lens" – is surely intended to be seen as ultimately excessive and self-pitying (Wilder might be drawn towards some aspects of the sentiment, but he has also been generous in his praise of directors like Coppola and Scorsese, both bearded and known to employ the zoom and hand-held camera). Above all, Detweiler did not make his film: Wilder has. Towards the end, having heard the full story, Detweiler says to Fedora: "This would have made a much better picture than the script I brought you." "Yes, but who would you get to play it?," she replies. Wilder, not Detweiler, has got the people to play it and has made the script; and the result is magnificent.

Nevertheless, there is sufficient kinship between Wilder and Detweiler to explain why *Fedora* seems closer in spirit to the melancholy of *The Private Life of Sherlock Holmes* than the Gothic extravagance of *Sunset Boulevard*. At the time of the latter film, Wilder was full of confidence and could be baroque and outrageous: his audacious picture of Hollywood is felt from a position of security within it. *Fedora* is more troubled and possibly even richer because of that, the vision of a man who knows the system inside out but who, like Detweiler, has been increasingly placed in the situation of the outsider looking in. Thus, the tone of the film is extraordinarily ambivalent, constantly pulling between nostalgia and bitterness, between sombreness and romance.

What is remarkable is that this ambivalence is thematically of the utmost relevance and importance. Just as we can hardly think of the Wilder and Holden of *Fedora* without the ghost of the Wilder and Holden of *Sunset Boulevard* in the background, we can similarly reflect that the whole film is about ghosts, mirror images and doubles – about the pull between truth and illusion, youth and age; between Detweiler as he was and Detweiler as he is; and, in particular, between Fedora I and Fedora II, and how one becomes the mirror image of the other. Even the structure has the same pattern, being in two distinct sections, the first dealing with Detweiler's strenuous attempts to meet Fedora and his subsequent concern for her safety; the second presenting the same story from a different perspective and resolving and rationalising all the ambiguities raised in the first. In the first part, Detweiler resembles a character in a mystery thriller, pitched headlong into a dark labyrinth. In the second part, as Fedora – literally and metaphorically – reveals a side to the mystery he has not seen, he is changed from participant to audience, from subject to object. Like Keyes in *Double Indemnity*, Sir Wilfrid Robarts in *Witness for the Prosecution* and Holmes in *The Private Life of Sherlock Holmes*, Detweiler is another Wilder investigator who misinterprets the evidence before him.

Occupying nearly two-thirds of the film, Detweiler's narration is concerned not only with his attempt to interest Fedora in returning to the screen in his new film. It also relates his mounting suspicion that she is being kept prisoner in her home, the Villa Calypso*, which is situated on a small island off Corfu and where she lives with the sinister Countess, Miss Balfour and Dr Vando. The tone of the first part of Detweiler's narration has closely resembled *Avanti!* as the American checks into a waterfront hotel whose owner (Mario Adorf) is a less refined but no less capable version of Carlucci, with a string of relatives or connections to help Detweiler go where he wishes. But unlike Wendell Armbruster, who assimilates a sun-drenched Ischia and European values, Detweiler is to experience violent storms and tragedy – not regeneration (which Fedora is striving for) but disillusionment.

His first glimpse of the villa's occupants is through a pair of binoculars and from behind the villa's barbed wire and 'Keep Out' signs. Worth noticing here is the care with which Wilder undercuts Detweiler's certainty by interposing barriers between him and the things he sees. By occasionally shooting through a long lens in wet and misty weather, Wilder gives a shimmering insubstantial quality to the image which eliminates all sense of surrounding landscape and, as an extension of this, all sense of freedom: the effect of this is to alert us to the limitations placed on the hero's visual perception while he is becoming steadily convinced of Fedora's entrapment.

His first meeting with Fedora at a souvenir shop does nothing to allay his suspicions, since she seems in a trance-like state, borrows money from him, and is clearly frightened at being discovered by Miss Balfour and the chauffeur. Summoned to the villa after a number

---

*Again one marvels at the wealth of incidental detail in Wilder's films. In Tryon's original story the villa, situated on Crete, is not given a name. Wilder's choice of "Calypso" reflects the enormous pains he takes in elaborating his principal themes. According to Greek mythology, Calypso (meaning To Hide) ruled the small island of Ogygia in the Ionian Sea where Corfu is situated. When the exhausted Odysseus drifts ashore, the beautiful water-nymph Calypso takes care of him for seven years. "If you stay with me," she says, "you shall enjoy immortality and ageless youth."

of enquiries from him by 'phone and letter, he is told by the Countess that a comeback for Fedora is impossible since her health is failing, only for Fedora to appear on the staircase and express excitement at the project, an enthusiasm quickly stifled by her being dragged back to her room. In a later scene in his hotel room, when Fedora unexpectedly turns up to ask Detweiler to sell some of her fan mail, they are interrupted by the arrival of Dr Vando and the chauffeur, and he watches helplessly as they bundle Fedora off, straitjacketed, in a Rolls-Royce. His search of the deserted villa next day reveals clues that seem incongruous and baroque – exercise books with "I am Fedora" written all over them; a drawer full of white gloves (a startling detail which recalls Max von Mayerling's white gloves as he plays Bach on the wheezing organ in *Sunset Boulevard*). Discovered in his snoopings by the chauffeur and knocked unconscious, Detweiler awakens a week later in his hotel room and is shown a newspaper report of Fedora's death. His entire investigation, which began as an innocent – if desperate – business trip, has ended in violence and tragedy. His conclusion is that Fedora was being held captive by an invalided and eccentric Countess, a dedicated spinster and sinister quack and has been killed by them.

In the middle of this flashback, Detweiler sits down to write a personal letter to Fedora, recalling how they first met in 1947, and we move into a further recollection of the past. Wilder begins the sequence by cutting from a shot of the ageing Detweiler writing his letter to a panning shot as Fedora walks past the studio technicians, has her robe removed by Miss Balfour, and descends gracefully into an ornamental pool. It is a shot which, like Norma Desmond's visit to DeMille's set in *Sunset Boulevard*, takes us from the business realities of making motion pictures to a complete illusion in a single camera movement. As she lies naked in the pool, Detweiler, at that time an assistant director nicknamed "Dutch," is assigned the task of covering her nipples with water lilies. He stares down and yawns before the Goddess beneath him and slaps down the leaves to appease the Legion of Decency. Considerably piqued at his casual attitude to her body, Fedora has summoned "Dutch" to her dressing-room and they get into a conversation about his life-style. "What, may I ask, is a cheese-burger?," she enquires, an eloquent way of indicating her isolation and her imperious way of asking for a date. "Dutch" obliges: they have a one-night affair on a beach in his battered second-hand

Ford (contrasting with Fedora's vintage Rolls, just as Joe Gillis's vehicle has contrasted with Norma's Isotta Fraschini). Ostensibly, this flashback-within-a-flashback might seem rather abrupt and contrived, but the brief affair between Detweiler and Fedora is to have poignant overtones later; the evocation of the innocent vulgarity of Hollywood in the past is highly relevant to Detweiler's present desperation; and the connection in the flashback between flowers and artifice (Fedora's waterlilies) is a beautifully planted clue to the truth behind Fedora's lying-in-state. Almost subconsciously, Detweiler has uncovered a significant link between the film set of 1947 and the elaborate performance taking place now over Fedora's body in her Paris mansion, but the meaning of the evidence before his eyes eludes him.

All of this passes through Detweiler's mind as he looks down on Fedora in her open casket. There are two points to be made immediately about this narration. The first, as we have indicated, is that this interpretation of events is to be revealed as wholly inadequate: every scene with Fedora and the Countess is to take on a different meaning when we learn how thoroughly he has been misled. The second is the film's strategy in having the narration take place alongside Fedora's open coffin. The film never leaves the chamber in which Fedora lies in state: all the flashbacks begin and end here*.

The film is saturated with the imagery of death and, indeed, the whole structure takes on the form of an inquest. The lavish lying-in-state is a sort of masque to conceal and diminish the ravages of death. Even Fedora's face, crushed by the train, has been repaired for the occasion, an action which recalls Dr Vando's experiments and the magic performed by Hollywood make-up men. There is a phrase in John Webster's great Jacobean tragedy 'The White Devil' which could be said to summarise this aspect of *Fedora*: "a dead man's skull

---

*Many of Wilder's films border on the macabre, and coffins and cemeteries are used extensively: the very title of *Five Graves to Cairo*; Keyes's claim in *Double Indemnity* that, "straight down the line" leads to the cemetery; the monkey's burial in *Sunset Boulevard*; the cave as metaphorical coffin in *Ace in the Hole*; the coffin leaking booze and the funeral parlour/speakeasy in *Some Like it Hot*. It should also be noted that Wilder's previous films – *The Private Life of Sherlock Holmes*, *Avanti!*, *The Front Page* – are to a significant degree based on situations concerned with death and burial. There are the coffins in *The Private Life of Sherlock Holmes* intended for the midgets, Emile Valladon and the canaries; the entire plot of *Avanti!* is concerned with Armbruster's efforts to procure one zinc-lined coffin, then another; *The Front Page* takes place during the preparations for an execution and obliges the condemned man to spend much of the film incarcerated in a roll-top desk, another of Wilder's surrogate coffins from which there is little or no chance of escape. *Fedora* is another story of confinement; and, as in so many Wilder films, the coffin does not contain what people think it contains.

beneath the roots of flowers." Like the Webster play, *Fedora* has this strange confluence of beauty and decay, the sense of a luxuriance and glamour concealing something that is evil and horrible. The impression of terrifying truths lying under the surface of things pervades the film's imagery: Fedora's dark glasses and white gloves; the Countess's veil; Fedora's terrified eyes, alone visible under the bandages when Dr Vando's treatment seems to have gone wrong and he is cutting through the cloth to inspect the extent of the damage; even a minor detail like the chauffeur's friendly smile before he cracks Detweiler's skull hard enough to leave him concussed for a week. The film's sumptuous photography intensifies the contrast between surface beauty and underlying horror. Indeed, the film's most stunning single shot, that of a carriage and two horses, festooned with flowers like the coffin and neatly wrapped in cellophane to protect the horses from the rain, is a visual joke which, nevertheless, in its echo of Fedora's insulation from the outside world, strikes at the core of the film's meaning. This motif (the worm under the rose) could even be taken as a statement on the star system itself: what Detweiler characterises as "sugar and spice and, underneath that, cement and stainless steel."

Connected with the imagery of death is, inevitably, the theme of time, to which attention is drawn in the film through its extraordinarily intricate structure. "You can't cheat nature without paying the price," Dr Vando has said at one stage, subtly alluding to his own experiments which, we will discover, have gone grotesquely wrong. But it is another way of saying that you cannot cheat time. The inexorability of time, the characters, entrapment within it and yet their attempts to transcend it, are a constant preoccupation of the film. Its actual running time of 112 minutes corresponds almost exactly to the time scheme of the main action, when Detweiler approaches the open coffin at about noon and when he leaves at two; the rest is memory, reverie and explanation. The impression is of an attempt almost to halt time, to live in a world of memory, all the more ironic since all this takes place alongside Fedora's dead body: not only a potent reminder of mortality itself but of a character who has refused to submit to the demands of time and contrived her own death. The flashback structure defines people who want to turn back the clock, who are living in the past and reluctant to relinquish their grip on old glories, whose answer to the frighteningly inevitable fact of ageing is to try to defy time itself: Fedora's submission to Dr Vando's gruesome experiments, the tragic effects of which generate the whole plot. One recalls Fedora's comment to Detweiler in the souvenir shop when he is describing the disappearance of the old Hollywood: "Time catches up with all of us." Even the impression of time's standing still as they talk around Fedora's coffin is an illusion since, in a brilliant stroke at the very end of the film, Wilder reveals that Detweiler's presence at the lying-in-state is *itself* a flashback, time having moved on a further six weeks. In other words, the film's 'present tense' is actually the past.

But in addition to highlighting the importance of time in the film, the flashback structure – and, in particular, the use of multiple narrators – brings to the forefront another major theme: the relativity of truth. We have been alerted to this in the first meeting between Detweiler and Dr Vando when they converse at the hotel bar, Detweiler quizzing the Doctor about his legendary yet lurid reputation. "How much of it is true?," he asks. "All of it. None of it," replies the Doctor, "It depends on whom you ask." It is an early clue that Detweiler's narration might not be as reliable as he thinks. Now, at the coffin, he puts his suspicions before the Countess – that she and the others were keeping Fedora prisoner and are largely responsible for her death. Initially to silence him (but, in retrospect, for much more profound reasons), the Countess, later supported by the others, begins to tell Detweiler the truth. From this point we move into one of the most exquisitely sustained passages in modern cinema, in effect an ending that lasts over half an hour, a tightly organised series of sequences whose quickening tempo gives exactly the sense of a situation accelerating to an unforeseen point of climax, and an ending whose explanations change the meaning of every scene that has gone before.

"Never mind the face," says the Countess to Detweiler, "look at the hands." The white gloves, which for so long have concealed Fedora's real age, are removed, but the hands are quite without wrinkles. From behind the heavy veil, the Countess reveals her own terrible disfigurement. Detweiler is looking at the face of the real Fedora, now played by Hildegard Knef. (We suddenly realise a detail that had not registered before in the discreet subtlety of Wilder's mise-en-scène: we have until now been shown only one side of the Countess's face.) The body in the casket is that of her daughter,

Fedora: *William Holden, Frances Sternhagen, Hans Jaray, Hildegard Knef, Jose Ferrer*

Antonia, the illegitimate child of Fedora and Count Sobryanski. "You are Fedora," says Detweiler quietly, to which the Countess replies with scrupulous accuracy, "I *was* Fedora": the destruction of her face was the moment when her hold on the identity of Fedora vanished.

By choosing to reveal the 'twist' in the story at this juncture, Wilder makes his final radical departure from Tryon's original story which keeps its readers in suspense until much nearer the end. The film's 'sudden revelation,' coming after seventy minutes, has attracted some criticism. Reviewing the film briefly from the Cannes Festival for 'Sight and Sound,' Richard Roud, who found the film a "big disappointment," thought that the 'twist' "comes far too late in the film to do any good. Hitchcock was right: it is much better to let your audience in on the secret early in the game, so that they can enjoy the contrast between what they know and what one or more of the character's don't. Here we learn the secret at the same time as William Holden, and although we may salute the screenwriter's (*sic*) ingenuity, it is very difficult at that stage to make the necessary readjustment in our view of the main characters. Of course, there are many funny moments. . . ."

One must emphasise at once that Roud's reference to Hitchcock to illustrate Wilder's structural miscalculation could hardly be more injudicious. If there is a precedent for *Fedora* it is to be found pre-eminently in Hitchcock's masterpiece, *Vertigo* (1958), which also has the boldness to give away its ending two-thirds of the way through so that one can experience the last part of the film with the full weight and new understanding of what has gone before. Much criticised at the time, Hitchcock's decision, as is now widely agreed, was the right one: the effect is to intensify the film's depth and power, and we would argue that Wilder's tactic has the same effect in *Fedora*. Indeed, the two films have much in common: an investigator pursuing a figure who is actually a 'double, of the person he thinks she is, and being present at her 'death, which is not really her death; and in both, a profound exploration of the worlds of illusion and death and disintegrating personality.

Another weakness of Roud's position stems from that common failing of critics (*cf* Pauline Kael on *The Private Life of Sherlock Holmes*) who approach Wilder with certain misguided expectations and then attack the director for not conforming to them. "Of course" there are many funny moments, but *Fedora* will be a disappointment for anyone approaching it in the expectation of a cynical comedy. Clearly Wilder is striving for something more than dark humour and the unconventional structure of the film is indicative of his entire strategy. The fact that we only discover the deception at the same time as Detweiler is precisely the point. *Fedora* is concerned with gleaning truth from fiction (the themes of *Sunset Boulevard, Witness for the Prosecution* and *The Private Life of Sherlock Holmes*). Like Detweiler and, later in the film, like Henry Fonda and Michael York, we are lulled into misconceptions, a technique which draws attention to *Fedora* as structure, as illusion, as a system of fallible visual signs. Indeed, Detweiler does recognise the artificiality of the 'lying-in-state,' comparing it to "some goddamn première" and asking the Countess rudely, "How many shows a day are you planning to have?". But the deeper meaning of this performance escapes him. Wilder tricks us, and his hero, into taking things literally at face value. When the usher refers to the lying-in-state as a performance, he is not only describing Fedora's last role, but is invoking the theatricality of Wilder's mise-en-scène. The elegant tracking shots around the coffin seem self-consciously 'cinematic'; the high-angle shots of the fans filing in emphasise the setting as a film set; the wide-angle shots which reveal the television camera equipment force an association between a representation of reality and a movie-in-progress, referring directly to the flashback to the Hollywood studio dressed for a performance with flowers.

One further point should be made about the film's unconventional form. Normally, Wilder favours a triangular structure, with the central figure wavering between the two other sides of the triangle who symbolise the corrupt and innocent sides of his personality. But this kind of sexual tension is completely absent from *Fedora*. One never feels Detweiler hopes to resume his one-night stand with Fedora after a break of thirty years; and Antonia's love for Michael York seems as much a reflection of her despair and isolation as a genuine romantic feeling towards him. Unusually for Wilder, the film is completely dominated by women; the men – the Count, Dr Vando, Detweiler himself – are passive figures whose lives ebb and flow according to the whims of Fedora and Antonia.

The relationship between Fedora and Antonia is one of the most moving aspects of the film. Ironically, Dr Vando's disastrous operation on Fedora, resulting in disfigurement and a stroke which has confined her to a wheelchair, has had one beneficial effect: it has brought mother and daughter much closer together. The situation is dramatically changed when a letter informs Fedora that she has been cited for an honorary Academy Award. She is obviously reluctant to admit the President of the Academy, Henry Fonda, to the villa to make the presentation; but suddenly struck by the likeness of her daughter to Fedora's former self, she has an idea. What if Antonia should impersonate her and accept the Oscar on her behalf?

The presentation ceremony – just Fonda, a photographer, and Antonia as Fedora on the terrace with the sea in the background – is a scene of surpassing beauty. First of all, it is visually stunning, Gerry Fisher's glowing photography at its most atmospheric and sublime here: it is striking how Wilder finds a visual beauty in Europe that is entirely absent from his films set in America. Also, its poignant effect arises from the thematic precision of the scene's conception. Henry Fonda as himself contrasting with Marthe Keller's playing of Antonia who is *herself* playing Fedora is at the heart of the film's intricate pattern of illusion and reality, role-playing and deception. The scene is observed discreetly from an upstairs window by the Countess – the real Fedora – with Dr Vando behind her. Yet Wilder's

Fedora: *Marthe Keller, the Oscar and Henry Fonda*

visual arrangement has also an acute undertone of sadness. Far from being detached from the scene, The Countess, alias Fedora, should be down there receiving her Oscar, but she is not. The man behind her, Dr Vando – who has been behind her in various ways through her career – is a discreet reminder of the reason for her inability to accept this ultimate accolade: it is his ruinous medicine that has consigned her here to the role of spectator. When Antonia comes rushing up the stairs, the Oscar in her hand, and embraces her mother, the complexity of feeling is overwhelming: Antonia overjoyed with the success of her deception and not yet realising that its consequences are to destroy her; Fedora delighted with her Oscar at last, yet pained that she was unable to receive it in person. Watching Antonia collect the Oscar, Fedora says to Dr Vando, "For thirty-five years I had a speech ready. Now she gets to make it." For all her gratitude and love for Antonia, she cannot conceal her pain and envy. It is surely this which explains her decision to tell Detweiler the truth, rather than any fear she might have of his going to the police with his suspicions. It is not fear that prompts her; it is, characteristically, vanity. She wants part of the glory, the recognition. She wants him to see that this homage to the figure in the coffin is not for Antonia but for *her*. It is perhaps her only victory over time: she can be present at her own funeral to reap her laurels in person.

The photographs of the Oscar presentation have been published the world over; the temptation to continue the deception proves irresistible. What follows is a film-watching sequence and a montage of Antonia's gruelling cosmetic sessions to prepare her for the screen as Fedora, which cannot help but recall the similar sequences of *Sunset Boulevard*. When Norma Desmond screens her old movies, she believes that the Hollywood she knew in the Twenties still awaits her outside the walls of her mansion and that the much younger version of herself on the screen is still herself: the screen is a mirror, casting back flattering, misleading images. In contrast, Antonia watches Fedora's old movies to catch her mother's mannerisms and gestures. Fedora's mirror is, in fact, not the screen but her daughter. She does not have to watch her films to see herself as she was; and she can see it in Antonia's face. The sixty-three mirrors have been removed from the villa because, as she says, Antonia "had become my mirror." But as with *Sunset Boulevard* the whole thing is to end up in madness and death, the role of Fedora finally enfolding Antonia and destroying her own identity. For all the difference of presentation and detail, the two film-watching scenes have similar implications: the dangers of illusion invading reality, of the public life invading the private life and forcing, as in *The Private Life of Sherlock Holmes* as well, a duality in the individual which cannot be reconciled. Fedora might not be as mad as Norma Desmond but she shares something of her grandeur and obsessions; like Norma, she is possessed by the popular image of herself and attempts to defy nature in order to preserve it. The tragedy is that she brings down both herself and her daughter in her consuming egomania.

When Detweiler starts to attack Fedora for having exploited her daughter in this way, Fedora stops him: "What would you give to be reborn . . . To have a second chance?". It is a particularly pointed question to put to him. What is his project of *Anna Karenina*, or "The Snows of Yesteryear," but a remake and a chance to make a comeback; and is not Fedora the person he needs to make it work? Is his desire to use Fedora for his own aggrandisement very different from her use of her daughter? The underlying question is perhaps even more personal and severe: what has happened to the Detweiler she knew to age and embitter him so prematurely ("What would *you* give to be reborn . . .")?

At first it has been a kind of game, a masquerade. It is the moment when Antonia, disguised as Fedora, falls in love with Michael York during a film they are making together, "The Last Waltz," that the full implications of the deception become clear. She cannot reveal herself as Antonia without destroying her mother; and yet her mother is the Countess. Miss Balfour, who is as fanatical in her devotion to her mistress as the redoubtable Mrs Danvers in *Rebecca*, puts the dilemma succinctly. The masquerade must continue "until Fedora dies. And you are now Fedora." There is no Antonia anymore. Her youth has been taken away; also her identity and freedom. Even her kiss with Michael York is in the presence of a camera and microphone, against a painted studio backdrop of the Schönbrunn Palace at Vienna, which exactly conveys the illusory relationship and the definition and entrapment of her personal life within her screen identity. In desperation, she attempts suicide; she has also begun seeking solace in drugs which has accounted for her distracted behaviour in Detweiler's presence and her requests for money. "I hate this face!", she cries. She scrawls "Antonia" on the hospital window; the exercise books proclaim "I am Fedora." When Dr Vando has burst in on them in Detweiler's hotel room he has said to her: "You must not forget who you are. You are . . . Fedora." She straightens, intimidated, and is led out. At the time, Dr Vando's words seem a rebuke to a great star who has a reputation to live up to and protect. In the context of the deception, it is an instruction to Antonia to continue with the role. But from Antonia's own point of view, the line is a statement of doom, implying exactly the opposite of what is ostensibly said. For her, it can only mean that she *must* forget who she is; she is Antonia.

Antonia is one of Wilder's most tragic heroines and her death makes a discussion of suicide in Wilder's work inevitable. In 1969, Wilder was dismissive about the suggestion that suicides are recurrent events in his films: "Two suicides in forty years of film-making. I don't detect any trend there," he said to the interviewers of 'Cinema' who had mentioned Sabrina and Fran Kubelik. But there are several more instances of attempted suicides in Wilder's work, not to mention numerous *reported* suicides in his films (for example, the psychiatrist's patient in *The Seven Year Itch* and the lady musician in *Some Like It*

Hot who slashed her wrists when Valentino died). Characters such as Don Birnam in *The Lost Weekend*, Norma Desmond, Sabrina, Fran Kubelik and Bud Baxter in *The Apartment* and Molly Malloy in *The Front Page* all attempt or consider taking their own lives. Wilder's attitude, however sympathetically he might view the character, seems to be that the suicide attempt itself is the result of either lack of will, romantic indulgence or moral cowardice: it is a dramatic device for taking a character's self-contempt and humiliation to its most precarious point so that the reassertion of identity will be all the more intense, involving and affirmative. Antonia, however, has no identity to reassert. Hers is the only successful suicide bid, an attempt moreover that the film seems resignedly to understand and not condemn. Whereas the other characters have not reached the end of the line, still having the potential for life and love within them, Antonia has failed to exist as a person, and the only way out is to kill both herself and her *doppelgänger*. By throwing herself under the train, she can destroy her face. Ironically, the face can be reconstructed. Equally ironically, the people around the body, while exchanging recriminations about the poor girl's fate, can be seen as each in a different way her killers – Fedora for initiating the deception; the Count for not stopping it; Dr Vando for wrecking Fedora's face in the first place; Miss Balfour for forcing Antonia to confront the hopelessness of her situation; even Detweiler, whose abortive project and damaging investigations have pushed the situation to its tragic conclusion.

The palm-court orchestra begins to tune up as the real Fedora concludes her tale. The mansion is opened for business once more and Fedora and her entourage resume their positions on the balcony. The orchestra strikes up, with instructions from Fedora to play some Chopin and Ravel instead of the Sibelius which is a bit "tacky." The guards replace *their* white gauntlets, the usher looks severe, Antonia's make-up is checked and the crowds come in to pay their last respects to an adorable fake. Amongst the mourners this time is Michael York who places a single rose in the casket. Detweiler finally goes to the visitor's book, turns to a brand new page, and poignantly signs himself "Dutch." As he walks from the mansion he tells us that Fedora died on Corfu a few weeks later, rating a few lines in the local paper. Fedora I and Fedora II have run their course.

Detweiler has asked Fedora: why this lavish lying-in-state, the flowers, the music? Fedora explains "Endings are very important.

That's what people remember. The last exit. The final close-up." It is a beautiful statement, conjuring up a host of memories: Wilder's own much-criticised endings; the ending of *Sunset Boulevard*, with Norma asking for her close-up; the remarkable, unforgettable ending of this film, all half-an-hour of it.

Above all, it is a statement which seems to relate *Fedora* to the whole of Wilder's work. Like Chaplin's *Limelight* (1952), which also draws on the maker's own biography, or like Ford's *The Man Who Shot Liberty Valance* (1962), which is also about legend and truth and somebody claiming the charismatic credit for an act he is only indirectly responsible for – or, for that matter, like Shakespeare's 'The Tempest' and Mahler's 'Das Lied von der Erde' – the work has the authority and the feeling of an artistic testament. As in all the works previously cited, the poignancy of the occasion is oddly transcended by the exalted expression.

We talked earlier of the dualities in the film which carry such thematic resonance. It is appropriate now to talk of the duality of the film's effect, its sense of tensions held in exquisite balance, which so enriches its impact. On the one hand, *Fedora* is a mesmerising narrative and superb entertainment in its own right without need of any reference external to itself. On the other, it is Wilder's intensely personal synthesis of the preoccupations of a life-time: film-making, Hollywood, Europe, masquerades and grand deceptions, stars, regeneration, charisma, reality and illusion, truth and legend. In one sense it has a very personal ache, which Detweiler expresses when his project has been rejected: "As Sam Goldwyn said, in life you have to take the bitter with the sour." But it also has an irony and wit that puncture self-pity and self-indulgence and morose bitterness. When Detweiler signs himself "Dutch" at the end, he has regained an identity he thought forever lost, identified himself with the Hollywood of the past, and transcended his own bitterness in his sympathy for another's tragedy. It could be seen as one of Wilder's blackest films, charting the complete destruction of a human being through the selfish delusions of others. But it is equally true that no film of Wilder's is more visually entrancing nor more moving, its relationships – between mother and daughter, between Detweiler and Fedora – having a poignant sense of potentiality and waste, of opportunities for contact momentarily grasped then tragically lost. On the one hand, there is harsh reality and human corruption and egomania. On the other, there is artifice, legend, art, which can always triumph over mere mortality. The show goes on, for the screen can conquer age, even conquer life.

Chapter VI

"WE ALL HAVE OCCASIONAL FAILURES"

— Sherlock Holmes to Queen Victoria in *The Private Life of Sherlock Holmes*

The Lost Weekend
The Emperor Waltz
The Seven Year Itch
The Spirit of St Louis

The Lost Weekend (1945)

With its four Academy Awards – for Best Picture, Best Director, Best Screenplay, Best Actor – *The Lost Weekend* might be regarded as the archetypal Oscar movie, dealing with an important social theme *and* appealing to a mass audience. When it first appeared its grim observation of an alcoholic's desperate weekend search for drink was hailed (legitimately enough) as a significant breakthrough, in sharp contrast to the wartime diet of escapism and propaganda, yet strongly linked to the low-budget thrillers that many of the major studios were producing. Today, however, when the contemporary impact has worn off, its virtues seem incidental rather than central and ironically serve to highlight the superficiality and the hectoring quality at the film's heart. Thus, the characterisation is much more interesting on the fringes of the film than in the centre; and its formal adventurousness seems in conflict with its bleak, deglamourised portrait of New York, pushing the film from gritty realism to expressionist nightmare, an inflation it cannot always support: the stylistic associations with the tormented worlds of *film noir* make the optimistic ending all the more suspect.

Don Birnam's (Ray Milland) famous despairing walk down Third Avenue in search of a pawnshop where he can trade in his typewriter is a little too much like an updated march to Calvary, particularly when he is accompanied by Miklós Rózsa's theremin-intoxicated music. In *Sunset Boulevard*, the visual elaboration corresponded perfectly with the grandeur of the subject; in *The Lost Weekend*, the emphatic visual pointing has the air of the director forcing his material to counterfeit a concern that he does not really feel. Usually, Wilder's intensity is felt when he is at his least demonstratively visual. In this film, when the camera is almost immersed in a glass of whisky (the kind of "phoney set-up" Wilder has deplored elsewhere and almost entirely eschewed in his other work), we are surely invited to be more impressed with the visual virtuosity than given any useful insight into the hero's condition. The conspicuous tracking-shot towards the rim of Birnam's glass at this point draws attention to the chief example of the film's insistent patterning: the recurrent use of the circle. Consider also the huge close-up of Birnam's eye as he wakes at the beginning of another humiliating morning, a close-up which, uniquely in Wilder, seems irrelevant and self-consciously applied, almost an acknowledgement of the film's failure to make you share the hero's heightened sensitivity through integral detail rather than excessive posturing by the camera.

The circle could be said to relate to a number of aspects of the hero's alcoholism. At the most basic level, it suggests his physical intoxication and dizziness and his inability to progress whilst under the influence of drink – his prospects being, as he puts it, "zero, zero, zero." "I'm on that merry-go-round and have to ride it all the way . . . round and round," he says. The balls outside the pawnbroker's shop are his guiding lights. At one point his secret supply of liquor is even hidden in a saucer-shaped light-shade. The sense of his life being controlled with an unending circle is even consciously endorsed in his contemptuous dismissal of the heroine's insistence that there must be a cure: "This has a familiar *ring*."

"Let me have my vicious circle," cries Birnam to the bartender Nat (Howard da Silva), referring to the circles of wet rings left by his glass on the bar (which ominously form a chain at one point). The "vicious circle" – that is, Birnam's obsessive need of stimulation through drink – allows him to be "Horowitz playing the Emperor Concerto, John Barrymore before the movies got him by the throat, and Jesse James and his brothers, all three of them, and W Shakespeare . . . And out there is not Third Avenue, it is the Nile, man, the Nile, and down it comes the barge of Cleopatra." The "vicious circle" allows Birnam the temporary satisfaction of being a dreamer, a poet, an artist. At moments like these, the film becomes less about alcoholism as a disease than about the failure of a man to sustain an image of himself which he can only reach through drink. Unfortunately, Wilder's restriction within the genre of 'social problem picture' means that the particular complexities of Birnam tend to be suppressed in favour of a less interesting generalisation about the horrors of alcoholism. Whenever he wants to interest us in the character, the conventions of the genre compel Wilder also to display Birnam as an exhibit, which means that he is torn between analysing a man and denouncing a sickness. Other Wilder characters have drink problems (Sugar in *Some Like it Hot*, for example) and others are drug addicts (Sherlock Holmes; Antonia in *Fedora*), but these are the symptoms of more complex areas of the characters' feelings of inadequacy or insecurity. The drink overwhelms Don Birnam, making his plight more desperate, perhaps, but also less complicated. Whereas Wilder would really like to get inside a man who just happens to be an alcoholic, he seems compelled to present an alcoholic who just happens to be a troubled individual. The film is more of a case-history than a character study. One of the negative aspects of the recurrent circle imagery is to make you all the more aware of the hollowness of the hero.

Birnam says of the circle that it is the most perfect shape because it has no beginning and no end. In a sense, neither has the film, whose own structure is cyclical, and this too presents certain ambiguities which the film cannot coherently contain. The opening shot pans across New York to Birnam's open window, with the liquor bottle hanging outside: the closing shot reverses this pattern as Birnam wonders about people like him "out there" and decides to recreate in a novel his experiences during the weekend. The camera's return to the point from where it started not only matches the hero's decision to recall events from that point; it is almost as if the film is being rewound, emphasising its own structure, just as Birnam is to construct the film again in his novel.

Previously he has been a man split between the writer and the drunk. The drink feeds his fantasies and illusions but paradoxically takes him further away from the achievement of the writer, to the point where he becomes an alcoholic and, in the famous *delirium tremens* sequence, has a terrifying vision of a mouse crawling through the wall of his apartment and being attacked by a bat. Wilder has explained this symbolism: "Birnam's hallucination is a result of his schizophrenic, or split, personality. The mouse represents the everyday Birnam; the bat – or mouse with wings – the artist he dreams of being." These are the two warring elements in his soul and by the end one way out of his dilemma has been suggested: in writing about his trauma and thus becoming the centre of his *own* drama, he might succeed in reconciling the writer with the man.

"We don't say that the man is cured," said Wilder, coming to the defence of his much criticised conclusion, "We just try to suggest that if he can lick his illness long enough to put some coherent words down on paper, then there must be hope." As it happens, Wilder inadvertently identifies a weakness of the film, an uncomfortable suspicion that special pleading is being made on behalf of this particular alcoholic because of the fact that he is a writer.* It is greatly to Ray Milland's credit that his performance has an edge and an irritability that prevents the character from being too sentimentalised in this way. Nevertheless, Wilder's conception does seem compromised and flawed: the implication is that if Birnam were not a potential writer sympathy would be appreciably withdrawn; the other implication is that Birnam as failed writer interests Wilder much more than Birnam as 'successful' alcoholic, which in turn means that the shape and weight of the film fail to allow Wilder to develop that interest.

In the light of Wilder's statement, the cyclical structure makes the ending more confusing rather than less. It could be argued that the ostensibly facile optimism is offset by the structure in the sense that the hero is in the same location at the end as at the beginning and that he is being compelled to re-live his experience, Ancient Mariner-like, before it can be fully exorcised. The evocations of *film noir* in this context of 'no escape' would then be highly appropriate. But Wilder's insistence on "hope" seems to indicate that such was not the intention and so one is forced back to the conclusion that he found difficulty in matching style with theme because of his uneasiness with the subject.

Even if one could justify the thematic rightness of the ending it would be difficult to defend the clumsy way in which it is handled. The barman Nat who has played a somewhat ambiguous role throughout (Birnam's most severe critic as well as being his most reliable source of supply) suddenly turns up on the doorstep and returns Birnam's typewriter, which the hero had dropped on a fall

*It has been suggested that *The Lost Weekend* arose from Wilder's partnership with the hard-drinking Raymond Chandler the year before on *Double Indemnity*.

The Lost Weekend: *Ray Milland gets his typewriter back*

downstairs and had thought was lost. This "miracle," as his girlfriend Helen (Jane Wyman) insists on referring to it, will enable Birnam to get on with his novel. To believe that he can lick his illness long enough to write, we need to be convinced by some transformation of character, not circumstance; some significant psychological development, not a structural sleight-of-hand. Birnam's inability to write, after all, is a bit more complex than not having a typewriter.

Another reason why Birnam's rehabilitation fails to convince is Wilder's inability to give any life at all to the 'good girl' Helen who is trying through the example of her pure and unselfish character to negotiate the corrupted hero back along the straight and narrow. Wilder seems unable to defeat the generic stereotype of this staple Hollywood woman of the Forties, and his irritation with her might explain his otherwise mystifying decision to caricature her parents in the savage way he does, and explain why the movement of the film seems to be bringing her down to Birnam's level more than elevating him to hers (her prim instruction to Birnam to "bend down" whenever she wants a kiss from him might, in that scheme, be highly ironic: it is she, after all, who has to sleep outside his front door). The fact is that there is much more warmth in Birnam's relationship with Gloria, the barmaid (Doris Dowling) than in his relationship with Helen, Gloria being attracted to the everyday Birnam and having a wit and generosity of spirit which often attaches itself to Wilder's 'earthy' women. In dress, in manner, in musical tastes, Gloria is the complete antithesis to Helen, who appeals to Birnam's artistic, aspirational side. He and Helen even meet at a performance of Verdi's "La Traviata." The contrast between the two women is also felt as a conflict within the hero himself, which anticipates the situation of the failed writer in *Sunset Boulevard*. But the triangle in that film has genuine tension, whereas in *The Lost Weekend* the righteousness and invulnerability of Helen produce a fatal slackness. Rather than being a complex and appealing character in her own right, her function in the film seems to be to act as an unofficial agent for Alcoholics Anonymous. Because of the concentration on this fateful weekend, we are compelled to take her love for Birnam as a person, as distinct from her sympathy for him as an alcoholic, very much on trust. This is compounded by the strange and surely misconceived choice of flashbacks which show how they meet and the initial stress when Helen discovers Birnam's problem but does not show how their relationship has blossomed into love. What attracts one to the other remains something of a mystery to the very end.

It might be rather unfair to compare the film with Blake Edwards' *Days of Wine and Roses* (1962), in which Jack Lemmon and Lee Remick play a married couple who drift into alcoholism. Edwards, after all, had had a long time to absorb and learn from Wilder's mistakes. Yet given the fame of both films as classic studies of alcoholism in the cinema, the comparison seems inevitable. (Actually, the casting of Jack Lemmon as the public relations man consumed with self-hatred for the pimping he is required to do seems to have been specifically influenced by the example set by Wilder's work, particularly *The Apartment*). Also, the comparison does illuminate certain strengths and weaknesses in both films.

The Lost Weekend certainly scores over its rival in its delineation of the secondary characters. Philip Terry's performance as Birnam's brother, Wick, might not be likeable but it does possess an unusual truth: the exasperation felt by many an upright man whose own strength is being sapped through having to support someone culpably weaker than himself. Indeed, Birnam recognises this and it is noticeable that the suicide note he writes is addressed to Wick and not to Helen: he obviously feels that his brother has suffered more than she. Frank Faylen's performance as the sadistic male nurse of "Hangover Plaza," as he calls the alcoholic ward, is unexpectedly, sardonically nasty. The supporting characterisations in *Days of Wine and Roses*, particularly Jack Klugman's saintly AA man, look singularly conventional in comparison. In general, the hospital scenes in the Wilder film have a tension and a horror that Edwards aspires to without having the visual imagination to achieve.

But the overall structure of the later film seems to be better judged. Its stretching of the time factor over a period of several years is skilfully managed and seems to allow Edwards more scope for developing his principal characters, while also permitting him to convey a tragic sense of *unnoticed* waste and decay. Wilder's most imaginative stroke in his handling of the time element is to suggest its passage by the gradual, rather amusing, accumulation of milk bottles outside Birnam's door. Otherwise, his compression of time essentially to this traumatic weekend has a limiting effect on his analysis of character. Similarly, the quiet, melancholic ending of *Days of Wine and Roses*, where Lemmon is cured but Remick isn't, has a moving sense of uncertainty and struggle that tellingly exposes the simplistic rhetoric of Wilder's conclusion.

Both directors characteristically attempt to inject humour into the pervading gloom, but in the Edwards film, it seems more closely integrated. The structure of the film – indeed, the structure within individual scenes – is a gradual movement from comedy to tragedy, a progress which, as Paul Mayersberg has observed, exactly conveys the effect of alcohol: at first it stimulates, later it depresses. Wilder's injections of humour are personal and peripheral, evidence of a suppressed directorial sensibility rather than expressive of the character's predicament.

As one might expect, however, these moments of grim humour provide the liveliest and most interesting moments of the film, when Wilder's sprightly personality escapes from the straitjacket of solemnity to which the theme has consigned it. The first meeting between Birnam and Helen at the opera, in particular, is a delightfully conceived scene. Each has picked up the other's coat check by mistake which prevents Birnam from retrieving a bottle from his pocket until she arrives to claim her coat. There are several characteristic touches here.

The introductory meeting of two people who each has a garment the other wants is a variation on the celebrated opening sequence in *Bluebeard's Eighth Wife*. Birnam's pursuit of Helen at this point is provoked not by burning passion but by burning thirst, he having dropped his last bottle and she on her way to a cocktail party: it is a typical example of the suspect ulterior motives by which a Wilder hero invariably initiates a romantic relationship. There is a particularly mordant humour in Wilder's conception of how the drinking song in "La Traviata" might effect an alcoholic – an irreverent joke worthy of *A Night at the Opera*. Flashes of offbeat humour and personality like this momentarily allow this rather faceless film to crackle into life. When Birnam is being ejected from a nightclub for attempting to steal a lady's purse (he has left a carnation in its place, which says a lot about his soft, over-florid personality), the pianist suddenly strikes up a mocking rendition of "Somebody stole my purse" to the tune of "Somebody stole my gal," provoking an explosion of public hilarity which intensifies the hero's humiliation. Even Birnam's walk down Third Avenue has its own lugubrious mocking humour – the whole situation of a search for a pawnbroker's shop on a Jewish holiday. Touches like this help to extend the range of mood of a film otherwise oppressed by a tone of academic sanctimoniousness.

So, even if alcoholism as a subject does not bring out the vintage in Wilder, the film has some freshly observed details and powerful moments. The Hollywood Academy – and the public – have undoubtedly rewarded many worse films and its impact was obviously considerable. It is hard to find any review of a film dealing with the problem of alcoholism which does not mention *The Lost Weekend*. Its popularity and its impact were such that its imagery could be alluded to in the most unlikely contexts with the expectation that an audience would immediately grasp the reference. At the height of a dangerous and possibly fatal situation in *My Favourite Brunette* (1947), Bob Hope is startled to find a bottle hidden in a chandelier. Not even the perilousness of his plight can suppress Hope's astonishment. "Ray Milland's been here," he says.

The Emperor Waltz (1947)

There is a wonderful moment in Ernst Lubitsch's *The Love Parade* (1929) when a group of American tourists are driven around the mythical kingdom of Sylvania in an open coach. The guide brings the coach to a halt so that the tourists might appreciate the view of the Royal Palace on the hill above the town and then describes with a deep sense of pride the great art treasures to be seen in the palace. But the Americans are not in the least bit interested in the cultural heritage of Sylvania and they rudely bury their heads in copies of 'The Wall Street Journal'. Only when the guide puts a monetary value on the art treasures do the Americans spring to life, turning their heads in unison to gaze at the source of Sylvania's wealth. But it is just a moment – less than a minute – and the film then proceeds on its course without further interruption. It is as if Lubitsch was intent on showing us the 'outside world', simply in order to banish it as quickly and as contemptuously as possible.

The Emperor Waltz could be described as Wilder's 101-minute elaboration of that brief interlude in Lubitsch's film, for it details the turbulent effect an American intruder has on the Viennese court of the Emperor Franz Josef. A witty caption at the beginning tells us that the action takes place "Forty years ago" which, if taken literally, was the year of Wilder's birth in 1906* in a town east of Vienna in what is now part of Poland. In a way, the film can be read as Wilder's nostalgic reconstruction of his own cultural heritage and his acknowl-

---

**The Emperor Waltz* was shot between June–September 1946, had its copyright filed in 1947 but was not released until 1948.

edgement, as an American, that that world of courtly leisure and elegant indiscretion was in its death throes by the turn of the century, that it had been totally destroyed by the end of the First World War, and that the map of Europe had been changed dramatically by 1946.

Although the film contains some of Wilder's most accomplished displays of mise-en-scène to that date, it is also something of a failure. Fifteen or twenty years ago, at the time of the worst excesses of *auteur* criticism, *The Emperor Waltz* might have been hailed as a masterpiece (had Wilder been a member of the Pantheon) for it offers a remarkably clear expression of his ambivalent feelings towards America and Europe. But sandwiched between the gritty 'realism' of *The Lost Weekend* and the rasping wit of *A Foreign Affair* it must have looked like an aberration, and whilst *Sabrina, Love in the Afternoon* and *Avanti!* have made *The Lost Weekend* seem aberrational, *The Emperor Waltz* is commonly regarded as Wilder's worst movie, a consensus that the director has made no attempt to dispute: "As for *The Emperor Waltz*," he told 'Cinema,' "I never want to see it again." Whilst we would not want to elevate the film to a status it doesn't deserve, we would argue that Wilder has made a far worse film (*The Seven Year Itch*) and less interesting ones (*The Lost Weekend*, *The Spirit of St Louis*). However, it must be admitted that the film loses its way rather badly in the middle and though it recovers for a magnificently stylish and witty finale we realise that the conflicting interests involved – Paramount's conception of the film as a Bing Crosby musical and what Andrew Sarris described in 'Film Comment' as an "overly fluffy Franz Josef conceit out of the cuisine of Chez Ernst" – prevent the film's most potentially rewarding areas from being fully explored. But even this stylistic compromise represents a thematically apposite contradiction, characterised by the opening caption's description of a Viennese ball as a "clambake', and by the music played over the main credits: Johann Strauss's "Emperor Waltz" conducted at such breakneck speed that, given Wilder's appreciation of music, must be regarded as a statement of the film's theme rather than the tastelessness of a studio orchestrator. Much of the film is trite and sentimental, but as Wilder's tribute to Lubitschian frivolity we would argue that it is every bit the equal of its critically revered progenitors. The toughness in Wilder is here forcibly suppressed (despite Maurice Zolotow's extraordinary claim that *The Emperor Waltz* shows Wilder "spewing out a black hatred of humanity") but as Wilder's previous and subsequent work has shown, direct comparisons with Lubitsch are invariably misleading and can turn out to be nothing more substantial and just as serpentine as a shaggy dog story.

The film opens as American phonograph salesman Virgil Smith (Bing Crosby) breaks into the Royal Palace as a lavish ball is in progress. He walks purposefully down a grand staircase and across the dance floor to meet Countess Johanna von Stolzenburg-Stolzenburg (Joan Fontaine). Somewhat reluctantly she dances a few steps with him and then they leave the room for a private conversation. At this point Wilder cuts to a group of elderly guests who have been observing these events from a balcony. The Dowager Princess Bitotska (Lucile Watson) says that Virgil and Johanna have a "love affair that has rocked Vienna these past four months." "Who is he?" asks someone. "The most vulgar, impossible, obnoxious . . ." begins someone else, only to be interrupted by the Dowager who puts it more succinctly: "In a word," she spits, "he's an American." The film then begins the first of three flashbacks, broken only by single shots of the group on the balcony to remind us that the story is being told by the Dowager who cannot yet know its outcome. As with *Fedora*, which never leaves the Paris mansion where the actress lies in state, and like *Double Indemnity*, which never leaves the insurance building, *The Emperor Waltz*, as befits its title, never leaves the ball. But unlike *Fedora* and *Double Indemnity*, the present film does not consist of personal disclosures and memories but comprises of social chit-chat. Although the Dowager can be seen in a few scenes, she is a peripheral character and, indeed, is absent from the most important scenes. This unusual structural device alerts us to the film as myth, as flimsy perhaps as the foundations of the Empire in which the film is set. The Dowager is the comic flip-side of the Emperor's stoicism, both representatives of the aristocracy whose security Virgil's intervention will threaten.

Virgil has come to Vienna to persuade the Emperor (Richard Haydn) personally to endorse the phonograph and so give Virgil's company the prestige to enhance their exports. Virgil has brought his dog Buttons with him, enabling him to present the popular image of the phonograph with a dog peering inquisitively into the loudspeaker. As Virgil waits for his audience with the Emperor the phonograph starts ticking in its wooden box which makes the guards assume he's carrying a time bomb. Virgil is thrown into a courtyard where Buttons gets into a fight with Scheherazade, a large French poodle owned by Johanna. Hearing that Scheherazade is to be mated with the Emperor's dog, Virgil decides to stay close to Johanna, waiting for an opportunity to put his sales pitch to the Emperor. At a Tyrolean village Buttons and Scheherazade fall in love, after being thrown forcibly together since Buttons has given the poodle psychological problems which prevent her from mating, and soon Virgil and Johanna are in love as well. The Emperor, however, frowns on their romance and refuses to give them permission to marry, buying Virgil off by endorsing the phonograph. Johanna then becomes engaged to a handsome Marquis and is given a celebratory ball. It is at this point that Virgil returns with the knowledge that Scheherazade is about to give birth to Buttons' puppies – an event which makes the Emperor realise that a marriage between Virgil and Johanna might not be too dangerous after all and the film ends with a shot of the couple dancing happily together at the ball.

It will probably be assumed from this brief outline that the canine love affair is the source of the film's whimsy and sentimentality. Although there is an element of truth in this, it must be stressed how important the dogs are to the film's narrative; and if Wilder realised the risks he was taking he tries to make up for it at the end by placing a basketful of puppies in a sink and nearly drowns them in water. If anything, the main objection to the dogs is the overly schematic way they are used. If the characters in *The Major and the Minor* talk to each other as children, or if the characters in *The Apartment* discuss life in terms of insurance jargon, the characters in *The Emperor Waltz* conceal their real emotions by using their dogs as surrogates, endowing them with human attributes and feelings. Scheherazade wears perfume and is offered sleeping pills and then brandy to help her over her romantic traumas; "Are we talking about the Countess or the dogs in that basket?" asks the Emperor irritably at the end. "It amounts to the same thing," says Virgil earnestly. At the beginning, when the mating of Scheherazade is proposed by the Emperor, Johanna is initially led to believe that the Emperor wishes to mate *with her*, before he gets too old (when in fact his dog is getting past it). The connection between human and canine psychology is taken to its absurdist extreme by Sig Ruman's glorious cameo as Dr Semmelgries, the palace vet who studied with Freud and who diagnoses a "mental block" for Scheherazade which can only be cured

The Emperor Waltz: *Bing Crosby, Joan Fontaine, Richard Haydn and puppies*

by close contact with Buttons. The love affair that develops between Virgil and Johanna is itself to involve the destruction of mental and cultural barriers.

The function of the dogs is to signify the class differences between the hero and heroine. After the fight in the courtyard, Virgil strides up to Johanna to demand an apology – Buttons has bled all over his rented suit. They compare notes on the pedigree of their respective pets – Scheherazade can trace her ancestry back to Napoleon, whilst Buttons is a mongrel of dubious origin. Scheherazade represents Europe's culture, aristocracy and history; Buttons represents America, democracy and the Twentieth Century. Johanna has a family tree as long as the Empire itself; Virgil comes from *New*ark, *New* Jersey. Virgil's general disposition, his refusal to be intimidated by the glitter and formality, is an open threat to the social equilibrium that the court has consciously created whilst his romantic overtures to Johanna are as much a danger as Buttons' easy conquest of Scheherazade. The seeds of this social instability are sown early on, when Virgil doesn't even pause before breaking the window to gain access into the palace, and the guard's assumption that the phonograph is a time bomb is actually not far from the truth: the American military music which blares from it, disrupting the Emperor's hunting party, and the ideology which stands behind it ("Teddy Roosevelt still carries a big stick," says Virgil at one point, threatening the Emperor's safe passage through the Panama Canal) will cause these men of the past to surrender to the present. When Virgil and Johanna meet for the first time in the courtyard she comments to him, "If the low-bred has the impertinence to come distastefully close what can he expect but to be bitten?" Virgil's response is to kiss her full on the lips, his first action in a process which is to turn her assertion on its head.

Part of the problem with the film is in the portrayal of its hero and heroine. Naturally, this is partly to do with the fact that both characters are played by Americans: Joan Fontaine fails to convince us of her pedigree even though she would give an exquisite performance as the tragic Viennese heroine of Max Ophuls's *Letter from an Unknown Woman*, made the following year. Perhaps this reflects Wilder's indifference to the character as anything more than a decorative object and his fascination with Virgil and the Emperor. Wilder has considerable success with the Emperor but the film's main fault lies in Bing Crosby's performance. It is not that Crosby performs badly or that the screenplay fails to provide him with sufficient material to build a character; it is simply that Crosby's whole style of acting (he has only ever given *one* performance in his long career) is wrong for the picture. The film is a shining example of Paramount's attempt to portray and idealise American ideology whilst remaining faithful to their European style: the film's unmistakable European mise-en-scène is not sufficiently contrasted by Crosby's acting. David Thomson, in 'A Biographical Dictionary of the Cinema', accurately describes Crosby's appeal: "He was the proof that unexceptional, lazy pleasantry was more desirable than prickly, difficult originality. It would be unjust to call him dull. More accurate to say that for forty years he skirted risk. His ease is the soft option." This persona of Crosby's can be one of the most engaging in movies given the right context for it (*High Society*, for example) but these are precisely the qualities which Wilder needed to avoid if he was to make Virgil convincing as a hustling American salesman. One need only compare Bing Crosby's methods with James Cagney's in *One, Two, Three* to appreciate that even half the latter's energy would have made *The Emperor Waltz* really sparkle.

This failure to inject the character of Virgil with the required dynamism, or *chutzpah*, undermines Wilder's otherwise evocative portrayal of an Empire on the wane. A line from one of Virgil's songs, "I'm in slumberland" might refer appropriately to the state of the nation but it also refers inappropriately to Virgil himself. Nevertheless, the Emperor's world is a touchingly melancholy and precarious one. An early shot shows him turning slowly on his feet on a spiral pattern on a marble floor. At first one draws a connection between the pattern and the grooves of a gramophone record which seem to suggest that the Emperor is destined to endorse the "mechanical orchestra," as he calls Virgil's machine. But a later scene brings another, sadder connection. It is the scene when Virgil finally gets his audience with the Emperor. Virgil has gone to ask for Johanna's hand in marriage but in his case he carries the phonograph, a further complication which makes his motives unclear. Virgil begins to describe his modest home in New Jersey, which he shares with his mother and a dentist, and says that Johanna will move in with them since at her palace they have so many forks: "I wouldn't know which one to pick up." The Emperor – who is always suffering from a cold, establishing his vulnerability – is not against Virgil for being an American but for being the wrong type of American: he finds the name 'Smith' objectionable and would have preferred him to be an "Astor or a Rocker . . . whatever it is." The Emperor is resisting what he (and Wilder) know to be the inevitable and after buying Virgil off he delivers one of the most poignant speeches in Wilder's films: "Ultimately the world will be yours," he begins, only to be interrupted by Virgil who says boastfully, "You bet it will." The old man continues as if he hasn't heard, "We are different. We are like snails living in lovely twisted shells. Have you ever observed a snail, Mr Smith? They are majestic creatures, with small coronetted heads that peer very proudly from their tiny castles. They move with dignity. I imagine they have a great sense of their own importance. But you take them from their shells and they die. That is us, Mr Smith. Take Johanna with you and you destroy her." The earlier image, of the Emperor turning on the floor, is that of a snail writhing in its shell.

Virgil's reaction to this is to walk out backwards, in a deep bow (Buttons adopting the same pose), and then saunter up to the anxious Johanna to boast of his success with the endorsement of the phonograph, saying (and confirming everyone else's view of him), "You know us Americans, anything for a dollar." One can't help but leap forward eight years to Linus Larrabee in *Sabrina*, pretending love for the heroine in the interests of his product, and how he eventually comes to recognise the superficiality and callousness of his actions. Virgil, too, comes to recognise this, with the aid of the lovesick Buttons, and he returns to Johanna at the ball. But Wilder's ambivalence remains in the final sequence, when he leaves Virgil to walk down another staircase to claim Johanna on the dance floor. The Emperor has given them his blessing but Wilder chooses to leave them dancing in graceful circles rather than face up to the decision of whether to move to America or remain in Vienna. It seems that either decision is possible, for if Johanna and the Emperor have surrendered to the inevitable, Virgil has travelled no less great a spiritual distance. As with *Sabrina*, the real victor is democracy.

There are, finally, the musical numbers and the visual quality of the film to be discussed. Although the songs are another part of the film's failure, in that they intrude upon the narrative flow and slow up the action, they also have an important thematic role to play, almost as important as the dogs. There is a fine joke when Johanna and her friend hear a man singing and yodelling as they drive to the Emperor's country estate. "This Tyrol," Johanna's friend says, "It's like a vast oxygen tent." "It's the voice of Austria," concurs Johanna moments before Virgil appears around the bend, crooning away. It is noticeable that all the songs involve not the court society but the villagers – Virgil's song, as he walks across the beautiful mountain scenery, is at one point accompanied by two dairy maids who appear out of nowhere – which echoes the film's impulse towards democracy: Virgil might inspire the wrath and contempt of high society but his crooning inspires even his police guard to suddenly produce a couple of violins which makes the entire village burst into spontaneous song and dance. These sequences, of which there are countless equivalents in Lubitsch's work, demonstrate the difficulty one has in reconciling context with effect, normally so precisely judged in Wilder: one admires the coherence of the narrative of *The Emperor Waltz*, in which every sequence has a symbolic function, but one can criticise its aesthetic conception.

The Emperor Waltz was Wilder's first film in colour and his last until *The Seven Year Itch*: "even the dialogue sounds phoney in colour" he said once, explaining his resistance to the process. Axel

Madsen and Maurice Zolotow devote most of their discussions of *The Emperor Waltz* to the extraordinary and exorbitant lengths Wilder went in 'improving' his location in the Canadian Rockies – planting trees, painting roads a darker colour, even building an island for a short sequence when Scheherazade escapes to find Buttons. Our concentration in this analysis on the thematic interest of *The Emperor Waltz* has, we hope, reclaimed the film from its unenviable position in the critical consensus on Wilder, but our approach also betrays the fact that we were regrettably unable to acquire a colour print for viewing. Even in black and white, the film looks wonderful, and as we stressed in our Introduction, all the placing of films in this book are tentative and none more so than *The Emperor Waltz*, despite its faults. Given a colour print it can only rise in one's estimation.

The Seven Year Itch (1955)

Next to *Some Like it Hot*, Wilder's most famous comedy is probably *The Seven Year Itch*, its title immediately entering the English language as a euphemism for (predominantly male) sexual infidelity and emotional insecurity. Ironically, no such infidelity takes place in Wilder's film and the set of characters are not so much insecure as immature. *The Seven Year Itch* presents particular problems for the viewer which can be attributed to a fundamental difference in the artistic temperaments of Wilder and the play's author, George Axelrod. Although the theme explored in the film can be intellectually justified (the hero's extreme passivity representing the enslavement of the modern American male to media-created fantasy women), the film simply fails to work on a comic and dramatic level. In a sense, Richard Sherman, played by Tom Ewell, is a typical Wilder hero who does not succeed in his ambition: when on the brink of triumph he rejects the role he has created for himself; but unlike the quintessential Wilder hero, such as Walter Neff, C C Baxter or Wendell Armbruster, whose role reversals are the result of a sudden self-awareness of moral truths and spiritual regeneration, Sherman is a negative figure throughout.

The Seven Year Itch is curiously lacking in atmosphere and inspiration – its few pleasures reside solely in Marilyn Monroe's performance as the archetypal Girl Upstairs – which might be accounted for in the fact that Wilder had moved away from the familiar company and production procedures of the Paramount studio where he had made his first ten features. Wilder's relationship with Paramount had been strained following the reception of *Ace in the Hole*, and *Sabrina* had been a very troubled and difficult production for him, but Wilder had been persuaded to purchase Axelrod's Broadway hit by an astute literary agent and the deal obliged him to make the film for 20th Century-Fox since Marilyn Monroe eventually became the most important part of the package. Wilder needed a major success and *The Seven Year Itch* was the most financially successful film released that year by 20th Century-Fox.

The central failure of *The Seven Year Itch* is due to a weak leading man who never does anything decisive. This is only partly the fault of Tom Ewell's mannered and shallow portrait of a typically American crisis of middle-aged and middle-class fading masculinity. It is unlikely, however, that Walter Matthau, Wilder's original choice for the part, would have made much difference since George Axelrod's original is firmly anchored to its bed of sand, and Wilder had to contend with severe censorship restrictions not unlike those encountered by Stanley Kubrick on his film of *Lolita* (1961). And like Kubrick, Wilder chooses comedy as a surrogate to eroticism but without Kubrick's bitter sense of irony and tragedy.

The screen adaptation, jointly written by Wilder and Axelrod, is far too theatrical (the use of CinemaScope, *de rigeur* in Fox movies of this period, emphasises the 'invisible' proscenium arch) and when compared with other films made at the same time, such as Nicholas Ray's *Bigger Than Life* (1956), Robert Aldrich's *The Big Knife* (1955), Delbert Mann's *Marty* (1955) or Charles Laughton's *The Night of the Hunter* (1955), its latter attempts at psychological analysis seem misplaced and naive. Yet Axelrod wants it both ways; *The Seven Year Itch* was the play of an unknown writer which went out of its way to be decently salubrious and facile, but Axelrod is also concerned that his work should be taken as a serious comment on the times. "All of Axelrod's most important films," Richard Corliss says, "are fantasies involving dreams that, more often than not, turn into nightmares. In his love-hate attitude toward both his horny, ineffectual writers and his all-American girls who 'express the total vulgarity of our time,' Axelrod comes close to defining the post-Kinsey, pre-Reichian male who has become aware of sexual alternatives to which neither Hollywood nor society would let him respond – except with brittle wisecracks, bashful leers, and bleeding ulcers."

This accurately describes the thematic pattern of *The Seven Year Itch*, yet it remains an obstinately old-fashioned work, well aware of its sociological roots and contemporary relevance, but constantly avoiding a head-on collision. The film's main strategy for avoiding such a confrontation is the casting of Marilyn Monroe, whose dominant presence overshadows the dilemma of the hero. Fox was well aware of Monroe's appeal and they were giving her the full publicity treatment. She was invariably cast with unattractive leading men which is why so many of her films lack tension, even though this strategy had the required effect of making her America's and the world's most obvious sex symbol. An exception to the rule is Henry Hathaway's *Niagara* (1953) in which Monroe's power over her vulnerable husband, played by Joseph Cotten, produced a thriller of remarkable subversion. But in *The Seven Year Itch* the imbalance of interest between hero and heroine is disastrous, leading to faintly embarrassing jokes at Ewell's expense. Wilder seems to realise this around the halfway stage as the film becomes frantic in its efforts to remain funny as well as socially significant. It soon degenerates into a sub-Feydeau farce (hinted at in Saul Bass's credit titles which are designed as a confusion of opening and closing doors) but since the centre is hollow Ewell's slapstick antics and *faux pas* become tiresome and Monroe seems as bored with him as we are.

When Richard Sherman packs his wife and young son off on a country holiday to escape the inferno of a New York summer we instinctively feel he would take his voluptuous neighbour to bed at the first available opportunity. Monroe is so preposterously innocent and vulnerable (a model from Colorado who appears in toothpaste commercials with the commitment of a Lee Strasberg graduate) that for a well-seasoned New Yorker she would seem an easy sexual conquest. After he has managed to invite Monroe down to his apartment he puts some Rachmaninov on the record player (in *hommage* to *Brief Encounter*, perhaps, but David Lean's film, made ten years earlier, deals far more maturely with a similar subject) because he imagines an out-of-town girl would be impressed by his level of sophistication and would expect a 'classical' seduction, such as those she would have seen in the movies. But all Monroe can say, in the film's most memorable line, is that she can recognise classical music because it lacks a vocal. This completely disarms Sherman and he never recovers from the blunder for it destroys the image he is trying to cultivate. As he fumbles about making cocktails and improvises with Monroe on the piano we begin to sense in Monroe's character an element of role-playing, a subtle shift of emphasis which perhaps indicates where Wilder's interest lies. But her character is never allowed to develop past the studio manufactured dumb blonde image which Monroe never really escaped until *Some Like It Hot* and John Huston's *The Misfits* (1960) fully revealed the helpless actress who appreciated all along the precise effect she had on men, even though she was incapable of controlling it. In *The Seven Year Itch* we are asked to believe that Monroe's ingenuousness is real.

She lounges invitingly beside Sherman's noisy air-conditioning unit (his sole status symbol and the pretext for inviting her down to cool off in the stifling heat) with her low neckline, white dress flapping around her thighs. But a timely knock on the door saves Sherman the necessity of confronting his repressed sexuality. "This has never happened to me before," confesses Sherman after a clumsy pass on the piano stool, to which Monroe replies, "Oh, it happens to me all the time." Monroe's supposed innocence – like Lolita's – makes Sherman's crisis all the more acute and instead of making a concerted effort to overcome his nervousness he wanders off into adulterous fantasies lifted from the movies (the mocking rendition of the 'classical' beach seduction in Fred Zinnemann's *From Here To Eternity* (1953)), or from the cheap paperback fiction that Sherman markets for a living. All through the movie one senses Wilder goading his hero into an affair because only then will Sherman become interesting. But while Wilder's dramatic instincts are pushing in one direction the censorship codes and Axelrod's original are pushing in another; and when the action fights itself into a tight corner a knock on the door or a spilt drink saves the day.

The plot contrivance of *The Seven Year Itch* had appeared in various guises before. In Fritz Lang's *The Woman in the Window* (1944), for example, Edward G Robinson, playing a meek and respectable lecturer in criminal psychology, finds himself a 'summer widower' and falls prey to a nightmare in which he murders the jealous lover of a woman who accosts him in the street. Lang's great *film noir*, made the same year as *Double Indemnity*, described the pessimism and romantic disillusion common to many American males during the 'Forties. Because of the war, women had been forced to adopt a more positive role in society, becoming more aggressive and self-sufficient and undermining the males' superiority and authority. Coming a decade later in Eisenhower's era of innocence, confidence and paternalism, *The Seven Year Itch* is a representative of that ideology: since no decent married man who entered into an adulterous affair with the ultimate of Hollywood sex-objects would be tolerated by contemporary audiences, it is prevented from exploring the situation in a way that is realistic or meaningful. It is in this context that one appreciates the deliberate mis-casting of Monroe. She is made to appear childlike – witness her girlish joy as the wind from a subway ventilation shaft causes her dress to billow around her waist – and sexually unattainable – "In this heat I always keep my undies in the icebox." The film's ideological obsession with rendering Monroe innocent and frigid, together with Wilder's unusually blatant use of phallic symbolism (the subway train which raises Monroe's dress, the child's oar which Sherman brandishes suggestively, the trouble over uncorking a bottle of champagne) makes Monroe into a fantasy figure beyond the reach of mortal men – a sex goddess, in fact, which would place *The Seven Year Itch* alongside *Sunset Boulevard* and *Fedora* as a comment on Hollywood were it not for the film's massive deficiencies.

We never believe that Sherman seriously intended being unfaithful to his wife; nor does Monroe really influence his return to 'normality' at the end. Monroe offers him a chance to test his sexual prowess

The Seven Year Itch: *Marilyn Monroe, Tom Ewell*

when he felt it might be dwindling. Instead of taking up the challenge he suffers from guilt and paranoia (he imagines his wife is having an affair on holiday) and becomes sexually and intellectually impotent, acquiring the leer of a voyeur who wanders the streets looking at girls in their revealing summer dresses and lowering the necklines on the fantasy women who adorn the covers of his paperbacks. These conflicts and ironies are certainly an essential part of Axelrod's world, sensitively elaborated in *The Secret Life of an American Wife* (1968) which reverses the situation and places it within an explicit Hollywood context, but Wilder clearly has no time for such a passive character.

In the 1976 'American Film' interview, Wilder honestly acknowledged the difficulties. "Unless the husband, left alone in New York while the wife and kid are away for the summer, has an affair with the girl there's nothing. But you couldn't do that in those days, so I was just straitjacketed. It just didn't come off one bit and there's nothing I can say about it except I wish I hadn't made it. I wish I had the property now."

The Spirit of St Louis (1957)

Following the huge commercial success of *The Seven Year Itch*, Wilder again changed studios and made *The Spirit of St Louis* for Warner Brothers at a cost of six million dollars. There are two conflicting published accounts describing how Wilder became involved in the project. He told Robert Mundy that "Sometimes I do pictures for friends. My friend Leland Hayward (who was also the film's producer) asked me to do this film, so I did it." But Ernest Lehman, who had collaborated with Wilder on the screenplay of *Sabrina*, offered the following theory to Maurice Zolotow: "I have this feeling that Wilder was conscious of people thinking of him as European and I think he wanted to do *The Spirit of St Louis* because it was a very American subject. He wanted to take the most American of all subjects and make it his." Seen in the context of Wilder's thematic preoccupations this notion of Lehman seems plausible enough, though Wilder has never concealed his dissatisfaction with the finished film. He told Axel Madsen that it was "A bad decision. I succeeded with a couple of moments but I missed creating the character." He discussed with Maurice Zolotow the technical problems and frustrations: "We could not communicate with a plane when it was up there. So when we had to do another take it had to land, get the instructions, and take off again. We had other planes in the air to film the plane we were shooting. God, it was horrendous. I never should have made this picture. It needed a director like John Frankenheimer, a man with enormous patience for technical details."

A semi-documentary account of Charles A Lindbergh's historic non-stop solo flight from New York to Paris in 1927, *The Spirit of*

St Louis involved Wilder and his largely inexperienced collaborator Wendell Mayes in many months of research in adapting Lindbergh's autobiographical account of the flight and many more months of location shooting and process work. But despite the creative and physical effort, supported by an extensive advertising campaign, the film was a commercial disaster; its total failure to make an impression on international audiences remains to this day something of a Hollywood legend. The critical reception was generally favourable, if not ecstatic, and the film contained an abundance of CinemaScope thrills and featured a very popular actor, James Stewart, in the role of Lindbergh.

It isn't particularly difficult to suggest possible reasons for the film's commercial failure. Lindbergh himself was a controversial figure whose image had been badly tarnished when he went on a visit to Hitler's Berlin in 1939 advocating an isolationist stance which Wilder and Charles Brackett condemned the following year in *Arise My Love*, but which Lindbergh himself repudiated in 1942 after the attack on Pearl Harbour. Perhaps more rationally, the film's failure can be attributed to the public's acceptance of advanced technology; in an age of regular passenger air services across the Atlantic, with in-flight movies, it is perfectly understandable for general audiences not to be very interested or excited by the exploits of early aviators, even though their courage has left us with a considerable legacy. To support this argument, one need only point to the commercial failure of George Roy Hill's superb *The Great Waldo Pepper* (1975) which starred Robert Redford, then the world's most bankable actor.

Although *The Spirit of St Louis* is certainly marginal to Wilder's career, it is seriously undervalued as a movie; indeed, it is a magnificent piece of entertainment and as technically skilful as Hollywood was capable of at the time. The aerial photography is outstanding and intricate (at one point, the back-projection screen shows the shadow of Lindbergh's plane racing along a hillside with James Stewart looking down on it) and the overall design and muted colour conveys a remarkable period atmosphere.

As we have seen, Wilder is at pains to minimise his involvement, but one can readily elaborate Ernest Lehman's theory to see what attracted Wilder, perhaps unconsciously, to "the most American of all subjects." The film celebrates a pioneer (most of Wilder's heroes are pioneers of one sort or another) and the will to break through existing barriers of achievement (this is the driving force behind Chuck Tatum, Willie Gingrich, Sherlock Holmes); even Lindbergh's goal – to fly to Paris – must have appealed to Wilder's sensibility.

The opening scenes are very much in Wilder's scheme of things. The camera prowls through the lobby of a hotel crowded with journalists working at their typewriters or yelling down temporary telephone lines in order to catch that morning's front page. Wilder gently satirises the journalists' cheerful copy ("SLEEPING LIKE A BABY," runs a typical dispatch) by going upstairs to reveal Lindbergh lying nervously awake, counting the hours to dawn and idly recalling the bizarre and fortuitous chain of events which led up to the fruition of his ambition. The realities behind the headlines, as it were, and the juxtaposing of fact and legend has always been a favourite theme of Wilder's (reaching its apotheosis in *The Private Life of Sherlock Holmes*) but here he ignores many of the possibilities offered by Lindbergh's curious situation (it has been alleged that Lindbergh was actually losing his virginity that night) and after the promising opening the film corresponds to the conventions of the action adventure laid down by Ford, Hawks, and Walsh.

The Spirit of St Louis is an invigorating patchwork of flashbacks which continue after Lindbergh has taken off from the Roosevelt airfield. We see him as an air-mail pilot, reluctantly bailing out of his plane in dense mist; as a young man barnstorming his way through the rural mid-West; the day he traded in his motorcycle for his first plane; his good-humoured though hazardous attempt to teach a plucky priest to fly so that he might be nearer the Lord; and of course the construction of "The Spirit of St Louis" itself. These flashbacks seem rather arbitrarily chosen at first and have been criticised because their effect is largely comic and add little to our understanding of Lindbergh's inner motivations and tensions. It would appear that Wilder endorses this view. But the humour of the flashback episodes – which is often executed in a kind of Keystone slapstick, appropriately enough for a film set in the Twenties – serves two important functions. The comedy inherent in the ricketty planes and the eccentric characters underlines the fairground image that aviation had at the time: an image which men like Lindbergh were to change. The colourful company Lindbergh keeps throughout the film, such as the priest and the plane's designer who grills fish with his acetylene torch, serve to heighten the solitude of the trans-Atlantic flight. While James Stewart's portrayal of Lindbergh outwardly suggests an introspective and private individual, it is clear that he needs the company and, most importantly, the technical expertise and the spiritual encouragement of other people. Soon after he takes off Lindbergh discovers a fly in his cockpit and immediately starts talking to it. When the insect is finally released over Newfoundland ("This is the last dry land, fella") Wilder manages to imply the real start of the flight. By cutting to a magnificent shot of Lindbergh's plane winging low across the harbour at St John towards the vast and empty ocean, the film's heroic spirit asserts itself gracefully.

It is in this section of the film dealing with the flight that James Stewart's performance finds its strongest challenge. Stewart was around twenty years older than Lindbergh but this doesn't seem to matter; the actor captures the sense of excitement mixed with fear which transcends the need for historical and physical accuracy. Cocooned inside the narrow cockpit with no home comforts or even a radio in his obsession to keep weight to an absolute minimum, Stewart keeps the film entirely gripping. He manages to convey his

The Spirit of St Louis: *James Stewart takes off*

increasing fatigue and boredom through the look in his weary eyes and the restricted movements of his gangling frame. And when he actually falls asleep Wilder's dramatic cutting between Stewart's peacefully nodding head and the rapidly falling plane makes the viewer feel powerless to intervene as the ocean rushes upwards. This feeling of unease pervades the entire flight, as Wilder has cleverly emphasised in the flashbacks the ever-present dangers of the largely untried machinery and the limits of human endurance. Lindbergh's take-off, a particularly dramatic affair through heavy rain, thick mud and electric cables, is a constant memory.

Lindbergh's flight lasted 33 hours, 30 minutes, 29.8 seconds and occupies about an hour of the film's 135-minute running time. It is during this central section that the flashbacks become increasingly slapstick (as in the scene when Lindbergh nearly runs down the salesman and almost demolishes a barn in his efforts to get his first plane airborne) as Lindbergh is confronted with the grim realities of his ambition. In common with Kon Ichikawa's *Alone on the Pacific* (1963), which dramatised a young man's solo voyage from Yokohama to San Francisco, Wilder utilises the flashback technique not merely as a device to avoid monotony but as a deliberate strategy to heighten drama. By making the flashbacks noisy and funny he is able to emphasise solitude and fear.

The brilliant formal organisation of *The Spirit of St Louis* has not been properly acknowledged. It gradually builds in momentum towards the climax when Lindbergh sights land, not entirely certain where he is and ruminating, almost in a state of trance, over the possibilities of icebergs or the Canary Islands. When he flies low over a group of off-shore fishermen, culminating in his famous yell "Which way to Ireland?," the astonished look on the fishermen's faces and Lindbergh's own euphoria releases the tension as the plane wings across Dingle Bay, down across England to the French coast, to the mouth of the River Seine, and finally to Paris. One senses here in the closing sequences, with the hordes of people gathered at Le Bourget suddenly and dramatically revealed in the beams of the searchlights, the same immutable heroic optimism which attended Wilder's vivid depiction of the construction and the testing of the plane. And when Lindbergh, elated and exhausted, finally touches down and sees "The Spirit of St Louis" safely into an empty hangar, the film emerges as a fitting tribute to a remarkably dedicated man.

Wilder told Robert Mundy that "The ending of the picture is not mine – I didn't even shoot it" which might imply that Wilder had other ideas about getting Lindbergh down to earth, both literally and as myth, or simply that by that time Wilder himself was exhausted and entrusted these scenes to a second unit. So if Lindbergh began very much in the Wilder mould as a reluctant hero and ends up with a ticker-tape welcome in New York, it describes both a popular piece of American mythology and the absolute professionalism of Hollywood of which Billy Wilder has always been part. If *Double Indemnity, Ace in the Hole, The Apartment* and *Kiss Me, Stupid* are variously virulent hate-letters to America, then *The Spirit of St Louis* is perhaps the nearest Wilder has ever come to writing a love-letter to the country of his adoption.

Filmography

1929 **MENSCHEN AM SONNTAG** (screenplay)
1931 **DER MANN, DER SEINEN MORDER SUCHT** (co-screenplay)
1931 **IHRE HOHEIT BEFIEHLT** (co-screenplay)
1931 **DER FALSCHE EHEMANN** (co-screenplay)
1931 **EMIL UND DIE DETEKTIVE** (screenplay)
1932 **ES WAR EINMAL EIN WALTZER** (screenplay)
1932 **EIN BLONDER TRAUM** (co-screenplay)
1932 **SCAMPOLO, EIN KIND DER STRASSE** (co-screenplay)
1932 **DAS BLAUE VOM HIMMEL** (co-screenplay)
1933 **MADAME WUNSCHT KEINE KINDER** (co-screenplay)
1933 **WAS FRAUEN TRAUMEN** (co-screenplay)
1933 **MAUVAISE GRAINE** (co-director; co-screenplay)
1934 **MUSIC IN THE AIR** (co-screenplay)
1935 **LOTTERY LOVER** (co-screenplay)
1938 **BLUEBEARD'S EIGHTH WIFE** (co-screenplay)
1939 **WHAT A LIFE** (co-screenplay)
1940 **ARISE MY LOVE** (co-screenplay)
1941 **BALL OF FIRE** (co-screenplay)

1939 **MIDNIGHT**

Paramount. Producer: Arthur Hornblow jun. Director: Mitchell Leisen. Screenplay: Charles Brackett, Billy Wilder. Based on an original story by Edwin Justus Mayer and Franz Schulz. Director of Photography: Charles Lang. Editor: Doane Harrison. Art Directors: Hans Dreier, Robert Usher. Music: Frederick Hollander. Leading Players: Claudette Colbert (Eve Peabody), Don Ameche (Tibor Czerny), John Barrymore (Georges Flamarion), Francis Lederer (Jacques Picot), Mary Astor (Helen Flamarion). Running time: 94 mins.

1939 **NINOTCHKA**

Metro-Goldwyn-Mayer. Producer-Director: Ernst Lubitsch. Screenplay: Charles Brackett, Billy Wilder, Walter Reisch. Based on the original story by Melchior Lengyel. Director of Photography: William Daniels. Editor: Gene Ruggiero. Art Director: Cedric Gibbons. Music: Werner R Heymann. Leading Players: Greta Garbo (Ninotchka), Melvyn Douglas (Leon), Ina Claire (Swana), Bela Lugosi (Razinin), Sig Rumann (Iranoff), Felix Bressart (Buljanoff), Alexander Granach (Kopalski). Running time: 110 mins.

Filmography

1941 **HOLD BACK THE DAWN**
Paramount. Producer: Arthur Hornblow jun. Director: Mitchell Leisen. Screenplay: Charles Brackett, Billy Wilder. Based on a story by Ketti Frenggs. Director of Photography: Leo Tover. Editor: Doane Harrison. Art Directors: Sam Comer, Hans Dreier, Robert Usher. Music: Victor Young. Leading Players: Charles Boyer (Georges Iscovescu), Olivia de Havilland (Emmy Brown), Paulette Goddard (Anita Dixon), Victor Francen (Professor Van Den Leuchen), Walter Abel (Hammock). Running time: 115 mins.

1942 **THE MAJOR AND THE MINOR**
Paramount. Producer: Arthur Hornblow jun. Director: Billy Wilder. Screenplay: Charles Brackett, Billy Wilder. Suggested by the play *Connie Goes Home* by Edward Childs Carpenter and the story *Sunny Goes Home* by Fannie Kilbourne. Director of Photography: Leo Tover. Editor: Doane Harrison. Art Directors: Hans Dreier, Roland Anderson. Music: Robert Emmett Dolan. Leading Players: Ginger Rogers (Susan Applegate), Ray Milland (Major Philip Kirby), Rita Johnson (Pamela Hill), Diana Lynn (Lucy Hill), Edward Fielding (Colonel Hill), Robert Benchley (Mr Osborne). Running time: 100 mins.

1943 **FIVE GRAVES TO CAIRO**
Paramount. Producer: Charles Brackett. Director: Billy Wilder. Screenplay: Charles Brackett, Billy Wilder. Based on a play by Lajos Biro. Director of Photography: John F Seitz. Editor: Doane Harrison. Art Directors: Hans Dreier, Ernst Fegte. Music: Miklós Rózsa. Leading Players: Franchot Tone (Corporal Bramble), Anne Baxter (Mouche), Akim Tamiroff (Farid), Erich von Stroheim (Field Marshall Erwin Rommel), Peter Van Eyck (Lieutenant Schwegler), Fortunio Bonanova (General Sebastiano). Running time: 96 mins.

1944 **DOUBLE INDEMNITY**
Paramount. Producer: Joseph Sistrom. Director: Billy Wilder. Screenplay: Billy Wilder, Raymond Chandler. Based on the story by James M Cain. Director of Photography: John F Seitz. Editor: Doane Harrison. Art Directors: Hans Dreier, Hal Pereira. Music: Miklós Rózsa. Leading Players: Fred MacMurray (Walter Neff), Barbara Stanwyck (Phyllis Dietrichson), Edward G Robinson (Barton Keyes), Jean Heather (Lola Dietrichson), Byron Barr (Nino Zachette), Tom Powers (Mr Dietrichson). Running time: 107 mins.

1945 **THE LOST WEEKEND**
Paramount. Producer: Charles Brackett. Director: Billy Wilder. Screenplay: Charles Brackett, Billy Wilder. Based on the novel by Charles Jackson. Director of Photography: John F Seitz. Editor: Doane Harrison. Art Directors: Hans Dreier, Earl Hedrick. Music: Miklós Rózsa. Leading Players: Ray Milland (Don Birnam), Jane Wyman (Helen St James), Howard da Silva (Nat), Philip Terry (Wick Birnam), Running time: 99 mins.

1947 **THE EMPEROR WALTZ**
Paramount. Producer: Charles Brackett. Director: Billy Wilder. Screenplay: Charles Brackett, Billy Wilder. Director of Photography: George Barnes (Technicolor). Editor: Doane Harrison. Art Directors: Hans Dreier, Franz Bachelin. Music: Victor Young.

Leading Players: Bing Crosby (Virgil Smith), Joan Fontaine (Johanna), Roland Culver (Baron Holenia), Lucile Watson (Princess Bitotska), Richard Haydn (Emperor Franz Josef), Sig Ruman (Dr Semmelgries). Running time: 106 mins.

1948 **A FOREIGN AFFAIR**
Paramount. Producer: Charles Brackett. Director: Billy Wilder. Screenplay: Charles Brackett, Billy Wilder, Richard L Breen. Based on an original story by David Shaw. Director of Photography: Charles B Lang jun. Editor: Doane Harrison. Art Directors: Hans Dreier, Walter Tyler. Music: Frederick Hollander. Leading Players: Jean Arthur (Congresswoman Phoebe Frost), Marlene Dietrich (Erika von Schluetow), John Lund (Captain John Pringle), Millard Mitchell (Colonel Rufus J Plummer). Running time: 116 mins.

1950 **SUNSET BOULEVARD**
Paramount. Producer: Charles Brackett. Director: Billy Wilder. Screenplay: Charles Brackett, Billy Wilder, D M Marshman jun. Director of Photography: John F Seitz. Editor: Arthur Schmidt. Art Directors: Hans Dreier, John Meehan. Music: Franz Waxman. Leading Players: Gloria Swanson (Norma Desmond), William Holden (Joe Gillis), Erich von Stroheim (Max von Mayerling), Nancy Olson (Betty Schaeffer), Fred Clark (Sheldrake), Jack Webb (Artie Green), Cecil B DeMille, Hedda Hopper, Buster Keaton, Anna Q Nilsson, H B Warner (themselves). Running time: 111 mins.

1951 **ACE IN THE HOLE**
Paramount. Producer-Director: Billy Wilder. Screenplay: Billy Wilder, Lesser Samuels, Walter Newman. Director of Photography: Charles Lang jun. Editors: Doane Harrison, Arthur Schmidt. Art Directors: Hal Pereira, Earl Hedrick. Music: Hugo Friedhofer. Leading Players: Kirk Douglas (Charles Tatum), Jan Sterling (Lorraine Minosa), Bob Arthur (Herbie Cook), Porter Hall (Jacob Q Boot), Richard Benedict (Leo Minosa), Ray Teal (Sheriff), Frank Cady (Mr Federber). Running time: 111 mins.

1953 **STALAG 17**
Paramount. Producer-Director: Billy Wilder. Screenplay: Billy Wilder, Edwin Blum. Based on the play by Donald Bevan and Edmund Trzcinski. Director of Photography: Ernest Laszlo. Editor: George Tomasini. Art Directors: Hal Pereira, Franz Bachelin. Music: Franz Waxman. Leading Players: William Holden (Sergeant J J Sefton), Don Taylor (Lieutenant Dunbar), Neville Brand (Duke), Peter Graves (Price), Otto Preminger (Oberst Von Scherbach), Sig Ruman (Schulz). Running time: 121 mins.

1954 **SABRINA**
Paramount. Producer-Director: Billy Wilder. Screenplay: Billy Wilder, Samuel Taylor, Ernest Lehman. Based on the play *Sabrina Fair* by Samuel Taylor. Director of Photography: Charles Lang jun. Editor: Arthur Schmidt. Art Directors: Hal Pereira, Walter Tyler. Music: Frederick Hollander. Leading Players: Humphrey Bogart (Linus Larrabee), Audrey Hepburn (Sabrina Fairchild), William Holden (David Larrabee), John Williams (Fairchild), Martha Hyer (Elizabeth Tyson), Walter Hampden (Oliver Larrabee). Running time: 114 mins. (GB title: *Sabrina Fair*)

1955 **THE SEVEN YEAR ITCH**
20th Century-Fox. Producers: Charles K Feldman, Billy Wilder. Director: Billy Wilder. Screenplay: Billy Wilder, George Axelrod. Based on the play by George Axelrod.

Director of Photography: Milton Krasner (CinemaScope, DeLuxe Color). Editor: Hugh S Fowler. Art Directors: Lyle Wheeler, George W Davis. Music: Alfred Newman. Leading Players: Marilyn Monroe (The Girl), Tom Ewell (Richard Sherman), Evelyn Keyes (Helen Sherman), Sonny Tufts (Tom McKenzie). Running time: 105 mins.

1957 **THE SPIRIT OF ST LOUIS**

Warner Bros. Producer: Leland Hayward. Director: Billy Wilder. Screenplay: Billy Wilder, Wendell Mayes. Based on the book by Charles A Lindbergh. Directors of Photography: Robert Burks, J Peverell Marley (CinemaScope, Warner Color). Editor: Arthur Schmidt. Art Director: Art Loel. Music: Franz Waxman. Leading Players: James Stewart (Charles A Lindbergh), Murray Hamilton (Bud Gurney), Patricia Smith (Mirror Girl), Bartlett Robinson (B F Mahoney). Running time: 135 mins.

1957 **LOVE IN THE AFTERNOON**

Allied Artists. Producer-Director: Billy Wilder. Screenplay: Billy Wilder, I A L Diamond. Based on the novel *Ariane* by Claude Anet. Director of Photography: William Mellor. Editor: Leonid Azar. Art Director: Alexander Trauner. Music: Franz Waxman. Leading Players: Gary Cooper (Frank Flannagan), Audrey Hepburn (Ariane Chevasse), Maurice Chevalier (Claude Chevasse), John McGiver (Monsieur X), Van Doude (Michel). Running time: 125 mins.

1957 **WITNESS FOR THE PROSECUTION**

Theme Pictures. Producer: Arthur Hornblow jun. Director: Billy Wilder. Screenplay: Billy Wilder, Harry Kurnitz. Based on the play by Agatha Christie. Director of Photography: Russell Harlan. Editor: Daniell Mandell. Art Director: Alexander Trauner. Music: Matty Malneck. Leading Players: Tyrone Power (Leonard Vole), Marlene Dietrich (Christine Vole), Charles Laughton (Sir Wilfrid Robarts), Elsa Lanchester (Miss Plimsoll), John Williams (Brogan-Moore), Una O'Connor (Janet McKenzie). Running time: 116 mins.

1959 **SOME LIKE IT HOT**

Mirisch. Producer-Director: Billy Wilder. Screenplay: Billy Wilder, I A L Diamond. Director of Photography: Charles Lang jun. Editor: Arthur Schmidt. Art Director: Ted Haworth. Music: Adolph Deutsch. Leading Players: Marilyn Monroe ('Sugar Kane'), Tony Curtis (Joe), Jack Lemmon (Jerry), George Raft (Spats Columbo), Joe E Brown (Osgood Fielding III), Joan Shawlee (Sweet Sue). Running time: 121 mins.

1960 **THE APARTMENT**

Mirisch. Producer-Director: Billy Wilder. Screenplay: Billy Wilder, I A L Diamond. Director of Photography: Joseph LaShelle (Panavision). Editor: Daniel Mandell. Art Director: Alexander Trauner. Music: Adolph Deutsch. Leading Players: Jack Lemmon (C C Baxter), Shirley MacLaine (Fran Kubelik), Fred MacMurray (J D Sheldrake), Ray Walston (Mr Dobisch), David Lewis (Mr Kirkeby), Jack Kruschen (Dr Dreyfuss), Joan Shawlee (Sylvia), Edie Adams (Miss Olson), Hope Holiday (Margie). Running time: 125 mins.

1961 **ONE, TWO, THREE**

Mirisch. Producer-Director: Billy Wilder. Screenplay: Billy Wilder, I A L Diamond. Based on a play by Ferenc Molnar. Director of Photography: Daniel Fapp (Panavision).

Editor: Daniel Mandell. Art Director: Alexander Trauner. Music: André Previn. Leading Players: James Cagney (C R MacNamara), Horst Buchholz (Otto Ludwig Piffl), Pamela Tiffin (Scarlett), Arlene Francis (Mrs MacNamara), Lilo Pulver (Ingeborg), Hans Lothar (Schlemmer). Running time: 115 mins.

1963 **IRMA LA DOUCE**
Mirisch. Producer-Director: Billy Wilder. Screenplay Billy Wilder, I A L Diamond. Based on the play by Alexandre Breffort. Director of Photography: Joseph LaShelle (Panavision, Technicolor). Editor: Daniel Mandell. Art Director: Alexander Trauner. Music: André Previn. Leading Players: Jack Lemmon (Nestor), Shirley MacLaine (Irma la Douce), Lou Jacobi (Moustache). Running time: 147 mins.

1964 **KISS ME, STUPID**
Mirisch. Producer-Director: Billy Wilder. Screenplay: Billy Wilder, I A L. Diamond. Director of Photography: Joseph LaShelle (Panavision). Editor: Daniel Mandell. Production Designer: Alexander Trauner. Music: André Previn. Leading Players: Dean Martin (Dino Martini), Kim Novak (Polly the Pistol), Ray Walston (Orville J Spooner), Felicia Farr (Zelda Spooner), Cliff Osmond (Barney Millsap). Running time: 124 mins.

1966 **THE FORTUNE COOKIE**
Mirisch. Producer-Director: Billy Wilder. Screenplay: Billy Wilder, I A L Diamond. Director of Photography: Joseph LaShelle (Panavision). Editor: Daniel Mandell. Art Director: Robert Luthardt. Music: André Previn. Leading Players: Jack Lemmon (Harry Hinkle), Walter Matthau (Willie Gingrich), Ron Rich (Boom-Boom Jackson), Cliff Osmond (Chester Purkey), Judi West (Sandi Hinkle). Running time: 126 mins. (GB title: *Meet Whiplash Willie*).

1970 **THE PRIVATE LIFE OF SHERLOCK HOLMES**
Mirisch. Producer-Director: Billy Wilder. Screenplay: Billy Wilder, I A L Diamond. Based on characters created by Sir Arthur Conan Doyle. Director of Photography: Christopher Challis (Panavision, DeLuxe Color). Editor: Ernest Walter. Production Designer: Alexander Trauner. Music: Miklós Rózsa. Leading Players: Robert Stephens (Sherlock Holmes), Colin Blakely (Dr John H Watson), Irene Handl (Mrs Hudson), Genevieve Page (Ilsa von Hoffmanstahl/Gabrielle Valladon), Christopher Lee (Mycroft Holmes), Tamara Toumanova (Petrova), Clive Revill (Rogozhin). Running time: 125 mins.

1972 **AVANTI!**
Mirisch. Producer-Director: Billy Wilder. Screenplay: Billy Wilder, I A L Diamond. Based on a play by Samuel Taylor. Director of Photography: Luigi Kuveiller (DeLuxe Color). Editor: Ralph E Winters. Art Director: Ferdinado Scarfioti. Music: Carlo Rustichelli. Leading Players: Jack Lemmon (Wendell Armbruster III), Juliet Mills (Pamela Piggot), Clive Revill (Carlo Carlucci), Edward Andrews (J J Blodgett), Gianfranco Barra (Bruno). Running time: 144 mins.

1974 **THE FRONT PAGE**
Universal. Producer: Paul Monash. Director: Billy Wilder. Screenplay: Billy Wilder, I A L Diamond. Based on the play by Ben Hecht and Charles MacArthur. Director of Photography: Jordan S Cronenweth (Panavision, Technicolor). Editor: Ralph E

Winters. Art Directors: Henry Bumstead, Henry Larrecy. Music: Billy May. Leading Players: Jack Lemmon (Hildy Johnson), Walter Matthau (Walter Burns), Carol Burnett (Molly Malloy), Allen Garfield (Kruger), Susan Sarandon (Peggy), Austin Pendleton (Earl Williams), Harold Gould (Mayor), Vincent Gardenia (Sheriff). Running time: 105 mins.

1978 **FEDORA**

Geria-Bavaria-Atelier. Producer-Director: Billy Wilder. Screenplay: Billy Wilder, I A L Diamond. Based on the story "Fedora" from *Crowned Heads* by Thomas Tryon. Director of Photography: Gerry Fisher (Technicolor). Editor: Frederick Steinkamp. Production Designer: Alexander Trauner. Music: Miklós Rózsa. Leading Players: William Holden (Barry Detweiler), Marthe Keller (Fedora/Antonia), Hildegard Knef (Countess Sobryanski), Jose Ferrer (Dr Vando), Frances Sternhagen (Miss Balfour), Hans Jaray (Count Sobryanski), Henry Fonda, Michael York (themselves). Running time: 112 mins.

Index

Index

Index

Note: "Wilder, Billy" is not indexed for obvious reasons